Warm Air Heating for Climate Control

FOURTH EDITION

William B. Cooper
Professor, Mechanical Technology
Macomb Community College

Raymond E. Lee
Professor, Mechanical Technology
Macomb Community College

Raymond A. Quinlan
Mechanical Contractor, State of Michigan
Air Conditioning, Heating, Refrigeration

Martin W. Sirowatka
Professor, Mechanical Technology
Macomb Community College

Robert Featherstone
Mechanical Contractor, State of Michigan
Instructor, Environmental Systems Technology
Oakland Community College

Prentice Hall
Upper Saddle River, New Jersey   *Columbus, Ohio*

Library of Congress Cataloging-in-Publication Data

Warm air heating for climate control.—4th ed. / Robert Featherstone
 . . . [et al.]
  p. cm
 Includes index.
 ISBN 0-13-095964-2
 1. Hot-air heating. 2. Heat pumps. 3. Dwellings—Heating and
ventilation. I. Featherstone, Robert.
 TH7601.W37 2000
697'.3—dc21   98-53501
                                                CIP

Editor: Ed Francis
Production Editor: Christine M. Buckendahl
Production Coordinator: Laura Citro, Custom Editorial Productions, Inc.
Design Coordinator: Karrie Converse-Jones
Cover Designer: Jason Moore
Production Manager: Patricia A. Tonneman
Marketing manager: Chris Bracken

This book was set in Times by Custom Editorial Productions, Inc., and was printed and bound by
R. R. Donnelley & Sons Company. The cover was printed by Phoenix Color Corp.

Photo Credits: Model LUI refrigerant recovery unit, courtesy of National Refrigeration Products.
Exploded view of Bryant Model 398AAU, courtesy of Bryant Heating and Cooling Products.

Printed in the United States of America

10 9 8 7 6 5 4 3 2 1

ISBN: 0-13-095964-2

Prentice-Hall International (UK) Limited, *London*
Prentice-Hall of Australia Pty. Limited, *Sydney*
Prentice-Hall Canada Inc., *Toronto*
Prentice-Hall Hispanoamericana, S. A., *Mexico*
Prentice-Hall of India Private Limited, *New Delhi*
Prentice-Hall of Japan, Inc., *Tokyo*
Prentice-Hall (Singapore) Pte. Ltd., *Singapore*
Editora Prentice-Hall do Brasil, Ltda., *Rio de Janeiro*

Preface

This fourth edition of *Warm Air Heating for Climate Control* is a useful tool to the student as well as to the technician. The information contained in this text assists the technician in the understanding, installation, and servicing of the forced-air furnace. The following is a list of changes that have been made from the third to the fourth edition.

The chapters were reorganized to aid the student in a sequential understanding of the heating system. First, the text will direct the student through climate control and comfort, then through combustion and common furnace components. After the student understands the fundamentals of furnace operation, the text covers the theory of electricity from basic electricity to electrical meter usage. From the electrical chapters, the text advances into furnace wiring, furnace control circuits, and high-efficiency furnaces. After discussing high-efficiency furnaces, the text thoroughly covers oil-fired furnaces. From oil furnaces, the text covers electric heat, equipment sizing and installation procedures, energy conservation, indoor air quality, zoning, hydronic heating, and heat pumps.

Along with reorganizing the chapters, many outdated pictures were removed and replaced with up-to-date photographs of electrical controls in Chapters 4, 6, and 10.

Common flame-sensing methods that are being used today for gas-fired furnaces were added to Chapter 5.

A complete furnace and air conditioning electrical diagram and installation procedure were added to Chapter 9.

The operational sequence and electrical diagrams of the following control circuits were added to Chapter 11: Honeywell S8610U system, Fenwal hot surface ignition system, Johnson G779 ignition system, White Rodgers ignition system, and Bryant HHA-4AA-011 System.

The operational sequence and electrical diagrams of the White Rodgers 50A50 furnace control and Honeywell Smart Valve ignition control system were added to Chapter 12.

The authors would like to thank the reviewers of this edition: Bennie Barnes, Live Oaks Community College; Robert S. Bates, Delaware Technical and Community College; and Carl F. Maulbank, Lincoln Technical Institute.

Contents

1

Climate Control

OBJECTIVES

After studying this chapter, the student will be able to:

- Describe the fundamental concepts that form the basis of this book

INDOOR CLIMATE CONTROL

One of the most challenging professions offered to students today is indoor climate control: not because it is a new occupation, but because it is an old business that has changed radically. It now requires a high degree of knowledge and skill, intensive study, and carries a large responsibility. At the same time it makes a valuable contribution to the health and welfare of the community.

In the past we have considered a satisfactory installation to be one that primarily controlled temperature, humidity to some degree, and did some filtering of the air. In the new technology we are better equipped to provide comfortable conditions, superior indoor air quality, and equipment and systems that conserve our valuable supply of energy. As an introduction to our study, let's review some of the important fundamental scientific principles that form the basis of indoor climate control:

1. Temperature
2. Pressure
3. Heat
4. Humidity
5. Air
6. Water
7. Laws of thermodynamics

TEMPERATURE

Temperature is a relative term that can be defined as something that is responsible for the sensations of hot and cold. Temperature can be measured accurately using a thermometer.

Example 1–1

70°F is converted to Celsius degrees as follows:

$$°C = \frac{5}{9} \times (°F - 32°)$$

$$= \frac{5}{9} \times (70° - 32°)$$

$$= \frac{5}{9} \times (38)$$

$$= \frac{190}{9}$$

$$= 21°C$$

Example 1–2

27° C is converted to Fahrenheit degrees as follows:

$$°F = \left(\frac{9}{5} \times °C\right) + 32°$$

$$= \left(\frac{9}{5} \times 27°\right) + 32°$$

$$= \left(\frac{243}{5}\right) + 32°$$

$$= 49 + 32$$

$$= 81°F$$

Thermometers

A *thermometer* is a device for measuring temperature. There are many shapes and sizes of thermometers that use a variety of scales. In general, two types of thermometers are most frequently used. One type is used in the British or English system and is known as the Fahrenheit thermometer. The other type is used in the metric system and is called the Celsius thermometer. Both of these thermometers measure temperature, but the scales are different. A comparison of the two thermometer scales is shown in Figure 1–1.

The scale selected for the Celsius thermometer is the easier of the two to understand. Zero degrees (0°) on the Celsius scale refers to the freezing point of water and 100° refers to the boiling of water. There are 100 equal divisions between the zero

FIGURE 1–1   Comparison of Fahrenheit and Celsius thermometer scales.

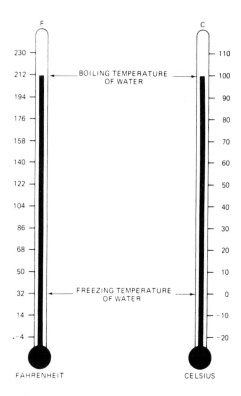

point and the 100° mark on the scale. On the Fahrenheit scale, the freezing point of water is 32° and the boiling point of water is 212°. The Fahrenheit thermometer has 180 equal divisions between the freezing point of water and its boiling point.

It is important to understand both of these thermometer scales. Some temperature information is given in Fahrenheit degrees and some in Celsius degrees. To prevent confusion about which scale is involved, a capital C is placed after the number of Celsius degrees and a capital F is placed after the number of Fahrenheit degrees. For example: 40°C means 40 degrees Celsius; 40°F means 40 degrees Fahrenheit.

When working continuously with one scale or the other, there is no problem in recording and using the information. However, there are times when it is necessary to change from one scale to the other. Such *conversions* can be done by using the following formulas:

$$\text{degrees Fahrenheit} = \frac{9}{5} \times \text{degrees Celsius}) + 32°$$

$$\text{degrees Celsius} = \frac{5}{9} \times \text{degrees Fahrenheit}) - 32°$$

PRESSURES

Pressure is the weight or force exerted by a substance per unit of area. For example, we speak of city water having a pressure of 75 psi (pounds per square inch). Correctly stated, we should indicate the pressure in terms of psig (the "g" standing for gauge pressure).

There are two general types of pressure: atmospheric and gauge. At sea level we consider the gauge pressure to be 0 psig and all gauge pressure readings relate to this base. The normal atmospheric pressure at sea level is 14.7 psi, usually rounded off to 15 psi. Zero atmospheric pressure is a theoretical place in space where no pressure exists.

In climate control measurements we often use compound gauges (Figure 1–2). On these gauges when we measure pressures below 0 psi, the gauge indicates a vacuum. Instead of measuring a vacuum as a negative pressure, the gauge reads inches of mercury (in. Hg). The "in. Hg" refers to pressure measurements made using a mercury manometer. Atmospheric pressure read on a mercury manometer is 29.92 in. Hg (usually rounded off to 30 in. Hg). Figure 1–2 shows a compound gauge. For a perfect vacuum the gauge would read 30 in. Hg.

There is another scale commonly used to express pressure measurements. Since atmospheric pressure will support a water column 34 ft. high (equivalent to 14.7 psi), pressures can be expressed in inches or feet of water. For example, a water pump may have a capacity of 6 gpm (gallons per minute) at a pressure of 10 ft. A fan may have a capacity to deliver 1000 cfm (cubic feet per minute) at a pressure of 1 in.

HEAT

Heat is the quality that causes an increase in the temperature of a body when heat is added or a decrease in the temperature of a body when heat is removed, provided there is no change in state in the process. The stipulation "no change in state" requires some explanation. A substance changes its state when it changes its physical form. For example, when a solid changes to a liquid, that is a change in state. When a liquid changes to a vapor, that is also a change in state. *Sublimation* is the change in state from a solid

FIGURE 1–2   Compound gauge with scale 30 in. Hg vacuum and pressures 0–250 psi, including equivalent boiling temperatures for refrigerator R–12, R–22 and R–502. (Courtesy of Mueller Industries, Inc.)

to a vapor without passing through the liquid state. A good example of this is the evaporation of mothballs or the evaporation of dry ice (solid carbon dioxide).

The unit of measurement of heat in the British system is the *British thermal unit* (Btu). One Btu is the amount of heat required to raise 1 pound (lb.) of water 1°F, as shown in Figure 1–3. In the original metric system the unit of heat was the *kilocalorie* (kcal). This is the amount of heat required to raise the temperature of 1 *kilogram* (kg), or 1000 *grams* (g), of water 1°C. This unit of heat is still in use. However, the present metric unit or International System (SI) unit for heat, comparable to a Btu, is the joule (J). The joule is defined in terms of work and is equivalent to the movement of a force of one newton for a distance of 1 meter (m). When the unit of heat includes a time element comparable to Btu per hour, the metric unit is watt (W), which is equivalent to joules per second.

It is important in most cases to note the rate of heat change. How fast or how slow does a piece of heating equipment produce heat? Therefore, a more precise term is *Btu per hour* (Btuh). Sometimes figures become quite large. Using M to represent 1000, the abbreviation *MBh is* used to represent *thousands of Btu per hour.* For example, a furnace may have an output of 100,000 Btu per hour or 100 MBh.

Types of Heat

There are two types of heat. One type changes the temperature of a substance and the other changes its state. The type that changes the temperature is called *sensible heat.* The type that changes the state is called *latent heat.* The formula used to determine the sensible heat added or removed from a substance is

$$Q = W \times SH \times TD$$

where: Q = quantity of heat, Btu
W = weight, lb.
SH = specific heat, Btu/lb./°F
TD = temperature difference or change, °F

FIGURE 1–3   One Btu is the amount of heat required to raise 1 lb. of water 1°F.

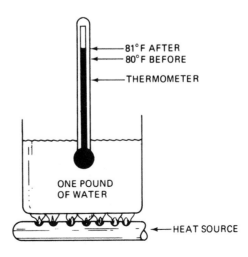

81°F AFTER
80°F BEFORE
THERMOMETER
ONE POUND OF WATER
HEAT SOURCE

The formula used to determine the change in latent heat is

$$Q = W \times L$$

where L is the change in latent heat per pound.

When heat is added to a solid to change it to a liquid, the latent heat is called *heat of melting*. When a liquid is changed to a solid, the latent heat is called *heat of fusion*. When a liquid is changed to a vapor, the latent heat is called *heat of vaporization*. When a vapor is changed to a liquid, the latent heat is called *heat of condensation*. Latent heat is always related to a change in state.

A good example to indicate the effects of heat is its reaction on water, as shown in Figure 1–4. In this figure, ice is taken at 0°F and heated to steam. Note that there are five parts to the diagram, and the following is a description of what takes place.

Part 1   Ice at 0°F is heated to 32°F; 16 Btu is added. The amount of heat required is found by substituting values in the sensible heat formula.

$$Q = 1 \text{ lb.} \times 0.5 \text{ Btu/lb./°F} \times (32°F - 0°F)$$
$$= 1 \times 0.5 \times 32$$
$$= 16 \text{ Btu}$$

Part 2   Ice at 32°F is changed to water at 32°F. Using the latent heat formula, since the heat of melting of water is 144 Btu/lb., 144 Btu is added:

$$Q = 1 \text{ lb} \times 144 \text{ Btu}$$
$$= 144 \text{ Btu}$$

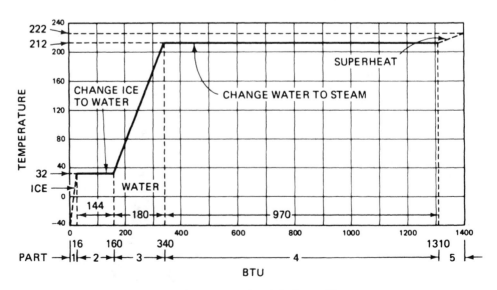

FIGURE 1–4   Temperature-heat diagram showing the effects of heat on water.

Part 3   Water at 32°F is heated to 212°F by adding 180 Btu. Using the formula and substituting in the values yields

$$Q = 1 \text{ lb.} \times 1.0 \text{ Btu/lb./°F} \times (212° - 32°F)$$
$$= 1 \times 1 \times 180$$
$$= 180 \text{ Btu}$$

Part 4   Water at 212°F is changed to steam by adding 970 Btu. Since the heat of vaporization of water is 970 Btu/lb., using this formula we obtain

$$Q = 1 \text{ lb.} \times 970 \text{ Btu (latent heat)}$$
$$= 970 \text{ Btu}$$

Part 5   The steam is superheated. *Superheating* means heating steam (vapor) above the boiling point. If the steam is superheated 10°F, the amount of heat added is 5 Btu. Since the specific heat of steam is 0.48 Btu/lb./°F, the amount of heat added is determined by the formula

$$Q = 1 \text{ lb.} \times 0.48 \text{ Btu/lb./°F} \times (222°F - 212°F)$$
$$= 1 \times 0.48 \times 10$$
$$= 5 \text{ Btu (rounded to the nearest whole number)}$$

Both heat of fusion and heat of vaporization are reversible processes. The change in state can occur in either direction. Water can be changed to ice or ice to water. The amount of heat added or subtracted is the same in either case. Tables giving the heat of fusion and the heat of vaporization for various substances are available.

Specific Heat

Except where a change in state occurs, when most substances are heated, they absorb heat, thereby raising their temperatures. The temperature of the substance increases rapidly or slowly, depending on the nature of the material. Since the standard heating unit is defined in terms of the temperature rise of water, it is fitting to use water as a basis for comparison for the heat-absorbing quality of other substances.

The definition of specific heat is much like the definition of Btu. The specific heat of a substance is the amount of heat required to raise 1 lb. of a substance 1°F. Figure 1–5 lists specific heat values for various substances.

These specific heat values make it easy to calculate the amount of heat added to or removed from a substance when the temperature rise or drop is known. The amount of heat required is equal to the weight of the substance, times the specific heat, times the rise in temperature in degrees Fahrenheit.

Example 1–3   How much heat is required to heat 10 lb. of aluminum from 50°F to 60°F?

Solution   Btu = pounds of aluminum × specific heat × °F temperature rise

$$= 10 \text{ lb.} \times 0.22 \text{ Btu/1b./°F} \times (60°F - 50°F)$$
$$= 10 \times 0.22 \times 10$$
$$= 22$$

□

FIGURE 1–5 Specific heat values for some common substances.

SPECIFIC HEAT VALUES	
MATERIAL	SPECIFIC HEAT BTU/LB./DEG F
Water	1.00
Ice	0.50
Air (dry)	0.24
Steam	0.48
Aluminum	0.22
Brick	0.20
Concrete	0.16
Copper	0.09
Glass (pyrex)	0.20
Iron	0.10
Paper	0.32
Steel (mild)	0.12
Wood (hard)	0.45
Wood (pine)	0.67

These values may be used for computations which involve no change of state.

Transfer of Heat

Three different ways to transfer heat are by convection, conduction, and radiation, as shown in Figure 1–6. Modern heating plants make use of all three ways to transfer heat.

Convection is the circulatory motion in air due to the warmer portions rising and the denser cooler portions sinking. For convection to take place, there must be a difference in temperature between the source of heat and the surrounding air. The greater the difference in temperature, the greater the movement of air by convection. The greater the movement of air, the greater the transfer of heat.

Conduction is the flow of heat from one part of a material to another part in direct contact with it. The rate at which a material transmits heat is known as its conductivity. The amount of heat transmitted by conduction through a material is determined by the surface area of the material, the thickness, the temperature between two surfaces, and the conductivity.

Radiation is the transfer of heat through space by wave motion. Heat passes from one object to another without warming the space in between. The amount of heat transferred by radiation depends on the area of the radiating body, the temperature difference, and the distance between the source of heat and the object being heated.

HUMIDITY

Humidity is the amount of water vapor within a given space. There are two types of humidity: absolute and relative. *Absolute humidity is* the weight of water vapor per unit

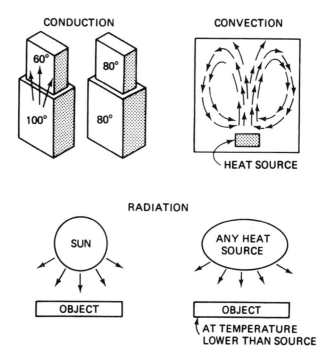

FIGURE 1–6 Three ways to transfer heat: conduction, convection, and radiation.

of volume. *Relative humidity* is the ratio of the weight of water vapor in 1 lb. (or in 1 kg) of dry air compared to the maximum amount of water vapor 1 lb. (or 1 kg) of air will hold at a given temperature, expressed in percent.

During the winter months in a heating system, it is usually desirable to increase the percentage of humidity within the space being conditioned. For every pound of water that is evaporated, approximately 970 Btu is required. Humidity is measured using a *sling psychrometer,* an instrument for determining the moisture content of air. The use of a sling psychrometer is discussed in Chapter 2.

AIR

In most heating applications, transferring heat to air is an important part of the conditioning process. It is desirable, therefore, that we consider some of the properties of air. Pure air is an invisible, odorless, and tasteless gas. It contains about 21% oxygen, 78% nitrogen, and 1% other gases, including water vapor. Standard air at sea-level pressure (14.7 psia) and at a temperature of 72°F, weighs 0.0725 lb. per cubic foot. One pound occupies about 14 ft^3. The specific heat of air is approximately 0.24 Btu per pound.

Moisture in air is in vapor form. Standard air at 72°F that is saturated with moisture contains 118.4 grains of water vapor per pound (7000 grains = 1 pound). When the same air contains half the moisture (59.2 gr/lb.), it could be stated that the relative humidity is 50%. Heating air causes it to expand and weigh less per cubic foot, thus causing it to rise by gravity action. As heat is transferred to objects in the space, the temperature of the air drops and the cooler air falls toward the floor.

It is important in heating applications that the circulation of air in the space involves the entire volume of the room, to prevent stratification and uneven temperatures. In most installations this is achieved by forced circulation. Since air is invisible, it can be contaminated and not be noticeable. An extreme case of this type is described in Chapter 21. A number of people died and many were ill at a convention of the American Legion at a large hotel in Philadelphia in 1976. The cause was airborne bacteria circulated through the air-conditioning system. Good air quality measures could have prevented this.

WATER

Water is another substance that can be used to transfer heat from the source to the space being conditioned, as shown in Chapter 23, Hydronic Heat. It is therefore important to consider some of the properties of water.

Pure water is transparent to some degree, depending on the thickness and surrounding light conditions. The appearance of water can be misleading. It can contain foreign substances that greatly affect its possible uses. Most communities have access to testing facilities. Water weighs 62.5 lb. per cubic foot. One cubic foot is equivalent to 8.33 gallons. Water may be found in any one of its three states: solid, liquid, or gas. The specific heat of water is 1.0. The specific heat of ice is 0.5.

There are two conditions that cause the HVAC technician special concern:

1. When water is heated, as in a hot water heating system, it expands. There must be expansion space in a closed system with an air cushion to allow for this increase in volume. In addition it is required by code to have an automatic relief valve. Both of these protective devices must be in good operating condition at all times.
2. When water freezes, it expands. The expansion can be so great that it will break almost any container, including piping.

There are numerous methods of preventing damage due to freeze-up, depending on the application. One way is to drain the system before it is subjected to freezing conditions. Another way is to add an antifreeze solution to the water being circulated in a hot water heating or cooling system. The amount of antifreeze added will be determined by the percent by volume necessary to prevent freezing in the region where the system is installed.

LAWS OF THERMODYNAMICS

Thermodynamics is the science that deals with the relationship between heat and mechanical energy. Energy is the ability to do work. If a force is applied to an object that moves it a given distance, work has been performed. Heat is a form of energy. Other forms of energy include light, chemical, mechanical, and electrical.

FIGURE 1–7   Heat flows from hot to cold.

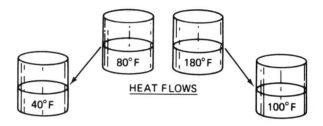

Since heat is a form of energy, it follows the natural laws that relate to energy. These laws are useful in the study of heating. From the laws of thermodynamics, two helpful facts are derived:

1. Energy can be neither created nor destroyed, but it can be converted from one form of energy to another.
2. Heat flows from hot to cold.

An example of the conversion of energy is the changing of electrical energy to heat in an electric heating unit. An example of heat flowing from hot to cold is illustrated in Figure 1–7.

STUDY QUESTIONS

Answers to the study questions may be found in the sections noted in brackets.

1–1. What are the three important requirements in the construction of indoor climate systems? *[Indoor Climate Control]*

1–2. Define *temperature*. *[Temperature]*

1–3. Describe the two types of scales for measuring temperature. *[Thermometers]*

1–4. Give the formula for converting degrees Fahrenheit to degrees Celsius and degrees Celsius to degrees Fahrenheit. *[Thermometers]*

1–5. Give two definitions of a British thermal unit (Btu), one for Fahrenheit temperatures, and one for Celsius temperatures. *[Heat]*

1–6. What are the formulas for calculating sensible and latent heat? *[Types of Heat]*

1–7. Define *specific heat* in terms of British units. *[Specific Heat]*

1–8. Name the three ways to transfer heat. *[Transfer of Heat]*

1–9. What is the difference between absolute and relative humidity? *[Humidity]*

1–10. Define *energy*. *[Laws of Thermodynamics]*

1–11. What is meant by *change of state*? *[Types of Heat]*

1–12. Give the specific heats of ice, water, and steam. *[Specific Heat]*

2
Comfort

OBJECTIVES

After studying this chapter, the student will be able to:

- Describe the conditions produced by the warm air heating system that are necessary for human comfort

CONDITIONS THAT AFFECT COMFORT

Comfort is the absence of disturbing or distressing conditions—it is a feeling of contentment with the environment. The study of human comfort concerns itself with two aspects:

1. How the body functions with respect to heat
2. How the area around a person affects the feeling of comfort

HUMAN REQUIREMENTS FOR COMFORT

The body can be compared to a heat engine. A heat engine has three characteristics:

1. It consumes fuel.
2. It performs work.
3. It dissipates heat.

The body consumes fuel in the form of food which produces energy to perform work. The body also dissipates heat to the surrounding atmosphere. The body has a

12

FIGURE 2–1   Heat from people.

ACTIVITY	TOTAL HEAT ADJUSTED* BTUH	SENSIBLE HEAT BTUH	LATENT HEAT BTUH
SCHOOL	420	230	190
OFFICE	510	255	255
LIGHT WORK	640	315	325
DANCING	1280	405	875
HEAVY WORK	1600	565	1035

*Adjusted Total Gain is based on normal percentage of men, women, and children for the application listed.

unique characteristic in that it maintains a closely regulated internal body temperature of 97 to 100°F (36 to 38°C). Any excess energy that is not used to produce work or to perform essential body functions is expelled to the atmosphere. It is therefore important that any loss of body heat be at the proper rate to maintain body temperature. If the body loses heat too fast, a person has the sensation of being cold. If the body loses heat too slowly, a person has the sensation of being too warm.

There are two additional factors that must be taken into consideration:

1. *Amount of activity of a person.* The greater the activity, the more heat produced by the body that must be dissipated to the atmosphere (Figure 2–1).
2. *Amount of clothing worn by a person.* Clothing is a form of insulation and insulation slows down the transfer of heat. Therefore, the warmer the clothing, the greater the insulation value and the less the amount of heat is dissipated. Thus, heat that would normally be lost to the atmosphere is used to warm the surface of the body.

Heat Transfer

Excess heat must be transferred from the body to the area around it. This is accomplished in three ways (Figure 2–2).

1. Convection
2. Radiation
3. Evaporation

Convection   For convection to take place, the area around the body must be at a lower temperature. The greater the difference in temperature, the greater the movement of convection currents around the body and the greater the heat transfer. If the temperature difference is too great, a person will feel the sensation of being cold. If the temperature difference is too small, a person will feel the sensation of being hot.

Radiation   The body radiates heat to cooler surfaces just as the sun radiates heat to the earth. The greater the temperature difference between the body and the exposed

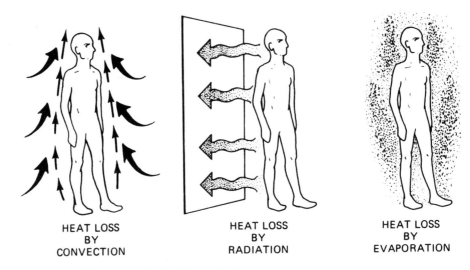

HEAT LOSS
BY
CONVECTION

HEAT LOSS
BY
RADIATION

HEAT LOSS
BY
EVAPORATION

FIGURE 2–2   Three ways the body loses heat.

surfaces, the greater the rate of heat transfer. It has been found that the most comfortable conditions are maintained if the inside surface of the outside walls and windows are heated to the room temperature. If these surface temperatures are too low, the body radiates heat to them too fast and this produces a feeling of discomfort.

Evaporation   Water (or moisture) on the surface of the skin enters the surrounding air by means of evaporation. Evaporation is the process of changing water to vapor by the addition of heat. As the water absorbs heat from the body, it evaporates, thus transferring heat to the air. If the rate of evaporation is too great, the skin has a dry, uncomfortable feeling. The membranes of the nose and throat require adequate humidity to maintain their flexible condition. If the rate of evaporation is too slow, the skin has a clammy, sticky feeling. Evaporation of moisture requires approximately 970 Btu of heat per pound of water evaporated. Heat required for evaporation is lost from the body, thereby cooling it.

Space

Space is defined as the enclosed area in which one lives or works. Conditions for comfort are maintained within the space by mechanical heating. The requirement for comfort is that the space supplies a means for dissipating the heat from the body at the proper rate to maintain proper body temperature.

The conditions for comfort in the space may be divided into two groups: thermal and environmental. The thermal conditions include temperature, relative humidity, and air motion. The environmental conditions include clean air, freedom from disturbing noise, and freedom from disagreeable odors. Because of the importance of the thermal factors, these will be discussed first.

Temperature

The ability to produce the correct space temperature is probably the most important single factor in providing comfortable conditions. Two types of temperature are considered:

1. Temperature of the air that surrounds the body
2. Temperature of the exposed surface enclosing the room

For the maximum degree of comfort, both the air temperature and the surface temperature should be the same. Air temperature is measured with an ordinary thermometer. Surface temperature is more difficult to measure and is usually read by using either an electronic thermometer or a special surface temperature thermometer. The best comfort temperature level for both air and surface within the space is 76°F (24.5°C), according to the American Society of Heating, Refrigerating, and Air Conditioning Engineers (ASHRAE) Comfort Standard 55–80.

In view of the need to conserve energy, however, interior temperature levels for heating have been lowered. In this book we use 70°F (2.1°C) as a design inside temperature. In cases when energy must be conserved, lower temperatures are recommended. It is acknowledged that some people will have to put on additional clothing to remain comfortable at this temperature.

Relative Humidity

For our purposes, *relative humidity* indicates the percent of water vapor actually in the air compared to the maximum amount that the air could hold at the same temperature. There are two types of psychrometers used to determine the relative humidity. The sling psychrometer and the power psychrometer are shown in Figure 2–3. The difference between the instruments is that the sling psychrometer is manual and the power psychrometer utilizes a fan powered by a battery.

To take readings using a sling psychrometer, dip the wick on the wet bulb thermometer in water (distilled, if possible). (Use only one dipping per determination of relative humidity, but never dip between readings.) The evaporation of the moisture on the wick is the determining factor of the wet bulb reading. Whirl the sling psychrometer for 30 seconds. Quickly take the reading on the wet bulb thermometer first; then read the dry bulb and record the readings. Continue to whirl the psychrometer, taking readings at 30-second intervals for five successive readings, recording the temperatures each time until the lowest readings for wet bulb and dry bulb have been obtained.

The power psychrometer is designed to provide a 15-ft./s airflow over the thermometers. When the fan operates, the wet bulb temperature will be rapidly lowered. A reading should not be taken until the temperature drops to its lowest point. This may take from 1 to 2 minutes, depending on the dryness of the air. Take two readings. Use a psychrometric chart or table to obtain the relative humidity (rh).

Figure 2–4 is a simplified psychrometric chart that can be used to determine the relative humidity of a sample of air. Note that the wet bulb lines slope downward to the

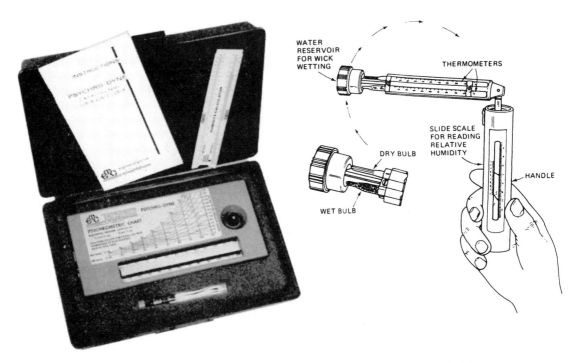

PSYCHRO-DYNE POWER PSYCHROMETER.
(COURTESY, ENVIRONMENTAL TECTONICS CO.)

SLING PSYCHROMETER.
(COURTESY, BACHARACH, INC.)

FIGURE 2–3   Two types of psychrometers.

right, the dry bulb lines are vertical, and the relative humidity lines curve upward to the right. Any point on the chart, therefore, represents some wet bulb, dry bulb, and relative humidity condition.

Example
2–1

What is the relative humidity for the condition of 75°F db (dry bulb) and 60°F wb (wet bulb)?

Solution
Locate 75°F db on the baseline and trace vertically upward until it meets the 60°F wb line. The relative humidity at this point is 40%.   □

Air Motion

Most heating systems require some air movement to distribute heat within the space. In a forced air heating system, air is supplied through registers and returned to the heating unit through grilles. High-velocity air, measured in feet per minute (ft./min.), enters the room through the supply registers. Air at these velocities may be required to heat cold exterior walls properly. The velocity is greatly reduced by natural means before the air reaches the occupants of the room. According to the ASHRAE Comfort Standard,

FIGURE 2–4 Simplified psychrometric chart.

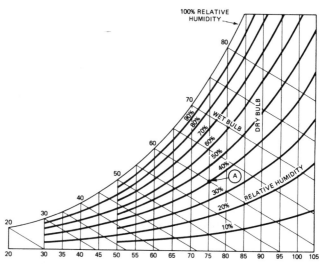

provided that other recommended conditions are maintained (76°F db, 40% rh), the air
that comes in contact with people should not exceed a velocity of 45 ft/min or 0.23 m/s.

Air Quality

Filtration is very important today because residential and commercial buildings are
more energy efficient. Consequently, there is less infiltration. To compensate, more
outdoor ventilation air must be brought in. However, if the indoor air can be cleaned
through filtration, less outdoor air needs to be brought in. Since the outdoor air must
be heated in the winter and cooled in the summer, less outdoor air means lower operational costs. ASHRAE has established the standards for ventilation for acceptable indoor air quality. The standard establishes a recommended outdoor air minimum of 15
cfm per person. For offices the minimum is 20 cfm per person. The outdoor air may
enter because of infiltration, ventilation, or a combination of both. Filters must be selected with care if the quality of the indoor air is to be maintained.

Freedom from Disturbing Noise

Noise or objectionable sound can be airborne or travel through the structure of a
building. Airborne noise can be caused by mechanical equipment being located too
near a building's occupants or by the mechanical noise being transmitted through connecting air ducts. Noise that travels through the structure of a building is caused by the
vibration of equipment mounted in direct contact with the building.

   To remove noise problems, equipment should be properly selected from a noise-level
standpoint. Where noise or vibration does exist, equipment should be properly isolated
(separated from sound-transmitting materials) (Figure 2–5). Sound can be measured by
acoustical instruments. The unit of sound-level measurement is the decibel (dB).

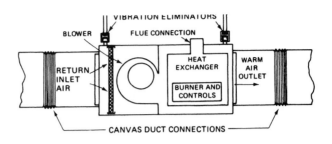

FIGURE 2–5 Noise and vibration eliminators. (By permission of *ASHRAE Handbook.*)

HORIZONTAL FORCED WARM AIR FURNACE

Freedom from Disagreeable Odors

Any closed space occupied by people will develop odors. Ventilation is the most effective means of reducing odors. Some outside air leaks into a building through the cracks around windows and through the building construction. In modern construction, occasionally this is not enough to provide adequate ventilation.

A provision can be made to provide an additional quantity of outside air. Ventilation air should not be confused with combustion air, since combustion air must be provided to burn the furnace fuel properly. This must not in any way subtract from the air (oxygen) available for the occupants of the house.

STUDY QUESTIONS

Answers to the study questions may be found in the sections noted in brackets.

2–1. Define comfort. *[Conditions That Affect Comfort]*

2–2. How can the body be compared to a heat engine? *[Human Requirements for Comfort]*

2–3. What is normal body temperature? *[Human Requirements for Comfort]*

2–4. What are the conditions for body comfort from the standpoint of heat loss? *[Human Requirements for Comfort]*

2–5. How does the body transfer heat? *[Human Requirements for Comfort]*

2–6. How does the temperature of exposed room surfaces affect comfort? *[Temperature]*

2–7. How much heat is required to evaporate 1 lb. of water? *[Evaporation]*

2–8. How does the activity of a person affect the amount of heat dissipated? *[Human Requirements for Comfort]*

2–9. What is a sling psychrometer? How do you use it to measure relative humidity? *[Relative Humidity]*

2–10. Referring to the psychrometric chart, what is the relative humidity for 75° db and 60° wb? *[Relative Humidity]*

3

Combustion and Fuels

OBJECTIVES

After studying this chapter, the student will be able to:

- Compare the heating qualities of various fuels
- Determine the conditions necessary for efficient utilization of fuels
- Use combustion test instruments
- Evaluate the results of combustion testing
- Determine the changes that must be made to reach maximum combustion efficiency

COMBUSTION

Combustion is the chemical process in which oxygen is combined rapidly with a fuel to release the stored energy in the form of heat. There are three conditions necessary for combustion to take place:

1. *Fuel:* consisting of a combination of carbon and hydrogen
2. *Heat:* sufficient to raise the temperature of the fuel to ignition (burning) point
3. *Oxygen:* from the air, combined with the elements in the fuel

Figure 3–1 illustrates the conditions necessary for combustion. The fuel can be gas (such as natural gas), liquid (such as fuel oil), or solid (such as coal). Two elements all fuels have in common are hydrogen and carbon. Fuel must be heated to burn. For example, a pilot burner (small flame) can be used to ignite gas burners; electric ignition (an electric spark) is used to ignite oil; and usually, a wood-burning fire is used to ignite coal. An example of a pilot burner and spark igniter is shown in Figure 3–2. Air containing oxygen must be present for burning of fuel to take place. As an example, a

FIGURE 3-1 Conditions necessary for combustion.

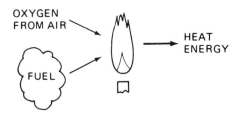

OXYGEN
FROM AIR

HEAT
ENERGY

FUEL

burning candle can be extinguished by placing a glass jar around it to enclose it (Figure 3–3). The candle goes out when it no longer has oxygen to burn.

Types of Combustion

There are two types of combustion: complete combustion and incomplete combustion. Complete combustion must be obtained in all fuel-burning devices. Incomplete combustion is dangerous. *Complete combustion* results when carbon combines with oxygen to form carbon dioxide (CO_2), which is nontoxic and can be readily exhausted to the atmosphere. The hydrogen combines with oxygen to form water vapor (H_2O), which also can be exhausted harmlessly to the atmosphere. *Incomplete combustion* results when a lack of sufficient oxygen causes the formation of undesirable products, including:

- Carbon monoxide (CO)
- Pure carbon or soot (C)
- Aldehyde, a colorless volatile liquid with a strong unpleasant odor (CH_3CHO)

Both carbon monoxide and aldehyde are toxic and poisonous. Soot causes coating of the heating surface of the furnace and reduces heat transfer (useful heat). Thus, the heating service technician must adjust the fuel-burning device to produce complete combustion of the fuel.

FIGURE 3-2 Example of pilot burner and spark igniter. (Courtesy of White-Rodgers, Division of Emerson Electric Company.)

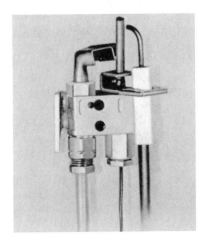

FIGURE 3–3   Candle flame extinguished by lack of oxygen

During complete combustion the fuel combines with oxygen in the air to produce carbon dioxide and water vapor:

$$CH_4 + O_2 \rightarrow CO_2 + 2H_2O$$

Caution: To prevent the dangers of incomplete combustion sufficient air must be provided for proper combustion to take place.

Air consists of about 21% oxygen and 79% nitrogen by volume (Figure 3–4). The nitrogen in air dilutes oxygen, which would otherwise be too concentrated to breathe in its pure form. Nitrogen is an *inert* element. The inert quality in an element means that it remains in a pure state without combining with other elements under ordinary conditions. For example, in a furnace when nitrogen is heated to temperatures higher than 2000°F, it does not react with the elements of the fuel. It enters the furnace with the combustion air and leaves through the chimney as pure nitrogen.

Flue Gases

The flue gases of a furnace operating to produce complete combustion contain:

- Carbon dioxide
- Water vapor
- Nitrogen
- Excess air

FIGURE 3–4   Chemical composition of air.

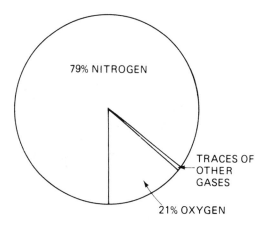

Carbon dioxide and water vapor are the products of complete combustion. Nitrogen remains after oxygen in the combustion air is consumed by the fuel. Excess air is supplied to the fuel-burning device to guard against the possibility of producing incomplete combustion. Normally, furnaces are adjusted to use 5 to 50% excess air. The effect of the amount of excess air on the CO_2 in the flue gases is shown in Figure 3–5.

Heating Values

Each fuel, when burned, is capable of producing a given amount of heat, depending on the constituents of the fuel. This information is useful in determining the heating capacity of a furnace. If the heating value of a unit of fuel produces a given amount of Btu, and the number of units of fuel burned per hour is known, the input rating of the furnace can be calculated. The Btu ratings for units of natural gas are shown in Figure 3–6. The typical gravity and heating value of fuel oil is shown in Figure 3–7, and the approximate Btu ratings for coal are shown in Figure 3–8.

Example 3–1

An oil furnace burning No. 2 fuel oil uses 0.75 gal/h. What is the input rating of the furnace?

Solution

The heating value of No. 2 oil from Figure 3–7 is between 141,800 and 137,000 Btu/gal. To simplify calculations, rating is rounded to 140,000 Btu/gal. Therefore, the input rating of the furnace would be

140,000 Btu/gal × 0.75 usage rate = 105,000 Btuh input   ☐

Note: The Btu ratings for gas are given in Btu/ft$_3$, for oil in Btu/gal, and for coal in Btu/lb. The units used differ for each fuel because of the form in which they are delivered (Figure 3–9).

Losses and Efficiencies

When fuel is burned in a furnace, a certain amount of heat is lost in the hot gases that rise through the chimney. Although this function is necessary for disposal of the products of combustion, the loss should be minimized to allow the furnace to operate at its highest efficiency. Air entering the furnace at room temperature, or lower, is heated to fuel gas temperatures. These temperatures range from 350 to 600°F, depending on the design of the furnace and its adjustment by a service technician.

If the amount of heat lost is 20%, the efficiency of the furnace would be 80%. Figure 3–20 shows a combustion efficiency slide rule. The calculation of the combustion efficiency is based on knowing the temperature and the carbon dioxide content of the flue gases. Knowing the efficiency of the furnace makes it possible for a heating service technician to calculate the output of the furnace. The following formula is used:

Btuh input × % efficiency = Btu output

APPROXIMATE MAXIMUM CO_2 VALUES FOR VARIOUS FUELS WITH DIFFERENT
PERCENTAGES OF EXCESS AIR

TYPE OF FUEL	MAXIMUM THEORETICAL CO_2 PERCENT	PERCENT CO_2 AT GIVEN EXCESS AIR VALUES		
		20%	40%	60%
GASEOUS FUELS				
NATURAL GAS	12.1	9.9	8.4	7.3
PROPANE GAS (COMMERCIAL)	13.9	11.4	9.6	8.4
BUTANE GAS (COMMERCIAL)	14.1	11.6	9.8	8.5
MIXED GAS (NATURAL AND				
CARBURETED WATER GAS)	11.2	12.5	10.5	9.1
CARBURETED WATER GAS	17.2	14.2	12.1	10.6
COKE OVEN GAS	11.2	9.2	7.8	6.8
LIQUID FUELS				
NO. 1 AND 2 FUEL OIL	15.0	12.3	10.5	9.1
NO. 6 FUEL OIL	16.5	13.6	11.6	10.1
SOLID FUELS				
BITUMINOUS COAL	18.2	15.1	12.9	11.3
ANTHRACITE	20.2	16.8	14.4	12.6
COKE	21.0	17.5	15.0	13.0

FIGURE 3–5   Effect of excess air on the CO_2 in the flue gases. (By permission from the *ASHRAE Handbook.*)

Example 3–2   The input of an oil furnace is 105,000 Btuh. Its efficiency is 80%. What is its output?

Solution

$$105,000 \text{ Btu} \times 0.80 \text{ efficiency} = 84,000 \text{ Btuh output}$$ ☐

Types of Flames

Basically, there are two types of flames: yellow and blue (Figure 3–10). Pressure-type oil burners burn with a yellow flame. Modern Bunsen-type gas burners burn with a blue flame. The difference is due mainly to the manner in which air is mixed with the fuel. A yellow flame is produced when gas is burned by igniting fuel gushing from an open end of a gas pipe, such as may be seen in fixtures used for ornamental decoration. A blue flame is produced when approximately 50% of the air requirement is mixed with the gas prior to ignition. This is called primary air. A Bunsen burner uses this arrangement. The balance of air, called *secondary air,* is supplied during combustion to the exterior of the flame. Air adjustments are discussed in Chapter 5.

Improper gas flames are the result of inefficient or incomplete combustion and can be caused by:

- Excess supply of primary air
- Lack of secondary air
- Impingement of the flame on a cool surface (Figure 3–11)

NO.	CITY	HEAT VALUE, BTU/CU FT	SPECIFIC GRAVITY
1	ABILENE, TEX.	1121	0.710
2	AKRON, OHIO	1037	0.600
3	ALBUQUERQUE, N.M.	1120	0.646
4	ATLANTA, GA.	1031	0.604
5	BALTIMORE, MD.	1051	0.590
6	BIRMINGHAM, ALA.	1024	0.599
7	BOSTON, MASS.	1057	0.604
8	BROOKLYN, N.Y.	1049	0.595
9	BUTTE, MONT.	1000	0.610
10	CANTON, OHIO	1037	0.600
11	CHEYENNE, WYO.	1060	0.610
12	CINCINNATI, OHIO	1031	0.591
13	CLEVELAND, OHIO	1037	0.600
14	COLUMBUS, OHIO	1028	0.597
15	DALLAS, TEX.	1093	0.641
16	DENVER, COLO.	1011	0.659
17	DES MOINES, IOWA	1012	0.669
18	DETROIT, MICH.	1016	0.616
19	EL PASO, TEX.	1082	0.630
20	FT. WORTH, TEX.	1115	0.649
21	HOUSTON, TEX.	1031	0.623
22	KANSAS CITY, MO.	945	0.695
23	LITTLE ROCK, ARK.	1035	0.590
24	LOS ANGELES, CALIF.	1084	0.638
25	LOUISVILLE, KY.	1034	0.506
26	MEMPHIS, TENN.	1044	0.608
27	MILWAUKEE, WIS.	1051	0.627
28	NEW ORLEANS, LA.	1072	0.612
29	NEW YORK CITY	1049	0.595
30	OKLAHOMA CITY, OKLA.	1080	0.615
31	OMAHA, NEB.	1020	0.669
32	PARKERSBURG, W. VA.	1049	0.592
33	PHOENIX, ARIZ.	1071	0.633
34	PITTSBURGH, PA.	1051	0.595
35	PROVIDENCE, R.I.	1057	0.601
36	PROVO, UTAH	1032	0.605
37	PUEBLO, COLO.	980	0.706
38	RAPID CITY, S.D.	1077	0.607
39	ST. LOUIS, MO.	–	–
40	SALT LAKE CITY, UTAH	1082	0.614
41	SAN DIEGO, CALIF.	1079	0.643
42	SAN FRANCISCO, CALIF.	1086	0.624
43	TOLEDO, OHIO	1028	0.597
44	TULSA, OKLA.	1086	0.630
45	WACO, TEX.	1042	0.607
46	WASHINGTON, D.C.	1042	0.586
47	WICHITA, KAN.	1051	0.690
48	YOUNGSTOWN, OHIO	1037	0.600

*Average analyses obtained from the operating utility company supplying the city; the supply may vary considerably from these data — especially where more than one pipeline supplies the city. Also, as new supplies may be received from other sources, the analyses may change.

FIGURE 3–6   Btu ratings for units of natural gas. (By permission from the *ASHRAE Handbook.*)

GRADE NO.	GRAVITY, API	WEIGHT, LB PER GALLON	HEATING VALUE, BTU PER GALLON
1	38–45	6.95 –6.675	137,000–132,900
2	30–38	7.296–6.960	141,800–137,000
4	20–28	7.787–7.396	148,100–143,100
5L	17–22	7.94 –7.686	150,000–146,800
5H	14–18	8.08 –7.89	152,000–149,400
6	8–15	8.448–8.053	155,900–151,300

(API AMERICAN PETROLEUM INSTITUTE RATING)

FIGURE 3–7 Typical gravity and heating values for standard grades of fuel oil. (By permission from the *ASHRAE Handbook.*)

FUELS

Fuels are available in three forms: gases, liquids, and solids. Gases include natural gas and liquid petroleum; fuel oils are rated by grades 1, 2, 4, 5, and 6; and coals are of various types, mainly anthracite and bituminous. Each fuel has its own individual Btu heat content per unit and its own desirable or undesirable characteristics. The fuel selection is usually based on availability, price, and type of application.

Types and Properties of Gaseous Fuels

There are three types of gaseous fuels:

1. Natural gas
2. Manufactured gas
3. Liquid petroleum (LP)

Natural gas comes from the earth in the form of gas and often accumulates in the upper part of the oil wells. Manufactured gases are combustible gases, usually produced from solid or liquid fuel and used mainly for industrial process. LP is a by-product of the oil refining process. It is so named because it is stored in liquid form. LP, however, is vaporized when burned.

FIGURE 3–8 Approximate Btu ratings for various types of coal. (By permission from the *ASHRAE Handbook.*)

RANK	BTU PER LB AS RECEIVED
ANTHRACITE	12,700
SEMIANTHRACITE	13,600
LOW-VOLATILE BITUMINOUS	14,350
MEDIUM-VOLATILE BITUMINOUS	14,000
HIGH-VOLATILE BITUMINOUS A	13,800
HIGH-VOLATILE BITUMINOUS B	12,500
HIGH-VOLATILE BITUMINOUS C	11,000
SUBBITUMINOUS B	9,000
SUBBITUMINOUS C	8,500
LIGNITE	6,900

FIGURE 3–9 Units of measurements for gas, oil, and coal.

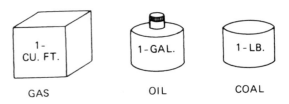

GAS OIL COAL

Natural gas Natural gas is nearly odorless and colorless. Therefore, an odorant such as a mercaptan (any of various compounds containing sulfur and having a disagreeable odor) is added so that a leak can be sensed. The content of gases differs somewhat according to locality. Information should be obtained from the local gas company relative to the specific gravity and the Btu/ft. content of the gas available.

The specific gravity affects piping sizes. *Specific gravity* is the ratio of the weight of a given volume of substance to an equal volume of air or water at a given temperature and pressure. Thus gas with a specific gravity of 0.60 weighs $^6/_{10}$ or $^3/_5$ as much as air for an equal volume. The Btu/ft.^{3} content of gas varies from 900 to 1200, depending on the locality, but it is usually in the range 1000 to 1050 Btu/ft.^{3}.

The chief constituent of natural gas is methane. Commonly called marsh gas, methane is a gaseous hydrocarbon that is a product of decomposition of organic matter in marshes or mines or of the carbonization of coal. Natural gas is comprised of 55 to 95% methane and is combined with other hydrocarbon gas.

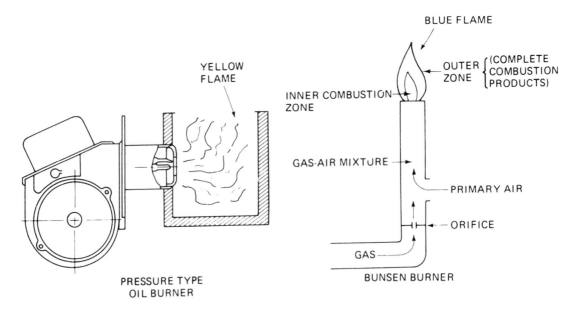

FIGURE 3–10 Types of flames produced by pressure-type oil burner and Bunsen burner. [Courtesy of Robertshaw Control Company (Bunsen Burner).]

FIGURE 3–11 Soot caused by impingement of flame on cool wall of heat exchanger.

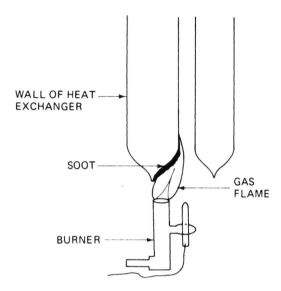

WALL OF HEAT
EXCHANGER

SOOT

GAS
FLAME

BURNER

Manufactured gas   Manufactured gas is produced from coal, oil, and other hydrocarbons. It is comparatively low in Btu/ft.^{3}, usually in the range of 500 to 600. It is not considered an economical space-heating fuel.

Liquid petroleum   There are two types of liquid petroleum: propane and butane. Propane is more useful as a space-heating fuel since it boils at –40°F and, therefore, can readily be vaporized for heating in a northern climate. Butane boils at about 32°F.

Propane has a heating value of 21,560 Btu/lb. or about 2500 Btu/ft.^{3}. Butane has a heating value of 21,180 Btu/lb. or about 3200 Btu/ft.^{3}. When LP gas is used as a heating fuel, the equipment must be designed to use this type of gas. When ordering equipment, the purchaser must indicate which type of gaseous fuel is being used. Conversion kits are available to convert natural gas furnaces to LP gas when necessary. It is important to follow the manufacturer's instructions with great care.

Note: Propane and butane vapors are generally considered more dangerous than those of natural gas, since they have higher specific gravities (propane 1.52, butane 2.01). Because the vapor is heavier it tends to accumulate near the floor, thereby increasing the danger of an explosion upon ignition.

Types and Properties of Fuel Oils

Fuel oils are rated according to their Btu/gal. content and API gravity (shown in Figure 3–7). The API gravity is an index selected by the American Petroleum Institute. There are six grades of oil: Nos. 1, 2, 4, 5 (light), 5 (heavy), and 6. Note that the lighter-weight oils have a higher API gravity.

Grade No. 1: light-grade distillate prepared for vaporizing-type oil burners.

Grade No. 2: heavier distillate than grade No. 1. It is manufactured for domestic pressure-type oil burners.

Grade No. 4: light residue or heavy distillate. It is produced for commercial oil burners using a higher pressure than domestic burners.

Grade No. 5 (light): residual-type fuel of medium weight. It is used for commercial burners that are specially designed for its use.

Grade No. 5 (heavy): residual-type fuel for commercial oil burners. It usually requires preheating

Grade No. 6: also called Bunker C; a heavy residue used for commercial burners. It requires preheating in the tank to permit pumping and additional preheating at the burner to permit atomization (breaking up into fine particles).

Types and Properties of Coals

There are four different types of coal: anthracite, bituminous, subbituminous, and lignite. Coal is constituted principally of carbon, with the better grades having as much as 80% carbon. The types vary not only in Btu/lb. but also in their burning and handling qualities.

Anthracite   Anthracite is a clean, hard coal. It burns with an almost smokeless short flame. It is difficult to ignite but burns freely when started. It is noncaking, leaving a fine ash that does not clog grates and ash removal equipment.

Bituminous   Bituminous coals include a wide range of coals, varying from high grade in the East to low grade in the West. It is more brittle than anthracite coal and readily breaks up into small pieces for grading and screening. The length of the flame is long, but varies for different grades. Unless burning is carefully controlled, much smoke and soot can result.

Subbituminous   This coal has a high moisture content and tends to break up when dry. It can ignite spontaneously when stored. It ignites easily and burns with a medium flame. It is desirable for its noncaking characteristic and for the fact that it forms little soot and smoke.

Lignite   Lignite coal has a woody consistency, is high in moisture content and low in heating value, and is clean to handle. Lignite has a greater tendency to break up when dry than subbituminous coal. Because of its high moisture content, it is difficult to ignite. It is noncaking and forms little smoke and soot.

EFFICIENCY OF OPERATION

Combustion is a chemical reaction resulting in the production of a flame. The fuels used for heating consist chiefly of carbon. In combustion, carbon and oxygen are combined to produce heat. Instruments are used to measure how well the equipment performs the process of combustion. The heating service technician makes whatever adjustments are necessary to produce the most efficient operation. The products of combustion that leave the oil-heating unit through the flue are:

- Carbon dioxide (CO_2)
- Carbon monoxide (CO)
- Oxygen (O)
- Nitrogen (N)
- Water vapor (H_2O)

An outline of the products of combustion is shown in Figure 3–12.

Measurement of the CO_2 in the flue gases is an indication of the amount of air used by the fuel-burning equipment. It is desirable to have a high CO_2 measurement, as this indicates a hot fire. The maximum CO_2 measurement for oil with no excess air is 15.6%; for natural gas, 11.8%. However, it is not practical, with field-installed equipment, to reach these high CO_2 readings. In practice, oil furnaces should have a CO_2 reading of between 10 and 12%; natural gas furnaces should read between $8^1/4$ and $9^1/2$%. The CO_2 in the flue gases is the indicator used (along with stack temperature) to measure the efficiency of combustion.

INSTRUMENTS USED IN TESTING

Instruments used for combustion testing are available from a number of manufacturers. While the illustrations for the instruments described below have been provided by specific companies, instruments that perform similar functions can be obtained from various other manufacturers. The instruments and their functions are:

Instruments Used in Testing

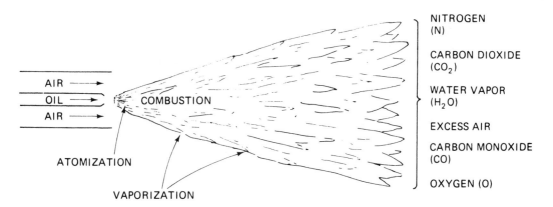

FIGURE 3–12   Products of combustion.

- *Draft gauge:* used for measuring draft (Figure 3–13)
- *Smoke tester:* used for determining smoke scale (Figure 3–14)
- *Flue gas analyzer:* used for testing CO_2 content (Figure 3–15)
- *Stack thermometer:* used for determining stack temperature (Figure 3–16)

Complete combustion kits (Figure 3–17) are available with many of the items listed above. The location of the various parts of the heating plant equipment, and sample holes for testing, are shown in Figure 3–18.

TESTING PROCEDURES

Tests should be made in the following order:

1. Draft measurement
2. Smoke sample
3. CO_2 content
4. Stack temperature

The equipment should be run for a minimum of 5 to 10 min. before testing to stabilize operating conditions. A record should be kept both before adjustments are made and after the tests.

Draft Test

The draft gauge reads in inches of water column. For example, a reading of 0.02 in. W.C. means 2 hundredths of an inch of water column. Always calibrate the instrument before using it. Place the instrument on a level surface and adjust the indicator needle to read zero.

Drill a $^1/_4$-in. hole in the firebox door (Figure 3–19) and two $^1/_4$-in. holes in the flue at the point just after it leaves the heat exchanger. The holes in the flue must be placed

FIGURE 3–13 Draft gauge model MZF, dry type, range +0.05 to –0.25 in. water, supplied with 5-in. draft tube and 9 ft. of rubber tubing. (Courtesy of Bacharach, Inc.)

between the heat exchanger and the draft regulator on an oil furnace and between the heat exchanger and the draft diverter on a gas furnace. One of the two holes in the flue is used for the stack thermometer, the other is used for the CO_2 and smoke tests. Occasionally, an additional $1/4$-in. hole is drilled in the flue pipe near the chimney to measure chimney draft. This is normally used only when it is necessary to troubleshoot draft problems.

The draft should always be negative when measured with the draft gauge, since the flue gases are moving away from the furnace. The draft-over-the-fire, measured at the firebox door, should be –0.01 to –0.02 in. W.C. The difference between the draft reading in the flue at the furnace outlet, and the draft-over-the-fire reading, indicates the heat-exchanger leakage.

Carbon Dioxide Test

An analyzer for CO_2 uses potassium hydroxide (KOH), a chemical that has the property of being able to absorb large quantities of CO_2. A known volume of flue gas is run

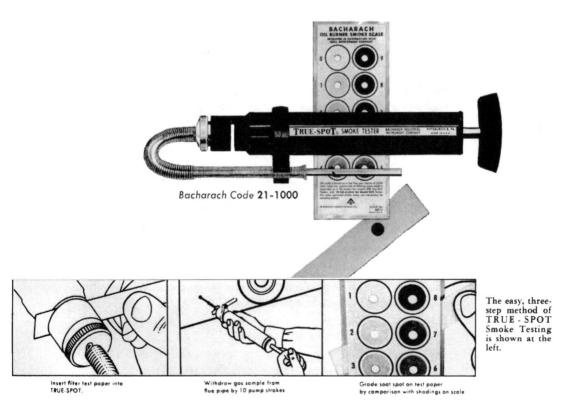

Bacharach Code 21-1000

The easy, three-step method of TRUE - SPOT Smoke Testing is shown at the left.

Insert filter test paper into TRUE-SPOT.

Withdraw gas sample from flue pipe by 10 pump strokes

Grade soot spot on test paper by comparison with shadings on scale

FIGURE 3–14 21–7007 True-Spot smoke test set determines efficient combustion. It is recognized as the standard method for evaluating smoke density of the flue gases of oil-burning equipment and includes test pump, smoke scale, and filter strips. (Courtesy of Bacharach, Inc.)

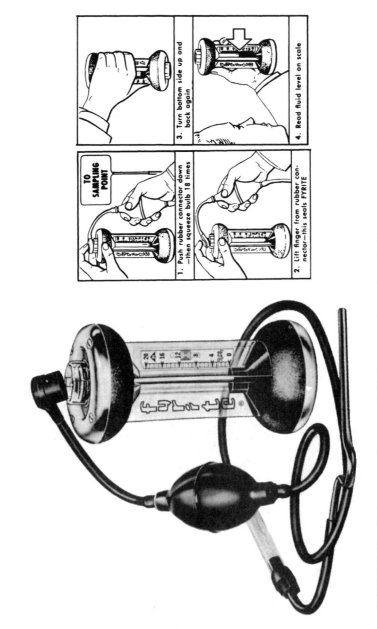

FIGURE 3–15 Fyrite gas analyzers, available for measuring carbon dioxide or oxygen, can be exposed to temperatures from –30 to 150°F, and gases up to 850°F may be tested. Kit 10–5001 CO_2 (range 0 to 20%) and Kit 10–5012 O_2 (range 0 to 21%). Case is included. (Courtesy of Bacharach, Inc.)

FIGURE 3–16 Tempoint dial thermometer, bimetal type, accurate from −40 to +1000°F. Designed to read stack temperatures; recalibration possible. (Courtesy of Bacharach, Inc.)

into the tester. Since KOH will absorb only CO_2, the reduction in volume of the flue gas is an indication of the amount of CO_2 absorbed by the KOH solution. Instructions for using the tester shown in Figure 3–15 are as follows:

1. Set the instrument to zero by adjusting the sliding scale to the level of the fluid in the tube.
2. Insert the sample tube in the flue opening. Place the rubber connector on top of the instrument and depress to open the valve. Collapse the bulb 18 times to fill the instrument with flue gas and then release the valve.

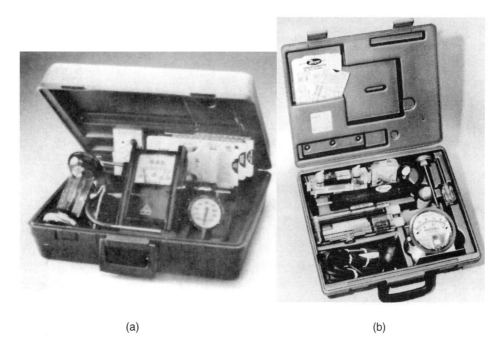

(a)   (b)

FIGURE 3–17 Combustion testing kits:
(a) Oil burner combustion testing kit: Fyrite CO_2 indicator, True-Spot smoke tester, Fire Efficiency finder/stack loss slide rule, dial thermometer, MZF draft gauge, Draftrite draft gauge, and carrying case. Gas burner combustion kits are also available. (Courtesy of Bacharach, Inc.)
(b) Combustion testing kit for gas-, oil-, and coal-fired installations: includes CO_2 indicator, draft gauge 0 to 0.25 in. W.C., smoke gauge pump, smoke chart, stack thermometer, combustion efficiency slide rule, portable magnehelic gauge with 4-in. dial 0 to 0.25 in. W.C. and 300 to 2000 fpm, carrying case, and operating instructions. (Courtesy of Dwyer Instruments, Inc.)

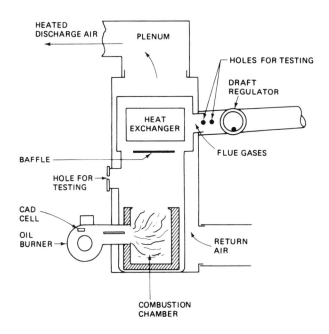

FIGURE 3–18   Heating plant equipment, showing holes for testing.

3. Tip the instrument over and back twice and hold at a 45-degree angle for 5 seconds.
4. Hold the instrument upright and read the CO_2 content on the scale. Release the pressure by opening the valve when the test is complete.

Stack Temperature Test

A stack thermometer is used to determine stack temperature. Insert the thermometer in the flue hole as shown in Figure 3–18. Operate the burner unit until the temperature rise, as read on the thermometer, is no more than 3°F/min. (indicating stability); then read the final stack temperature.

Smoke Test

The burner flame should not produce excessive smoke. Smoke causes soot (carbon) to collect on the surfaces of the heat exchanger, reducing its heat-transfer rate. A soot deposit of $1/8$ in. can cause a reduction of 10% in the rate of heat absorption. Measurement of smoke is performed by using a smoke tester. A sample is collected by pumping 2200 cm³ (10 full strokes with the sampling pump) through a 0.38-cm² area filter paper. The color of the sample filter paper spot is compared to a standard graduated smoke scale (Figure 3–14). Spot No. 0 is white and indicates no smoke. Spot No.

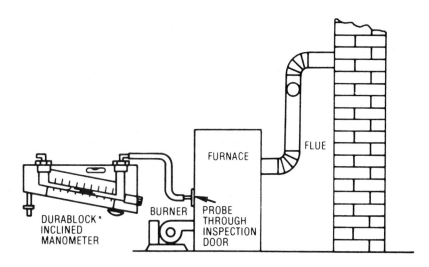

FIGURE 3–19   Using a draft gauge to adjust for efficient combustion. (Courtesy of Dwyer Instruments, Inc.)

9 is darkest and represents the most extreme smoke condition. Between 0 and 9 the scale has 10 different grades. It is most desirable to produce smoke at a scale of No. 1 or 2 but not 0. Older-style or conversion units could read at high as No. 4. No. 0 indicates excess air supply to the burner and low efficiency. Readings higher than No. 2 indicate the production of excessive carbon and soot. Normally, this test is performed only on oil-burning equipment.

COMBUSTION EFFICIENCY

Combustion efficiency, expressed in percentage, is a measure of the useful heat produced in the fuel compared to the amount of fuel available. A furnace that operates at 80% efficiency is therefore one that loses 20% of the fuel value in the heat that goes out through the chimney. High-efficiency furnaces have an operating efficiency of up to 96%.

A combustion efficiency slide rule is a useful tool (Figure 3–20). After determining the stack (flue) temperature and CO_2 content, and by using the appropriate slide on the rule, the combustion efficiency can be determined. Note that combustion efficiency is based on net stack temperature. Net stack temperature is the reading taken on the stack thermometer minus the room temperature (the temperature of the air entering the furnace). For example, assume that the net stack temperature for an oil burner is found to be 500°F and the CO_2 content is determined as 9%. Using the slide rule, move the large slide to the right so that 500 appears in the small window at the upper right marked "net stack temperature." Then move the

FIGURE 3–20 Combustion efficiency slide rule.
(Courtesy of Bacharach, Inc.)

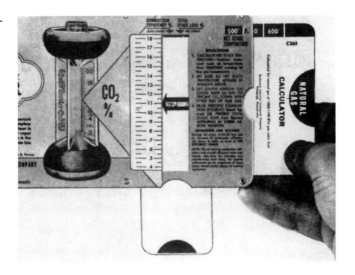

FROM AN ORIGINAL EFFICIENCY OF	TO AN INCREASED COMBUSTION OF:							
	55%	60%	65%	70%	75%	80%	⑧⑤%	90%
50%	9.10	16.70	23.10	28.60	33.30	37.50	41.20	44.40
55%	—	8.30	15.40	21.50	26.70	31.20	35.30	38.90
60%	—	—	7.70	14.30	20.00	25.00	29.40	33.30
65%	—	—	—	7.10	13.30	18.80	23.50	27.80
70%	—	—	—	—	6.70	12.50	17.60	22.20
75%	—	—	—	—	—	6.30	11.80	16.70
⑧⓪%	—	—	—	—	—	—	⑤.⑨⓪	11.10
85%	—	—	—	—	—	—	—	5.6

FIGURE 3–21 Fuel saved by increasing efficiency. (Courtesy of R. W. Beckett Corporation.)

small vertical slide until the arrow points to reading 9 on the CO_2 scale. Through the window in the arrow, read the figures 80 (black) and 20 (red). This means that the combustion efficiency is 80% and the stack loss is 20%. Figure 3–21 shows, for example, how increasing the combustion efficiency from 80% to 85% would save $5.90 of every $100 of fuel cost.

ANALYSIS AND ADJUSTMENTS

Usually, the tests are made after routine maintenance has been performed. The combustion tests indicate the condition of the equipment and point to further service or adjustments that may be necessary.

Oil-Burning Equipment

On oil-burning equipment, adjustments are made in the air supply to the burner. Air is reduced to maintain a smoke test within the No. 1 to No. 2 limits while providing the highest possible CO_2 content in the flue gases. If an efficiency rating of 75% or better cannot be obtained as a result of adjustments in the air supply, further service on the burner is required. Listed below are some common causes of low CO_2 content and smoky fires (Figure 3–22).

1. Incorrect air supply
2. Combustion chamber air leaks
3. Improper operation of draft regulator
4. Insufficient draft
5. Burner "on" periods too short
6. Oil does not conform to burner requirements
7. Air-handling parts defective or incorrectly adjusted
8. Firebox cracked
9. Spray angle of nozzle unsuitable
10. Nozzle worn, clogged, or incorrect type
11. Gallons/hour rate too high for size of combustion chamber
12. Ignition delay due to defective stack control
13. Nozzle spray or capacity unsuited to type of burner
14. Oil pressure to nozzle improperly adjusted
15. Nozzle loose or not centered
16. Electrodes dirty, loose, or incorrectly set
17. Cutoff valve leaks
18. Rotary burner motor running under speed

Some conditions that produce poor efficiency, such as those indicated below, can be determined by visual inspection.

1. Check burner shutdown. A flame should last no longer than 2 seconds after the burner shuts down.
2. Check the flame. It should be symmetrically shaped and centered in the combustion chamber. It should not strike the walls or floor of the combustion chamber.
3. Check for air leaks. There should be no leakage around the burner tube where it enters the combustion chamber.
4. Check the burner operating period. Burning periods of less than 5 min. duration usually do not produce efficient operation.

Gas-Burning Equipment

On gas-burning equipment, the primary air is reduced by adjusting the air shutter to provide a blue flame. The secondary air is a fixed quantity on most furnaces. Inspection should be made, however, to determine if the secondary air restrictor has become loose or perhaps removed. A correction should be made. If the flame does not adjust

1. Improper fan delivery or incorrect air shutter opening.

2. Furnace or boiler has excessive air leaks.

3. Draft regulator is improperly installed or sticking.

4. Draft is insufficient due to defective flue or insufficient height of chimney.

5. Burner "on" periods are too short.

6. Oil does not conform to burner requirements.

7. Air handling parts defective or incorrectly adjusted.

8. Firebox is cracked or of improper refractory material.

9. Spray angle of nozzle unsuited to air pattern of burner or shape of firebox.

10. Nozzle is worn, clogged or of incorrect type.

11. Gph. rate is too high for size of combustion chamber.

12. Ignition is delayed due to defective stack control.

13. Nozzle spray or capacity unsuited to the particular type of burner being used.

14. Oil pressure to nozzle improperly adjusted causing poor spray characteristics.

15. Nozzle is loose or not centered.

16. Electrodes are dirty, loose or incorrectly set.

17. Cut-off valve leaks, allowing after-drip of fuel oil.

18. Rotary burner motor is running underspeed.

FIGURE 3–22   Common causes of low CO_2 content and smoky fires. (Courtesy of Bacharach, Inc.)

properly to produce a blue flame and an efficiency rating of 75% or better cannot be obtained, further service is required.

Some causes of poor efficiency are:

1. Unclean burner ports. To clean the burner ports, remove the lint and dirt.
2. Insufficient gas pressure. The draft diverter should be checked with the burner in operation. Air should be moving into the opening, thus indicating a negative pressure at the inlet. This can be verified by holding a lighted match at the opening.
3. Improper gas pressure. The gas pressure should be $3^1/_2$ in. W.C. at the manifold for natural gas. Check the gas meter for input into the furnace. It should read the same as the input indicated on the furnace nameplate. If the gas pressure reads between 3 and 4 in. W.C. and still does not produce the rated input, the orifice should be cleaned or replaced with one of proper size. For LP the gas pressure should be 11 in. W.C. at the manifold on the furnace.
4. Improper "on" and "off" periods of the furnace. "On" periods of less than 5 min. are too brief to produce high efficiency.

STUDY QUESTIONS

Answers to the study questions may be found in the sections noted in brackets.

3–1. What type of process is combustion? Describe the action that takes place. *[Combustion]*

3–2. What are the three conditions necessary for combustion? *[Combustion]*

3–3. What action takes place during complete combustion? What elements are combined and what products are produced? *[Types of Combustion]*

3–4. What is the cause of incomplete combustion? What are the products formed? *[Types of Combustion]*

3–5. What is the percent of oxygen in the air? *[Types of Combustion]*

3–6. What is the range of heating values for natural gas, fuel oil, and coal? *[Heating Values]*

3–7. What is the maximum efficiency for natural gas and oil fuels? *[Losses and Efficiencies]*

3–8. What is the proper color for an oil flame? a gas flame? *[Types of Flames]*

3–9. Should the draft-over-the-fire for an oil burner be positive, negative, or neutral? *[Draft Test]*

3–10. Using a draft regulator, with an oil furnace, what is the proper draft measurement over-the-fire? *[Draft Test]*

3–11. In testing for CO_2 in the flue gas with a potassium hydroxide analyzer, how many times should the bulb be collapsed? *[Carbon Dioxide Test]*

3–12. What should be the combustion efficiency on a standard oil-burning furnace? *[Combustion Efficiency]*

3–13. What dollar savings for every $100 of fuel cost would be saved in increasing the efficiency from 60% to 80%? *[Combustion Efficiency]*

3–14. Name 10 conditions that can cause an oil burner to produce low CO_2 and a smoky fire. *[Oil-Burning Equipment]*

3–15. Name three conditions that can cause a gas burner to operate at low efficiency. *[Gas-Burning Equipment]*

4

Parts Common to All Furnaces

OBJECTIVES

After studying this chapter, the student will be able to:

- Identify the various components of forced warm air heating furnaces
- Adjust the speed of a furnace fan
- Provide proper service and maintenance for common parts of a heating system

HOW A FURNACE OPERATES

A warm air furnace is a device for providing space heating. Fuel, a form of energy, is converted into heat and distributed to various parts of a structure. Fuel-burning furnaces provide heat by combustion of the fuel within a heat exchanger. Air is passed over the outside surface of the heat exchanger, transferring the heat from the fuel to the air. In a fuel-burning furnace, the products of combustion are exhausted to the atmosphere through the flue passages connected to the heat exchanger.

Since no products of combustion are formed in an electric furnace, air passes directly over the electrically heated elements without the use of a heat exchanger. A forced-air furnace uses a fan to propel the air over the heat exchanger and to circulate the air through the distribution system. A furnace is considered a residential type when its input is less than 250,000 Btuh.

BASIC COMPONENTS

There are six basic components of a forced warm air furnace:

1. Heat exchanger
2. Fuel-burning device
3. Cabinet or enclosure
4. Fan and motor
5. Air filters
6. Controls

The fuel-burning device is discussed in Chapters 5 and 13. The controls are discussed in Chapters 10, 11, and 14.

ARRANGEMENT OF COMPONENTS

Four different designs of forced air furnaces are in common use. Each requires a different arrangement of the basic components:

1. Horizontal
2. Upflow or highboy
3. Lowboy
4. Downflow or counterflow

The *horizontal* furnace is used in attic spaces or other locations, where the height of the furnace must be kept as low as possible (Figures 4–1 and 4–2). Air enters at one end of the unit through the fan compartment, is forced horizontally over the heat exchanger, and then exits at the opposite end.

The upflow or *highboy* design is used in the basement or a first-floor equipment room where floor space is at a premium (Figures 4–3 and 4–4). The fan is located below the heat exchanger. Air enters at the bottom or lower sides of the unit and leaves at the top through a warm air plenum.

The lowboy furnace occupies more floor space and is lower in height than the upflow design, which makes it ideally suited for basement installation (Figure 4–5). The fan is placed alongside the heat exchanger. A return air plenum is built above the fan compartment. A supply air plenum is built above the heat-exchanger compartment.

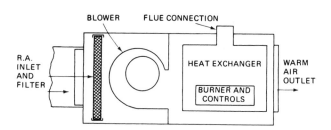

FIGURE 4–1 Horizontal forced warm air furnace. (By permission from the *ASHRAE Handbook*)

FIGURE 4–2   Horizontal forced warm air furnace, gas-fired. (Courtesy of ARCOAIRE, Inter-City Products Corporation, USA.)

PARTS IDENTIFICATION

1. FLUE CONNECTION.
2. BURNER ACCESS PANEL. LIFT UP AND OUT TO REMOVE.
3. FAN AND LIMIT CONTROL.
4. WIRING MAKE-UP BOX.
5. MAIN GAS VALVE.
6. PILOT BURNER.
7. MAIN BURNERS.
8. FILTER.
9. FAN MOTOR.
10. FAN AND FILTER ACCESS PANEL. LIFT UP AND OUT TO REMOVE.
11. DURACURVE HEAT EXCHANGER.
12. DIRECT DRIVE FAN.

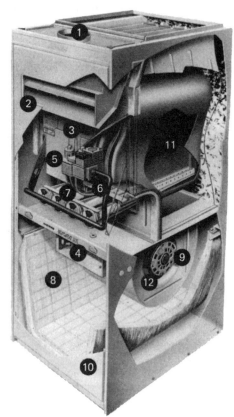

FIGURE 4–3   Upflow (highboy) forced warm air furnace, gas-fired. (Courtesy of Lennox Industries, Inc.)

FIGURE 4–4 Installed upflow warm air furnace, gas-fired, including air conditioner, air cleaner and humidifier. (Courtesy of Carrier Corporation.)

① AIR CONDITIONER   ② ELECTRONIC AIR CLEANER

①A HEAT PUMP   ③ HUMIDIFIER

The *downflow* or *counterflow* design is used in houses having an under-the-floor type of distribution system (Figure 4–6). The fan is located above the heat exchanger. The return air plenum is connected to the top of the unit. The supply air plenum is connected to the bottom of the unit.

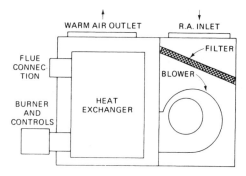

FIGURE 4–5 Lowboy forced warm air furnace. (By permission from the *ASHRAE Handbook.*)

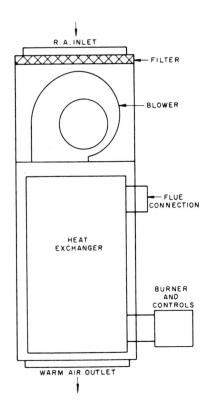

FIGURE 4–6   Downflow (counter-flow) forced warm air furnace. (By permission from the *ASHRAE Handbook.*)

DESCRIPTION OF COMPONENTS

Although forced warm air furnaces differ in their fuel-burning equipment and in many of the controls required for operation, many other components are the same or similar. These components vary somewhat, depending on the size of the furnace and the arrangement of parts, but basically they have characteristics and functions in common. Components of a typical gas-fired forced warm air furnace are shown in Figure 4–7.

Heat Exchanger

The heat exchanger is the part of the furnace where combustion takes place. It uses gas, oil, or coal as fuel. The heat exchanger is usually made of cold-rolled, low-carbon steel with welded or crimped seams. There are several general types of heat exchangers:

- Individual section
- Tubular
- Serpentine (clamshell)
- Cylindrical

Individual-section heat exchanger   This type of heat exchanger has a number of separate heat exchangers (Figure 4–8). Each section has individual burners (fuel-

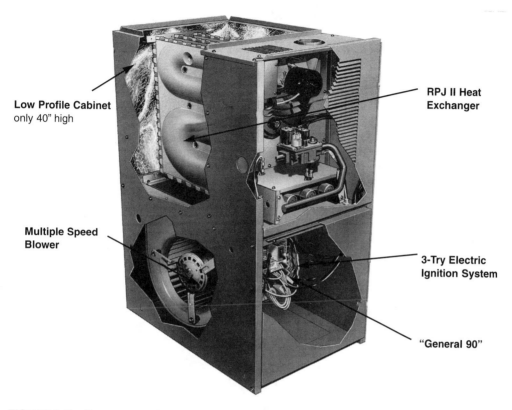

Low Profile Cabinet
only 40" high

Multiple Speed Blower

RPJ II Heat Exchanger

3-Try Electric Ignition System

"General 90"

FIGURE 4–7   Components of a typical gas-fired, upflow forced, warm air furnace. (Courtesy of ARCOAIRE, Inter-City Products Corporation, USA.)

burning devices). These sections are joined together at the bottom so that a common pilot can light all burners. The sections are joined together at the top so that flue gases are directed to a common flue. The individual section type of heat exchanger is used only on gas-burning equipment. The tubular and serpentine heat exchangers are variations of the individual section type (Figure 4–9 and 4–10).

Cylindrical heat exchanger   This type of heat exchanger has a single combustion chamber and uses a single-port, fuel-burning device (Figure 4–11). The cylindrical type of heat exchanger is used on gas, coal, and oil units. Many heat exchangers for coal, gas, and oil have two types of surfaces:

1. Primary
2. Secondary

The *primary surface* is in contact with or in direct sight of the flame and is located where the greatest heat occurs. The *secondary surface* follows the primary surface in the path between the burner and the flue. This is used to extract as much heat as possible from the flue gases before the products of combustion exit through the flue to the chimney.

FIGURE 4–8 Individual-section heat exchanger. (Courtesy of ARCOAIRE, Inter-City Products Corporation, USA.)

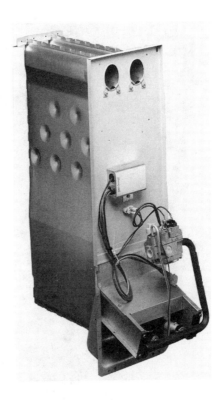

FIGURE 4–9 Serpentine (clamshell). (Courtesy of ARCOAIRE, Inter-City Products Corporation, USA.)

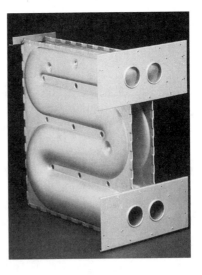

The fuel used by the furnace has a definite relation to the amount of chimney draft required. Coal, because of the high resistance of its fuel bed, requires a relatively high draft. Oil requires a relatively low draft. Gas requires a balanced draft, which is effective only when the furnace provides heat.

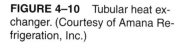

FIGURE 4–10 Tubular heat exchanger. (Courtesy of Amana Refrigeration, Inc.)

Cabinet

Cabinets for forced warm air furnaces serve many functions. They provide:

- An attractive exterior
- Insulation in the area around the heat exchanger
- Mounting facilities for controls, fan and motor, filters, and other items which they enclose
- Access panels for parts requiring service
- Connections for the supply and return air duct
- An airtight enclosure for air to travel over the heat exchanger

Cabinets for gas and oil furnaces are usually rectangular in shape and have a baked enamel finish. Cabinets are insulated on the interior with aluminum-based mineral wool, fiberglass, or a metal liner so that the surface will not be too hot to the touch. Insulation also makes it possible to place flammable material in contact with the cabinet without danger of fire.

Complete units are furnished so that a minimum amount of assembly time is required for installation. Usually, only duct and service connections need be made by the installer. Knockouts (readily accessible openings) are provided for gas and electric

FIGURE 4–11 Cylindrical heat exchanger.

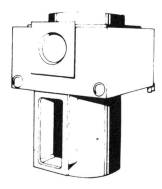

connections. The bolts used for holding the unit in place during shipment are also used for leveling the unit during installation. On highboy units, return air openings in the fan compartment can be cut in the cabinet sides or bottom to fit installation requirements.

Fans and Motors

Much of the successful performance of a heating system depends on the proper operation of the fan and fan motors. The fan moves air through the system, obtaining it from return air and outside air, and forces it over the heat exchanger and through the supply distribution system to the space to be heated.

Fans used are the centrifugal type with forward curved blades (Figure 4–12). Air enters through both ends of the wheel (double inlet) and is pumped or compressed (the buildup of air pressure) at the outlet. Fans and motors must be the proper size to deliver the required amount of air against the total resistance produced by the system. Depending on the quantity of air moved and the resistance of the system, a motor of the proper size is selected.

Because the resistance of the system cannot be fully determined beforehand, it is usually necessary to make some adjustment of the air quantities at the time of installation. Generally, the higher the speed of the fan, the greater the cubic-foot-per-minute output, thereby requiring more power and often a higher-horsepower motor.

Types of fans   Two types of fan motor arrangements are used:

1. Belt-drive
2. Direct-drive

FIGURE 4–12 Components of a direct-drive centrifugal fan. (Courtesy of DNP Company.)

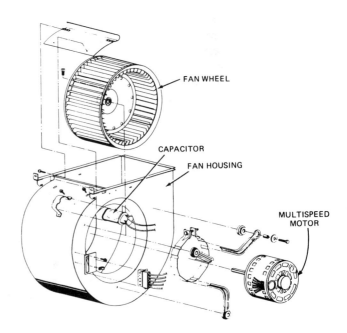

FAN WHEEL

CAPACITOR

FAN HOUSING

MULTISPEED MOTOR

The *belt-drive* arrangement uses a fixed pulley on the fan shaft and a variable-pitch pulley on the motor shaft (Figure 4–13). The speed of the fan is directly proportional to the ratio of the pulley diameters. The following equation is used:

$$fan\ speed\ (rev/min) = \frac{diameter\ of\ motor\ pulley\ (in.)}{diameter\ of\ fan\ pulley\ (in.)} \times motor\ speed\ (rev/min)$$

Example 4–1

What is the fan speed using a 3-in. motor pulley, a 9-in. fan pulley, and an 1800-rev/min motor?

Solution

$$fan\ speed\ (rev/min) = \frac{3\ in.}{9\ in.} \times 1800 = 600$$

The diameter of a variable-pitch pulley can be changed by adjusting the position of the outer flange of the pulley. This arrangement permits adjustment of the speed up to 30%. For changes greater than this, a different pulley must be used.

On the belt-drive arrangement, provision is made for regulating the belt tension and isolating the motor from the metal housing. The belt tension should be sufficient to prevent slippage. The motor mounts (usually rubber) provide isolation to prevent sound transmission.

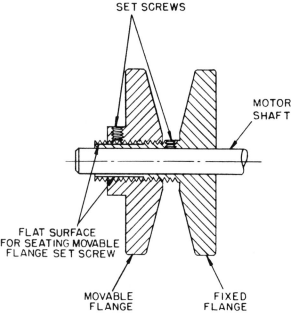

FIGURE 4–13   Belt-driven centrifugal fan with adjustable pitch motor pulley. (Photo courtesy of Lau Division, Phillips Industries, Inc.)

The amperage draw of the motor is an indication of the amount of loading of the motor. The maximum loading is indicated on the motor nameplate as full-load amperes (FLA). If the FLA value is exceeded, a larger motor must be used. Additional information on measuring amperage draw is given in Chapter 8. If the motor is not drawing its full capacity in FLA, it is an indication that the motor is underloaded. This may be caused by the additional resistance of dirty filters.

The *direct-drive* arrangement has the fan mounted on an extension of the motor shaft. Fan speeds can be changed only by altering the motor speed which is accomplished by the use of extra windings on the motor, sometimes called a *tap-wound,* or *multispeed,* motor (Figure 4–14). A tap-wound motor has a series of connections that provides a different speed. Often one speed is selected for heating and another speed is selected for cooling.

FIGURE 4–14 Tap-wound motor used for altering speed of direct-drive centrifugal fan. (Courtesy of Lau Division, Phillips Industries, Inc.)

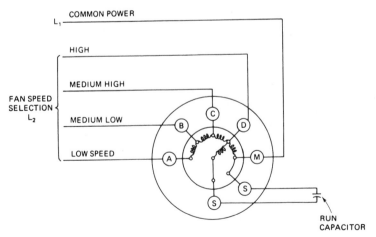

Filters

One of the desirable qualities of a forced warm air heating system is its ability, through air filters, to remove certain portions of the dust and dirt that are carried by the air. There are three types of residential air filters: disposable (throwaway), permanent (cleanable), and electronic, as shown in Figure 4–15.

Disposable filters are made of oil-impregnated fibers. When dirty, they are non-cleanable and are replaced with new ones. *Permanent filters* are made of metal or specially constructed fibrous material. The dirt is collected on the surface of the filtering material as the air passes through. When properly cleaned, these filters can be reused.

FIGURE 4–15   Three types of air filters: (a) disposable; (b) permanent; (c) electronic.

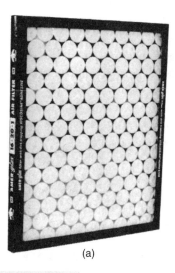

(a)

(b)

(c)

Electronic filters remove dust particles by first placing an electrical charge on the dust particle and then attracting the dust to collector plates having the opposite electrical charge. They are usually used with cleanable-type prefilters because the electronic filter removes only extremely small particles.

Figure 4–16 shows the size of various dust particles. The size is indicated in *microns* (pm). A micron is 1/25,400 inch (in.) [0.001 millimeter (mm)]. An ordinary throwaway or cleanable home air filter will remove particles down to 10 µm. An electronic air filter will remove particles from 0.1 to 10 µm.

Humidifiers and Humidistats

Humidifiers are used to add moisture to indoor air. The amount of moisture required depends on:

- Outside temperatures
- House construction
- Amount of relative humidity that the interior of the house will withstand without condensation problems

It is desirable to maintain 30 to 50% relative humidity. Too little humidity can cause furniture to crack. Too much humidity can cause condensation problems. From a comfort and health standpoint, a range as wide as 20 to 60% relative humidity is acceptable.

The colder the outside temperature, the greater the need for humidification. The amount of moisture the air will hold depends on its temperature. The colder the outside air, the less moisture it contains. Air from the outside enters the house through infiltration. When outside air is warmed, its relative humidity is lowered, unless moisture is added by humidification (Figure 4–17).

For example, air at 20°F and 60% relative humidity contains 8 grains of moisture per pound of air. When air is heated to 72°F, it can hold 118 grains of moisture per pound. Thus, to maintain 50% relative humidity in a 72°F house, the grains of moisture per pound must be increased to 59 (118 × .5 = 59). One pound of air entering a house from the outside will require the addition of 51 grains of moisture (59 – 8 = 51).

FIGURE 4–16   Particle size in microns. (Courtesy of Research Products Corporation.)

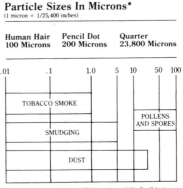

Particle Sizes In Microns*
(1 micron = 1/25,400 inches)

| Human Hair | Pencil Dot | Quarter |
| 100 Microns | 200 Microns | 23,800 Microns |

.01   .1   1.0   5   10   50   100

TOBACCO SMOKE

POLLENS AND SPORES

SMUDGING

DUST

*American Society of Heating, Refrigeration and Air Conditioning Engineers Guide

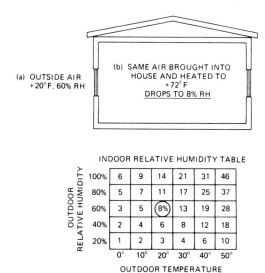

FIGURE 4–17 Effect of temperature on relative humidity. (Courtesy of Humid-Aire Corporation.)

The amount of infiltration depends on the tightness of the windows, doors, and other parts of the building's construction.

It is impractical in most buildings to maintain high relative humidity when the outside temperature is low. Condensation forms on the inside of the window when the surface temperature reaches the dew point temperature of the air. The *dew point temperature is* the temperature at which moisture begins to condense when the air temperature is lowered.

Types of humidistats It is desirable to control the amount of humidity in the house by the use of a humidistat. A *humidistat* is a device that regulates the "on" and "off" periods of humidification (Figure 4–18). The setting of a humidistat can be changed to comply with changing outside temperatures.

Types of humidifiers There are two popular types of humidifiers:

1. Evaporative
2. Vaporizing

There are three types of evaporative humidifiers:

1. Plate
2. Rotating drum or plate
3. Fan-powered

The *plate* evaporative humidifier (Figure 4–19) has a series of porous plates mounted in a rack. The lower section of the plates extends down into the water that is

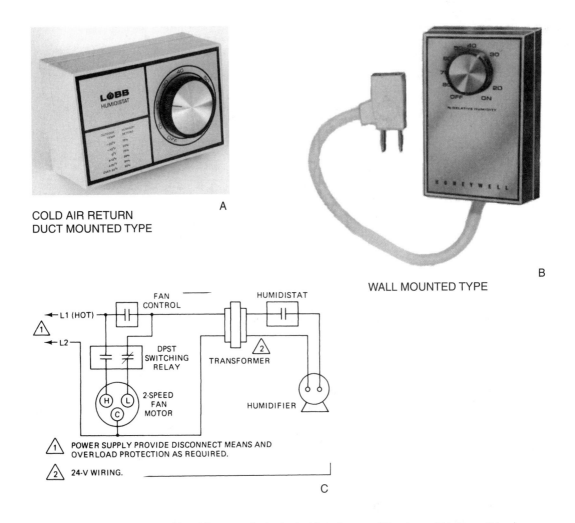

COLD AIR RETURN
DUCT MOUNTED TYPE

A

WALL MOUNTED TYPE

B

FIGURE 4–18 Two types of humidistats and a typical wiring diagram. (Courtesy of Honeywell Inc.)

contained in the pan. A float valve regulates the supply of water to maintain a constant level in the pan. The pan and plates are mounted in the warm air plenum.

The *rotating drum* evaporative humidifier (Figure 4–20) has a slowly revolving drum covered with a polyurethane pad partially submerged in water. As the drum rotates, it absorbs water. The water level in the pan is maintained by a float valve. The humidifier is mounted on the side of the return air plenum. Air from the supply plenum is ducted into the side of the humidifier. The air passes over the wetted surface, absorbs moisture, then goes into the return air plenum.

The *rotating plate* evaporative humidifier (Figure 4–21) is similar to the drum type in that the water-absorbing material revolves. However, this type is normally mounted on the underside of the main warm air supply duct.

FIGURE 4–19   Plate evaporative humidifier. (Courtesy of Skuttle Manufacturing Company.)

The *fan-powered* evaporative humidifier (Figure 4–22) is mounted on the supply air plenum. Air is drawn in by the fan, forced over the wetted core, and delivered back into the supply air plenum. The water flow over the core is controlled by a water valve. A humidistat is used to turn the humidifier on and off, controlling both the fan and the water valve. The control system is set up so that the humidifier can operate only when the furnace fan is running. Wiring diagrams are shown in Figures 4–23, 4–24, and 4–25. A current sensing relay, shown in Figure 4–25, is used to detect the amperage of the blower's speed that is used for heating. Once current is sensed, a set of normally open contacts close, completing the path to the transformer for the humidifier circuit.

The *vaporizing* type of humidifier (Figure 4–26) uses an electrical heating element immersed in a water reservoir to evaporate moisture into the furnace supply air plenum. A constant level of water is maintained in the reservoir. These humidifiers can operate even though the furnace is not supplying heat. The humidistat not only starts the water heater but also turns on the furnace fan if it is not running.

Note: Problems can arise in the use of humidifiers when the water hardness (mineral content) is too great. Water treatment and tablets can be added to humidifiers when the water hardness is more than 10 grains of dissolved mineral particles per gallon. A kit is available for testing the hardness of water.

Steam humidification units are similar to the vaporizing type shown in Figure 4–26, with the exception of the method used for distribution of the steam vapor. This type of steam system is chosen primarily because of its fast response time. The water vapors are introduced directly into the airsteam or conditioned space. Steam is sterile and therefore contains no contaminants, thus minimizing microorganism growth and odors. Figures 4–27 and 4–28 illustrate a unit normally used in commercial applications.

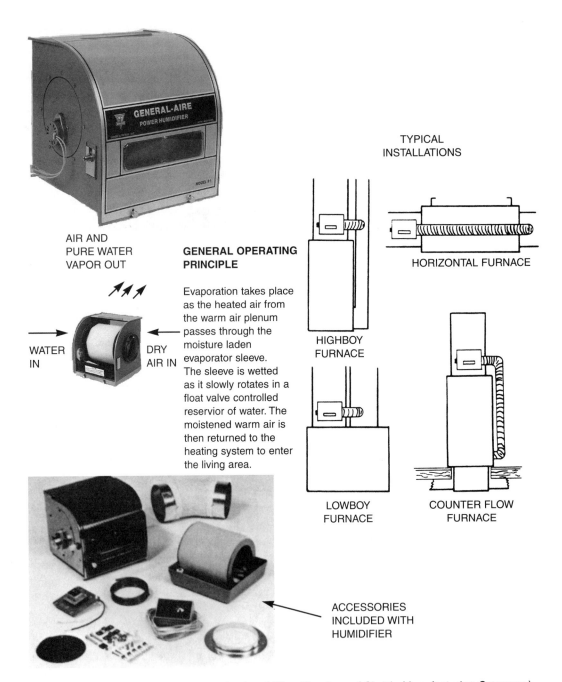

AIR AND
PURE WATER
VAPOR OUT

WATER
IN

DRY
AIR IN

**GENERAL OPERATING
PRINCIPLE**

Evaporation takes place
as the heated air from
the warm air plenum
passes through the
moisture laden
evaporator sleeve.
The sleeve is wetted
as it slowly rotates in a
float valve controlled
reservior of water. The
moistened warm air is
then returned to the
heating system to enter
the living area.

TYPICAL
INSTALLATIONS

HORIZONTAL FURNACE

HIGHBOY
FURNACE

LOWBOY
FURNACE

COUNTER FLOW
FURNACE

ACCESSORIES
INCLUDED WITH
HUMIDIFIER

FIGURE 4–20 Rotating drum evaporative humidifier. (Courtesy of Skuttle Manufacturing Company.)

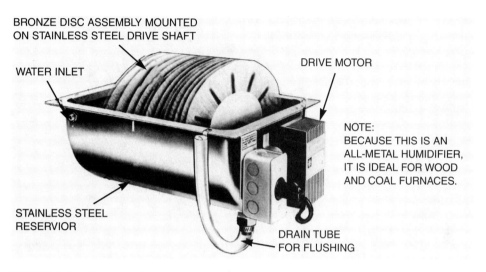

BRONZE DISC ASSEMBLY MOUNTED
ON STAINLESS STEEL DRIVE SHAFT

WATER INLET

DRIVE MOTOR

NOTE:
BECAUSE THIS IS AN
ALL-METAL HUMIDIFIER,
IT IS IDEAL FOR WOOD
AND COAL FURNACES.

STAINLESS STEEL
RESERVOIR

DRAIN TUBE
FOR FLUSHING

FIGURE 4–21   Rotating plate evaporative humidifier. (Courtesy of Humid-Aire Corporation.)

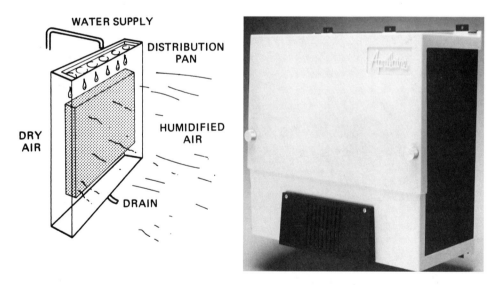

WATER SUPPLY

DISTRIBUTION
PAN

DRY
AIR

HUMIDIFIED
AIR

DRAIN

FIGURE 4–22   Fan-powered evaporative humidifier. (Courtesy of Research Products
Corporation.)

FIGURE 4–23   Wiring diagram for system with single-speed motor. (Courtesy of Skuttle Manufacturing Company.)

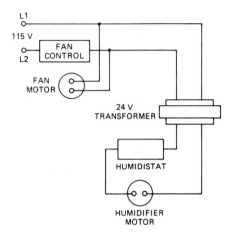

FIGURE 4–24   Wiring diagram for fan-powered evaporative humidifier. (Courtesy of Research Products Corporation.)

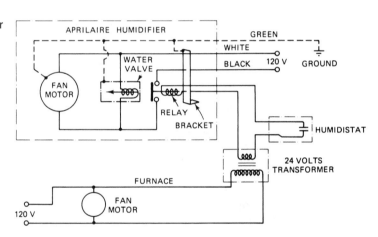

FIGURE 4–25   A typical wiring diagram using a current sensing relay.

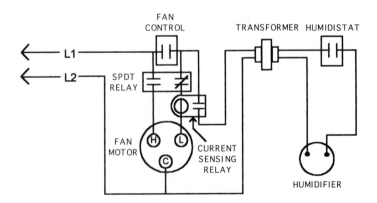

HEAT PUMP AND ELECTRIC FORCED AIR FURNACE HUMIDIFIERS
DESIGNED SPECIFICALLY FOR
MAXIMUM EFFICIENCY
ON THESE SPECIAL
SYSTEMS.

INSTALLS ANYWHERE ON THE SYSTEM –
BECAUSE THIS HUMIDIFIER HAS
ITS OWN HEAT SOURCE, IT CAN
BE MOUNTED IN THE "COLD AIR"
RETURN SECTION, AS WELL AS
IN THE "HOT AIR" SUPPLY. OFTEN,
THE "RETURN" PLENUM IS MORE
CONVENIENT BECAUSE THERE ARE
NO AIR CONDITIONING COILS TO
INTERFERE. THIS UNIT REQUIRES
A HUMIDISTAT CONTROL. THIS
CONTROL MAY BE ROOM MOUNTED,
OR IN THE RETURN AIR SECTION OF
THE SYSTEM.

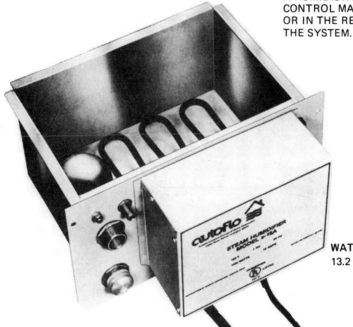

WATER VAPOR OUTPUT:
13.2 TO 19.1 GAL PER DAY

THIS IS A HIGH CAPACITY HUMIDIFIER FOR TODAY'S
HEAT PUMP AND ELECTRIC FURNACES . . . WHERE
LOW AIR TEMPERATURES DO NOT PROVIDE ENOUGH
HEAT FOR AN EVAPORATIVE TYPE HUMIDIFIER TO
FUNCTION PROPERLY.
THE STAINLESS STEEL RESERVOIR IS INSTALLED IN
THE RETURN OR SUPPLY PLENUM, OR DUCT. THE
CONTROLS ARE IN A COMPACT MODULE ON THE
EXTERIOR PANEL, WHERE ALL ELECTRICAL AND
WATER CONNECTIONS ARE MADE. A REMOTE
HUMIDISTAT TURNS ON AN INCALOY HEAT ELEMENT
TO HEAT THE WATER IN THE RESERVOIR. WHEN
THE WATER REACHES 170°F., THE FURNACE FAN
IS TURNED ON TO DISTRIBUTE THE PURE STEAM
THROUGHOUT THE HOME. WHEN THE SELECTED
HUMIDITY IS REACHED, THE HEAT ELEMENT TURNS
OFF. WHEN THE WATER COOLS, THE FAN CONTROL
TURNS OFF.

FIGURE 4–26   Vaporizing steam humidifier. (Courtesy of Autoflo, a division of Masco Corporation.)

FIGURE 4–27 Electronic steam humidifier with 100% demand, filling with water to maintain steam output. (Courtesy of Armstrong International, Inc.)

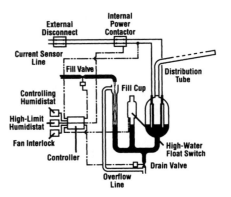

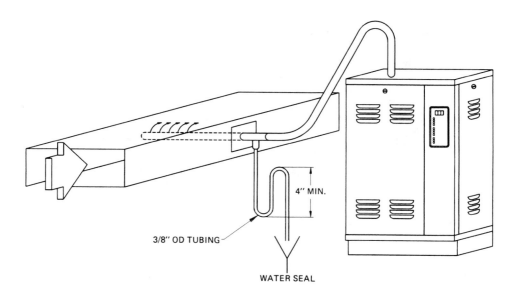

FIGURE 4–28 Cabinet housing and ductwork for steam humidifier. (Courtesy of Armstrong International, Inc.)

STUDY QUESTIONS

Answers to the study questions may be found in the sections noted in brackets.

4–1. What are the four different configurations of parts available on forced warm air furnaces? *[Arrangement of Components]*

4–2. Where is the fan located in respect to the heat exchanger on each type of furnace? *[Arrangement of Components]*

4–3. Describe the two types of heat exchangers on standard furnaces. *[Heat Exchanger]*

4–4. What material is used to construct the standard heat exchanger? *[Heat Exchanger]*

4–5. What are the two types of fan-motor arrangements? *[Fans and Motors]*

4–6. If a motor has a 3-in. pulley and the blower a 12-in. pulley, using a motor operating at 1200 rev/min, what is the speed of the fan? *[Types of Fans]*

4–7. How much can the fan speed be adjusted with a variable-pitch motor pulley? *[Types of Fans]*

4–8. Name and describe the three types of air filters. *[Filters]*

4–9. What is the range of particles removed by the electronic air filter? *[Filters]*

4–10. How is the inside humidity requirement affected by the outside temperature? *[Humidifiers and Humidistats]*

4–11. Describe the construction of various types of humidistats. *[Types of Humidistats]*

4–12. What are the three types of evaporative humidifiers? *[Types of Humidifiers]*

5

Components of Gas-Burning Furnaces

OBJECTIVES

After studying this chapter, the student will be able to:

- Identify the components of a gas-burning assembly
- Adjust a gas burner for best performance
- Provide service and maintenance for a gas burner assembly

GAS-BURNING ASSEMBLY

The function of a gas-burning assembly is to produce a proper fire at the base of the heat exchanger. To do this, the assembly must:

- Control and regulate the flow of gas
- Assure the proper mixture of gas with air
- Ignite the gas under safe conditions

To accomplish these actions, a gas burner assembly consists of four major parts or sections. These parts are:

1. Gas valve
2. Flame proving circuit
3. Manifold and orifice
4. Gas burners and adjustment

An illustration of a complete gas burner manifold assembly is shown in Figure 5–1.

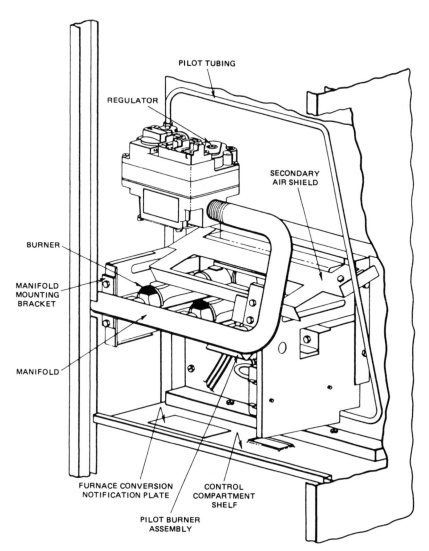

PILOT TUBING

REGULATOR

SECONDARY
AIR SHIELD

BURNER

MANIFOLD
MOUNTING
BRACKET

MANIFOLD

FURNACE CONVERSION
NOTIFICATION PLATE

CONTROL
COMPARTMENT
SHELF

PILOT BURNER
ASSEMBLY

FIGURE 5–1   Complete gas burner manifold assembly. (Courtesy of Bryant Air Conditioning.)

Gas Valve

The gas valve section consists of a number of parts with each performing a different function. On older units these operations were entirely separate. On more modern units these parts are all contained in a combination gas valve (CGV) and include:

- Hand shutoff valve
- Pressure-reducing valve
- Safety shutoff equipment
- Operator-controlled automatic gas valve

Figure 5–2 shows the separate parts of the gas valve section installed along the manifold, sometimes called a gas regulator train. Figure 5–3 shows the combination valve (CGV) that includes these separate parts, each of which is replaceable if trouble should develop.

Hand shutoff valves   Referring to Figure 5–2, note that the main shutoff valve or gas cock is composed of two parts, an A cock and a B cock. The A cock is used to turn the main gas supply on and off manually. The B cock is used to turn the gas supply to the pilot on and off manually.

These gate or ball-type valves are open when the handle is parallel to the length of the pipe and closed when the handle is perpendicular to the length of the pipe. They should be either on or off and not placed in an intermediate position. If it is desirable to regulate the supply of gas, it should be done by adjusting the pressure regulator.

Pressure-reducing valve   The pressure-reducing valve, or pressure regulator, decreases the gas pressure supplied from the utility meter at approximately 7 in. W.C. to $3^1/2$ in. W.C. The regulator maintains a constant gas pressure at the furnace to provide a constant input of gas to the furnace. On an LP system a regulator is supplied at the tank and at the gas valve on the furnace.

As shown in Figure 5–4, the spring exerts downward pressure on the diaphragm which is connected to the gas valve. The spring pressure tends to open the valve. When the gas starts to flow through the valve, the downstream pressure of the gas creates an upward pressure on the diaphragm tending to close it. Thus the spring pressure and the downstream gas pressure oppose each other and must equal each other for the pressure to remain in equilibrium. To adjust the gas pressure the cap is removed and the spring tension is adjusted. Also note that the vent maintains atmospheric pressure on the top of the diaphragm.

Safety shutoff equipment   The safety shutoff equipment consists of:

- Pilot burner
- Thermocouple or thermopile
- Pilotstat power unit

FIGURE 5–2   Older-style gas manifold showing separate components. (Courtesy of Honeywell Inc.)

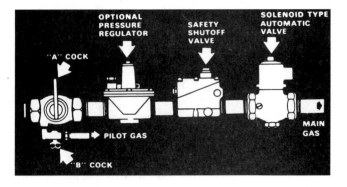

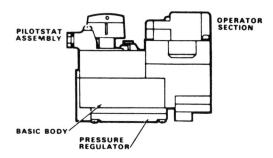

FIGURE 5–3   Combination gas valve (CGV). (Courtesy of Honeywell Inc.)

The pilot burner and the thermocouple or thermopile are assembled into one unit as shown in Figures 5–12 to 5–14. This unit is placed near the main gas burner. The thermocouple is connected to the pilotstat power unit. The pilotstat power unit may be located in the CGV or installed as a separate unit in the gas regulation train, as shown in Figure 5–2.

The pilot burner has two functions:

1. It directs the pilot flame for proper ignition of the main burner flame.
2. It holds the thermocouple or thermopile in correct position with relation to the pilot flame.

The thermocouple or thermopile extends into the pilot flame and generates sufficient voltage to hold in the pilotstat. The thermopile generates additional voltage, which also operates the main gas valve.

The pilotstat power unit is held in by the voltage generated by the thermocouple. If the voltage is insufficient, indicating a poor or nonexistent pilot light, the power unit drops out, shutting off the main gas supply. These units are of two types: one that shuts off the gas supply to the main burner only, and one that shuts off the supply of gas to both the pilot and the main burner. Units burning LP gas always require 100% shutoff.

Principle of the Thermocouple   Two dissimilar metal wires are welded together at the ends to form a thermocouple (Figure 5–5). When one junction is heated and the other remains relatively cool, an electrical current is generated which flows through the wires. The voltage generated is used to operate the pilotstat power unit.

FIGURE 5–4   Pressure-reducing valve and its operation. (Courtesy of Honeywell Inc.)

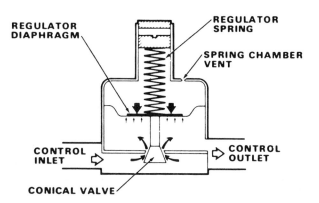

Thermopile   The thermopile is a number of thermocouples connected in series (Figure 5–6). One thermocouple may generate 25 to 30 millivolts (mV). A thermopile may generate as high as 750 or 800 mV (1000 mV equals 1 V).

Power Unit   The power unit is energized by the voltage generated by the thermocouple or thermopile. This voltage operates through an electromagnet. The voltage generated is sufficient to hold in the plunger against the pressure of the spring. The position of the plunger against the electromagnet must be manually set. If the thermocouple voltage drops due to a poor or nonexistent pilot, the plunger is released by the spring. This action either causes the plunger itself to block the flow of gas or operates an electrical switch that shuts off the supply of gas. The plunger must be manually reset when the proper pilot is restored. Figure 5–7 shows the pilotstat mechanism installed in a CGV.

Operator-controlled automatic gas valve   The main function of the operator is to control the gas flow. Some operators control the gas flow directly; some regulate

FIGURE 5–5   Basic construction. (Courtesy of Honeywell Inc.)

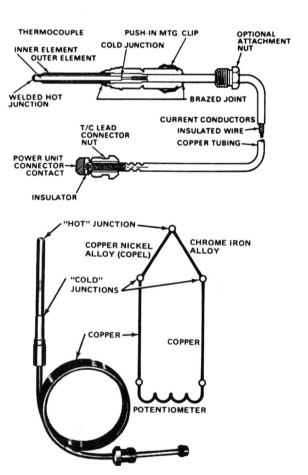

FIGURE 5–6   Basic thermopile construction. (Courtesy of Honeywell Inc.)

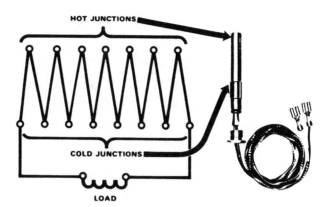

the pressure on a diaphragm, which in turn regulates the gas flow. The various types of operators are:

- Solenoid
- Diaphragm
- Bulb

Solenoid Valve Operators   These units (Figure 5–8) employ electromagnetic force to operate the valve plunger. When the thermostat calls for heat, the plunger is raised, opening the gas valve. These valves are often filled with oil to eliminate noise and to serve as lubrication.

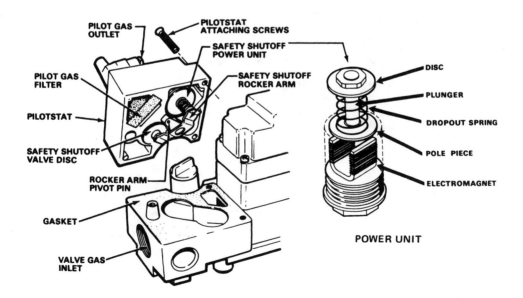

FIGURE 5–7   Pilotstat mechanism in a CGV. (Courtesy of Honeywell Inc.)

FIGURE 5–8 Solenoid valve operator. (Courtesy of Honeywell Inc.)

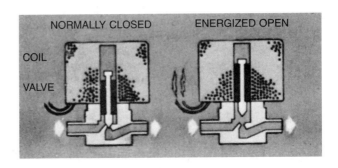

Diaphragm Valve Operators   On these operators (Figure 5–9) gas is used to control the pressure above and below the diaphragm. The diaphragm is attached to the valve. To close the valve, gas pressure is released above the diaphragm. With equal pressure above and below the diaphragm, the weight of the valve closes it. To open the valve, the supply of gas is cut off above the diaphragm and gas pressure is vented to atmosphere. The pressure of the gas below the diaphragm opens the valve. These valves also can be filled with oil.

Bulb Valve Operators   Bulb operators (Figure 5–10) use the expansion of a liquid-filled bulb to provide the operating force. A snap-action disk is also incorporated to speed up the opening and closing action.

Redundant gas valve   The redundant gas valve, shown in Figure 5–11, is used

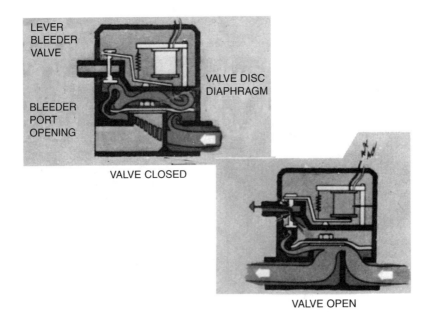

FIGURE 5–9 Magnetic diaphragm valve operator. (Courtesy of Carrier Corporation.)

FIGURE 5–10   Bulb valve operator. (Courtesy of Honeywell Inc.)

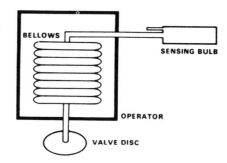

on furnaces with electronic ignition and circuit boards. This valve has two or more internal valves operating in series. All of the main burner gas must flow through both valves before reaching the gas manifold. Either valve, operating independently of the other, can interrupt all main burner gas flow if the need arises. Usually, the first valve is operated by a solenoid, while the second valve is opened like a diaphragm valve or with a bimetal heat motor. A knob is provided for manual shutoff and must be kept in the "on" position at all times during normal operation.

When the furnace is equipped with a spark ignition pilot, the pilot tap is normally located between the two valves. The circuit board energizes the first valve on a call for heat, prior to pilot ignition. The second valve is energized when the pilot has been verified.

On furnaces where an electric heating element, called a hot surface ignitor (HSI), lights the main burner directly, the internal valves are often energized simultaneously. Therefore, the redundancy is for safety only.

Safety Pilot

The function of the safety pilot is to provide an ignition flame for the main burner and

FIGURE 5–11   Redundant gas valve for intermittent and direct spark application. (Courtesy of White Rogers Division, Emerson Electric Co.)

to heat the thermocouple to provide safe operation.

Pilot burner   There are two types of pilot burners:

1. Primary-aerated
2. Non-primary-aerated

On the *primary-aerated pilot* (Figure 5–12), the air is mixed with the gas before it enters the pilot burner. The disadvantage of this is that dirt and lint tend to clog the screened air opening. The air opening must be cleaned periodically.

On the *non-primary-aerated pilot* (Figure 5–13), the gas is supplied directly to the pilot, without the addition of primary air. All the necessary air is supplied as secondary air.

This eliminates the need for cleaning the air passages.

Pilot burner orifice   The orifice is the part that controls the supply of gas to the burner. The drilled opening permits a small stream of gas to enter the burner. The amount that enters is dependent on the size of the drilled hole and the manifold pressure. Some cleaning of this opening may be required. This can be done by blowing air through the orifice or by using a suitable non-oily solvent.

Pilot flame   The pilot flame should envelop the thermocouple $3/8$ to $1/2$ in. at its top, as shown in Figure 5–14. The gas pressure at the pilot is the same as the inlet pressure to the gas valve. Too high a pressure decreases the life of the thermocouple. Too low a

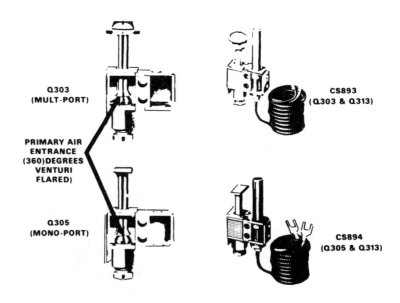

FIGURE 5–12   Primary-aerated pilot designs. (Courtesy of Honeywell Inc.)

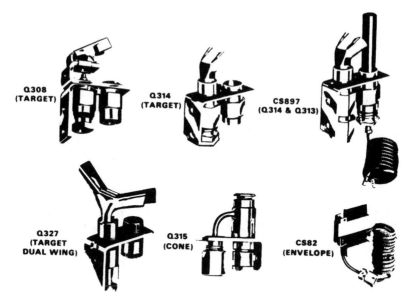

FIGURE 5–13   Non-primary-aerated pilot designs. (Courtesy of Honeywell Inc.)

pressure provides unsatisfactory heating of the thermocouple tip. Poor flame conditions are shown in Figure 5–15.

Mercury Flame Sensor

A mercury flame sensor (Figure 5–16) is a mechanical device that proves the existence of a pilot flame. It converts the heat of the pilot flame to motion which is used to open and close a set of electrical contacts. The sensor consists of a bulb, capillary, diaphragm, snap-switch mechanism, and mercury. When the bulb is heated by the pilot

FIGURE 5–14   Pilot flame adjustment. (Courtesy of Honeywell Inc.)

3/8 TO 1/2 INCH

ADJUST PILOT FLOW ADJUSTMENT SCREW
TO GIVE A SOFT, STEADY FLAME ENVELOPING
3/8 TO 1/2 INCH OF THE TIP OF THE
THERMOCOUPLE OR GENERATOR.

FIGURE 5–15 Poor pilot
flame conditions. (Courtesy of
Honeywell Inc.)

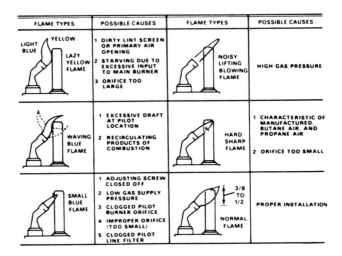

FLAME TYPES	POSSIBLE CAUSES	FLAME TYPES	POSSIBLE CAUSES
LIGHT BLUE / YELLOW / LAZY YELLOW FLAME	1 DIRTY LINT SCREEN OR PRIMARY AIR OPENING 2 STARVING DUE TO EXCESSIVE INPUT TO MAIN BURNER 3 ORIFICE TOO LARGE	NOISY LIFTING BLOWING FLAME	HIGH GAS PRESSURE
WAVING BLUE FLAME	1 EXCESSIVE DRAFT AT PILOT LOCATION 2 RECIRCULATING PRODUCTS OF COMBUSTION	HARD SHARP FLAME	1 CHARACTERISTIC OF MANUFACTURED, BUTANE AIR, AND PROPANE AIR 2 ORIFICE TOO SMALL
SMALL BLUE FLAME	1 ADJUSTING SCREW CLOSED OFF 2 LOW GAS SUPPLY PRESSURE 3 CLOGGED PILOT BURNER ORIFICE 4 IMPROPER ORIFICE (TOO SMALL) 5 CLOGGED PILOT LINE FILTER	3/8 TO 1/2 NORMAL FLAME	PROPER INSTALLATION

flame, the mercury is vaporized causing pressure in the capillary and the diaphragm. Movement of the diaphragm causes the snap-switch to open to one set of contacts and close to another set. These contacts control the pilot valve and the main valve.

Bimetal Flame Sensor

A bimetal flame sensor (Figure 5–17) is a mechanical device that proves the existence of a pilot flame. It converts the heat of the pilot flame to motion which is used to open and close a set of electrical contacts. The sensor consists of a set of contacts and a bimetal snap-switch mechanism. When the sensor is heated by the pilot flame, the bimetal warps in one direction. Movement of the bimetal causes the snap-switch to open to one set of contacts and close to another set. These contacts control the pilot valve and the main valve.

Electronic Flame Sensor (Flame Rectification System)

A flame rectification system (Figure 5–18) is the most common flame proving system being used today. It is used universally with many heating control companies. They are

FIGURE 5–16 A mercury flame sensor.

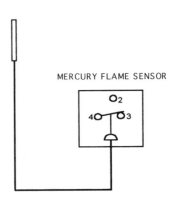

MERCURY FLAME SENSOR

FIGURE 5–17   A bimetal flame sensor.

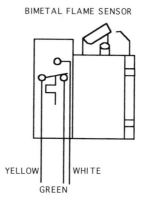

BIMETAL FLAME SENSOR

YELLOW   WHITE
GREEN

seen on furnaces of the indirect ignition (utilizing a pilot) and direct ignition (no pilot) types.

Flame rectification systems use an electronic control module that sends an a.c. voltage to the flame sensor. Through the flame, alternating current is converted to a direct current which flows through the pilot or burner flame and completes the circuit to the grounded burner. From the burner, current flows back to the grounded control module thus completing a circuit. The flow of current through the flame completes and proves burner operation and the system will stay lit for the complete cycle of the furnace. The current that flows in this circuit is measured in micro amps, one millionth of an amp. Many systems range from .2 up to 15 micro amps.

Manifold and Orifice

The manifold delivers gas equally to all the burners. It connects the supply of gas from the gas valve to the burners. It is usually made of $1/2$ to 1-in. pipe. Connections can be made either to the right or left, depending on the design, as shown in Figure 5–19.

The orifice used for the main burners is similar to the pilot orifice, but larger. The drilled opening permits a fast stream of raw gas to enter the burner. The orifice is sized to permit the proper flow of gas. Items to be considered in sizing the orifice are:

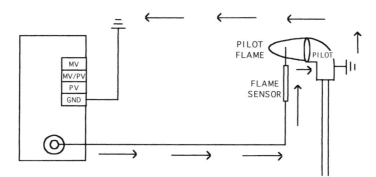

FIGURE 5–18   A flame rectification system.

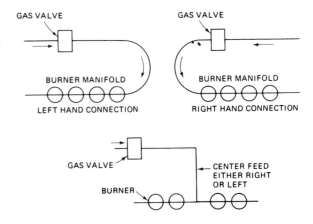

FIGURE 5–19   Gas manifold piping arrangements. (Courtesy of White Rogers Division of Emerson Electric Co.)

- Type of gas
- Pressure in manifold
- Input of gas required for each burner

Gas Burners and Adjustment

Primary and secondary air   Most gas burners require that some air be mixed with the gas before combustion. This air is called *primary air* (Figure 5–20). Primary air constitutes approximately one-half of the total air required for combustion. Too much primary air causes the flame to lift off the burner surface. Too little primary air causes a yellow flame.

Air that is supplied to the burner at the time of combustion is called *secondary air* (Figure 5–21). Too little secondary air causes the formation of carbon monoxide. To be certain that enough secondary air is provided, most units operate on an excess of secondary air. An excess of about 50% is considered a good practice. To produce a good flame it is essential to maintain the proper ratio between primary and secondary air.

FIGURE 5–20   Primary air to gas burner. (Courtesy of Carrier Corporation.)

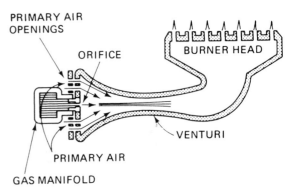

FIGURE 5–21   Secondary air to gas burner. (Courtesy of Carrier Corporation.)

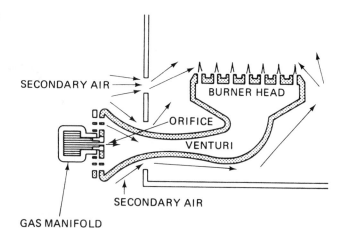

Venturi   In a multiport burner, gas is delivered into a venturi (mixing tube) creating a high gas velocity. The increase in gas velocity creates a sucking action which causes the primary air to enter the tube and mix with the raw gas.

Crossover ignitors   The crossover or carryover ignitor is a projection on each burner near the first few ports that permits the burner that lights first to pass flame to the other burners. There is a baffle, as shown in Figure 5–24, which directs gas to the first few ports of the burner to assure the proper supply of fuel to the area of the ignitor.

Note: Burners that fail to light properly can cause rollout, a dangerous condition where flames emerge in the area containing the gas valve.

Draft diverter   The draft diverter (Figure 5–22) is designed to provide a balanced draft (slightly negative) over the flame in a gas-fired furnace. The bottom of the diverter is open to allow air from the furnace room to blend with the products of combustion. In case of blockage or downdraft in the chimney, the flue gases vent to the area around the furnace.

Note: The American Gas Association (AGA) requires a rigid test to be certain that under these conditions complete combustion occurs and there is no danger of suffocation of the flame.

Types of burners   There are four types of burners, classified according to the type of burner head:

1. Single-port or inshot
2. Drilled port
3. Slotted port
4. Ribbon

Single-Port or Inshot Burner   The single-port is the simplest type. Fuel and air are mixed inside of the burner tube and ignited at the outlet of the burner. After ignition, the flame is directed into the heat exchanger.

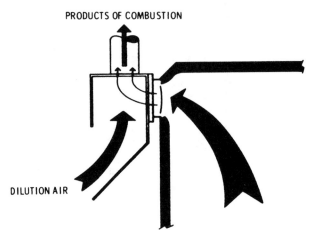

FIGURE 5-22   Draft diverter.
(Courtesy of Carrier Corporation.)

PRODUCTS OF COMBUSTION

DILUTION AIR

Drilled-Port Burner   The drilled-port burner is usually made of cast iron with a series of small drilled holes. The size of the hole varies for different types of gas.

Slotted-Port Burner   The slotted-port burner (Figure 5–24) is similar to the drilled port burner, but in place of holes, it uses elongated slots. It has the advantage of being able to burn different types of gas without change of slot size. It is also less susceptible to clogging with lint.

Ribbon Burner   The ribbon burner has a continuous opening down each side, and when it is lit, the flame has the appearance of a ribbon. The burner itself is made either of cast iron or fabricated metal. The ribbon insert is usually corrugated stainless steel.

Adjusting gas pressure

It is extremely critical to have the properly designed gas pressure to the furnace. This will ensure the correct Btu rating output for which the furnace is designed. If a furnace has too high a gas pressure, it will overheat and could possibly crack the heat exchanger. If a furnace has too low a gas pressure, it could cause condensation and corrosion to form in the heat exchanger.

To test and adjust gas pressure on an LP or natural gas-fired furnace, use the following procedures:

1. Check the furnace's name plate for required operating gas pressure. (Commonly 3.5" W. C. for natural gas and 10" to 11" W. C. for LP)
2. Turn the main gas valve to the off position.
3. Locate the set screw for the outlet gas pressure on the combination gas valve,

FIGURE 5–23   Single-port or Inshot burner.

FIGURE 5–24   Slotted-port burners. (Courtesy of Carrier Corporation.)

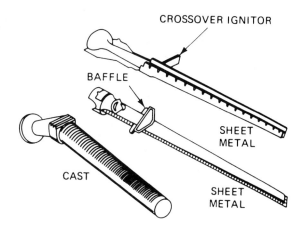

shown in Figure 5–25. (The reading can also be taken at the manifold if a pressure tap is present.)

4. Remove the set screw and install the manometer.

5. Turn the main gas valve to the on (in line) position and start the furnace.

6. When the furnace ignites, a pressure reading will be present on the gauge.

7. If the gas pressure is not the recommended gas pressure of the furnace, locate the gas pressure regulator adjustment screw on the gas valve (Figure 5–26). Remove the cap and adjust the gas pressure. (Clockwise increases pressure and counter clockwise decreases pressure.)

8. After adjusting the gas pressure turn the furnace off and turn main gas valve to the

FIGURE 5–25 Measuring gas
manifold pressure.

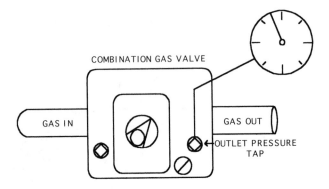

off position.

9. Remove the manometer from the gas valve and re-insert the plug to the outlet
   pressure tap.

MAINTENANCE AND SERVICE

The main items requiring service on gas-burning equipment are:

- Gas burner assembly
- Pilot assembly
- Automatic gas valve

After the equipment is in use for a period of time, each of these items may require
service, depending on the conditions of the installation.

Gas Burner Assembly

Problems that can arise include:

FIGURE 5–26 Adjusting gas
manifold pressure.

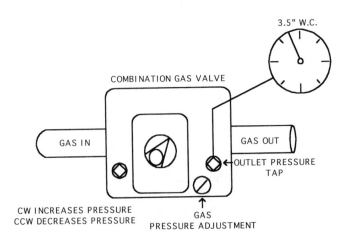

- Flashback
- Carbon on the burners
- Dirty air mixture
- Noise of ignition
- Gas flames lifting from ports
- Appearance of yellow tips in flames

When the velocity of the gas-air mixture is reduced below a certain speed, the flame will flash back through the ports. This is undesirable and must be corrected. The solution is to close the primary air shutter as much as possible and still maintain a clear blue flame (Figure 5–27). Burners that become clogged with carbon due to flashback conditions must be cleared in order not to interfere with the proper flow of gas.

If the burner flame becomes soft and yellow-tipped, it is an indication that cleaning is required. Items requiring cleaning are the shutter opening, venturi, and the burner head it-self. In some cases these can be cleaned with the suction of a vacuum cleaner. In other cases, a thin, long-handled brush may be used to reach completely inside the mixing tube.

Noise of ignition is usually caused by delayed or faulty ignition. Conditions that must be checked and corrected, if called for, are location of the pilot, poor flame travel, or poor distribution of the flame on the burner itself. Lifting flames are usually caused by gas pressure that is too high or improper primary air adjustment. The gas pressure for natural gas at the manifold should be 3.5" W.C. Primary air should be ad-justed to provide a blue flame.

The appearance of yellow tips on the flame indicate incomplete combustion,

FIGURE 5–27 Primary air adjustment.

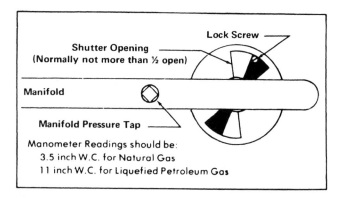

PRIMARY AIR ADJUSTMENT

To adjust primary air supply, turn main gas supply **ON** and operate unit for 15 to 20 minutes. Then loosen set screw and rotate shutter on burner bell. Open shutter until the yellow tips just disappear. Lock shutter in position by tightening set screw. Turn main gas supply **OFF**, let cool completely, and re-check operation and flame characteristics from a cold start.

which can cause sooting of the heat exchanger. The following items should be checked and corrected if necessary:

1. *Gas pressure.* Pressure should be 3.5" W.C. for natural gas.
2. *Clogged orifices.* Inspect and clean if required.
3. *Air adjustment.* Use minimum primary air required for blue flame.
4. *Alignment.* Gas stream should move down the center of the venturi tube.
5. *Flues.* Air passages must not be clogged.
6. *Air leaks.* Air from fan or strong outside air current can cause a yellow flame.

Pilot Assembly

Pilot problems can be caused by:

- Clogged air openings
- Dirty pilot filters
- Clogged orifice
- Defective thermocouples

Dirt and lint in the air opening are the most common problems. Cleaning solves these problems. Pilots for manufactured gases use pilot filters. The cartridge must be replaced periodically. Occasionally, it is necessary to clean the pilot orifice, which may become clogged from an accumulation of dirt, lint, carbon, or condensation in the lines.

If the pilot flame does not heat the thermocouple adequately, not enough d.c. voltage will be generated and the electromagnet will not energize sufficiently to permit the opening of the automatic gas valve. The thermocouple can be checked, as shown in Figure 8–3.

Automatic Gas Valve

Many gas valves are of the diaphragm type with an electromagnetic or heat motor-operated controller. The two principal problems that can occur with gas valves are:

1. A valve that will not open
2. Gas leakage through the valve

First, the pilot must be checked to be certain that the proper power is being produced by the thermocouple. If the gas valve will not open after following the lighting procedure shown on the nameplate, proceed as follows: Check to determine if power is available at the valve. If power is available, connect and disconnect the power and listen for a muffled click which indicates that the lever arm is being actuated. Check to be sure that the vent above the diaphragm is open. If the valve still does not operate, replace the entire operator or valve top assembly. If gas continues to leak through the valve outlet or the vent opening after the valve is de-energized, the entire valve head assembly should be replaced.

STUDY QUESTIONS

Answers to the study questions may be found in the sections noted in brackets.

5–1. What are the functions of the gas burner assembly, and what are its component parts? *[Gas-Burning Assembly]*

5–2. On the modern gas valve, there are two shutoff cocks. What are they used for? *[Hand Shutoff Valves]*

5–3. What is the proper natural gas pressure leaving the gas valve? *[Pressure-Reducing Valve]*

5–4. What are the component parts of the safety shutoff equipment? *[Safety Shutoff Equipment]*

5–5. What are the functions of the pilot burner? *[Safety Shutoff Equipment]*

5–6. How much voltage does the thermocouple generate? *[Safety Shutoff Equipment]*

5–7. What does CGV represent? *[Safety Shutoff Equipment]*

5–8. What type of valve operator has a delayed action feature? *[Operator-Controlled Automatic Gas Valve]*

5–9. Describe the operation of the two types of pilot burners. *[Pilot Burner]*

5–10. What type of valve requires 100% shutoff? *[Safety Shutoff Equipment]*

5–11. What is the function of the power unit? *[Safety Shutoff Equipment]*

5–12. Describe a proper pilot flame. *[Pilot Flame]*

5–13. What factors are considered in sizing the main burner orifice? *[Manifold and Orifice]*

5–14. Describe what is meant by primary and secondary main burner air. *[Primary and Secondary Air]*

5–15. What is the purpose of the venturi? *[Venturi]*

5–16. What is the function of the draft diverter? *[Draft Diverter]*

5–17. Name and describe the various types of main gas burners. *[Types of Burners]*

5–18. Describe the service required for gas-burning equipment. *[Maintenance and Service]*

5–19. Describe the various problems that can arise on the gas burner assembly, pilot assembly, and automatic gas valve. *[Maintenance and Service]*

6

Basic Electricity and Electrical Symbols

OBJECTIVES

After studying this chapter, the student will be able to:

- Identify the basic electrical symbols used in wiring diagrams for electrical load devices
- Determine the types of circuits used to connect electrical loads

ELECTRICAL TERMS

A knowledge of certain electrical terms is necessary in working with electrical power. Most power used for warm air heating systems is alternating current. Some of the common terms used in describing alternating current are:

Volts: measure of electromotive force (EMF) or pressure being supplied to cause the electrical current to flow

Amperes: measure of the flow of current (electrons) through a conductor

Ohms (Ω)*:* measure of the resistance to current flow through a conductor
Watts: measure of power consumed by an electrical load

Powerfactor: resulting fraction obtained by dividing watts by the product of volts times amperes

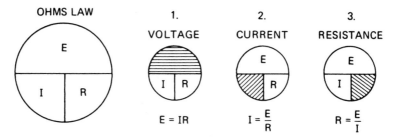

FIGURE 6–1   Ohm's law.

Ohm's Law

Ohm's law is used to predict the behavior of electrical current in an electrical circuit. Simply stated,

$$E = IR$$

where
E = electromotive force EMF, volts

I = intensity of current, amperes

R = resistance, ohms

Ohm's law can be stated in three ways (Figure 6–1). An example of the use of Ohm's law is shown in Figure 6–2. Given $E = 120$ V and $R = 10\ \Omega\ (I = E/R)$, the current flow in the circuit is 12 A.

A voltmeter can be used to measure the voltage between L_1 and L_2. An ohmmeter can be used to measure the resistance of the load but should be used *only when the power is turned off*. An ammeter can be used to measure amperes.

Series Circuits

A series circuit is one in which each resistance is wired end to end like a string of boxcars on a train. In a series circuit the amperage stays the same throughout the circuit. The voltage is divided between the various loads. The total resistance of the circuit is the sum of the various resistances in the circuit. Thus, using Figure 6–3,

FIGURE 6–2   Simple electrical circuit.

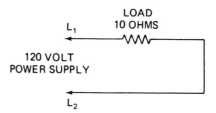

LOAD
10 OHMS

L_1

120 VOLT
POWER SUPPLY

L_2

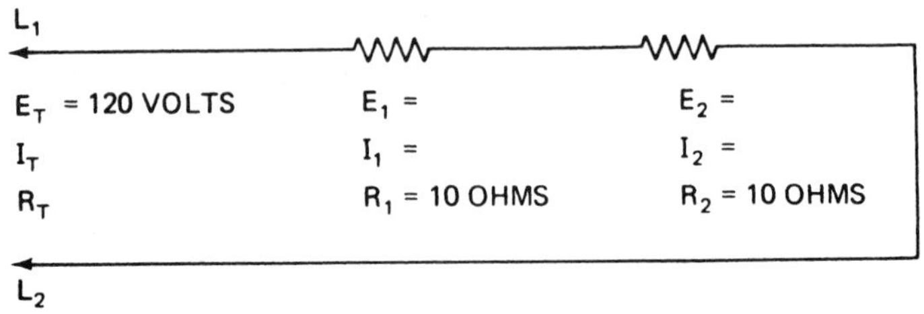

FIGURE 6–3   Series circuit.

$$E_T = E_1 + E_2$$
$$I_T = I_1 = I_2$$
$$R_T = R_1 + R_2$$

Given $E_T = 120$, $R_1 = 10$, $R_2 = 10$, then

1. $R_T = R_1 + R_2 = 10 + 10 = 20\ \Omega$
2. $I_T = \dfrac{E_T}{R_T}$ (Ohm's law) $= \dfrac{120}{20} = 6\ \text{A}$
3. $I_T = I_1 = I_2 = 6\ \text{A}$
4. $E_1 = I_1 \times R_1 = 10 \times 6 = 60\ \text{V}$
5. $E_2 = I_2 \times R_2 = 10 \times 6 = 60\ \text{V}$

Parallel Circuits

In a parallel circuit each load provides a separate path for electricity, and each path may have different current flowing through it. The amount is determined by the resistance of the load. The voltages for each load are the same. The total current is the sum of the individual load currents. The reciprocal of the total resistance is equal to the sum of the reciprocals of the individual resistances. Thus, using Figure 6–4, we have

$$E_T = E_1 = E_2$$
$$I_T = I_1 + I_2$$
$$\frac{1}{R_T} = \frac{1}{R_1} + \frac{R}{R_2}$$

or for two resistances,

$$R_T = \frac{R_1 \times R_2}{R_1 + R_2}$$

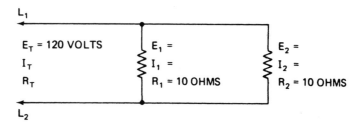

FIGURE 6–4   Parallel circuit.

Given $E_1 = 120$, $R_1 = 10$, $R_2 = 10$, then

1. $E_T = E_1 = E_2 = 120$ V

2. $I_1 = \dfrac{E_1}{R_1}\,(\text{Ohm' s law}) = \dfrac{120}{10} = 12$ A

3. $I_2 = \dfrac{E_2}{R_2} = \dfrac{120}{10} = 12$ A

4. $I_T = I_1 + I_2 = 12 + 12 = 24$ A

5. $R_T = \dfrac{E_T}{I_T} = \dfrac{120}{24} = 5\ \Omega$

   or

   $R_T = \dfrac{R_1 \times R_2}{R_1 + R_2} = \dfrac{10 \times 10}{10 + 10} = \dfrac{100}{20} = 5\ \Omega$

Electrical Potential

Electrical potential is the force that produces the flow of electricity. It is similar to the action of a pump in a water system that causes the flow of water. The battery in a flashlight is a source of electrical potential. The unit of electrical potential is a *volt*. Volts are measured with a voltmeter.

Resistance

Resistance is the pressure exerted by the conductor in restricting the flow of current. In a water system, the flow would be limited by the size of the pipe. In an electrical system, the flow of current is limited by the size of the conducting wire or by the electrical devices in the circuit. Resistance in an electrical circuit can be a means of converting electrical energy to other forms of energy, such as heat, light, or mechanical work. The unit of resistance is the ohm (Ω). Ohms are measured with an ohmmeter.

Power

Power is the use of energy to do work. An electrical power company charges its customers for the amount of energy used. The unit of power is the *watt*. Watts are measured with a wattmeter.

Electromagnetic Action

Magnetic action is the force exerted by a magnet (Figure 6–5). A magnet has two poles: north and south. Like poles repel, while unlike poles attract. The force of a magnet is dependent on its strength and the distance between the magnet and the metal it is affecting.

Current

Current is a term used in electricity to describe the rate of electrical flow. Electricity is believed to be the movement of *electrons,* small electrically charged particles, through a *conductor.* A conductor is a type of metal through which electricity will flow under certain conditions. These conditions are described later in the chapter. Current flow is measured in amperes with an electrical instrument called an ammeter.

There are two types of electric current: *direct current* and *alternating current.* In *direct current* (d.c.), the electrons move through the conductor in only one direction. This is the type of current produced by a battery. In *alternating current* (a.c.), the electrons move first in one direction and then in the other, alternating their movement usually 60 times per second [called 60 cycles or 60 hertz (Hz)]. Alternating current is the type available for residential use and is supplied by an electric power company.

Electromagnetic action is the force exerted by the magnetic field of a magnet (Figure 6–6). Current flowing through a conductor creates a magnetic field around the conductor. This action is extremely useful in construction of electrical devices.

If an insulated conductor is coiled and alternating current is passed through it, two important effects are produced:

FIGURE 6–5   Magnetic action.

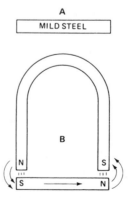

FIGURE 6–6 Electromagnetic action. (Courtesy of I-T-E Electrical Products.)

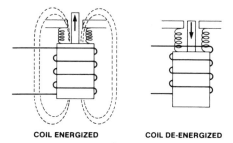

COIL ENERGIZED   COIL DE-ENERGIZED

1. A magnetic effect with directional force is produced in the field inside the coil. This force can move a separate metal plunger. The resultant action is called the *solenoid effect*. A solenoid is shown in Figure 6–7.
2. A magnetic field effect can transfer current to a nearby circuit, causing current to flow. This is called *electromagnetic induction* (Figure 6–8).

The solenoid effect is used to operate switches and valves. The electromagnetic induction effect is used to operate motors and transformers.

Capacitance

Capacitance is the charging and discharging ability of an electrical device, called a capacitor, to store electricity. Capacitors are made up of a series of conductor surfaces separated by insulation (Figure 6–9). The unit of capacitance is the farad (F).

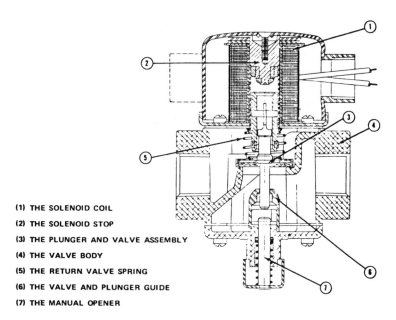

(1) THE SOLENOID COIL

(2) THE SOLENOID STOP

(3) THE PLUNGER AND VALVE ASSEMBLY

(4) THE VALVE BODY

(5) THE RETURN VALVE SPRING

(6) THE VALVE AND PLUNGER GUIDE

(7) THE MANUAL OPENER

FIGURE 6–7 Solenoid valve. (Courtesy of Robertshaw Controls Company.)

FIGURE 6–8   A flow of current in circuit A induces a flow of current in circuit B by electromagnetic induction.

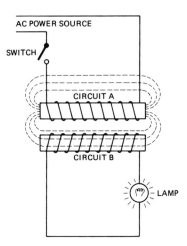

AC POWER SOURCE

SWITCH

CIRCUIT A

CIRCUIT B

LAMP

Most capacitors for furnace motors are used to increase the starting power of the motor. These capacitors are rated in microfarads (μF).

CIRCUITS

Electrical devices are used in a circuit to perform various functions. A circuit is an electrical system that provides the following:

- Source of power
- Path for power to follow
- Place for power to be used (load)

An electrical circuit is shown in Figure 6–10.

The source of power can be a battery that stores direct current or a connection to a power company's generator that supplies alternating current. The path is a continuous electrical conductor (such as copper wire) that connects the power supply to the load and from the load back to the power supply. The load is a type of electrical resistance that converts power to other forms of energy, such as heat, light, or mechanical work.

FIGURE 6–9   Capacitors. (Courtesy of Sprague Electric Co.)

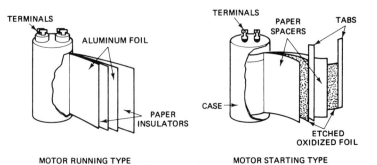

TERMINALS

ALUMINUM FOIL

PAPER INSULATORS

MOTOR RUNNING TYPE

TERMINALS

PAPER SPACERS

TABS

CASE

ETCHED OXIDIZED FOIL

MOTOR STARTING TYPE

FIGURE 6–10 Electrical circuit.

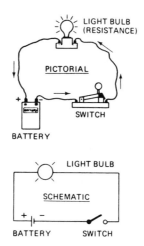

A switch can be inserted into the circuit to connect (make) or disconnect (break) the flow of current as desired, to control the operation of the load. Thus, a light switch is used to turn a light on and off by making or breaking its connection to the power supply.

A single-phase power supply, such as that used for heating equipment, always consists of two wires. For 120-V a.c. power, one wire is called *hot* (usually black) and the other wire is called *neutral* (usually white). The hot wire can be found by using a test light attached to two wire leads (Figure 6–11). Touch one lead to the hot wire and the other to the ground (a metal pipe inserted in the ground) and the bulb will light. Touch one lead to the neutral wire and the other to the ground and the bulb will not light.

In a circuit using a.c. power, the assumption is made that power moves from the hot wire through the load to the neutral wire (although the current does alternate). This assumption is made only to simplify tracing circuits and locating switches.

FIGURE 6–11 Use of test light.

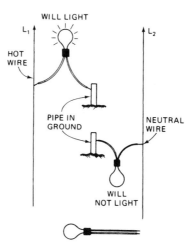

Caution: Switches are always placed between the hot wire and the load, not between the load and the neutral wire. Thus, when the switch is open (disconnecting the circuit) it is safe to work on the load. If the switch were on the neutral side of the load, touching the load could complete the circuit to ground. This dangerous condition could cause current to flow through a person's body with serious or fatal results.

A circuit consists of a source of electrical current, a path for it to follow, and a place for it to go (electrical load). Switches are inserted in the path of the current to control its flow either manually or automatically. Electrical devices are connected in circuits to produce a specific resultant action, such as operating a fan motor or a firing device on a furnace.

There are two basic types of circuits: series and parallel. Electrical devices can be connected in either of these ways or in a combination of both. Referring to Figure 6–12, using 120-V alternating current as a power source, the two wires are termed L_1 (hot) and L_2 (neutral). The hot wire is usually black and the neutral wire is usually white. Most 120-V installations include a third wire (color coded green) for the earth ground. These systems require a three-prong plug and outlet.

The fuse inserted in the hot side of the line is usually incorporated in the switching device known as a *fused disconnect*. Where the load is in some type of residence, a thermal fuse is used. In case of a shorted circuit or overload, the fuse melts and disconnects the power automatically. Where the type of load is a motor, a time-delay fuse is used.

ELECTRICAL DEVICES

Electrical devices are chiefly of two types (Figure 6–13):

1. Loads
2. Switches

Loads have resistance and consume power. Loads usually transform power into some other form of energy. Examples of loads are motors, resistance heaters, and lights. *Switches* are used to connect loads to the power supply or to disconnect them when they are not required.

Loads and Their Symbols

The common loads used on heating equipment are described next, along with the symbol used to represent them in the schematic wiring diagram.

FIGURE 6–12 Typical electrical circuit, including a source of power, a path for the current to flow in, and a load.

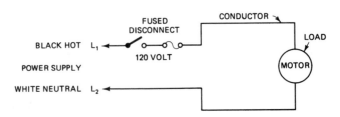

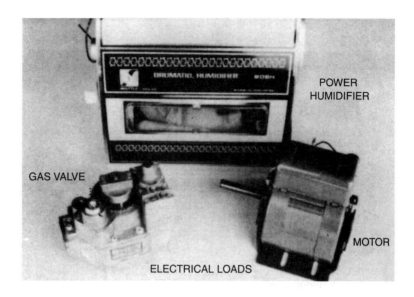

FIGURE 6–13 Loads and switches.

Motors   The electrical motor is usually considered the most important load device in the electrical system. It can be represented in two ways: by a large circle or by the internal wiring (Figure 6–14). To better understand the electrical motor application, refer to the legend on the wiring diagram. The symbol may represent a fan motor, an oil burner motor, or an automatic humidifier motor. When current flows through the motor, the motor should run.

Solenoids   The second most important device is the solenoid (Figure 6–15). When the current flows through the solenoid (coil or wire), magnetism is created. The solenoid is a device designed to harness and use magnetism. It is most frequently used to open and close switches. It is also used to open and close valves. It is common practice to use letters under the symbol to abbreviate the name of the device and to

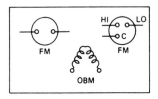

LEGEND

FM = FAN MOTOR
FM = FAN MOTOR, MULTIPLE SPEED
OBM = OIL BURNER MOTOR

FIGURE 6–14 Electric motor and symbols. (Courtesy of Essex Group, Controls Division, Steveco Products, Inc.)

provide reference to the legend. For example, GV under the symbol would be shown in the legend to mean gas valve.

Relays   A relay is a useful application of a solenoid. By flowing current through the solenoid coil, one or more mechanically operated switches can be opened or closed. The solenoid coil is located in one circuit, while the switches are usually in separate circuits. A relay is identified by the symbols shown in Figure 6–16 and 6–17. There are at least two parts to the relay: the coil and the switch (or switches). The switch may be

FIGURE 6–15   Solenoid and symbols.

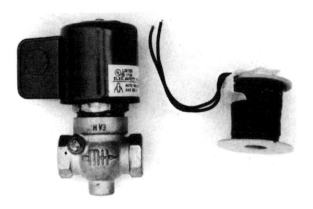

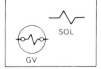

LEGEND

SOL = SOLENOID (RELAY COIL)

GV = SOLENOID (GAS VALVE)

FIGURE 6–16 Indoor fan relay switch and symbols, switch 1 open and switch 2 closed. (Courtesy of Essex Group, Controls Division, Steveco Products, Inc.)

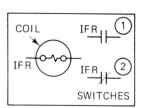

IFR = INDOOR FAN RELAY

RELAY SWITCH

in one part of the diagram and the coil in another. The two symbols are identified as belonging to the same electrical device by the letters above them.

When the switch has a diagonal line across it, it is a closed switch; without the diagonal line, the switch is open. All wiring diagrams show relay switches in their normal position, the position when no current is applied to the solenoid coil. Thus, in a diagram, where no current is flowing through the coil, the open switches are called *normally open* and the closed switches are called *normally closed*. When current is applied to the coil, all of the related switches change position (Figure 6–17). There are several types of relays used in heating work. They differ in the number of NO and NC switches.

Resistance heaters   Another form of load device commonly used is the resistance heater. In the resistance heater, electricity is converted to heat. Heat in an electric furnace is produced by electricity. Heat is also used to control switches. The higher the resistance, the greater the amount of heat that is produced. The symbol for a resistance heater is a zigzag line (Figure 6–18). A letter is used under the heater symbol to designate its use, as indicated in the legend.

Heat relays   The symbols and letters for a heat relay are shown in Figure 6–19. In heating circuits, particularly for electric heating, resistance heaters are used to operate switches. The advantage of this type of relay is that it provides a time delay in operating the switch. When current is supplied to the heater, it heats up a bimetal element located in another circuit. Bimetal elements are made by bonding together two pieces of metal that expand at different rates. As the bimetal heats, its shape is changed, thereby closing or opening a switch.

FIGURE 6–17 Indoor fan relay switch and symbols, switch 2 open and switch 1 closed. (Courtesy of Essex Group, Controls Division, Steveco Products, Inc.)

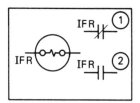

IFR = INDOOR FAN RELAY

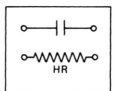

LEGEND

RH = RESISTANCE HEATER

FIGURE 6–18 Resistance heater and symbols.

FIGURE 6–19 Heat relay and symbols.

LEGEND

HR = RESISTANCE HEAT RELAY

FIGURE 6–20 Light and symbol.

LEGEND
G = GREEN LIGHT

Lights   Lights are a type of load. They have resistance to current flow. A signal light is often used to indicate an electrical condition that cannot otherwise be readily observed. The color of the light is often indicated by a letter on the symbol (Figure 6–20).

Transformers   In heating systems, it is often desirable to use two or more different voltages to operate the system. The fan must run on line voltage (usually 120 V), but the thermostat circuit (control circuit) can often best be run on low voltage (24 V). A transformer is used to change from one voltage to another. The legend and symbols for transformers are shown in Figure 6–21.

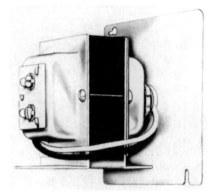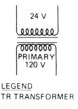

FIGURE 6–21 Transformer and symbol. (Courtesy of Essex Group, Controls Division, Steveco Products, Inc.)

Switches and Their Symbols

Loads perform many functions. However, switches perform only one: to start and stop the flow of electricity. Electrical switches are classified according to the force used to operate them: manual, magnetic (solenoid), heat, light, or moisture.

The terms *normally open* and *normally closed* refer to the position of the switch with no operating force applied. All wiring diagrams show the position of the switches when the operating solenoid (relay coil) or mechanism is deenergized.

A thermostat is assumed to be a normally open (NO) switch. A cooling thermostat makes (closes) an electrical circuit upon a rise in temperature. A heating limit switch is considered a normally closed (NC) switch since it is normally closed when the system is in operation and opens only when excessively high temperatures are reached in the furnace.

It is important to identify the type of force that operates a switch. Only then can its normal position be accurately determined. The simplest type of switch is one that makes (closes) or breaks (opens) a single electrical circuit. Other switches make or break several circuits. The switching action is described by:

- Number of poles (number of electrical circuits through the switch)
- The throw (number of places for the electrical current to go)

The following abbreviations are often used to designate the types of switching action.

SPST: single-pole single-throw
SPDT: single-pole double-throw
DPST: double-pole single-throw
DPDT: double-pole double-throw

These designations and their symbols are shown in Figure 6–22.

The common types of switches used for heating equipment controls are described, together with the symbols used to represent them.

Manual switches Manual disconnect switches are hand operated and are usually used to disconnect the electrical power supplying an air-conditioning unit. Disconnect

FIGURE 6–22 Designations and symbols for switching actions. (Courtesy of Carrier Corporation.)

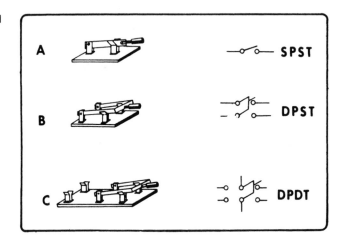

switches that contain no fuses, or the bladed type, are referred to as safety switches. These switches are used to shut off the electrical power to the unit whenever service is required or for seasonal shutdown.

The fusible disconnect shown in Figure 6–23 serves two functions. It is used as a safety switch and also contains fuses that are rated to protect the equipment from excessive electrical overload. Note that for proper equipment protection, the fuses must be sized for each unit's amperage draw.

Magnetic switches Magnetic or solenoid switches are electrically operated switches using the force of the magnetic effect to operate the switch. To produce the required amount of power to operate the switch, the wire is coiled, creating a strong magnetic effect on a metal core. Magnetic or solenoid switches have various names, depending on their use. Among these are relays (Figure 6–24), contactors (Figure 6–25), and starters (Figure 6–26).

Relays were described earlier in this chapter. Contactors are relatively large electric relays used to start motors. Starters are also relatively large relays that include overload (excess current) protection. The National Electrical Code® specifies whether a motor requires a manual, contactor, or starter switch. Solenoid switches may also be used to operate valves that regulate the flow of a fluid (liquid or vapor). An example of this type of valve is the gas valve, described in Chapter 5.

Some types of overloads can also be described as magnetic switches. An overload device protects a motor against excess current flow. Normal amounts of current will not energize the solenoid, but excess amounts of current will. When the solenoid is energized, it trips a mechanically interlocked switch that cuts off the power to the motor.

Heat-operated switches There are many types of heat-operated switches. In all cases, heat is the force that operates the switch. These switches include thermostats, fan and limit controls, heat relays, fuses, overloads, and circuit breakers.

Thermostats A heating thermostat (Figure 6–27) makes (closes) on a drop in room temperature. The intensity of heat affects the bimetal, changing its shape, which in

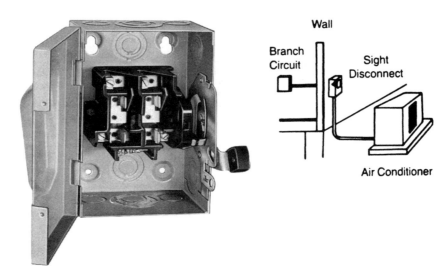

FIGURE 6–23 General-duty safety switches. (Courtesy of Square D Company.)

turn actuates a switch. The thermostat is usually shown as an NO switch. Thermostats are discussed in Chapter 10.

Fan and Limit Controls Fan and limit controls (Figure 6–28) have a bimetal sensing element that protrudes into the warm air passage of a furnace. The fan control makes on a rise in temperature. It is considered to be an NO switch because with the furnace shut down, the fan control will have an open switch. The limit control

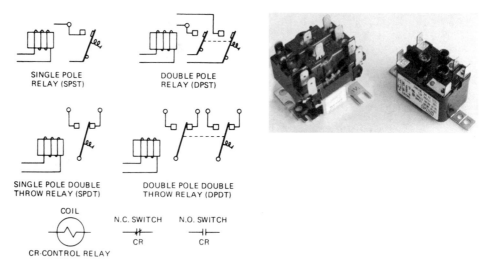

FIGURE 6–24 Relay switch, symbols, and switching action. (Courtesy of Essex Group, Controls Division, Steveco Products, Inc.)

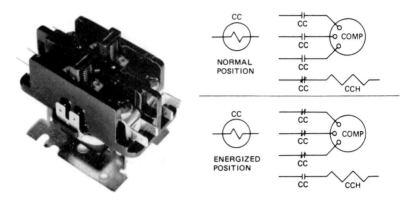

FIGURE 6–25   Contactor switch and symbol. (Courtesy of Essex Group, Controls Division, Steveco Products, Inc.)

FIGURE 6–26   Starter switch and symbol.

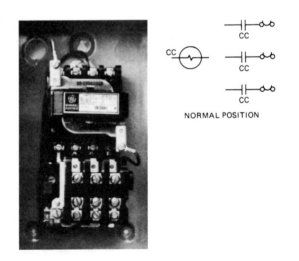

FIGURE 6–27   Thermostat switch and symbol. (Courtesy of Honeywell Inc.)

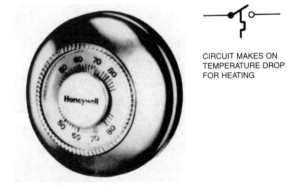

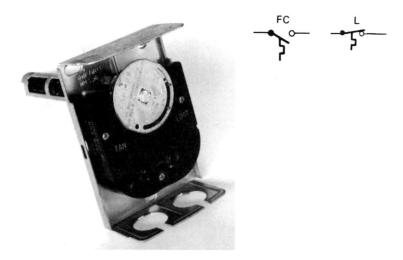

FIGURE 6–28   Combination fan and limit control switch and symbol.

protects the furnace against excessively high air temperatures, turning off the firing devices when a predetermined temperature is reached. The limit control is diagrammed as an NC switch.

Heat Relays   Heat relays (Figure 6–29) are similar to magnetic or solenoid relays in function. However, the mechanical action takes place as a result of heat produced in an electrical resistance. When the resistance coil is energized, heat is produced. This heat is applied to one or more bimetal elements. As the bimetal elements expand, they either break an electrical circuit or make an electrical circuit.

The heat relay is a delayed-action switch. This means that the switch requires some amount of time to change position. Depending on the construction, the time delay may be 15, 30, 45 seconds, or more. This feature permits staging or sequencing loads (turning loads on automatically at different times). Since the inrush current to a load, when first turned on, is usually many times greater than its running current, sequencing is important. Sequencing permits using a smaller power service to the appliance. A sequencer is used on an electric furnace to turn on the electric heating elements in steps.

Fuses   Fuses (Figure 6–30) are placed in an electrical circuit to cut off the flow of current when there is an overload or a short. An *overload* is current in excess of the circuit design. A *short* is a direct connection between the two wires of a power supply without having the current pass through a load. In either case, the fuse will heat and melt, breaking the circuit continuity and stopping the flow of current. Where the fault is overcurrent, the melting of the fuse takes place slowly. Where the fault is a short, the melting of the fuse takes place quickly.

Some circuits require a time-delay fuse. An example is a motor circuit. The inrush of current in starting (a fraction of a second) is so great that an ordinary fuse would "blow" before the motor reached running speed. This initial motor current is called *locked rotor amperes* (LRA). The running amperes or *full-load amperes* (FLA) are

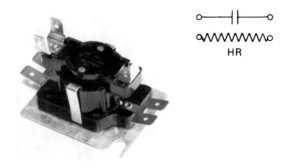

FIGURE 6–29   Heat relay switch and symbol. (Courtesy of Honeywell Inc.)

much less. Because of the special design of delayed-action fuses, they may be selected on the basis of FLA. According to the National Electrical Code®, fuses and wiring can be sized on the basis of 125% of FLA.

Overloads   Overloads (Figure 6–31) can be constructed in many ways. All overloads are designed to stop the flow of current when safe limits are exceeded. Overloads differ from fuses in that they do not have one-time use as does a fuse. When a fuse melts, it must be replaced to return the circuit to operation. When an overload senses excess current, a switch is opened, breaking the flow of current. Some of these switches are reset automatically when the current returns to normal; others must be manually reset. An overload is considered an NC switch, since it is closed when no current is flowing through the circuit and during normal operation of the equipment.

Circuit Breakers   The main power circuit to a heating furnace must be protected against excess current flow by a fuse or a circuit breaker (Figure 6–32). Either one of these switches will disconnect the power supply if the equipment draws excess current. The circuit breaker is a type of overload device placed in the power supply, which will "trip" (open the circuit) in the event of excessive current flow. When the fault is corrected, the circuit breaker can be reset manually to restore the circuit to its original condition.

Light-operated switches   Some switches are activated by light. An example is the cad cell used on the primary control of an oil burner. A *cad cell* is a cadmium sulfate sensing element. In the presence of light, the electrical resistance of a cad cell is about

FIGURE 6–30   Fuses.

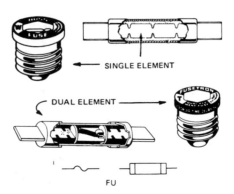

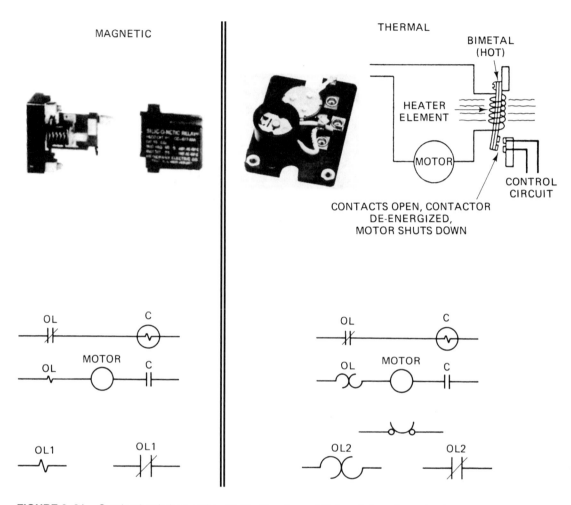

FIGURE 6–31   Overload switches and symbols. (Courtesy of Motors & Armatures, Inc.)

1000 Ω; in darkness, its resistance is about 100,000 Ω. The cad cell is located in the draft tube of an oil burner and senses the presence (or proof) of a flame. If the cad cell is in darkness, there is no flame; if the cad cell is lighted, the flame is proof that the burner has been started by the ignition system. It therefore acts as a safety device.

FIGURE 6–32   Circuit breaker switch. (Courtesy of Sears, Roebuck and Company.)

In the electrical circuit the cad cell is placed in series with a relay coil. If the cad cell does not sense adequate light from the flame, the relay will not be energized. If the cad cell senses the flame, its resistance is reduced and the relay is energized, which allows the burner to continue running.

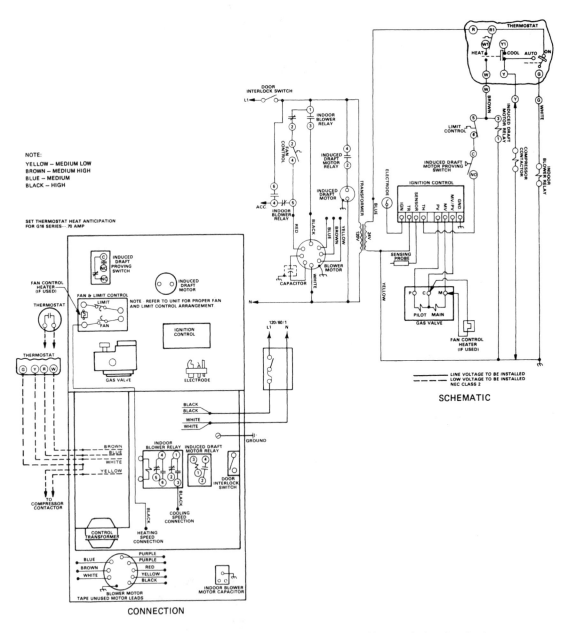

FIGURE 6–33 Connection and schematic wiring diagrams. (Courtesy of Lennox Industries, Inc.)

Moisture-operated switches   The presence of moisture in the air can be used to operate a switch. Certain materials, including human hair and nylon, expand when moist and contract when dry. These two materials are used to sense the relative humidity in the air. The change in the length of a strand of hair or nylon can be used to operate a suitable switch. The switch will turn a humidifier on or off to maintain the desired relative humidity in a space.

ELECTRICAL DIAGRAMS

The greatest advances in the design and use of forced warm air heating equipment came after the invention of automatic control systems. It was then no longer necessary to operate the equipment manually. Automatic controls regulate the furnace to maintain the desired temperature conditions. Forced air heating owes its very beginning to the use of electricity to drive the fan motor.

A wiring diagram describes an electrical system. There are generally two types of diagrams for warm air heating units. A *connection diagram* shows the electrical devices in much the same way as they are positioned on the equipment (Figure 6–33). Lines are connected to the electrical terminals to show the paths the electric current will follow. A *schematic diagram* (Figure 6–33) uses symbols to represent the electrical devices. The arrangement of the symbols in the diagram, using ladder-type connecting lines, indicates how the system works. It shows the sequence of operation. This diagram is essential to the service technician in troubleshooting problems in heating systems.

STUDY QUESTIONS

Answers to the study questions may be found in the sections noted in brackets.

6–1. Define volts, amperes, ohms, and watts. *[Electrical Terms]*

6–2. State Ohm's law and give an example of its use. *[Ohm's Law]*

6–3. How does a series circuit differ from a parallel circuit? *[Series Circuits; Parallel Circuits]*

6–4. State the formulas for series and parallel circuits. *[Series Circuits; Parallel Circuits]*

6–5. Describe how a solenoid coil uses electromagnetic action. *[Electromagnetic Action]*

6–6. How are capacitors rated? *[Capacitance]*

6–7. What is an electrical circuit? *[Circuits]*

6–8. How do loads differ from switches? *[Electrical Devices]*

6–9. Give the electrical symbols for motors, heaters, solenoids, relays, lights, and transformers. *[Loads and Their Symbols]*

6–10. How does a relay operate? *[Relays]*

6–11. What do SPST, SPDT, DPST, and DPDT mean? *[Electrical Switches and Their Symbols]*

6–12. What is the difference between a connection and a schematic wiring diagram? *[Electrical Diagrams]*

7

Schematic Wiring Diagrams

OBJECTIVES

After studying this chapter, the student will be able to:

- Read and construct a schematic electrical wiring diagram

PURPOSE OF A SCHEMATIC

A schematic wiring diagram consists of a group of lines and electrical symbols arranged in ladder form to represent the individual circuits controlling or operating a unit. The lines represent the connecting wires. The electrical symbols represent loads or switches. The rungs of the ladder represent individual electrical circuits. The unit can be an electrical-mechanical device such as a furnace.

UNDERSTANDING A SCHEMATIC

To understand a schematic diagram, a student must know:

- The purpose of each electrical component
- Exactly how the unit operates, both mechanically and electrically
- The sequence of operation of each electrical component

Sequence refers to the condition where the operation of one electrical component follows another to produce a final result. It represents the order of events as they occur in a system of electrical controls. All electrical systems must be wired by

FIGURE 7–1   Connection wiring diagram.

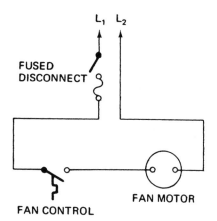

making connections to power and to each electrical device. A schematic diagram is important to assist a service technician in wiring the equipment, locating connections for testing circuits, and in analyzing the operation of the control system. Occasionally, however, a schematic diagram may be unavailable, so it is essential that a service technician is able to construct one.

Following is the legend to the schematic diagrams used in this chapter:

CR	Control relay	L	Limit
FC	Fan control	LA	Limit auxiliary
FD	Fused disconnect	L_1, L_2	Power supply
FM	Fan motor	NC	Normally closed
FR	Fan relay	NO	Normally open
FS	Fan switch	T	Thermostat
GV	Gas valve	TR	Transformer
IFR	Indoor fan relay	Y, R, G, W	Terminals of thermostat

SCHEMATIC CONSTRUCTION

Connection and schematic wiring diagrams are shown in Figures 7–1 and 7–2. To draw a schematic and to separate the individual circuits on the unit itself, a service

FIGURE 7–2   Schematic wiring diagram.

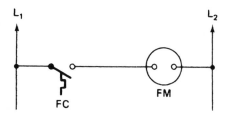

FIGURE 7–3 Relay coils and switches.

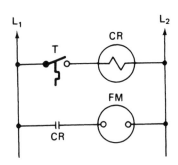

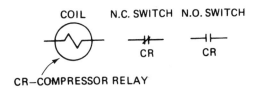

technician must be able to trace (or follow) the wiring of each individual circuit. The method of tracing a circuit is as follows:

1. Start at one side of the power supply (L_1), go through the resistance (load), and return to the other side of the power supply (L_2). This is a *complete circuit*.
2. If a technician starts at L_1 and goes through the resistance and cannot reach L_2 or returns back to L_1 this is an *open circuit*.
3. If a technician starts at L_1 and reaches L_2 without passing through a resistance (load), this is a *short circuit*.

Rules for Drawing: Vertical Style

1. Use letters on each symbol to represent the name of the component.
2. The names of all components represented by letters should be listed in the legend.
3. When using a 120-V a.c. power supply*, show the hot line (L_1) on the left side and the neutral line (L_2) on the right side of the diagram.
4. When using a 120-V power supply, the switches must be placed on the hot side (L_1) of the load.
5. Relay coils and their switches (Figure 7–3) should be marked with the same (matched) symbol letters.
6. Numbers can be used to show wiring connections to controls or terminals.
7. Always show switches in their normal (de-energized) position.

---

*In 208-, 230-, 240-, or 440-V single-phase circuits, there are two hot wires and no neutral wire. In these circuits, switches can be placed on either side of the load.

8. Thermostats with switching subbases, primary controls for oil burners, and other more complicated controls can be shown by terminals only in the main diagram. Sub-diagrams are used when necessary to show the internal control circuits.
9. It is common practice to start the diagram showing line-voltage circuits first and low-voltage (control) circuits second (Figure 7–4).

Rules for Drawing: Horizontal Style

Assuming that either a completely wired unit or a connection wiring diagram is available, the following is a step-by-step procedure for drawing a schematic:

Referring to the Connecting Wiring	Drawing the Schematic Diagram
Locate the source of power. Trace it back to the disconnect switch.	Draw two horizontal lines* representing L_1 and L_2, with sufficient space between them for the diagram. Draw in the disconnect switch.
Trace each circuit on the diagram, starting with L_1 and returning to L_2.	Draw each circuit on the diagram using a vertical line to connect L_1 through the switches, through the load to L_2.
Determine the names of each switch and load.	Make a legend by listing the names of the electrical components, together with the letters representing each. The letters are used on the diagram to identify the parts.

*Vertical lines could also be used to represent L_1 and L_2 in which case horizontal lines would then be used to represent the individual circuits.

A connection diagram usually shows the relative position of the various controls on the unit. A schematic diagram makes it possible to indicate the sequence of operation of the electrical devices. A verbal description of the electrical system may also reveal some useful facts about the operation of the unit. Thus, the connection diagram, the schematic diagram, and the verbal description are all useful in understanding how the unit operates electrically.

To show how these three are related, a connection diagram and a schematic diagram will be constructed from the description of each circuit.

FIGURE 7–4 Line-voltage and low-voltage circuits schematic diagram.

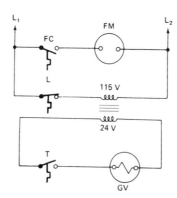

FIGURE 7–5 Power supply to
furnace.

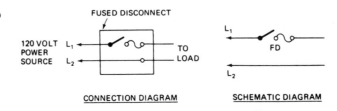

FIGURE 7–5 Power supply to
furnace.

Power supply *Description:* The power supply is 120-V, 60-Hz, single-phase
(Figure 7–5). A fused disconnect is placed in the hot line to the furnace to disconnect
the power when the furnace is not being used. The power supply consists of a hot wire
and neutral wire. The circuit has a 20-A fuse.

Circuits *Description:* A fan motor operating on 120 V is placed in circuit 1 of
Figure 7–6. It is controlled by a fan control. This fan control is located in the plenum
or in the furnace cabinet by the heat exchanger. It is adjustable, but to conserve energy
it is usually set to turn the fan on at 110°F (43°C) and off at 90°F (32°C). This permits
the furnace to heat up before the fan turns on to deliver heated air to the building.

   Note that the fan control is part of a combination fan and limit control. Both use
the same bimetal heat element. The limit control settings are higher than the fan control settings.

   Description: the primary of a transformer is placed in a separate 120-V circuit,
circuit 2 (Figure 7–7). The transformer will be used to supply 24-V (secondary) power
to the control circuits.

   Description: This is a 24-V gas valve circuit (Figure 7–8). Circuit 3 includes the
thermostat, gas valve, and limit control. When the thermostat calls for heat, the gas
valve opens. The limit control will shut off the flow of gas should the air temperature
leaving the furnace exceed 200°F (93°C).

   Description: A manual switch, located in the subbase of the thermostat, is connected to an indoor fan relay, circuit 4, so that the fan can be manually turned on for
ventilation even though the gas is off (Figure 7–9). The relay switch is in the 120-V

FIGURE 7–6 Fan circuit.

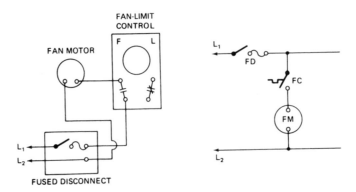

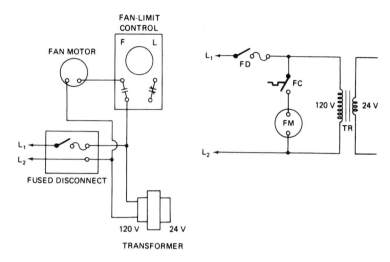

FIGURE 7–7 Transformer circuit.

FIGURE 7–8 Gas valve circuit.

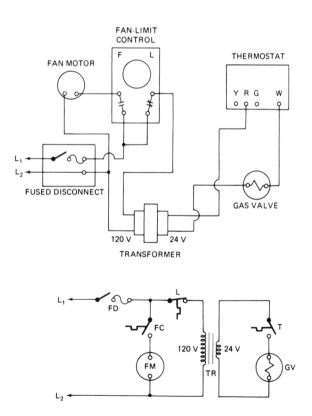

FIGURE 7–9   Manual fan circuit.

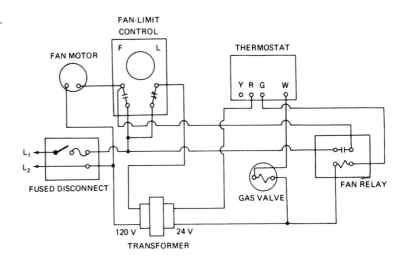

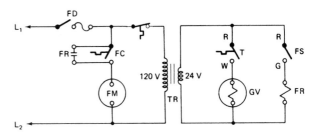

circuit parallel with the fan control, and the solenoid coil of the relay is in the 24-V circuit in series with the fan switch (FS).

Field wiring is shown in Figure 7–10 for high-efficiency heating only and for a combination heating and cooling unit.

REVIEW PROBLEM 1

Draw a connection diagram from the schematic diagram shown in Figure 7–11.

REVIEW PROBLEM 2

Draw a schematic wiring diagram from the connection diagram shown in Figure 7–12.

REVIEW PROBLEM 3

Copy the components from Figure 7–13 onto a separate sheet of paper, connect them into their proper circuits, and draw a schematic of the system.

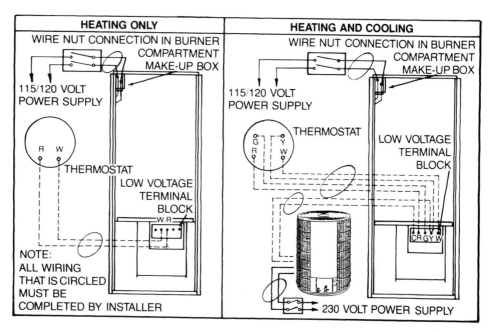

FIGURE 7–10   Typical wiring for a heating and cooling unit. (Courtesy of ARCOAIRE, Inter-City Products Corporation, USA.)

REVIEW PROBLEM 4

Copy the components from Figure 7–14 onto a separate sheet of paper, connect them into their proper circuits, and draw a schematic of the system.

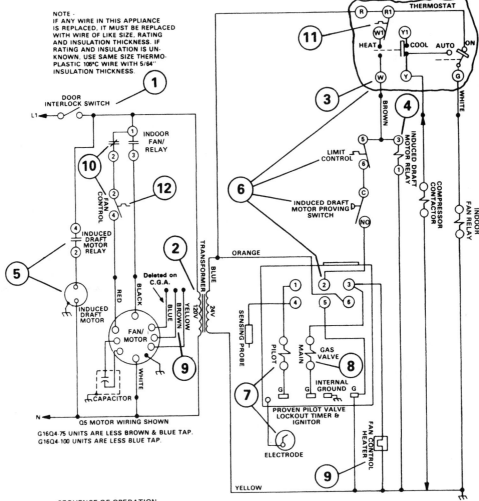

NOTE ·
IF ANY WIRE IN THIS APPLIANCE
IS REPLACED, IT MUST BE REPLACED
WITH WIRE OF LIKE SIZE, RATING
AND INSULATION THICKNESS. IF
RATING AND INSULATION IS UN-
KNOWN, USE SAME SIZE THERMO-
PLASTIC 105°C WIRE WITH 5/64''
INSULATION THICKNESS.

Q5 MOTOR WIRING SHOWN
G16Q4-75 UNITS ARE LESS BROWN & BLUE TAP.
G16Q4-100 UNITS ARE LESS BLUE TAP.

SEQUENCE OF OPERATION

1. LINE POTENTIAL FEEDS THROUGH DOOR INTER-
   LOCK. ACCESS PANEL MUST BE IN PLACE TO
   ENERGIZE UNIT.
2. TRANSFORMER PROVIDES 24 VOLTS TO POWER
   CONTROL CIRCUIT.
3. ON A HEATING DEMAND, THERMOSTAT BULB
   MAKES PROVIDING 24 V AT "W" LEG.
4. INDUCED DRAFT MOTOR RELAY IS ENERGIZED
   FROM "W" LEG.
5. INDUCED DRAFT MOTOR RELAY N.O. CONTACTS
   CLOSE AND ENERGIZE THE INDUCED DRAFT
   MOTOR.
6. WHEN THE INDUCED DRAFT MOTOR COMES UP
   TO SPEED, THE INDUCED DRAFT MOTOR
   PROVING SWITCH CLOSES COMPLETING THE
   CIRCUIT FROM "W" LEG OF THERMOSTAT
   THROUGH LIMIT CONTROL TO IGNITION
   CONTROL TERMINAL 2.
7. PILOT GAS VALVE AND PILOT IGNITION SPARK
   ARE ENERGIZED.

8. AFTER PILOT FLAME HAS BEEN PROVEN BY
   IGNITION CONTROL, MAIN GAS VALVE IS
   ENERGIZED AND SPARK IS DE-ENERGIZED.
   (MAIN GAS VALVE WILL OPEN ONLY ON PROOF
   OF PILOT FLAME.)
9. AS THE MAIN GAS VALVE IS ENERGIZED, THE
   FAN CONTROL HEATER IS ACTIVATED.
10. IN APPROXIMATELY 30-80 SECONDS N.O. FAN
    CONTROL CONTACTS CLOSE ENERGIZING
    BLOWER MOTOR FROM N.C. BLOWER MOTOR
    RELAY CONTACTS TO THE HEATING SPEED TAP.
11. AS HEATING DEMAND IS SATISFIED, THERMO-
    STAT HEAT BULB BREAKS DE-ENERGIZING
    IGNITION CONTROL, GAS VALVE, AND FAN
    CONTROL HEATER.
12. BLOWER MOTOR CONTINUES RUNNING UNTIL
    FURNACE TEMPERATURE DROPS BELOW FAN
    CONTROL SET POINT.

FIGURE 7–11 Gas-fired upflow furnace schematic diagram.

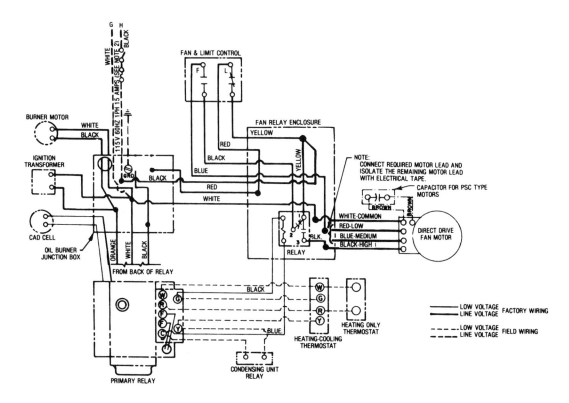

FIGURE 7–12   Heating-cooling connection diagram for oil-fired upflow furnace.

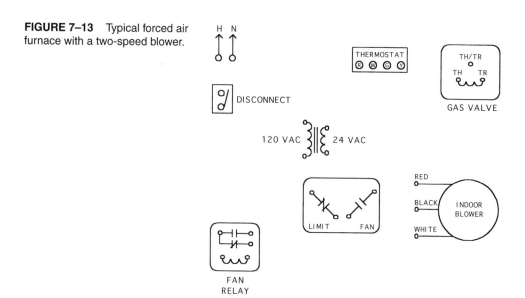

FIGURE 7–13   Typical forced air furnace with a two-speed blower.

FIGURE 7–14   Oil-fired furnace with burner mount stack control.

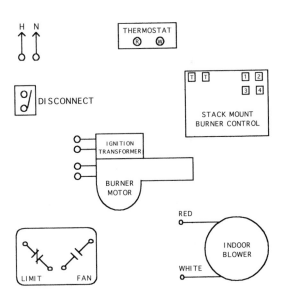

STUDY QUESTIONS

Answers to the study questions may be found in the sections noted in brackets.

7–1. What is the purpose of a schematic wiring diagram? *[Understanding a Schematic]*

7–2. If the power lines are vertical, what does each horizontal line represent? *[Rules for Drawing]*

7–3. What essential electrical devices must be shown in each circuit? *[Rules for Drawing]*

7–4. With two vertical lines representing the power supply, which line is usually shown "hot"? *[Rules for Drawing]*

7–5. With L_1 hot and L_2 neutral, where should the fused disconnect be placed? *[Rules for Drawing]*

7–6. How is the position of two switches shown if both must be on to have the load operate? *[Rules for Drawing]*

7–7. If one switch operates two loads, how is that drawn? *[Rules for Drawing]*

8

Using Electrical Test Instruments and Equipment

OBJECTIVES

After studying this chapter, the student will be able to:

- Use common electrical test instruments for service or troubleshooting

ELECTRICAL TEST INSTRUMENTS

To test the performance of a heating unit, or to troubleshoot service problems, requires the use of instruments. Since a heating unit has many electrical components, a heating service technician should:

- Know the unit electrically
- Be able to read and use schematic wiring diagrams
- Be able to use electrical test instruments

The reading and construction of schematic wiring diagrams was discussed in Chapter 7. The use of schematic diagrams is discussed in this chapter.

COMPONENT FUNCTIONS

To know the unit electrically means to understand exactly how each component functions. Figure 8–1 shows a simple electrical heating wiring arrangement for a forced air gas system. Two views are shown:

1. Schematic diagram
2. Connection diagram

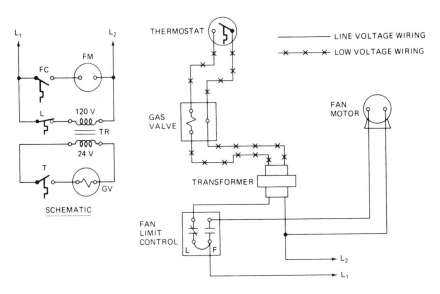

FIGURE 8–1 Electrical wiring for a 24-V forced warm air gas-fired furnace.

Three load devices are shown:

1. Fan motor
2. Transformer
3. Gas valve

The fan motor turns the fan when it is supplied with power, in this case 120-V, single-phase, 60-Hz current. The transformer, which has a primary voltage of 120 V and a secondary voltage of 24 V, is energized whenever power is supplied. A solenoid gas valve opens when it is energized and operates on 24-V power.

There is at least one automatic switch in each circuit. The fan has one, the transformer has one, and the gas valve has two. The following is a description of the types of switches used:

- The fan control turns on the fan when the bonnet temperature rises to the cut-in setting. It turns off the fan when the bonnet temperature drops to the cut-out setting.
- The limit control is a safety device that turns off the power to the transformer when the bonnet temperature rises to the cut-out setting. It turns on the power to the transformer automatically when the bonnet temperature drops to the cut-in setting.
- A combination gas valve has a built-in pilotstat. The pilotstat is a safety device operated by a thermocouple (not shown). When the pilot is burning properly, the NO contacts are closed, permitting the gas valve to open in response to the thermostat.
- The thermostat is a low-voltage (24-V) switch operated by a bimetal sensing element. When the room temperature drops, and the thermostat reaches its cut-in setting, the contacts close, and the gas valve opens (provided that the pilot flame is proven). When the room temperature rises to the cut-out setting of the thermostat, the contacts open and the gas valve closes.

INSTRUMENT FUNCTIONS

A number of instruments are required in testing. These include:

- A voltmeter to measure electrical potential
- An ammeter to measure rate of electrical current flow
- An ohmmeter to measure electrical resistance
- A wattmeter to measure electrical power
- A temperature tester to measure temperatures

Some meters measure a combination of characteristics. For example, a clamp-on ammeter that has provisions to measure amperes, volts, and ohms is available. A VOM multimeter that can measure volts, ohms, and milliamperes is available. The following scales are typical. However, before purchasing an instrument it is important to verify that its features match specific service needs. For example, do its scales allow the measured values to be clearly read?

1. *D.c. millivolt scales:* 0 to 50, 0 to 500, 0 to 1500. These scales are used to read voltages on thermocouples and thermopiles. A millivolt is a thousandth (1/1000) of a volt.
2. *A.c. voltage scales:* 0 to 30, 0 to 500. These scales are used to read low-voltage control circuits and line-voltage circuits.
3. *A.c. amperage scales:* 0 to 15, 0 to 75. These scales are used for measuring amperage drawn by various low-voltage and line-voltage loads.
4. *Ohm scales:* 0 to 400, 0 to 3000. These scales are used for resistance readings on all types of circuits and for continuity checks on all systems.
5. *Wattage scales:* 0 to 300, 0 to 600, 0 to 1500, 0 to 3000. These scales are used to measure power input to a circuit or system.
6. *Temperature scale:* 0° to 1200°F. This scale is used to check return air temperatures, discharge air temperatures, and stack temperatures.

USING METERS

When using meters, the following points should be considered:

1. Always use the highest scale first; then work down until midscale readings are obtained. This prevents damage to the meter.
2. Always check the calibration of a meter before using it. For example, on an ohmmeter the two test leads are shorted together and the zero adjust knob turned until the needle reads zero resistance.
3. When using a clamp-on ammeter, the sensitivity of the instrument can be increased by wrapping the conductor wire around the jaws. The sensitivity will be multiplied by the number of turns taken. For example: 10 loops of single-strand insulated thermostat wire can be wrapped around the jaws of an ammeter, as shown in Figure 8–2. If the meter is set to read on the 1 to 5-A scale, a reading of 2.5 A would be divided by 10 to arrive at the true reading 0.25 A.

FIGURE 8–2 Method used to read low-amperage values accurately using a clamp-on ammeter.

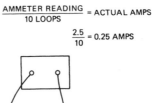

$$\frac{\text{AMMETER READING}}{10 \text{ LOOPS}} = \text{ACTUAL AMPS}$$

$$\frac{2.5}{10} = 0.25 \text{ AMPS}$$

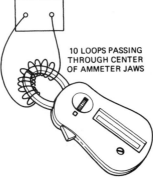

10 LOOPS PASSING THROUGH CENTER OF AMMETER JAWS

4. When using a clamp-on ammeter, be sure that the clamp is around only one wire. If it enclosed two wires, the current may be flowing in opposite directions, which could cause a zero reading even though current is actually flowing.
5. Always have a supply of the required meter fuses on hand. Certain special fuses may be difficult to obtain on short notice.
6. When measuring d.c. millivolts being delivered by a thermocouple in a circuit, an adapter is required to provide access to the internal connection. See Figure 8–3 for application.
7. The multimeter can be used when checking the output of pilot generators and thermocouples. See Figure 8–4.

FIGURE 8–3 Adapter being used for thermocouple measurements.

FIGURE 8–4 High performance auto-ranging multimeter, 11 different measurement functions, including frequency, capacitance, temperature, volts, amps, ohms and continuity. Digital and bargraph readouts. Programmable reference values. Single 9-V battery power source. Auto power off.
Ranges: 0–750 V a.c.
0–100 V d.c.
400 mu a–10 a
4 K–40 M ohm
–400° to 2,498°F
–400° to 1,3700°C
0–4000 pf
0–400 nF
0–40 mu F

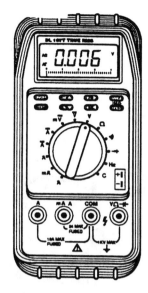

8. The digital multimeter shown in Figure 8–5 is used when testing burner equipment. It checks the flame signal current on systems using rectifying flame rod, photocell, infrared, or ultraviolet flame detectors.

Three types of readings that can be taken with an ohmmeter are shown in Figure 8–6:

1. *No resistance.* Closed switch is given full-scale deflection, indicating 0 Ω.
2. *Measurable resistance.* Measurable resistance is producing less deflection or a specific ohm reading on the meter.

FIGURE 8–5 Digital volt-ohm-ampere multitester.
Ranges: 0–200 mV, 0–2, 20, 200, 700 V a.c.
0–20/200 UA, 0–2/20 mA, 0–2/10 A a.c.
0–200 mV, 0–2/20/200/ 1000 V d.c.
0–20/200 pA, 0–2/20/200 mA, 0–2/10 A d.c.
0–200, 0–20/200 kΩ, 0–2/20 MΩ
20 µA d.c. range for measuring flame safeguard units
200 mV d.c. range for checking thermocouples, fused 10-A range. (Courtesy of Universal Enterprises.)

FIGURE 8–6   Three types of readings taken with an ohmmeter.

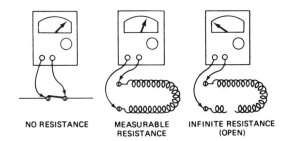

NO RESISTANCE   MEASURABLE   INFINITE RESISTANCE
                    RESISTANCE   (OPEN)

FIGURE 8–7   Ohm scale of multi-meter being used for testing fuses. (Courtesy of Simpson Electric Company.)

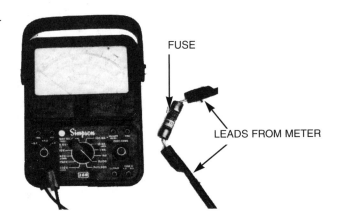

FUSE

LEADS FROM METER

3. *Infinite resistance (open).* There is no complete path for the ohmmeter current to flow through, so there is no deflection of the meter needle. The resistance is so high that it cannot be measured. The meter shows infinity (∞) representing an open circuit.

Note: It is important to remember when using an ohmmeter that it has its own source of power and must never be used to test a circuit that is "hot" (connected to power). All power must be off or the ohmmeter can be seriously damaged.

One good example of the use of an ohmmeter is in testing fuses (Figure 8–7). The fuse is removed from the power circuit and the ohmmeter is used to make a continuity check. If continuity (0 Ω) is obtained when the meter leads are touching the two ends of the fuse, the fuse is good.

SELECTING THE PROPER INSTRUMENT

The most helpful procedure for deciding which instrument to use in troubleshooting is to check as follows:

1. If any part of the unit operates, the voltmeter or ammeter is normally used.
2. If the unit is inoperable, caused by a blown fuse, an ohmmeter may be used to test the circuit for a short or a grounded condition.

FIGURE 8–8 Disconnecting one side of parallel circuit when testing resistance with ohmmeter.

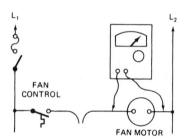

When attempting to measure the resistance of any component, the possibility of obtaining an incorrect reading always exists when a part is wired into the system. In a parallel circuit, when testing with an ohmmeter, it is necessary to disconnect one side of the component being tested to avoid the possibility of an incorrect reading of the resistance (Figure 8–8).

A wattmeter measures both amperage and volts simultaneously. This is necessary in an a.c. circuit because watts take into consideration the power factor. The *power factor* indicates the percent of the volts times the amperes that a consumer actually pays for. Since the peak of the volts and amperes does not usually occur at the same time, wattage is normally less than the product of the volts times the amperes.

Power Calculations

It may be necessary to calculate the power, measured in watts, consumed by a furnace or air-conditioning unit. This can be accomplished by taking both voltage and amperage readings at the equipment and then inserting these values into the following formula. The power factor can be obtained from the electric company.

$$P = E \times I \times PF$$

where P = power, watts

E = EMF, volts

I = current, amperes

PF = power factor

Substitute the sample values $E = 120$ V, $I = 12$ A, and $PF = 0.90$ into the formula:

$$P = 120 \text{ V} \times 12 \text{ A} \times 0.90 \text{ power factor} = 1296 \text{ W}$$

or approximately 1.3 kilowatts (kW), where $k = 1000$.

Clamp-on Volt-Ammeter-Ohmmeters

The clamp-on style of volt-ammeter-ohmmeter is popular with service personnel. The instrument is easy to use and the variable scales are easy to read. See Figure 8–9 to 8–11 for specifications. Figure 8–12 shows their application when troubleshooting motors.

FIGURE 8–9   Digital clamp-on volt-ohm-ammeter.
Ranges: 0–400/750 V a.c.
            0–300/400 A a.c.
            200–4000 Ω
(Courtesy of Amprobe Instruments.)

Voltprobe Tester

Figure 8–13 shows an instrument that is designed for measuring a.c./d.c. voltage and resistance only. Some checks that can be made with a Voltprobe tester are shown in Figure 8–14.

Digital Multimeters

The digital type meter is popular because it is considered accurate within ±0.05%. Some of the features of the digital meter are auto setting of zero for each change of range, auto change of polarity as the signal changes polarity, noise rejection, removal of an a.c. line-frequency signal riding on a d.c. voltage, and very high input resistance of 10 MΩ and higher, making it suitable for virtually any solid-state circuitry. Figures 8–15 and 8–16 are examples of digital multimeters.

Volt-Ampere Recorder

When a permanent record of volts and amperes is required, a portable recorder can be used. This is helpful for detecting and interpreting intermittent electrical problems. The recorder shown in Figure 8–17 can record up to three variables on the same paper chart.

FIGURE 8–10 Digital snap-around volt-ohm-ammeter.
Ranges: 0–200/750 V a.c.
0–200/2000 A a.c.
0–20/200/1000 V d.c.
0–200/2 WO A d.c.
0–200/1500 Q
Data hold switch freezes reading.
Output jack for recording.
(Courtesy of A.W. Sperry
Instruments, Inc.)

FIGURE 8–11 Digital clamp-on volt–ohm-ammeter.
Ranges: 0–1000 V a.c.
0–1000 A a.c.
0–8000 Ω
Measures and locks in peak surge current. (Courtesy of TIF
Instruments, Inc.)

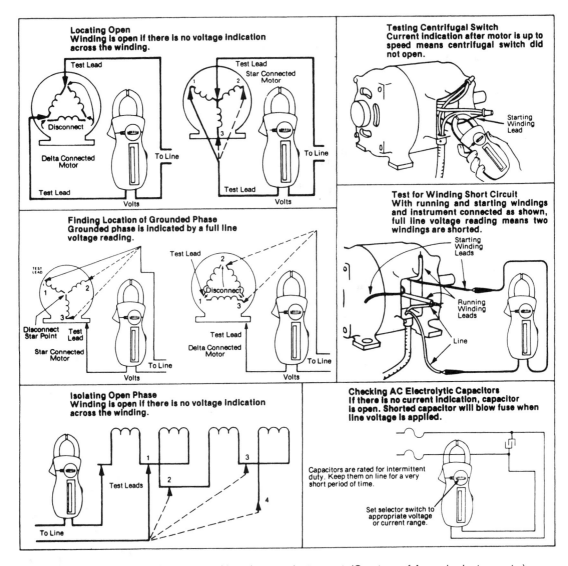

FIGURE 8–12 Troubleshooting motors with a clamp-on instrument. (Courtesy of Amprobe Instruments.)

TROUBLESHOOTING A FURNACE ELECTRICALLY

Testing Part of a Furnace

To troubleshoot a unit electrically, assume, for example, that service is required on a gas-fired forced-air furnace, with wiring shown in Figure 8–1. The complaint is that

FIGURE 8–13 Ac/dc voltage and resistance tester, with auto range selection.
Ranges: 0–2/20/200/500 V a.c.
　　　　0–200 mV, 0–2/20/200/500 V d.c.
　　　　0–200/2 kΩ/20 kΩ/200 kΩ
　　　　0–2/20 MΩ
(Courtesy of Universal Enterprises.)

the furnace does not heat properly. The fan will not run. The gas burner cycles as a result of the limit control cycling on and off.

The first step is to review the schematic wiring diagram and eliminate from consideration any circuits that appear to be operating properly. In this case the transformer and the gas valve circuits are eliminated. Now the testing can be confined to the fan motor circuit.

Since part of the furnace does run, a voltmeter should be used for testing. By the process of elimination the source of the trouble is found. First, measure the voltage across the ends of the circuit where the connection is made to L_1 and L_2 (Figure 8–18). The voltmeter reads 120 V, which is satisfactory. Second, with one meter lead on L_2, place the other meter lead between the fan control and the motor (Figure 8–19). The meter reads 120 V. The bonnet temperature is 150°F. The fan control is set to turn the fan on at 120°F. Therefore, the fan control should be made and this checks out as satisfactory.

If the fan motor still does not run after the proper power has been supplied, it is an indication that the fan motor is defective and must be replaced. The process of

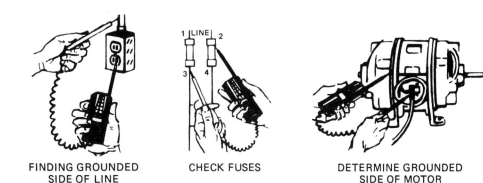

FINDING GROUNDED　　　CHECK FUSES　　　DETERMINE GROUNDED
SIDE OF LINE　　　　　　　　　　　　　　　SIDE OF MOTOR

FIGURE 8–14 Application of Voltprobe tester. (Courtesy of Amprobe Instruments.)

FIGURE 8–15 Digital volt–ohm-amp multi-meter, with temperature ranges.

Ranges: 200 mV/2/20/200/1000 V d.c.
200 mV/2/20/200/750 V a.c.
200 μA/2 m/200 m A/20 ADC
200 μA/2 m/20 m/200 mA/20 AAC
200/2 K/20 K/200 K/2 M/20 M ohm
−50° to 200°F/1400°F
−50° to 200°F/750°C
Continuity and Diode Test.
(Courtesy, A.W. Sperry
Instruments, Inc.)

FIGURE 8–16 Digital industrial volt-ohm-ampere multimeter, with 0.1 resolution for checking motor windings.
Ranges: 2–200/750 V a.c.
0–20/200/2000 mA a.c., 0–10 A a.c.
0–2000 mV d.c., 0–2/20/200/1000 V d.c.
0–2000 μA, 0–20/200/2000 mA d.c.
0–10 A d.c.
0–200/2000, 0–20/200/2000 kΩ
Temperature with optional probe is −50° to +250°F.
(Courtesy of Amprobe Instruments.)

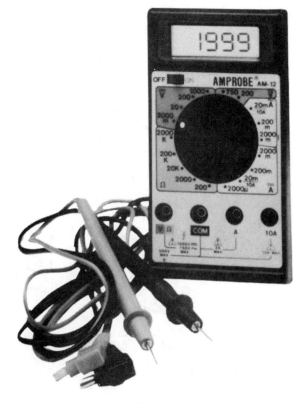

FIGURE 8–17   Portable stripchart volt/ammeter recorder.

Ranges: 0–15/300/600 V a.c.
          0–15/60/150/300 V a.c.
Voltage and amperage can be recorded on the same chart. Supplied with power cord, voltage meter cord, clamp on current transducer, roll of chart paper. (Courtesy of Amprobe Instruments.)

FIGURE 8–18   Measuring line voltage.

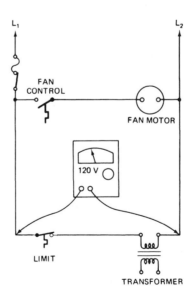

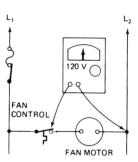

FIGURE 8–19   Placement of
meter leads.

METER LEADS ON L₂ AND LOAD SIDE OF FAN
CONTROL SWITCH TO CHECK POWER AVAILABLE
FOR LOAD (MOTOR).

elimination can be used on any circuit where troubleshooting is required, regardless
of the number of switches. Where power is being supplied to the load and the load
does not operate, the load device is defective and needs to be replaced.

Testing a Complete Unit

In troubleshooting a complete unit, there are numerous electrical tests that can be
made with the instruments. By the process of elimination, it is important to rule out as
many of the circuits as possible that are not causing trouble. The methods of testing
various heating systems are indicated in the following diagrams:

1. Thermopile, self-generating, gas heating control system (Figure 8–20)
2. 24-V gas heating control system (Figure 8–21)
3. Line-voltage gas heating control system (Figure 8–22)
4. Oil burner control system (Figure 8–23)
5. Electric heating system (Figure 8–24)

EFFICIENCY AND AIR-BALANCING INSTRUMENTS

Spark Ignition Tester

Figure 8–25 shows an instrument specifically designed to test residential intermittent
spark ignition devices and commercial flame safety controls.

Combustion Analyzer

To determine the combustion efficiency, an analyzer is required. A popular hand-held
model is shown in Figure 8–26. This tester quickly measures the oxygen in the flue
gas. With this information the furnace efficiency is calculated.

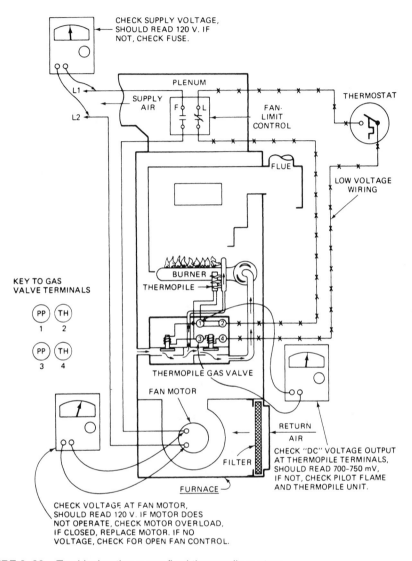

CHECK SUPPLY VOLTAGE,
SHOULD READ 120 V. IF
NOT, CHECK FUSE.

PLENUM

THERMOSTAT

SUPPLY
AIR

FAN-
LIMIT
CONTROL

L1

L2

F   L

FLUE

LOW VOLTAGE
WIRING

KEY TO GAS
VALVE TERMINALS

PP   TH
1   2

PP   TH
3   4

BURNER

THERMOPILE

THERMOPILE GAS VALVE

FAN MOTOR

RETURN
AIR

FILTER

FURNACE

CHECK "DC" VOLTAGE OUTPUT
AT THERMOPILE TERMINALS,
SHOULD READ 700-750 mV,
IF NOT, CHECK PILOT FLAME
AND THERMOPILE UNIT.

CHECK VOLTAGE AT FAN MOTOR,
SHOULD READ 120 V. IF MOTOR DOES
NOT OPERATE, CHECK MOTOR OVERLOAD,
IF CLOSED, REPLACE MOTOR. IF NO
VOLTAGE, CHECK FOR OPEN FAN CONTROL.

FIGURE 8–20   Troubleshooting a gas-fired thermopile system.

Combustible Gas Detector

The accurate detection of combustible gases is extremely important and can be accomplished with a solid-state electronic detector. Figure 8–27 shows a hand-held model capable of detecting leaks as small as 50 to 1000 parts per million (ppm) with audible and visual signals. Hydrocarbons, halogenated hydrocarbons, alcohols, ethers, and ketones are among the gases that can be detected. This detector is extremely useful as a general-purpose tool in any environment where gasoline, propane, natural gas, or fuel oil is used.

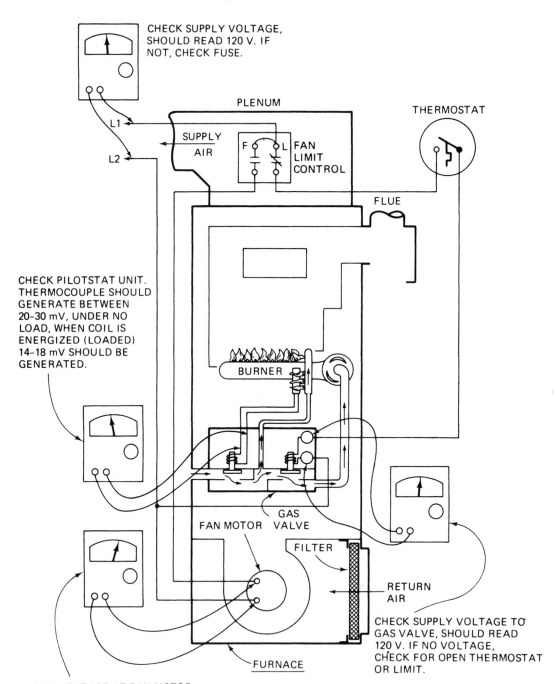

CHECK SUPPLY VOLTAGE, SHOULD READ 120 V. IF NOT, CHECK FUSE.

PLENUM

THERMOSTAT

L1

L2

SUPPLY AIR

F   L   FAN LIMIT CONTROL

FLUE

CHECK PILOTSTAT UNIT. THERMOCOUPLE SHOULD GENERATE BETWEEN 20-30 mV, UNDER NO LOAD, WHEN COIL IS ENERGIZED (LOADED) 14-18 mV SHOULD BE GENERATED.

BURNER

GAS VALVE

FAN MOTOR

FILTER

RETURN AIR

CHECK SUPPLY VOLTAGE TO GAS VALVE, SHOULD READ 120 V. IF NO VOLTAGE, CHECK FOR OPEN THERMOSTAT OR LIMIT.

FURNACE

CHECK VOLTAGE AT FAN MOTOR, SHOULD READ 120 V. IF MOTOR DOES NOT OPERATE, CHECK MOTOR OVERLOAD. IF CLOSED, REPLACE MOTOR. IF NO VOLTAGE, CHECK FOR OPEN FAN CONTROL.

FIGURE 8–21   Troubleshooting a 24-V gas-fired system.

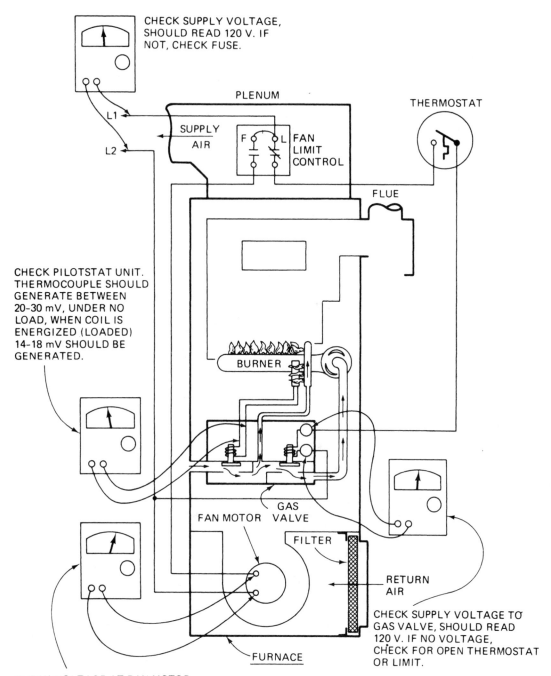

CHECK SUPPLY VOLTAGE, SHOULD READ 120 V. IF NOT, CHECK FUSE.

PLENUM

THERMOSTAT

L1

SUPPLY AIR

F L FAN LIMIT CONTROL

L2

FLUE

CHECK PILOTSTAT UNIT. THERMOCOUPLE SHOULD GENERATE BETWEEN 20-30 mV, UNDER NO LOAD, WHEN COIL IS ENERGIZED (LOADED) 14-18 mV SHOULD BE GENERATED.

BURNER

GAS VALVE

FAN MOTOR

FILTER

RETURN AIR

CHECK SUPPLY VOLTAGE TO GAS VALVE, SHOULD READ 120 V. IF NO VOLTAGE, CHECK FOR OPEN THERMOSTAT OR LIMIT.

FURNACE

CHECK VOLTAGE AT FAN MOTOR, SHOULD READ 120 V. IF MOTOR DOES NOT OPERATE, CHECK MOTOR OVERLOAD. IF CLOSED, REPLACE MOTOR. IF NO VOLTAGE, CHECK FOR OPEN FAN CONTROL.

FIGURE 8–22 Troubleshooting a 120-V gas-fired system.

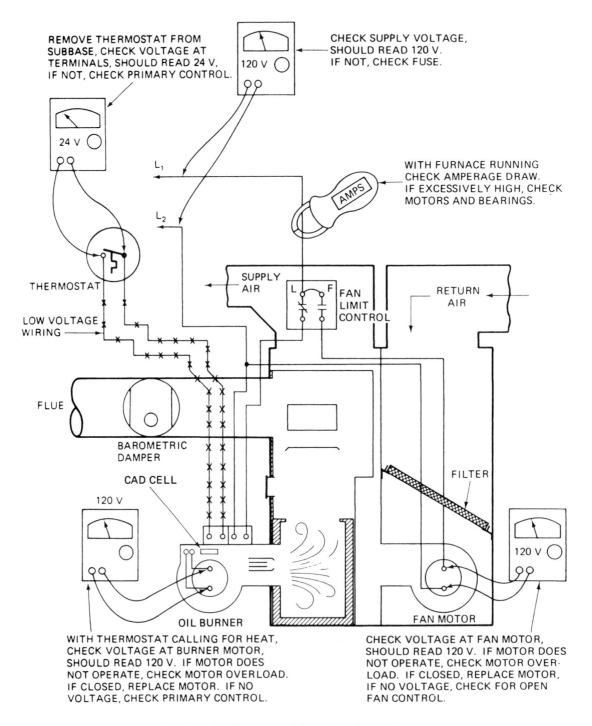

REMOVE THERMOSTAT FROM
SUBBASE, CHECK VOLTAGE AT
TERMINALS, SHOULD READ 24 V,
IF NOT, CHECK PRIMARY CONTROL.

24 V

CHECK SUPPLY VOLTAGE,
SHOULD READ 120 V.
IF NOT, CHECK FUSE.

120 V

L_1

L_2

WITH FURNACE RUNNING
CHECK AMPERAGE DRAW.
IF EXCESSIVELY HIGH, CHECK
MOTORS AND BEARINGS.

AMPS

THERMOSTAT

LOW VOLTAGE
WIRING

SUPPLY
AIR

L   F   FAN
LIMIT
CONTROL

RETURN
AIR

FLUE

BAROMETRIC
DAMPER

FILTER

CAD CELL

120 V

120 V

OIL BURNER

FAN MOTOR

WITH THERMOSTAT CALLING FOR HEAT,
CHECK VOLTAGE AT BURNER MOTOR,
SHOULD READ 120 V. IF MOTOR DOES
NOT OPERATE, CHECK MOTOR OVERLOAD.
IF CLOSED, REPLACE MOTOR. IF NO
VOLTAGE, CHECK PRIMARY CONTROL.

CHECK VOLTAGE AT FAN MOTOR,
SHOULD READ 120 V. IF MOTOR DOES
NOT OPERATE, CHECK MOTOR OVER-
LOAD. IF CLOSED, REPLACE MOTOR,
IF NO VOLTAGE, CHECK FOR OPEN
FAN CONTROL.

FIGURE 8–23 Troubleshooting the cad-cell primary safety control of an oil burner.

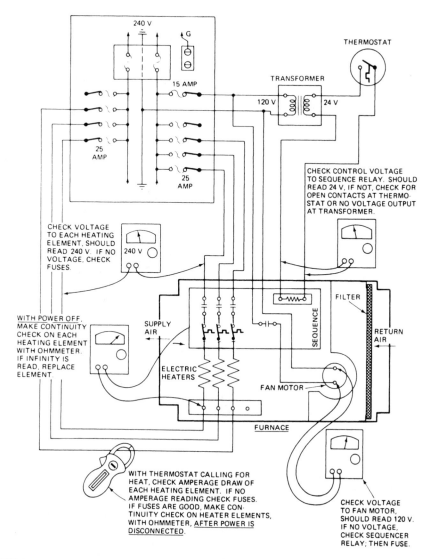

FIGURE 8–24   Troubleshooting an electric heating system.

Temperature Testers

Temperature readings are often required when performing service work. Three types of temperature testers are shown in Figure 8–28 to 8–30. The model shown in Figure 8–28 has 15-ft. remote probes and can read from –50° to 300°F. Both Fahrenheit and Celsius can be read on the digital model shown in Figure 8–29. The pocket thermometer shown in Figure 8–30 is also digital and reads from –40° to 300°F.

FIGURE 8–25 Spark ignition control tester.
Ranges: 0–2 µA, 0–8 µA
Volts a.c. and d.c.
Test lead package includes flame simulator lead, microampere probe, spare resistor for setting flame current on S86 controls. (Courtesy of JamesKamm Technologies.)

FIGURE 8–26 Digital electronic combustion tester that incorporates an electric sampler pump and a stainless steel probe; accuracy of ±2%. (Courtesy of JamesKamm Technologies.)

FIGURE 8–27   Solid-state electronic cordless combustible gas detector with audible signal and visual leak size indicators. (Courtesy of TIF Instruments, Inc.)

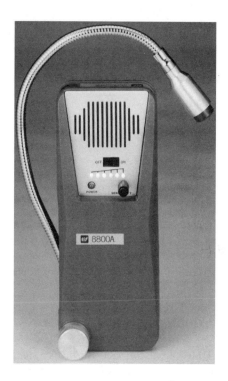

FIGURE 8–28   Temperature tester, thermistor type.
Ranges: –50° to 100°F
100° to 300°F
Includes two 15-ft. general-purpose probes. Additional leads are available for specific applications, battery powered. (Courtesy of Robinair Division, SPX Corporation.)

FIGURE 8–29   Digital thermometer, with retractable probe, °F and °C selector switch, battery powered. *Ranges:* –58° to 302°F
–50° to 150°C (Courtesy of A.W. Sperry Instruments, Inc.)

Air Meters

There are many types of testers used to read and measure air velocity, pressure, and volume. Readings possible can include supply or return: grille velocity, duct air velocity, and pressure drops across cooling coils or air filters. It is also possible to measure furnace drafts and exhaust hood face velocities (see Figures 8–31 to 8–34).

Manometer

To test a gas furnace for proper operating gas pressures, a manometer is used. There are two basic types of manometers, a gauge type and a U-tube type. The gauge type connects to the gas manifold and uses the gas pressure to deflect the needle to obtain a pressure reading (see Figure 8–35).

A U-Tube manometer is a plastic U-shaped tube that uses water for its measurement. The water is half way in the tube and set to a "0" reading before connecting to a system. When gas pressure is applied, this will push the water column up to readable pressure. The pressure reading is the difference in height, which is the sum of the readings above and below zero (see Figure 8–36).

FIGURE 8–30   Digital pocket thermometer, with large LCD display, battery operated, lower ranges available. *Range:* –40° to 300°F; accuracy, ±2%. (Courtesy of Universal Enterprises.)

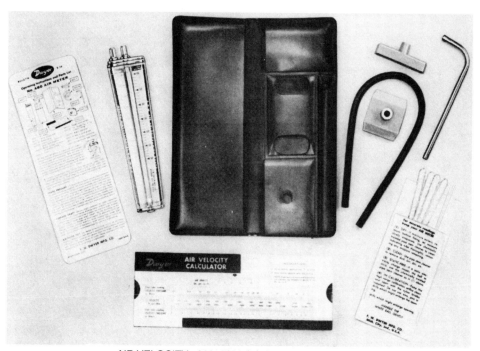

AIR VELOCITY: 260–1200 ft./min, 1000–4000 ft./min
STATIC PRESSURE: 0.005–0.09 in., 0.05–1.0 in. W.C

FIGURE 8–31   Direct-reading air meter kit; includes meter, probes, and air velocity calculator. (Courtesy of Dwyer Instruments, Inc.)

FIGURE 8–32   Pocket size, air-flow indicator.
Range: (0–1000 fpm, readability within 50 fpm; instant readings from any position, no leveling or zero balancing required. Carrying case included.
(Courtesy of Bacharach, Inc.)

RANGES: 0–600 FT./MIN.,
500–6000 FT./MIN.

FIGURE 8–33   Hand-held thermal anemometer, battery-powered with low-battery indicator. (Courtesy of Dwyer Instruments, Inc.)

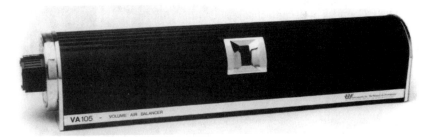

FIGURE 8–34   Volume-aire air balancer. Reads cubic feet per minute directly (70 to 3000 cfm); reads feet per minute directly (250 to 1100 fpm); will handle areas of 50 to 500 in.^{2}. (Courtesy of TIF Instruments, Inc.)

FIGURE 8–35 Measuring gas pressure using a gauge-type manometer.

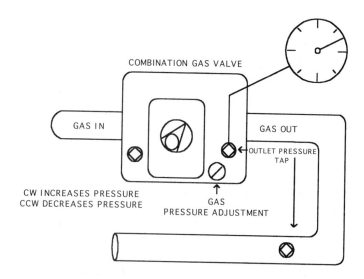

FIGURE 8–36 Measuring gas pressure using a U-Tube manometer.

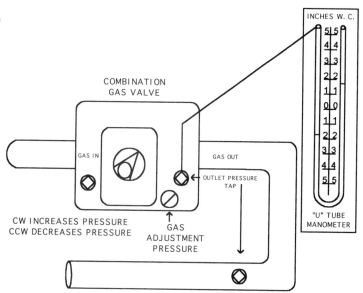

STUDY QUESTIONS

Answers to the study questions may be found in the sections noted in brackets.

8–1. Explain the functions of the voltmeter, ammeter, ohmmeter, and wattmeter. *[Instrument Functions]*

8–2. In purchasing a meter, which scales are important on each of the commonly used meters? *[Selecting the Proper Instrument]*

8–3. Name three important points in using electrical test instruments. *[Selecting the Proper Instrument]*

8–4. Describe the types of readings that can be taken with an ohmmeter. *[Using Meters]*

8–5. Which meter has its own source of power? *[Using Meters]*

8–6. Which meter is good for testing fuses? *[Using Meters]*

8–7. Which meter requires calibration each time it is used? *[Instrument Functions]*

8–8. How many wires should be placed in the jaws of a clamp-on ammeter? *[Selecting the Proper Instrument]*

8–9. When measuring d.c. millivolts delivered by a thermocouple, which special device is required? *[Selecting the Proper Instrument]*

8–10. If a voltmeter reads zero when placed across a switch when the power is on, what is the condition of the switch? *[Selecting the Proper Instrument]*

8–11. In troubleshooting a defective unit, which circuits can be eliminated from the testing procedure? *[Testing a Complete Unit]*

8–12. If no part of the unit operates, caused by a blown fuse, which instrument should be used for testing? *[Selecting the Proper Instrument]*

9

External Furnace Wiring

OBJECTIVES

After studying this chapter, the student will be able to:

- Evaluate the external electrical wiring of a forced, warm-air furnace and troubleshoot where necessary

FIELD WIRING

External furnace wiring usually includes the wiring connections to the power supply and the thermostat (Figure 9–1 and 9–2). These connections are also described as field wiring, to distinguish them from the wiring done at the factory by the manufacturer. Field wiring is completed by the installation crew or the electrician on the job. Where the furnace equipment includes accessories such as a humidifier, electronic air cleaner, or cooling, additional field wiring is required.

Since the performance of the furnace is dependent on proper field wiring, special attention must be given to this particular part of the installation. Most manufacturers supply detailed instructions for connecting the thermostat and accessories to the furnace. Most field-wiring problems occur because of improper or inadequate connections to the building's power supply.

Most gas and oil furnaces operate on a 20-A, 120-V single-phase a.c. branch circuit. Where electric heating or cooling equipment is installed, a 240-V single-phase a.c. circuit is required. The amperes of service needed depend on the size of the electric furnace or cooling unit.

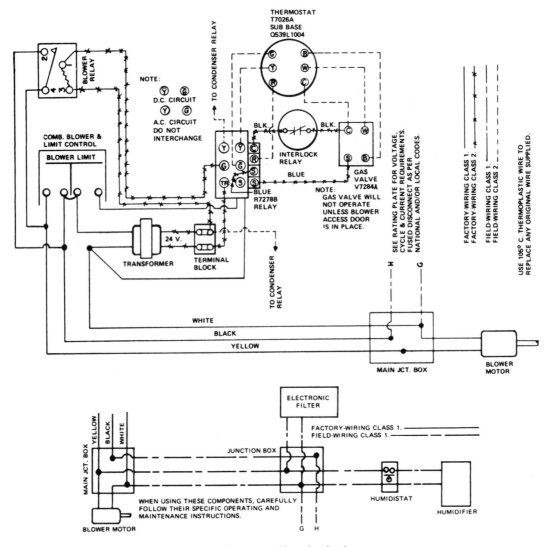

FIGURE 9–1 External gas furnace wiring. (Courtesy of Luxaire, Inc.)

ANALYZING THE POWER SUPPLY

A building's electrical system must be analyzed to determine whether or not the existing power supply is adequate. If it is found to be inadequate, additional service needs to be installed. A building's electrical system includes the entire wiring of the building, starting from the service entrance. The system can be studied from three standpoints:

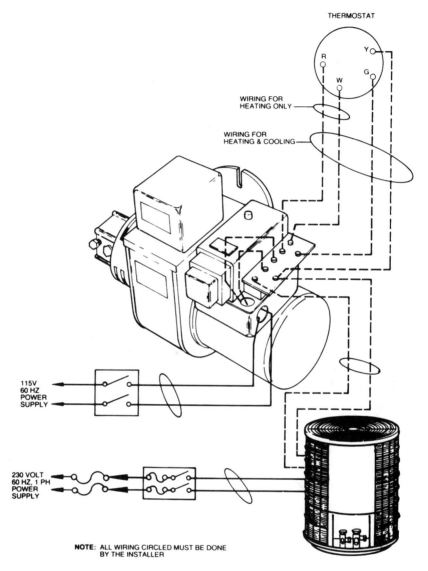

THERMOSTAT

WIRING FOR
HEATING ONLY

WIRING FOR
HEATING & COOLING

115V
60 HZ
POWER
SUPPLY

230 VOLT
60 HZ, 1 PH
POWER
SUPPLY

NOTE: ALL WIRING CIRCLED MUST BE DONE
BY THE INSTALLER

FIGURE 9–2   External wiring for oil furnace for heating and air conditioning. (Courtesy of AR-COAIRE, Inter-City Products Corporation, USA.)

1. Main power supply
2. Branch circuits
3. Materials and equipment

All wiring must be installed in accordance with the National Electrical Code® and any local codes or regulations that apply.

Main Power Supply

The usual source of the main power supply to a building is an entrance cable, consisting of three wires. On newer services one of these wires is black (hot), one is red (hot), and the third is white (neutral). The size of these entrance wires determines the maximum size of the service panel that can be installed.

Entrance cable   The wires in an entrance cable connect the incoming power lines with the building wiring. The cable is connected through the meter socket to the main service panel, as shown in Figure 9–3. Note that the neutral wire at the main panel is connected to a water pipe or other type of approved ground.

When it is necessary to increase the size or capacity of the service, an additional fuse panel or subpanel can be added to the main service panel. This is possible, however, only when the entrance wiring is large enough to permit the extra load.

Building's ampere service   A building's ampere service is the size or capacity of the power supply available from the main panel for electrical service within the building. The service is usually 60, 100, 150, or 200 A. If a home has an electric range, electric dryer, and central air conditioning, 150-A service is needed. For homes having electric heating, 200-A service is required. The minimum service for a modern home is 100 A. Many older homes have only 60-A service. The service must always be large enough to supply the needs of the connected loads.

All residential services require a three-wire electric power supply. The size of the wire for various ampere services is as follows:

Copper wire	Aluminum and copper-clad wire
60-A No. 6	No. 6
100-A No. 4	No. 2
150-A No. 1	No. 0
200-A No. 2/0	No. 3/0

Branch Circuits

Branch circuits are the divisions of main power supply that are fused and connected to the loads in a building. The main power supply is connected to the fuse or circuit breaker box, as shown in Figure 9–4. The two hot lines are fused. The voltage across the two hot lines is usually 208 or 240 V. The neutral line is grounded at the main service panel. The voltage from either of the hot lines to the neutral line is 120 V.

Types of branch circuits.   Branch circuits can be either 208/240 V (Figure 9–5) or 120 V (Figure 9–6). Branch circuits for 208/240 V have fuses in both hot lines. Branch circuits of 120 V have one fuse in the hot line and none in the neutral. The main fuse box or circuit breaker can have both 208/240-V and 120-V branch

FIGURE 9–3 Typical service entrance arrangements, including one with neutral ground. (Courtesy of ITE Electrical Products.)

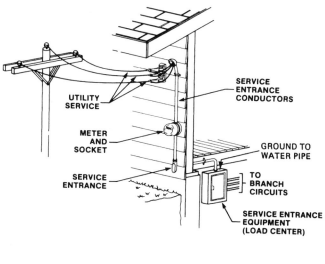

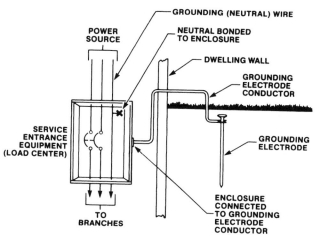

circuits. The maximum fuse size on a 120-V branch is 20 A. The 20-A 120-V branch requires No. 12 wire minimum. The 15-A 120-V branch requires No. 14 wire minimum, or as required by local codes.

Grounding   The electrical terms *grounding, grounded,* and *ground* may be confusing. *Grounding* is the process of connecting to the earth a wire or other conductor from a motor frame or metal enclosure to a water pipe, buried plate, or other conducting material. Grounding is done chiefly for safety, and all electrical equipment should be *grounded.* Modern three-pronged plugs and receptacles for 120-V circuits have a grounding wire (Figure 9–7).

A *ground* is the common return circuit in electric equipment whose potential is zero. A ground permits the current to get through or around the insulation to normally

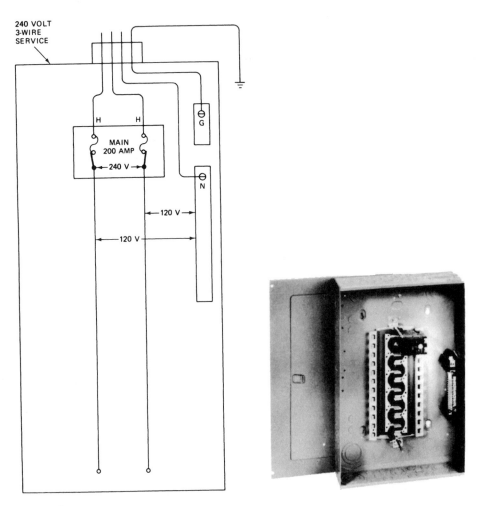

FIGURE 9–4   Electrical load center. (Courtesy of Bryant Electric.)

exposed metal parts that are hot, or "live." A proper ground protects a user from electrical shock should a short circuit occur.

Low voltage   All load devices are designed to operate at a specified voltage that is marked on the equipment. The voltage may be 120, 208, or 240 V. Most electrical equipment will tolerate a variation of voltage from 10% above to 10% below rated (specified) voltage. Thus, a motor rated at 120 V will operate with voltages between 108 and 132 V.

Low or high voltage is usually considered to be any voltage that is not within the tolerated range. Thus, if a 120-V motor is supplied with 100-V power, the voltage would be too low and the motor would probably fail to operate properly. Low

FIGURE 9–5 Electrical load
center providing 240-V service.

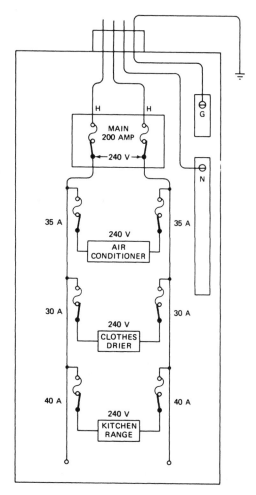

voltage is a much more common problem than high voltage for the reason that all
current-carrying wire offers a resistance to flow, which results in a voltage drop. For
example, a 50-ft. length of No. 14 wire would have a $3^{1}/_{2}$-V drop when carrying 15 A.
This is not excessive since the resultant voltage is within the 10% allowable limit. If
a circuit is overloaded, the current rises above the rated current-carrying capacity of
the wire and the voltage drop can easily exceed the 10% limit established for the
load. The low-voltage condition that results from overloaded circuits can cause motors to fail or burn out.

   All power supplies should be checked during peak load conditions to determine
if proper voltage is being supplied. This should be done at the service entrance, at
the furnace disconnect, and at load devices. If there is a problem at the service entrance, the power company should be contacted. If there is a problem of overloaded
circuits in the building, the owner should be notified and an electrician's services

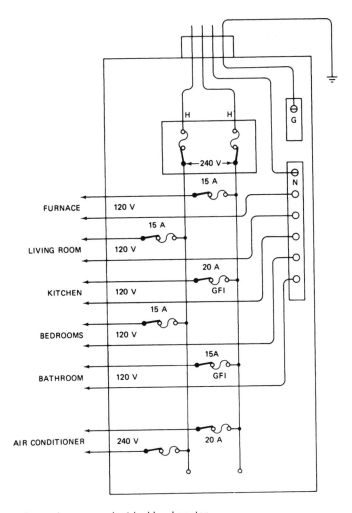

FIGURE 9–6 General-purpose electrical load center.

secured. If there is a problem in the furnace wiring, a service technician should look for defective wiring and/or check for proper sizes of wires and transformers.

Materials and Equipment

All electrical power devices are important when analyzing a building's electrical system. In addition, certain special equipment is required to complete the external electrical wiring system to the furnace. This equipment includes:

- Power takeoff
- Cable
- Adapter for wire service conversion

FIGURE 9–7 120-V, three-pronged plug and receptacles. (Courtesy of Sears, Roebuck and Company)

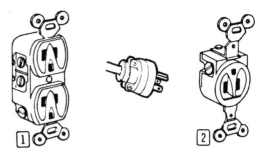

Main panel   The existing main electrical panel may be suitable or it may need replacing, depending on power requirements for the equipment being installed. On new installations, the building plans should include adequate main panel service.

There are two types of panels: those with fuses (old style; Figure 9–8), and those with circuit breakers for the individual circuits (Figure 9–9). The circuit breaker type of panel has the advantage of simply being able to reset the breaker rather than having to replace the fuses, making it more convenient to service when an overload occurs. Both types of panels are available with delayed-action tripping to permit loads to draw extra current when starting without shutting down the power supply.

Secondary load center   The secondary load center is connected below the service side of the main service breaker. This type has no main circuit breaker and is normally used downstream from the entrance panel. In Figure 9–10 the separate branch circuit breakers are wired in the same manner and serve the same purpose as the branch breakers in the main load center.

FIGURE 9–8 Fuse service panel. (Courtesy of Sears, Roebuck and Company.)

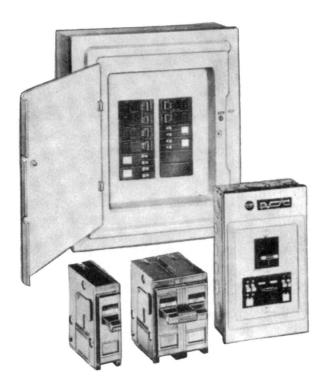

Fused disconnect   A fused disconnect is used to disconnect and protect a 120-V a.c. circuit and is located within a few feet from the unit it serves. It is sometimes called a *service switch* because it permits a convenient means for disconnecting the power to the furnace.

Cable   Cable has a protective shield that encloses electrical wires. In most areas, all line-voltage wiring must be enclosed in approved cable with wire connections made in an approved junction box.

There are four types of cable (Figure 9–11):

1. Indoor-type plastic-sheathed
2. Dual-purpose plastic-sheathed
3. Flexible armored
4. Thin-wall and rigid conduit

The dual purpose cable can be used outdoors or indoors without conduit. The method of connecting cable to junction boxes is shown in Figure 9–12 (nonmetallic cable) and Figure 9–13 (thin-wall conduit). Grounding is not required when using conduit.

Adapter   An adapter converts two-wire service to three-wire, 120-V service. After proper grounding of the receptacle, existing systems that include only two wires may be converted to three-wire systems by use of an adapter arrangement, shown in Figure 9–14.

INCOMING LINE FROM MAIN PANEL
1-PHASE, 3-WIRE, 120/240 VOLT CIRCUIT

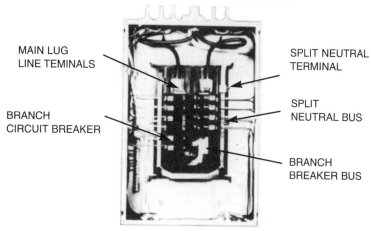

MAIN LUG
LINE TEMINALS

SPLIT NEUTRAL
TERMINAL

SPLIT
NEUTRAL BUS

BRANCH
CIRCUIT BREAKER

BRANCH
BREAKER BUS

FIGURE 9–10   Secondary electrical panel. (Courtesy of ITE Electrical Products.)

Indoor-type Plastic Sheathed Cable

Tough, flexible outer jacket is ivory color and flat in shape. Use for all indoor wire runs. Easy to pull and strip. Heavy inner thermo-plastic insulation. Solid copper conductors. New work or additions require use of grounded type receptacles, therefore, use "with ground" type cable. SPECIAL NOTE: When using aluminum cable or replacing devices on aluminum wired circuits use CO/ALR rated devices only.

Flexible Armored Cable

For use in dry indoor locations. Can be used on wall and ceiling surfaces, or for concealed runs in hollow spaces of walls, floors and ceilings.

Wires enclosed in heavy steel cover. Flexible .. often used for extensions of existing conduit systems. Usable with *steel* switch and junction boxes *only*.

Not for use in damp indoor locations, outdoor or underground.

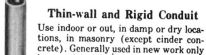

Dual-purpose Plastic Sheathed Cable

Our best plastic cable. Can be used underground, outdoors or indoors. Generally used without conduit unless there is possibility of mechanical damage. Flat shape and gray or ivory color makes it ideal for surface wiring where permitted. Resists moisture, acid, corrosion. Can be run through masonry or between studding. Solid copper conductors. If used for outdoor circuits use grounded type cable only and check local code for use of Ground Fault protection. See page 51.

Thin-wall and Rigid Conduit

Use indoor or out, in damp or dry locations, in masonry (except cinder concrete). Generally used in new work only because it is difficult and costly to install in old buildings.

Rigid conduit is made of steel with galvanized finish .. thin wall is much lighter, easily cut or bent.

FIGURE 9–11   Types of cable. (Courtesy of Sears, Roebuck and Company.)

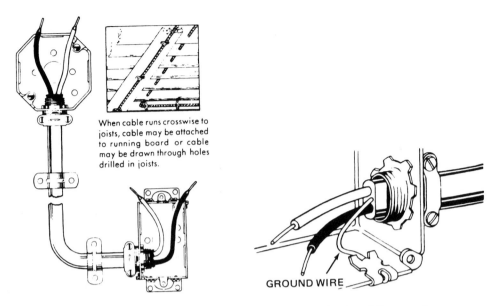

When cable runs crosswise to joists, cable may be attached to running board or cable may be drawn through holes drilled in joists.

GROUND WIRE

FIGURE 9–12   Nonmetallic cable connectors. (Courtesy of Sears, Roebuck and Company.)

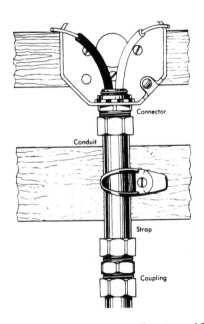

Connector

Conduit

Strap

Coupling

FIGURE 9–13   Thin-wall (metallic) cable connectors. (Courtesy of Sears, Roebuck and Company.)

FIGURE 9-14 Adapter for conversion of two-wire to three-wire system. (Courtesy of Sears, Roebuck and Company.)

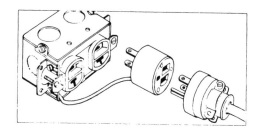

Ground-fault interrupters   Fuses and circuit breakers protect circuits and wire against overloads and short circuits but not against current leakage. Small amounts of leakage can occur without blowing a fuse or tripping a breaker. Under certain conditions the leakage can be hazardous.

A relatively new product adapted for residential use is called the *ground-fault circuit interrupter* (GFCI) (see Figures 9–15 and 9–16). The GFCI is designed to detect a small current leakage and interrupt the power supply quickly enough to prevent a serious problem. After the problem is corrected, the GFCI can be reset and power at that point will be restored.

The National Electrical Code® recommends the use of GFCIs on all outdoor circuits. Local codes are especially strong on their use in conjunction with swimming pools that have any electrical connections.

EXTERNAL WIRING OF A GAS FURNACE AND AN AIR-CONDITIONING SYSTEM

There are 3 power supplies that will be of concern when installing a furnace and air-conditioning system in a home. The 3 power supplies are 120 volts for the furnace circuit, 24 volts for the control circuit, and 220 volts for the outdoor air-conditioning condensing unit (see Figure 9–17).

120-Volt Circuit

The line voltage (120 volts) is brought to the furnace to operate the blower and the primary side of the transformer. A hot leg will be fed from a 20-amp circuit breaker accompanied with a neutral leg and a ground. At the furnace, the hot leg must be controlled by a disconnect switch. (Because many high-efficiency furnaces use condensate pumps to remove the water created in the combustion process, a switch with an electrical outlet may be used to supply voltage to the pump.)

For proper polarity, it is necessary to have the black wire, the white wire and the bare wire connected to the appropriate connections at the breaker panel. The black wire (hot leg) should be connected to the circuit breaker, the white wire (common or neutral leg) should be connected to the neutral bus at the breaker panel and a bare or green wire (ground) should be connected to the ground bus.

GROUND FAULT CIRCUIT INTERRUPTER
FOR BATHROOMS AND OTHER AREAS,
WHERE REQUIRED BY CODE.

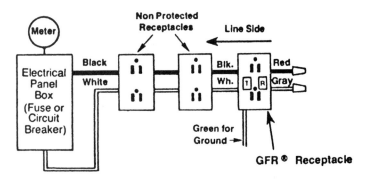

TYPICAL WIRING DIAGRAM FOR
ADDITION OF GFR RECEPTACLE.

FIGURE 9–15 Ground-fault circuit interrupters. (Courtesy of Bryant Electric.)

GFR FOR OUTDOOR USE,
WEATHERPROOF, 20 AMP,
DUPLEX RECEPTACLE.

BREAKER TYPE GFR, ONLY
FITS SPECIFIC PANEL

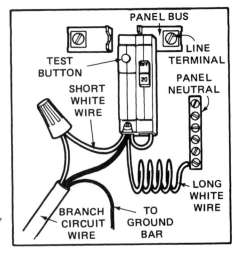

FIGURE 9–16 Ground-fault circuit interrupters. (Courtesy of Bryant Electric.)

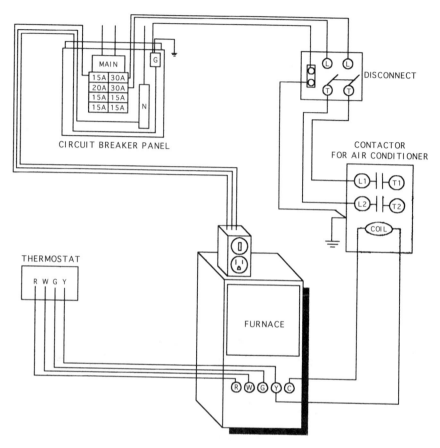

FIGURE 9–17   Complete wiring diagram of a furnace and air conditioner.

24-Volt Circuit

When the primary side of the transformer is energized with 120 volts, this will induce 24 volts on the secondary side of the transformer.

The 24-volt circuit is used to control the heating and cooling circuits by energizing a fan relay coil, a contactor coil, and a gas valve. When installing a furnace and air conditioning system, it is necessary to connect 4 strand thermostat wire from the thermostat to the terminal block on the furnace. The 4 wires are color coded for proper installation. The red wire supplies 24 volts to the thermostat from the secondary side of the transformer. The white wire directs current to the heating circuit at the furnace. The green wire brings current to the fan relay coil (to energize the high speed on the blower). The yellow wire energizes the contactor coil located in the condensing unit for the air-conditioning system.

220-Volt Circuit

The 220-volt circuit is used to power the compressor and the condenser fan at the air-conditioning condensing unit. Two hot legs of power and a bare grounding wire are brought from a circuit breaker panel to a fused disconnect. This fused disconnect is located near the outdoor condensing unit. The wires are then directed from the fused disconnect to the line side of the contactor. The ground wire is connected to the grounding screw on the condensing unit for safety purposes.

STUDY QUESTIONS

Answers to the study questions may be found in the sections noted in brackets.

9–1. What field wiring is usually low voltage? *[Field Wiring]*

9–2. What is the usual color coding for the three entrance wires? *[Main Power Supply]*

9–3. What is the service amperage for most gas furnaces? *[Field Wiring]*

9–4. What service amperage is required for residential electric heating? *[Building's Amperage Service]*

9–5. How many fuses are required for a 240-V branch circuit? *[Types of Branch Circuits]*

9–6. What is the range of voltage that can be used on a 120-V motor? *[Low Voltage]*

9–7. Name one circuit that requires a ground-fault interrupter. *[Ground-Fault Interrupters]*

9–8. When should the power supply be checked for low-voltage conditions? *[Low Voltage]*

9–9. What is the connection to the main panel called when an additional fuse panel is added? *[Entrance Cable]*

9–10. What action should be taken if the voltage is too low coming to the residence? *[Low Voltage]*

9–11. How should an adapter be grounded? *[Adapter]*

10

Controls Common to All Forced-Air Furnaces

OBJECTIVES

After studying this chapter, the student will be able to:

- Identify the common types of electrical control devices used on forced, warm-air furnaces
- Evaluate the performance of common types of controls in the system

FUNCTIONS OF CONTROLS

The function of automatic controls is to operate a system or unit in response to some variable condition. Automatic controls are used to turn the various electrical components (load devices) on and off. These devices operate in response to a controller that senses the room temperature or humidity, thereby activating the equipment to maintain the desired conditions. Load devices that make up a heating unit are:

- Fuel-burning device or heater
- Fan
- Humidifier
- Electrostatic air cleaner
- Cooling equipment

Each of these load devices has some type of switch or switches that automatically or manually causes the device to operate. The automatic switches respond to variable conditions from a *sensor*. A sensor is a device that reacts to a change in conditions and is then capable of transmitting a response to one or more switching devices. For example, a thermostat senses the need for heat and switches on the heating unit. When the thermostat senses that enough heat has been supplied, it switches off the heating unit.

COMPONENTS OF CONTROL SYSTEMS

Five elements comprise the control system for a forced, warm-air heating unit:

1. Power supply
2. Controllers
3. Limit controls
4. Primary controls
5. Accessory controls

Power supply   The power supply furnishes the necessary current at the proper voltage to operate the various control devices. The fused disconnect and the transformer are parts of the power supply.

Controllers   Controllers sense the condition being regulated and perform the necessary switching action on the proper load device. The controller group includes such devices as the thermostat, the humidistat, and the fan control.

Limit controls   Limit controls shut off the firing device or heater when the maximum safe operating temperature is exceeded.

Primary controls   The gas valve, the flame detector relay for an oil burner, and the sequencer for electric furnaces are types of primary controls. A primary control usually includes some type of safety device. For example, on an oil furnace primary control, the burner will be shut off if a flame is not produced or goes out.

Accessory controls   Used to add special features to the control system. One of these is the fan relay, which permits the fan switch on a 24-V thermostat to operate a 120-V fan.

THERMOSTATS

Thermostats control the source of heat to closely maintain the selected temperature in the space being conditioned. A heating system should provide even (consistent) temperatures for the comfort of a building's occupants. It is said that people can sense a change of approximately $1\frac{1}{2}°F$ in temperature. A well-regulated system will provide less than $1°F$ variation.

FIGURE 10–1   Bimetallic switches. (Courtesy of Honeywell Inc.)

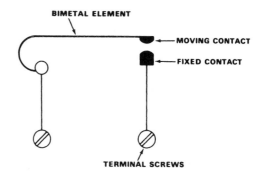

A sensing element is usually bimetallic. Thus, the element is composed of two different metals. One is usually copper and the other invar bonded together. When heated, copper has a more rapid expansion rate than invar. When the bimetal is heated, it changes shape. In a heating thermostat, this movement is mechanically connected to a switch that closes on a drop in temperature and opens on a rise in temperature (Figure 10–1). Bimetallic elements are constructed in various shapes (Figure 10–2). A spiral-wound bimetallic element (Figure 10–3) is compact in construction. For this reason it is the element used in many thermostats.

Switching action should take place rapidly to prevent arcing, which causes damage to the switch contacts. A magnet is used to provide rapid action. The most common type of switching action in use is the mercury tube arrangement (Figure 10–4). The electrical contacts of the switch are inside the tube together with a globule of mercury. The electrical contacts are located at one end of the tube. When the tube is tipped in one direction, the mercury makes an electrical connection between the contacts and the switch is closed. When the tube is tipped in the opposite direction, the mercury goes to the other end of the tube and the switch is opened.

Electronic Temperature Sensing

Thermistors use various materials whose resistance lowers when the temperature rises, and rises when their temperature lowers. Electronic sensing devices have no moving parts. As the temperature changes, their resistance changes. An electronic device (thermostat) converts these changes in resistance into a control signal that turns burners or compressors on and off. In Figure 10–5, different styles of thermistors and their symbol are shown.

Figure 10–6 shows another type of electronic temperature-sensing device, called a resistance bulb, which is a coil of fine wire wound around a bobbin.* The resistance of the wire increases as the temperature rises and decreases as the temperature falls, which is the opposite of a thermistor.

---

*A bobbin is a small round device or cylinder.

FIGURE 10–2 Bimetallic element shapes. (Courtesy of Honeywell Inc.)

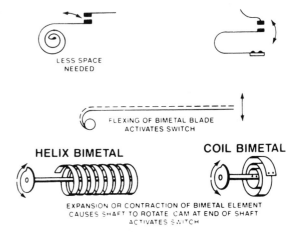

LESS SPACE NEEDED

FLEXING OF BIMETAL BLADE ACTIVATES SWITCH

HELIX BIMETAL   **COIL BIMETAL**

EXPANSION OR CONTRACTION OF BIMETAL ELEMENT CAUSES SHAFT TO ROTATE CAM AT END OF SHAFT ACTIVATES SWITCH

Types of Current

Most residential thermostats are of the low-voltage type (24 V). Low-voltage wires are easier to install between the thermostat and the heating unit. The construction of a low voltage thermostat provides greater sensitivity to changing temperature conditions than does a line-voltage (120-V) thermostat. The materials can be of lighter construction and easier to move, with less chance for arcing. Some self-generating systems (Figure 10–7) use a millivolt (usually 750 mV) power supply to operate the thermostat circuit. These thermostats are very similar in construction to low-voltage thermostats.

Purpose

Some thermostats are designed for heating only or for cooling only. Other thermostats are designed for a combination of both heating and cooling (Figure 10–8). With the

FIGURE 10–3 Spiral-bound bimetallic element. (Courtesy of Honeywell Inc.)

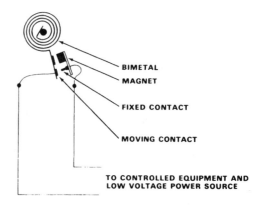

BIMETAL
MAGNET
FIXED CONTACT
MOVING CONTACT
TO CONTROLLED EQUIPMENT AND LOW VOLTAGE POWER SOURCE

FIGURE 10–4 Mercury tube switching action. (Courtesy of Honeywell Inc.)

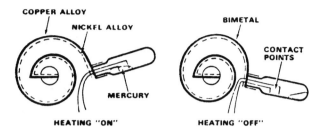

mercury tube design, a set of contacts is located at one end of the tube for heating and the other end for cooling. The cooling contacts make on a rise in temperature and break on a drop in temperature. The tube with both sets of contacts is attached to a single bimetallic element.

Anticipators

There is a lag (time delay) between the call for heat by the thermostat and the amount of time it takes for heat to reach a specific area. The differential of the thermostat plus the heat lag of the system could cause a wide variation in room temperature. There is always a differential (difference) between the temperature at which the thermostat makes and the temperature at which it breaks (opens). For example, the thermostat may call for heat when the temperature falls to 70°F and shut the furnace off when the temperature rises to 72°F.

To provide closer control of room temperature, a heat anticipator is built into the thermostat (Figure 10–9). A heat anticipator consists of a resistance heater placed in series with the thermostat contacts. On a call for heat, current is supplied to the heater. This action heats the bimetallic element, causing it to respond somewhat ahead of the actual rise in room temperature. By supplying part of the heat with the anticipator, less room heat is required to meet the room thermostat setting. Thus, the

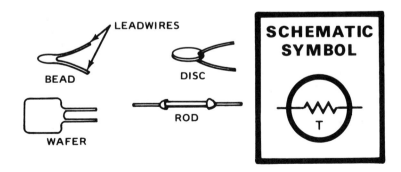

FIGURE 10–5 Typical thermistors and their schematic symbol. (Courtesy of Honeywell Inc.)

FIGURE 10–6 Resistance bulb. (Courtesy of Honeywell Inc.)

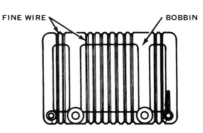

furnace shuts off before the actual room temperature reaches the cutout point on the thermostat. Although the furnace continues to supply heat for a short period after the unit shuts off, the actual room temperature does not exceed the setting of the thermostat because the anticipator assists in producing even heating and prevents wide temperature variations.

Anticipators are also supplied for thermostats that control cooling. A cooling anticipator (Figure 10–10) is placed in parallel with the thermostat contacts. Thus heat is supplied to the bimetal on the off cycle (when cooling is off) and serves to decrease the length of the shutdown period.

Thermostat anticipator setting Proper control of the indoor air temperature can only be achieved if the thermostat is calibrated to the heating and/or cooling cycle. A vital consideration of this calibration is related to the thermostat heat anticipator. Anticipators for the cooling operation are generally preset by the thermostat manufacturer and require no adjustment. Anticipators for the heating operation are of two types, preset and adjustable. Those that are preset will not have an adjustment scale and are generally marked accordingly.

Thermostat models having a scale as shown in Figure 10–11 must be adjusted to each application. The proper thermostat heat anticipator setting is a minimum of 0.8 A for furnace operation only. A lower setting will result in short cycling of the furnace and

FIGURE 10–7 Powerpile self-powered system. (Courtesy of Honeywell Inc.)

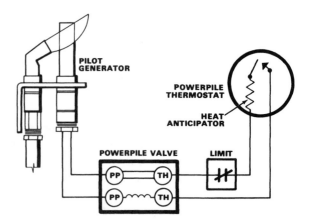

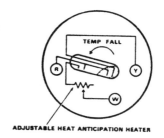

FIGURE 10–8 Contacts in the mercury bulb. (Courtesy of Honeywell Inc.)

in extreme cases will cause a complaint of "no heat." To increase the length of the cycle, increase the setting of the heat scale. To decrease the length of the cycle, decrease the setting of the heat scale.

A third type uses a cycle-rate adjustment (see Figure 10–12). Generally, the rate is factory set for forced air furnaces. Consult the thermostat instruction sheet for details. In many cases this adjustment setting can be found in the thermostat instruction sheet. If this information is not available, or if the correct setting is questioned, the following procedures should be followed:

Preferred Method. Use a low-scale ammeter such as an ampcheck or milliammeter. Connect the meter across terminals R and W on the subbase (RH and W1 on the multistage thermostat subbase).

Step 1. Wrap 10 loops of single-strand insulated thermostat wire around the prongs of an ammeter. Set the scale to the lowest ampere scale.

Step 2. Connect the uninsulated ends of this wire jumper across terminals R and W on the subbase (RH and W1 on the multistage thermostat subbase) (see Figure 10–13). This test must be performed without the thermostat attached to the subbase.

Step 3. Let the heating system operate in this position for about 1 min. Read the ammeter scale. Whatever reading is indicated must be divided by 10 (for 10 loops of wire). This is the setting at which the adjustable heat anticipator should be set.

Step 4. If a slightly longer cycle is desired, the heat anticipator pointer should be moved to a higher setting. Slightly shorter cycles can be achieved by moving to a lower setting.

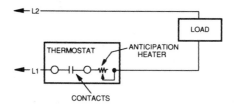

FIGURE 10–9 Series heat anticipator. (Courtesy of Honeywell Inc.)

FIGURE 10–10 Parallel cooling anticipator. (Courtesy of Honeywell Inc.)

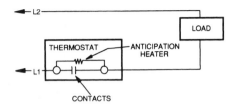

Step 5. Remove the meter jumper wire and reconnect the thermostat. Check the thermostat in the heating mode for proper operation.

If a digital ammeter is used, read the ampere draw direct from the meter. Steps 1 and 3 are then not required.

Note: the length of the heating cycle can also be affected by the fan control settings (of the combination fan and limit control). The fan "on" and "off" settings should be checked at this point.

Subbases

Most thermostats have some type of subbase, which serves as a mounting plate (Figure 10–14). A subbase provides a means for leveling and fastening a thermostat to the wall and contains electrical connections and manual switches. Manual switches offer a homeowner the choice of HEAT-OFF-COOL and FAN AUTO-ON. Switches on a subbase increase the number of functions that can be performed by a thermostat (Figure 10–15). Although a thermostat has only a sensing element and

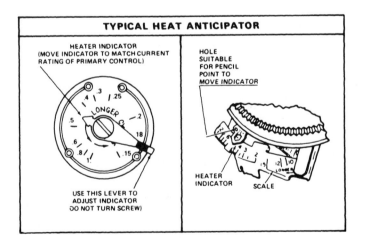

FIGURE 10–11 Typical heat anticipator. (Courtesy of ARCOAIRE, Inter-City Products Corporation, USA.)

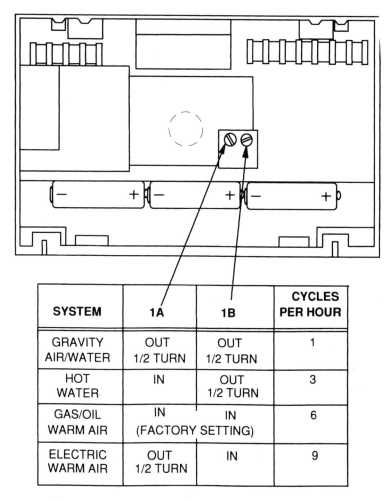

SYSTEM	1A	1B	CYCLES PER HOUR
GRAVITY AIR/WATER	OUT 1/2 TURN	OUT 1/2 TURN	1
HOT WATER	IN	OUT 1/2 TURN	3
GAS/OIL WARM AIR	IN (FACTORY SETTING)	IN	6
ELECTRIC WARM AIR	OUT 1/2 TURN	IN	9

FIGURE 10–12   Typical cycle-rate adjustment. (Courtesy of ARCOAIRE, Inter-City Products Corporation, USA.)

one or two automatic switches, with the addition of subbase manual switches it offers a choice of many switching actions.

Application and Installation

The following are recommended procedures in the application and installation of thermostats.

- Select the thermostat that best meets customers' needs.
- Select the thermostat designed for the specific type of application: heat only, heat-cool, heat pump, and so on.

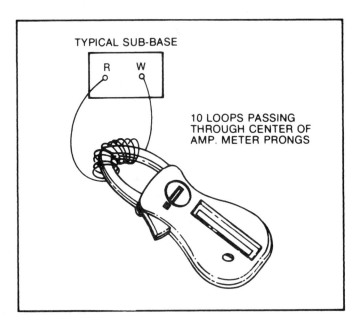

FIGURE 10–13 Taking an ampere reading with an ammeter. (Courtesy of ARCOAIRE, Inter-City Products Corporation, USA.)

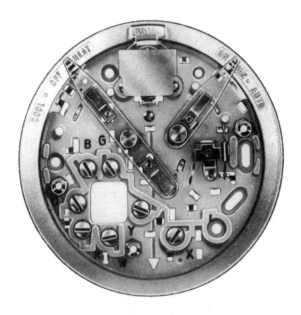

FIGURE 10–14 Thermostat subbase. (Courtesy of Honeywell Inc.)

FIGURE 10–15 Switching action that takes place in the thermostat subbase shown in Figure 10–14. (Courtesy of Honeywell Inc.)

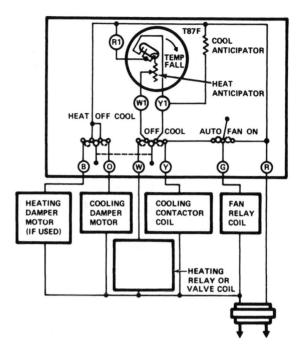

- Select the location.
- Mount the thermostat approximately 5 ft. above the floor.
- Select the anticipator setting that matches the equipment.
- Select proper location for outdoor sensor, if used.
- Seal up any openings in the wall under the mounting plate to eliminate infiltration.

Programmable Thermostats

The programmable thermostat is a solid-state microcomputer control with 7-day programming. This thermostat is designed with a full range of temperature setback-setup-offset capability. A battery is used to maintain the program and time during periods of power interruption. In Figure 10–16, there is a built-in cooling time delay to protect the compressor from damage due to short cycling.

The capability of setback/set-up maximizes energy savings during unoccupied periods and during the night hours. The thermostat and control module shown in Figure 10–17 contains optional features that perform several functions:

1. *Controls start-up times:* automatically varies the daily startup time depending on building load. If the outdoor air temperature is suitable the building can be precooled.
2. *Controls damper and fan operation:* closes outdoor air dampers and allows fan operation only on a call for heating or cooling during unoccupied periods.

FIGURE 10–16 Seven-day programmable thermostat with digital
display of temperature and time
settings. (Courtesy of Robertshaw
Controls Company.)

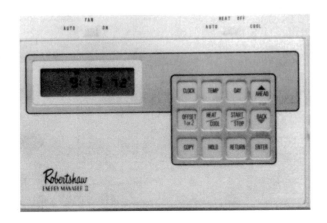

HUMIDISTATS

A humidistat (Figure 10–18) is a sensing control that measures the amount of humidity
in the air and provides switching action for the humidifier. The sensing element is either human hair or nylon ribbon. These materials expand when moist and contract
when dry. This movement is used to operate the switching mechanism.

The sensing element for the humidistat can be located either in the return air duct
or in the space being conditioned (Figure 10–19). The humidistat is wired in such a
way that humidity is added only when the fan is operating.

FAN AND LIMIT CONTROLS

Fan (blower) and limit controls have separate functions in the heating system. They are
discussed together since both can use the same sensing element and are therefore often
combined into a single control.

The insertion element (sensor) can be made in a number of forms (Figure 10–20).
Some are bimetallic and some are hydraulic. The hydraulic element is filled with liquid
which expands when heated, moving a diaphragm connected to a switch. The sensing element for these controls is inserted in the warm air plenum of the furnace. It must be located in the moving airstream where it can quickly sense the warm air temperature rise.
Sensing elements are made in different lengths to fit various applications. When replacing equipment, the original insertion length should always be duplicated.

Fan Controls

A fan control (Figure 10–21) senses the air temperature in the furnace plenum. To prevent discomfort, it turns on the fan when the air is sufficiently heated. There are two
general types of fan controls:

- Temperature-sensing
- Timed fan start

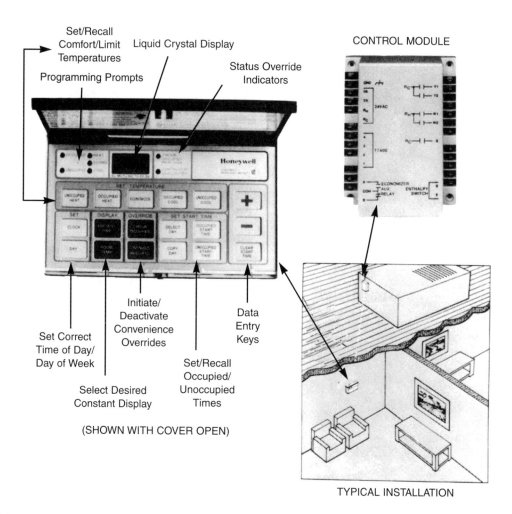

Set/Recall
Comfort/Limit   Liquid Crystal Display
Temperatures

Programming Prompts

Status Override
Indicators

CONTROL MODULE

Initiate/
Deactivate
Convenience
Overrides

Data
Entry
Keys

Set Correct
Time of Day/
Day of Week

Set/Recall
Occupied/
Unoccupied
Times

Select Desired
Constant Display

(SHOWN WITH COVER OPEN)

TYPICAL INSTALLATION

FIGURE 10–17   Seven-day programmable thermostat with control module for heating, ventilation, and air-conditioning equipment. (Courtesy of Honeywell Inc.)

Temperature-sensing fan control   These controls depend on the gravity heating action of the furnace to move air across the sensing element. When the air temperature reaches the fan-on temperature (usually, about 110°F), the fan starts. When the thermostat is no longer calling for heat, the fan continues to run to move the remaining heat out of the furnace. The fan stops at the fan-off temperature setting of the fan control (usually about 90°F). Most fan controls are adjustable so that changes in fan operation can be made to fit individual requirements. The fan control circuit is usually line voltage (120 V). The fan control switch is placed in series with the power to the fan motor. Some fan controls have a fixed differential. The fan-on temperature can be set but the differential (fan-on minus fan-off temperature) is set at the factory. The fixed differential is normally 20° to 25°F.

FIGURE 10–18 Humidistat.

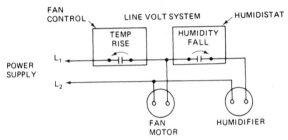

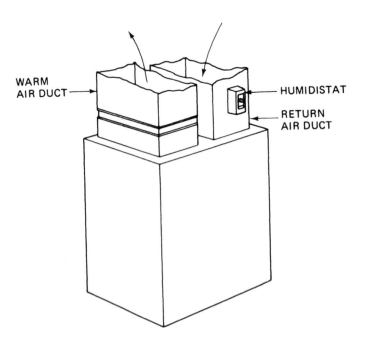

FIGURE 10–19 Duct installation of humidistat.

BIMETALIC
BLADE ELEMENT

BIMETALIC
FLAT SPIRAL ELEMENT

BIMETALIC HELIX ELEMENT

LOOPED TUBE ELEMENT

FIGURE 10–20   Types of insertion elements (sensors). (Courtesy of Honeywell Inc.)

Timed fan start   This control (Figure 10–22) is used in a downflow or horizontal furnace where gravity air movement over the heat exchanger cannot be depended on to warm the sensing element. This control has a low-voltage (24-V) resistance heater, which is energized when the thermostat calls for heat. The fan starts approximately 60 seconds after the heat is turned on. Usually, the fan is turned off by a conventional temperature-sensing fan control. It is important that the manufacturer's instructions be followed for setting the heat anticipator in the thermostat.

FIGURE 10–21   Fan control.

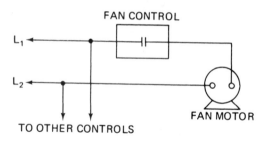

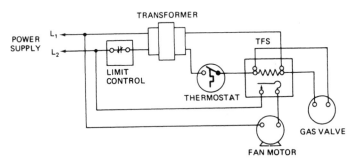

FIGURE 10–22 Timed fan start control.

Limit Controls

The limit control is a safety device that shuts off the source of heat when the maximum safe operating temperature is reached (Figure 10–23). Like the fan control, it senses furnace plenum temperature or air temperature at the outlet. Warm air furnace limit controls are usually set to cut out at 200°F and cut in automatically at 175°F.

On a gas furnace the line-voltage limit control is placed in series with the transformer. On an oil furnace the line-voltage limit control is placed in series with the primary control. On an electric furnace, the limit controls are placed in series with the heating elements. On a horizontal or downflow furnace, a secondary limit control is required (Figure 10–24). This control is located above the heating element and is usually set to cut out the source of heat when the sensing temperature reaches 145°F.

Where two limit controls are used, they are usually wired in series with each other. Thus, either limit control can turn off the source of heat. Some secondary limit controls have a manual reset (not automatic). Some have an arrangement for switching on the fan when the limit contacts are opened.

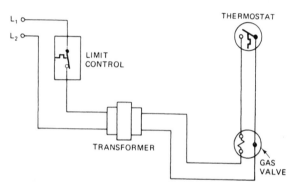

FIGURE 10–23   Limit Control.

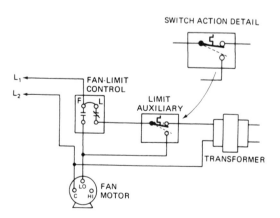

FIGURE 10–24   Secondary limit control.

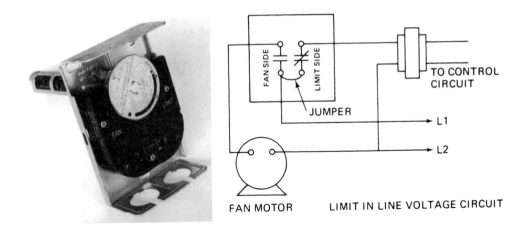

FAN MOTOR   LIMIT IN LINE VOLTAGE CIRCUIT

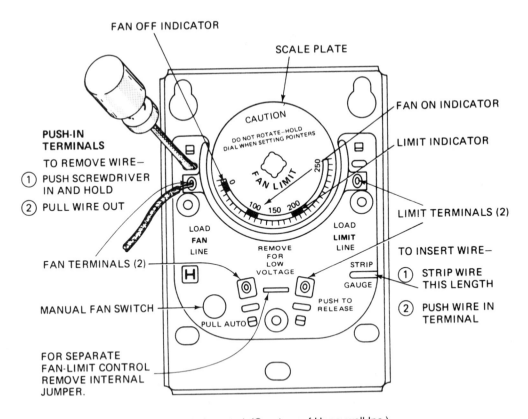

FIGURE 10–25 Combination fan and limit control. (Courtesy of Honeywell Inc.)

FIGURE 10–26   Two-speed fan
control.

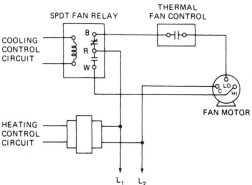

Combinations

Since the fan and limit controls both use the same type of sensing element, they are
often combined into one control (Figure 10–25). This is helpful when both the fan and
limit controls are of line-voltage type, since this simplifies the wiring. The fan and
limit controls, though, each have separate switches and separate terminals. The fan
control can be wired for line voltage and the limit control for low voltage, if desired.

Two-Speed Fan Controls

Two fan speeds can be obtained by adding a fan relay to a standard control system
(Figure 10–26). The fan is operated at low speed on heating and high speed for ventilation or air conditioning. Some high-efficiency furnaces operate the fan at a higher
speed for heating than for cooling. The relay has a low-voltage coil in series with the
G terminal on the thermostat. When the thermostat calls for cooling, the switch in the
relay opens and an NO switch closes. This switches the fan from low to high speed.

STUDY QUESTIONS

Answers to the study questions may be found in the sections noted in brackets.

10–1. Describe the function of an automatic control system. *[Functions of Controls]*

10–2. Name and describe the five elements of a control system. *[Functions of Controls]*

10–3. What is the smallest temperature difference that most people can sense? *[Thermostats]*

10–4. What metals are used in constructing bimetal sensors? *[Thermostats]*

10–5. What is the rating of the low-voltage circuit used on thermostat circuits? *[Thermostats]*

10–6. What voltage is used in a self-generating system? *[Types of Current]*

10–7. How is the differential of a thermostat determined? *[Anticipators]*

10–8. How are the terminals on a thermostat identified by color code? *[Thermostats]*

10–9. What are the additional features in a programmable thermostat? *[Programmable Thermostats]*

10–10. What type of sensing element does a humidistat have? *[Humidistats]*

10–11. Why are fan and limit controls both placed on the same electrical device? *[Fan and Limit Controls]*

10–12. Where is a timed fan-start switch used? *[Timed Fan Start]*

10–13. How does a two-speed fan control operate? *[Two-Speed Fan Controls]*

10–14. Where is the heat anticipator located, and how is it adjusted? *[Anticipators]*

11

Gas Furnace Controls

OBJECTIVES

After studying this chapter, the student will be able to:

- Identify the various electrical controls and circuits on a gas-fired furnace
- Determine the sequence of operation of the controls
- Service and troubleshoot the gas heating unit control system

USE OF GAS FURNACE CONTROLS

Broadly speaking, gas furnace controls are the electrical and mechanical equipment that operates the unit manually or automatically. The controls used depend on:

1. Type of fuel or energy
2. Type of furnace
3. Optional accessories

The controls differ for gas, oil, or electric heat sources. They differ somewhat for the upflow and downflow units. They also become more complex as accessories, such as humidifiers, electrostatic filters, and cooling, are added.

CIRCUITS

Control circuits for a gas warm air heating unit are:

1. Power supply circuit
2. Fan circuits

3. Pilot circuit
4. Fuel-burning or heater circuit
5. Accessory circuits

Both line-voltage and low-voltage circuits are required for some components. For example, a relay used to start a fan motor may have a low-voltage coil, but the switch that starts the fan motor operates on line voltage.

Schematic diagrams are used in the study of circuits. Following is the key to the legends used on schematics described in this chapter:

CAP	Capacitor
CC	Compressor contactor
DPDT	Double-pole double-throw switch
DPST	Double-pole single-throw
DSI	Direct spark ignition
EAC	Electrostatic air cleaner
EP	Electric pilot
FC	Fan control
FM	Fan motor
FD	Fused disconnect
FR	Fan relay
G	Fan relay terminal
GV	Gas valve
H	Humidistat
HS	Humidification system
HU	Humidifier
L	Limit
LA	Limit auxiliary
L_1, L_2	Power supply
N	Neutral
NC	Normally closed
NO	Normally open
PPC	Pilot power control
R	24-V power terminal
SPDT	Single-pole double-throw
SPST	Single-pole single-throw
TFS	Timed fan start
THR	Thermocouple
TR	Transformer
W	Heating terminal
Y	Cooling terminal

Power Supply

The power supply circuit (Figure 11–1) usually consists of a 15-A or 20-A source of 120-V a.c. power, a fused disconnect (FD) in the hot line, and a transformer (TR) to supply 24-V a.c. power to the low-voltage controls.

A single source of power is adequate unless a cooling accessory is added, in which case a separate source of 208/240-V a.c. power is required. Power for cooling requires a DPST disconnect with fuses in each "hot" line. Possibly an additional low-voltage transformer would be required if the one used for heating does not have sufficient capacity.

Fan

The line-voltage circuit for a single-speed fan consists of a fan control (FC in series with the fan motor (FM) connected across the power supply (Figure 11–2). Many heating units have multiple-speed fans. One speed is used for heating, while the other speed is used for cooling or ventilation. The operation of the fan with a two-speed motor requires two circuits (Figure 11–3). There is a line voltage circuit to power the fan motor, and a low voltage circuit to operate the switching relay.

Under normal operation in heating, the fan motor (FM) is controlled by the fan control (FC). When operating the fan on cooling speed, the fan switch on the subbase of the thermostat can be moved to the "on" position. This action closes a contact between R and G in the thermostat. Current flows through the coil of the cooling fan relay (FR), opening the NC switch and closing the NO switch operating the fan motor on cooling speed.

On a downflow or horizontal unit, the fan motor can be operated by a timed fan start relay (TFS) (Figure 11–4). On these units, with the fan not running and the sensing element of the fan control located in the air outlet, the standard fan control cannot be used to start the fan.

On a call for heating, R and W make in the thermostat. The heater of the timed fan start (TFS) is energized. After about 45 seconds, the fan motor is operated by the TFS switch. When the thermostat is satisfied and R and W break, the fan motor continues to operate until the leaving air temperature reaches the cutout temperature setting of the fan control (FC).

Pilot

The gas safety circuit is powered by a thermocouple (THR) (Figure 11–5). When a satisfactory pilot is established the thermocouple generates approximately 30 mV to energize the safety control portion of the combination gas valve. Thus, the gas

FIGURE 11–1 Power supply circuit with fused disconnection (FD) and transformer (TR).

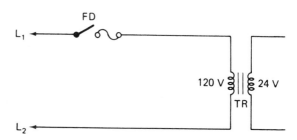

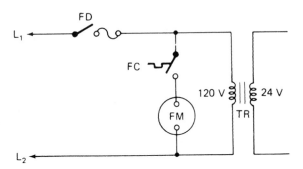

FIGURE 11–2 Fan circuit with fan control (FC) and fan motor (FM).

cannot enter the burner until a satisfactory pilot is established. Most wiring diagrams omit the pilot circuit, since it is common to all combination gas systems and need not be repeated in each diagram.

Gas Valve

The gas valve circuit is a low-voltage circuit (Figure 11–6). When the thermostat calls for heat, R and W make, energizing the gas valve (GV) because the limit control (L) is normally closed.

Should excessive temperatures occur (usually 200°F in the plenum), the limit control opens the circuit to de-energize and close the gas valve. The limit control automatically restarts the burner when its cut-in temperature (usually 175°F) is reached. On a downflow or horizontal furnace, a limit auxiliary (LA) control is used (Figure 11–7). The LA control is located in a position to sense gravity heat from the heating elements. If the fan fails to start, the LA control will sense excess heat (usually set to cut out at 145°F).

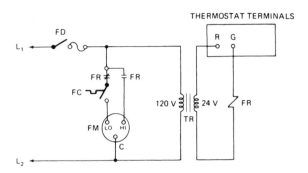

FIGURE 11–3 Two-speed fan motor with cooling fan relay (FR).

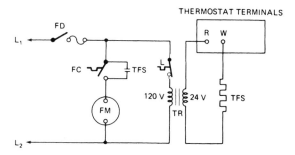

FIGURE 11–4   Fan control for downflow furnace using timed fan starts (TFS).

Limit controls can be line voltage and placed in series with the transformer (Figure 11–8). Some line-voltage limit controls have a separate set of contacts that make when the limit breaks, turning the fan on if, for any reason, it is not running. Limit controls can also be placed in series with the low-voltage heating control circuit. If the limit control opens, this will de-energize the heating circuit and close the gas valve.

Accessories

Figure 11–9 shows the schematic of accessory circuits. The humidistat (H) and humidifier (HU) are wired in series and connected to power only when the fan is running. The electrostatic air cleaner also operates only when the fan is running. These accessories are supplied with line-voltage power.

The cooling contactor (CC) is in series with the Y connection on the thermostat. When R and Y make, the cooling contactor coil is energized, operating the cooling unit.

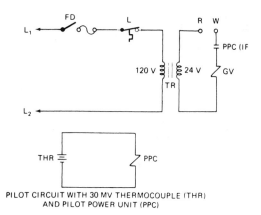

PILOT CIRCUIT WITH 30 MV THERMOCOUPLE (THR)
AND PILOT POWER UNIT (PPC)

FIGURE 11–5   Pilot circuit with 30-mV thermocouple (THR) and pilot power control (PPC).

FIGURE 11–6 Gas valve (GV) circuit with limit control (L).

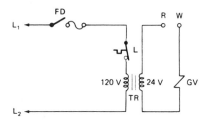

TYPICAL WIRING DIAGRAMS

The following schematic wiring diagrams illustrate the control circuits found on many heating furnaces. A schematic aids a service technician in understanding how the control system operates. Many manufacturers, however, supply only connection wiring diagrams for their equipment. It may therefore be necessary for a technician to construct a schematic in order to separate the circuits for testing and for diagnosing service problems.

Unfortunately, few standards exist that require manufacturers to conform in making connection wiring diagrams. If service technicians know the most common controls and their functions, with practice they can interpret almost any diagram. When a diagram is not available, a technician can also prepare one to suit the equipment found on the job.

The following is a review of some typical connection diagrams supplied by various manufacturers for their equipment.

Upflow

The controls in an upflow gas furnace (Figure 11–10) include:

- Thermostat
- Gas valve
- Combination fan and limit control
- Multispeed fan motor with run capacitor
- Transformer
- Fan relay

FIGURE 11–7 Gas valve (GV) circuit for downflow or horizontal furnace with limit control (L) and secondary limit (LA) in series with transformer.

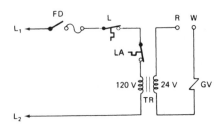

FIGURE 11–8 Single-pole double-throw (SPDT) limit control with set of contacts to operate fan on limit action.

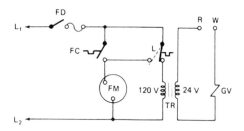

This system has been prepared for the addition of air conditioning, so cooling can be added with very little modification of the control system. A schematic diagram for this unit can be constructed as shown in Figure 11–11.

Downflow

The controls in a downflow gas furnace (Figure 11–12) include:

- Thermostat
- Gas valve
- Combination fan and limit control
- Auxiliary limit
- Fan motor with run capacitor
- Transformer

Note that Figures 11–12 and 11–13 do not show a timed fan start, which is common to many downflow (counterflow) units. On certain units, the fan control is located in such a position that it senses gravity heat from the heating elements, thus eliminating the need for a timed fan start.

Horizontal Flow

A connection drawing for a horizontal gas furnace with cooling accessory (Figure 11–14) includes:

- Thermostat
- Gas valve

FIGURE 11–9 Accessory circuits.

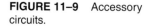

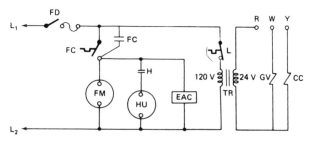

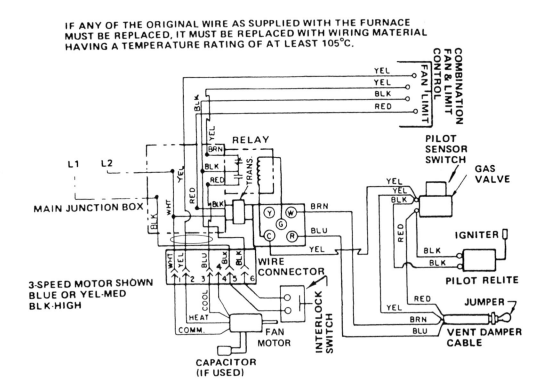

IF ANY OF THE ORIGINAL WIRE AS SUPPLIED WITH THE FURNACE MUST BE REPLACED, IT MUST BE REPLACED WITH WIRING MATERIAL HAVING A TEMPERATURE RATING OF AT LEAST 105°C.

FACTORY WIRING ——————
FIELD WIRING CLASS 1 —— · —— - —— - -

FIGURE 11–10 Connection wiring diagram for upflow gas furnace. (Courtesy of Borg Warner Central Environmental Systems, Inc.)

- Combination fan and limit control
- Auxiliary limit
- Fan motor
- Transformer

A schematic diagram for this unit can be constructed as shown in Figure 11–15.

One special feature of this control system is that the purchaser has the option of installing electronic air cleaner controls and equipment. The schematic diagram, Figure 11–16, shows the proper locations to connect the wiring for the electronic air cleaner.

The connection diagram shown in Figure 11–17 displays the wiring connections to the printed circuit board. Note the vent damper breakaway tab provided for installation of a vent damper. The printed circuit board is designed for ease of service in the field.

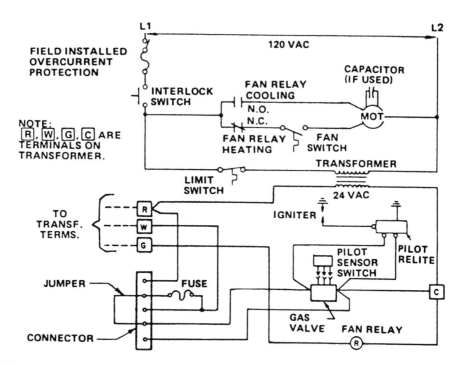

FIGURE 11–11 Schematic diagram for upflow gas furnace in Figure 11–10. (Courtesy of Borg Warner Central Environmental Systems, Inc.)

TESTING AND SERVICING

When performing service on a furnace, every effort is made to pinpoint the problem to a specific part or circuit. This avoids extra work in checking over the complete control system to find the problem. For example, if all parts of a furnace operate properly except the fan, the fan circuit can be tested separately to locate the malfunction.

In electrical troubleshooting, it is good practice to "start from power," that is, to start testing where power comes into the unit and continue testing in the problem area until power is either no longer being supplied, or with power available, the load does not operate. When reaching either point, the difficulty is located. For example, referring to Figure 11–11, if the complaint is that the fan will not run on cooling speed, the step-by-step troubleshooting procedure would be as follows:

1. Check power supply at load side of fused disconnect.
2. Remove thermostat and jump terminals R and G to determine if the relay will "pull in."
3. If the relay operates satisfactorily, check power supply at cooling-speed terminals of fan.
4. If power is available at fan, and it still will not run, motor is defective.

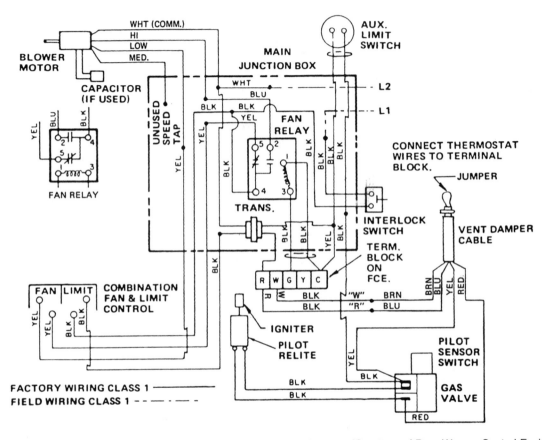

FIGURE 11–12 Connection wiring diagram for downflow gas furnace. (Courtesy of Borg Warner Central Environmental Systems, Inc.)

Use of Test Meters

Figure 11–18 shows five locations where a test meter can be used on a 24-V gas heating control system. These meters check out the following circuits:

- Power
- Fan
- Pilot
- Gas valve
- Transformer

No accessories are shown, but if these circuits exist on equipment being serviced, meter readings can be taken at these parts in addition to the ones shown.

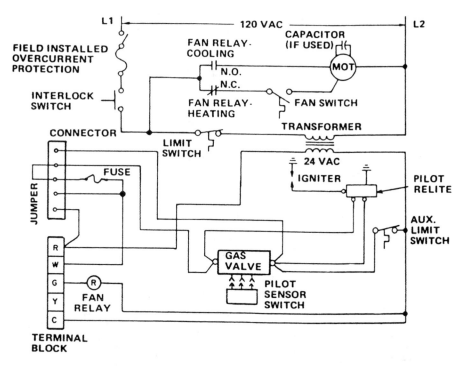

FIGURE 11–13 Schematic diagram for downflow gas furnace shown in Figure 11–12. (Courtesy of Borg Warner Central Environmental Systems, Inc.)

Component Testing and Troubleshooting

In troubleshooting, each component (or circuit) has the potential for certain problems that the service technician can check for or test. Some of these potential problems are:

1. Power supply
   (a) Switch open
   (b) Blown fuse or tripped breaker
   (c) Low voltages
2. Thermostat
   (a) Subbase switch turned off
   (b) Set too low
   (c) Loose connection
   (d) Improper anticipator setting
3. Pilot
   (a) Plugged orifice on pilot
   (b) Pilot blowing out due to draft
   (c) Too little or too much gas being supplied to pilot
4. Thermocouple
   (a) Loose connection

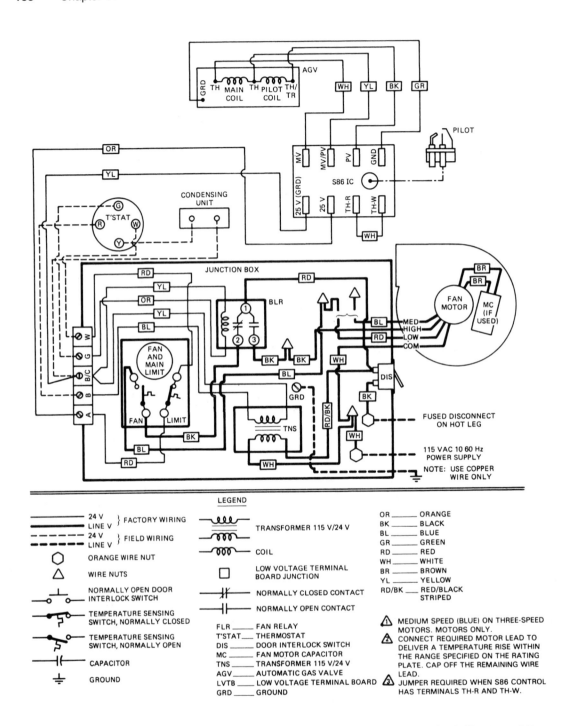

FIGURE 11–14 Connection wiring diagram for horizontal gas furnace with cooling added. (Courtesy of Borg Warner Central Environmental Systems, Inc.)

FIGURE 11–15 Schematic wiring diagram for horizontal gas furnace with cooling added. (Courtesy of Borg Warner Central Environmental Systems, Inc.)

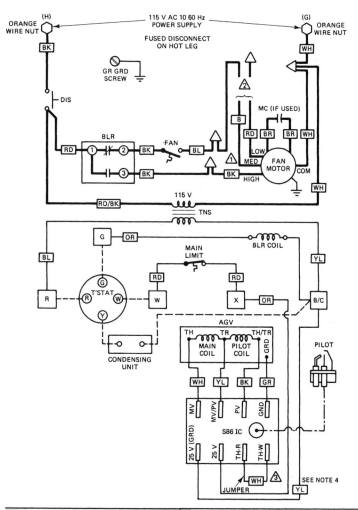

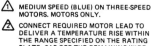

△1 MEDIUM SPEED (BLUE) ON THREE-SPEED MOTORS. MOTORS ONLY.

△2 CONNECT REQUIRED MOTOR LEAD TO DELIVER A TEMPERATURE RISE WITHIN THE RANGE SPECIFIED ON THE RATING PLATE. CAP OFF THE REMAINING WIRE LEAD.

△3 JUMPER REQUIRED WHEN S86 CONTROL HAS TERMINALS TH-R AND TH-W.

━━━━━ FACTORY HIGH-VOLTAGE WIRING

───── FACTORY LOW-VOLTAGE WIRING

▄ ▄ ▄ ▄ FIELD HIGH-VOLTAGE WIRING

NOTES:

(1) JUMPER FROM R TO G_H – REMOVED WHEN SPECIAL THERMOSTAT SUBBASE IS USED.

(2) ⊘ – SCREW TERMINALS FOR FIELD WIRING CONNECTIONS.

(3) ▭ – $\frac{1}{4}$-IN. QUICK CONNECT TERMINALS.

(4) ▉▐●▌▉ – HEATING FAN RELAY CONTACT IS
      2A   NORMALLY CLOSED UNTIL 115 V AC IS APPLIED TO FURNACE.

(5) TO CHANGE MOTOR SPEED, MOVE BLK OR RED WIRE TO DESIRED SPEED SETTING.

(6) IF ANY OF THE ORIGINAL WIRE AS SUPPLIED WITH THE APPLIANCE MUST BE REPLACED, IT MUST BE REPLACED WITH AWM(105°C) WIRE OR ITS EQUIVALENT.

(7) MOTOR IS THERMALLY OVERLOAD PROTECTED.

(8) FACTORY SPEED SELECTION IS FOR AVERAGE CONDITIONS, SEE INSTALLATION INSTRUCTIONS FOR OPTIMUM SPEED SELECTION. MOTOR MAY BE 3 OR 4 SPEED.

(9) SYMBOLS ARE AN ELECTRICAL REPRESENTATION ONLY.

FIGURE 11–16 Wiring diagram for upflow gas furnace with printed circuit control center. (Courtesy of Bryant Air Conditioning/Heating.)

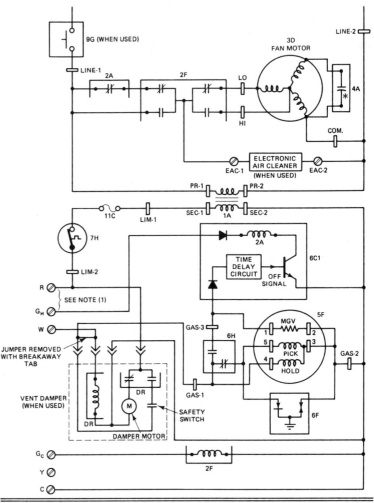

NOTES:

(1) JUMPER FROM R TO G_H – REMOVED WHEN SPECIAL THERMOSTAT SUBBASE IS USED.

(2) ⊘ – SCREW TERMINALS FOR FIELD WIRING CONNECTIONS.

(3) ▭ – $\frac{1}{4}$-IN. QUICK CONNECT TERMINALS.

(4) |●┤┤●| – HEATING FAN RELAY CONTACT IS
  2A   NORMALLY CLOSED UNTIL 115-V AC IS APPLIED TO FURNACE.

(5) TO CHANGE MOTOR SPEED, MOVE BLK OR RED WIRE TO DESIRED SPEED SETTING.

(6) IF ANY OF THE ORIGINAL WIRE AS SUPPLIED WITH THE APPLIANCE MUST BE REPLACED, IT MUST BE REPLACED WITH AWM(105°C) WIRE OR ITS EQUIVALENT.

(7) MOTOR IS THERMALLY OVERLOAD PROTECTED.

(8) FACTORY SPEED SELECTION IS FOR AVERAGE CONDITIONS, SEE INSTALLATION INSTRUCTIONS FOR OPTIMUM SPEED SELECTION. MOTOR MAY BE 3 OR 4 SPEED.

(9) SYMBOLS ARE AN ELECTRICAL REPRESENTATION ONLY.

1A – TRANSFORMER 115/24
2A – RELAY - HEAT (SPST-NC)
2F – RELAY - COOL (DPDT)
3D – FAN MOTOR
4A – RUN CAPACITOR
5F – GAS VALVE
6C1 – PRINTED CIRCUIT BOARD
6F – PILOT IGNITER
6H – SAFETY PILOT (FLAME SENSING)
7H – LIMIT SWITCH (SPST-NC)
9G – FAN DOOR SWITCH (SPST-N.O.)
11C – FUSIBLE LINK
11E – GROUND LUG

━━━━━ FACTORY HIGH-VOLTAGE WIRING
──── FACTORY LOW-VOLTAGE WIRING
▬ ▬ ▬ FIELD HIGH-VOLTAGE WIRING

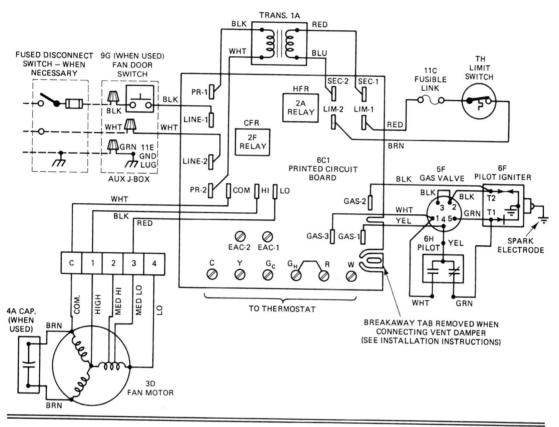

1A – TRANSFORMER 115/24
2A – RELAY - HEAT (SPST-NC)
2F – RELAY - COOL (DPDT)
3D – FAN MOTOR
4A – RUN CAPACITOR
5F – GAS VALVE
6C1 – PRINTED CIRCUIT BOARD
6F – PILOT IGNITER
6H – SAFETY PILOT (FLAME SENSING)
7H – LIMIT SWITCH (SPST-NC)
9G – FAN DOOR SWITCH (SPST-N.O.)
11C – FUSIBLE LINK
11E – GROUND LUG

————— FACTORY HIGH-VOLTAGE WIRING
——— FACTORY LOW-VOLTAGE WIRING
- - - - - FIELD HIGH-VOLTAGE WIRING

NOTES:
(1) JUMPER FROM R TO G_H - REMOVED WHEN SPECIAL THERMOSTAT SUBBASE IS USED.
(2) ⊘ – SCREW TERMINALS FOR FIELD WIRING CONNECTIONS.
(3) ▭ – $\frac{1}{4}$-IN. QUICK CONNECT TERMINALS.
(4) [•)|•] 2A – HEATING FAN RELAY CONTACT IS NORMALLY CLOSED UNTIL 115 V AC IS APPLIED TO FURNACE.
(5) TO CHANGE MOTOR SPEED, MOVE BLK OR RED WIRE TO DESIRED SPEED SETTING.
(6) IF ANY OF THE ORIGINAL WIRE AS SUPPLIED WITH THE APPLIANCE MUST BE REPLACED, IT MUST BE REPLACED WITH AWM(105°C) WIRE OR ITS EQUIVALENT.
(7) MOTOR IS THERMALLY OVERLOAD PROTECTED.
(8) FACTORY SPEED SELECTION IS FOR AVERAGE CONDITIONS, SEE INSTALLATION INSTRUCTIONS FOR OPTIMUM SPEED SELECTION. MOTOR MAY BE 3 OR 4 SPEED.
(9) SYMBOLS ARE AN ELECTRICAL REPRESENTATION ONLY.

FIGURE 11–17 Connection diagram for upflow gas furnace with printed circuit control center. (Courtesy of Bryant Air Conditioning/Heating.)

FIGURE 11–18 Use of electrical test meters on a gas furnace.

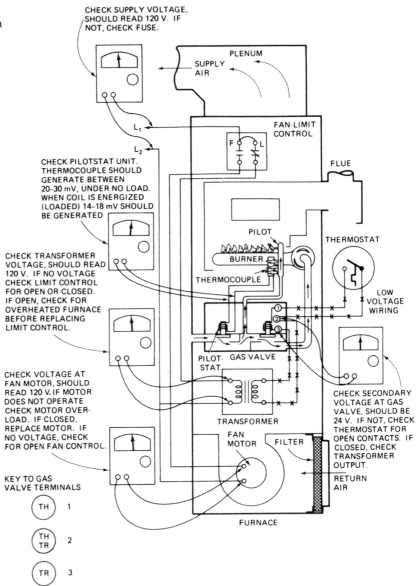

CHECK SUPPLY VOLTAGE, SHOULD READ 120 V. IF NOT, CHECK FUSE.

PLENUM

SUPPLY AIR

FAN-LIMIT CONTROL

FLUE

F   L

CHECK PILOTSTAT UNIT. THERMOCOUPLE SHOULD GENERATE BETWEEN 20-30 mV, UNDER NO LOAD. WHEN COIL IS ENERGIZED (LOADED) 14-18 mV SHOULD BE GENERATED

L_1

L_2

PILOT

THERMOSTAT

BURNER

CHECK TRANSFORMER VOLTAGE, SHOULD READ 120 V. IF NO VOLTAGE CHECK LIMIT CONTROL FOR OPEN OR CLOSED. IF OPEN, CHECK FOR OVERHEATED FURNACE BEFORE REPLACING LIMIT CONTROL.

THERMOCOUPLE

LOW VOLTAGE WIRING

PILOT. GAS VALVE STAT

CHECK VOLTAGE AT FAN MOTOR, SHOULD READ 120 V. IF MOTOR DOES NOT OPERATE CHECK MOTOR OVER-LOAD. IF CLOSED, REPLACE MOTOR. IF NO VOLTAGE, CHECK FOR OPEN FAN CONTROL.

TRANSFORMER

FAN MOTOR

FILTER

CHECK SECONDARY VOLTAGE AT GAS VALVE, SHOULD BE 24 V. IF NOT, CHECK THERMOSTAT FOR OPEN CONTACTS. IF CLOSED, CHECK TRANSFORMER OUTPUT.

RETURN AIR

KEY TO GAS VALVE TERMINALS

TH   1

TH TR   2

TR   3

FURNACE

(b) Too close or too far from flame
(c) Defective thermocouple
5. Transformer
(a) Low primary voltage
(b) Defective transformer
(c) Blown fuse in 24-V circuit
6. Limit control
(a) Switch open

      (b) Loose connection

      (c) Defective control

  7. Gas valve

      (a) Defective pilot safety power unit

      (b) Defective main gas valve

  8. Fan control

      (a) Switch open

      (b) Improper setting

      (c) Defective control

Thermocouple Circuit

Millivoltmeter probes can be connected in the thermocouple circuit, as shown in Figure 11–19, using the special adapter. If the meter reading is less than 17 mV, there is insufficient power to operate the pilot safety power unit. This must be

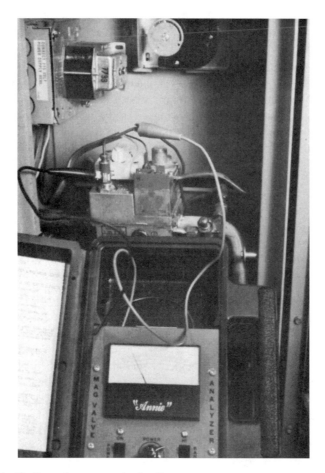

FIGURE 11–19   Testing a thermocouple circuit.

corrected by either improving the flame impingement on the thermocouple or by replacing the thermocouple.

BURNER IGNITION

There are three types of gas burner ignition systems:

1. Pilot ignition system (intermittent)
2. Direct-spark ignition system
3. Silicon carbide ignition system

Pilot Ignition

The pilot ignition system (intermittent) is designed for low-voltage application on all types of residential, gas-fired heating equipment.

Principle of operation   The thermostat powers the control to open the pilot burner gas valve and provide the ignition spark simultaneously. As soon as the pilot flame is established, the spark ceases and the main burner gas valve is energized. Should the flame not be established within a predetermined period, the system provides safety shutdown. (Sparking stops and pilot gas flow is interrupted.)

Electronic flame-sensing circuitry in the ignitor detects the presence or absence of the pilot burner flame. If the flame is not established during the trial-for-ignition period, the system closes the pilot gas valve and locks out. If the burner flame is extinguished during the duty cycle, the main gas valve will close and the ignitor will retry ignition before going into lockout.

Proper location of the electrode assembly is important for optimum system performance. It is recommended that there be approximately a $1/8$-in. gap between the electrodes and the pilot, as shown in Figure 11–20. This figure also shows the typical retrofit wiring for a pilot ignition system. In Figure 11–21 the ignition system is used in a heat-cool application. This type of installation can be used with a two-stage gas valve.

Direct-Spark Ignition

Direct-spark ignition (DSI) does away with the pilot altogether and lights the main burner with an electric spark. Operation of the burner depends on continuous detection of the main burner flame by an electronic flame-sensing system. Unlike the intermittent pilot ignition, DSI is required to light a significantly larger gas flow. Safety demands that ignition and flame detection occur in a few seconds.

Principle of operation   If the main burner lights, a circuit is completed from the flame sensor through the flame to the burner head and ground. This current flow

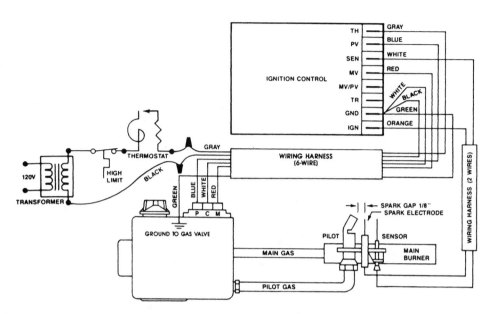

FIGURE 11–20   Typical retrofit wiring of an electronic ignition control. (Courtesy of Robertshaw Controls Company.)

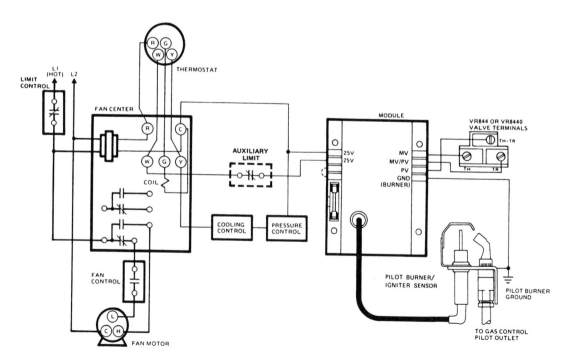

FIGURE 11–21   Wiring diagram for heat-cool application of a pilot spark ignition system. (Courtesy of Honeywell Inc.)

proves the presence of the main burner flame and resets the lockout timer and at the same time interrupts the spark ignition circuit. The gas valve remains open as long as there is a call for heat and as long as the module continues to detect the presence of the main flame. Should the current flow be interrupted (flame-out), trial for ignition begins again.

If the safety lockout timing period ends before the main burner lights or before the flame sensor establishes enough current, the control module will go into safety lockout. When the module goes into safety lockout, power to the pulse generator is interrupted, the gas control circuit is interrupted, and the alarm circuit relay (if the module is so equipped) is energized. The module will stay locked out until it is reset by turning the thermostat down below room temperature for 30 seconds. Applying a DSI system is a complex engineering task best accomplished by the equipment manufacturer. Field-retrofitting the DSI controls is not a practical procedure. There are, however, times when components of DSI systems need replacing. Parts are available for this kind of job.

Ignition control units are sometimes installed with vent dampers. When a vent damper is in the system, the thermostat wire is connected to one side of the *end switch* circuit. The end switch is closed only when the damper is fully open. Figure 11–22 shows the wiring connection for the damper end switch.

Warning: the vent damper must be in the full-open position before the ignition system is energized. Failure to verify this may cause a serious health hazard to occupants.

In some furnace wiring, one terminal of the secondary side of the transformer may be grounded. This could damage the transformer. Therefore, it is important to determine

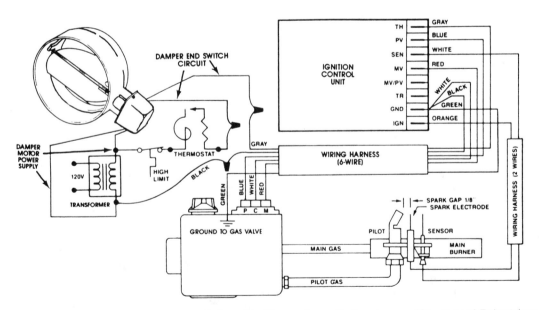

FIGURE 11–22 Wiring diagram for installation of ignition system with flue damper. (Courtesy of Robertshaw Controls Company.)

which gas valve wire is grounded before making the connection to the wiring harness. This procedure is shown in Figure 11–23.

Ignition and flame-sensing hardware for direct spark ignition systems is available in different configurations. One of these is shown in Figure 11–24. In Figure 11–25 the diagram shows a combined system is which the igniter and the sensor are one unit.

Silicon Carbide Ignition System

Principle of operation   The system utilizes a silicon carbide element that performs a dual function of ignition and flame detection. The igniter is an electrically heated resistance element that thermally ignites the gas. The flame detector circuit utilizes flame rectification for monitoring the gas flame.

The igniter serves two functions. Upon a call for heat, the element is powered from the 120-V a.c. line and allowed to heat for 45 seconds (typical). Then the main valve is powered, permitting gas to flow to the burner for the trial-for-ignition period, which is typically 7 seconds long, although other timings are available. At the end of this period, the igniter is switched from its heating function to that of a flame probe which checks for the presence of flame. If flame is present, the system will monitor it and hold the main valve open. If flame is not established within the trial-for-ignition period, the system will lock out, closing the main valve and shutting off power to the igniter. If a loss of flame occurs during the heating cycle, the system will recycle through the ignition sequence.

Silicon carbide ignition   Proper location of the silicon carbide igniter is important for optimum system performance. It is recommended that the igniter be mounted temporarily using clamps or other suitable means so that the system can be tested before permanent mounting is accomplished. The igniter should be located so that its tip extends $1/4$ in. through the center of the flame and about $1/2$ in. above the base of the flame, as shown in Figure 11–26. Wiring diagrams for the silicon carbide systems are shown in Figures 11–27 and 11–28.

Operation and Troubleshooting of a
Honeywell Universal Intermittent Pilot Module S8610U

The Honeywell S8610U module in Figure 11–29 is a general replacement control for many pilot spark ignition modules used on furnaces today. It provides ignition sequence, flame monitoring, and safety shutoff for central heating systems.

Sequence of Operation for the Honeywell S8610U

1. On a call for heat the heating thermostat will close from R to W and bring 24 volts to the TH-W terminal on the S8610U control module.

FIGURE 11–23   Procedure for checking ground side of transformer. (Courtesy of Robertshaw Controls Company.)

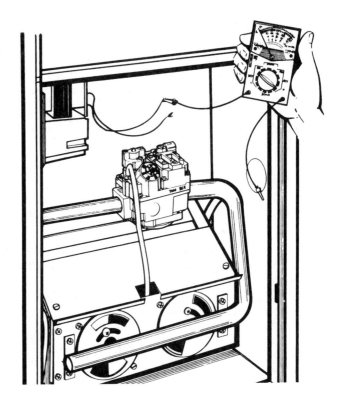

FIGURE 11–24   Connection wiring diagram of system with separate igniter and sensor. (Courtesy of Honeywell Inc.)

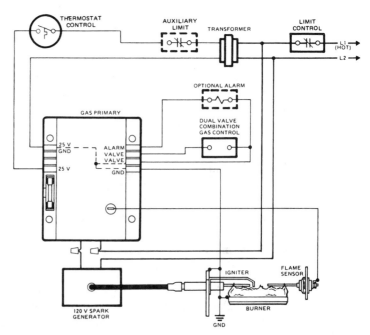

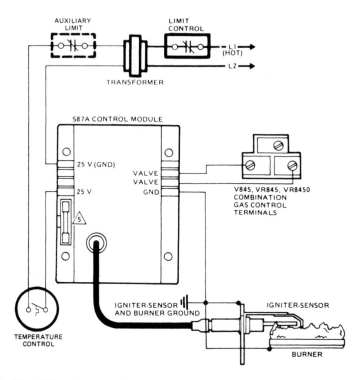

FIGURE 11–25 Wiring diagram of system with combined igniter-sensor. (Courtesy of Honeywell Inc.)

2. 24 volts will energize the pilot valve from the PV and MV/PV terminals on the S8610U control module. At the same time 13,000 volts will be fed to the igniter from the SPARK terminal on the S8610U control module.
3. When the pilot lights, the flame rectification system will prove the pilot by sending a micro amp signal (minimum of 1 μA) to the SENSE terminal on the S8610U.
4. After the pilot has been proven, 24 volts will energize the main gas valve from terminals MV and MV/PV on the S8610U control module.
5. When the thermostat is satisfied, its contacts will open, the pilot and main gas valve will close and this will end the burner cycle.

Operation of a Johnson G779 Universal Intermittent Pilot Ignition Control

The Johnson G779 control (see Figure 11–30) replaces many existing intermittent pilot ignition controls made by various manufacturers. It is a safety control designed for indirect ignition systems that provides precise timing functions, draft tolerant burner supervision, ignition retries, and a choice of separate or integral spark and sensor combination.

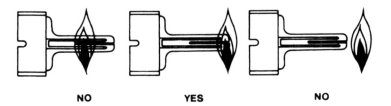

NO   YES   NO

FIGURE 11-26 Proper location of silicon carbide igniter element in relation to flame. (Courtesy of Fenwal Incorporated.)

Sequence of Operation for the Johnson G779

1. On a call for heat the heating thermostat will close from R to W and bring 24 volts to the THS-2 terminal on the G779 control module. (If an automatic vent damper is used it will open fully and then energize the ignition control system.)
2. Once the module is energized, the diagnostic LED lights, and the control begins its trial for ignition.
3. The pilot valve is energized with 24 volts from the PV1 terminal and the Ground terminal on the G779 control module. At this time, the igniter is energized for 3 seconds to ignite the pilot gas.

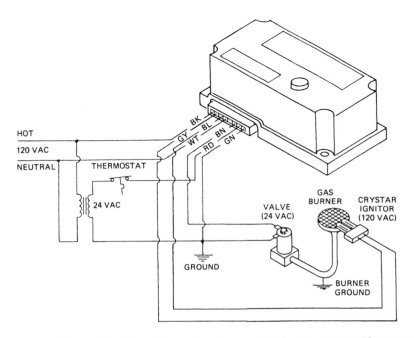

FIGURE 11-27 Connection wiring diagram for silicon carbide ignition system. (Courtesy of Fenwal Incorporated.)

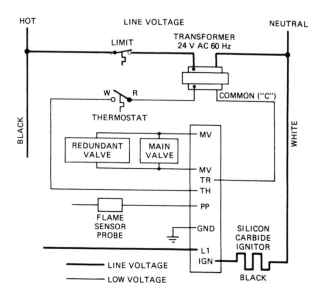

FIGURE 11–28   Schematic wiring diagram for silicon carbide ignitor system. (Courtesy of White-Rodgers Division of Emerson Electric Co.)

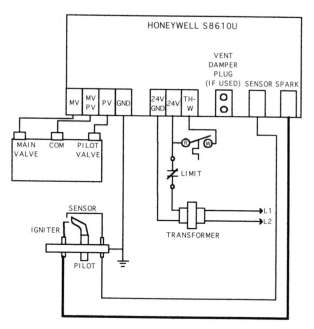

FIGURE 11–29   Honeywell general replacement module. (Courtesy of Honeywell Inc.)

FIGURE 11–30 Johnson G779 Universal intermittent pilot ignition control system. (Courtesy of Johnson.)

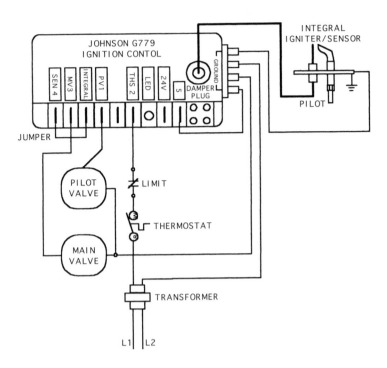

4. After pilot ignition, the pilot flame is detected by the flame sensor (separate spark/sensor) or by the igniter (integral spark/sensor). A minimum of .3 μA must be sensed or the system will enter into 100% lockout. At this time the system will repeat a sequence of trial-delay-retry until the pilot lights or the thermostat is satisfied. The LED will flash during the retry/delay period.

5. After the pilot has been proven, 24 volts will energize the main gas valve from terminals MV3 and No. 5 on the G779 control module.

6. When the thermostat is satisfied, the contacts will open, the pilot and main gas valve will close, which will end the burner cycle.

Operation of a Fenwal 05-31 Hot Surface Ignition System

The Fenwal 05-31 HSI system control (see Figures 11–31 and 11–32) is widely used for many residential furnaces today. This control uses a hot surface igniter to directly ignite the main burners of a gas fired system. It is an ignition control that, through a patented technique, uses a hot surface element to ignite and sense the main burner flame. It provides ignition sequence, flame monitoring, and safety shutoff for central heating systems.

Sequence of Operation for the Fenwal 05-31

1. On a call for heat the heating thermostat will close from R to W and bring 24 volts to the TH terminal on the 05-31 control module.

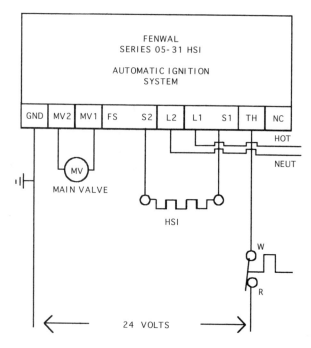

FIGURE 11–31   Local Sensing Wiring Diagram. (Courtesy of Fenwal.)

2. Once the TH terminal has been powered by 24 volts, the hot surface igniter is energized for 20 seconds. This will allow the igniter to reach ignition temperature.
3. Twenty-four volts will be brought to the main gas valve from terminals MV1 and
   MV2 on the Fenwal 05-31 control module. This will open the gas valve, the igniter will light the gas and the main burners will be established.
4. After main burner ignition, the Fenwal 05-31 switches the hot surface element
   from the ignition mode to the sensing mode for the duration of the cycle. If the
   flame is not sensed during this trial for ignition period, the system will go into a
   lockout mode after three ignition attempts.
5. A minimum of .75 μA must be sensed by the sensor igniter or the system will
   enter into 100% lockout.
6. When the thermostat is satisfied, terminals R and W will open and the main gas
   valve will close, shutting down the burner cycle.

Operation of a Bryant HHA4AA-011 Printed Circuit Board

The HHA4AA-011 printed circuit board (see Figure 11-33) is only used on Bryant
and Carrier furnaces. The circuit board is used on an indirect ignition system that will,
on a call for heat, control pilot ignition, monitor pilot flame, energize the main gas
valve, and control blower operation by the use of a solid state control circuit.

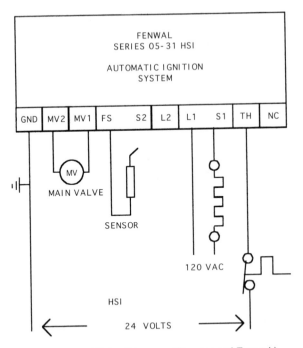

FIGURE 11–32   Remote Sensing Wiring Diagram. (Courtesy of Fenwal.)

Sequence of Operation for the Bryant HHA4AA-011 Printed Circuit Board

1. On a call for heat, the heating thermostat will close from R to W and bring 24 volts to the W terminal on the HHA4AA-011 printed circuit board.

2. Once the W terminal has been powered by 24 volts, this will start the sequence of operation by energizing the GAS1 and GAS2 terminals with 24 volts. This will, through the normally closed set of contacts on the bimetal pilot sensor, energize the pick coil on the gas valve. At the same time, it will energize the pilot igniter and the hold coil on the gas valve.

3. With the pick coil and pilot igniter energized, gas will flow to the pilot and be ignited by a spark from the pilot igniter. The pilot flame will heat the bimetal pilot sensor and, after approximately 45 seconds, a set of normally closed contacts will change to the open position. This will de-energize the pick coil and the pilot igniter. The hold coil will stay energized, since it is directly controlled from the GAS1 terminal and is not controlled by the bimetal flame sensor. The hold coil will keep the pilot valve open which will in turn keep the pilot lit and ready for the ignition of the main gas burners.

4. The bimetal pilot sensor also has a set of normally open contacts that will close once the pilot flame is sensed, approximately 45 seconds after pilot ignition. This proves the existence of the pilot and energizes the main gas valve. The main gas valve will feed gas to the main burners and the gas will be ignited by the pilot.

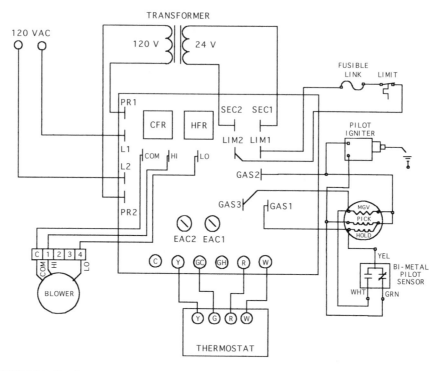

FIGURE 11–33   Bryant HHA4AA-011 printed circuit board.

5. When the main gas valve is energized, 24 volts is sent to terminal GAS3 from the main gas valve which will start the solid state timed delay circuit. After 45 seconds, the fan will energize on the heating speed.
6. When the thermostat is satisfied, terminals R and W will open, which will de-energize the (hold) pilot valve and the main gas valve. The blower will then operate for 45 seconds and then shut down, completing the cycle.

White Rodgers Mercury Flame Sensor

The White Rodgers mercury flame sensor (see Figure 11–34) is used on an indirect ignition system that will, on a call for heat, control pilot ignition, monitor pilot flame, and energize the main gas valve.

Sequence of Operation for the White Rodgers Mercury Flame Sensor Ignition System

1. On a call for heat, the heating thermostat will close from R to W and bring 24 volts to the ignition transformer. This will create a spark for the ignition of the pilot gas. At the same time, current will flow to the number 4 terminal on the mercury flame

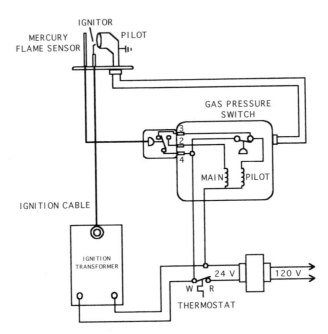

FIGURE 11–34   White Rodgers mercury flame sensor. (Courtesy of White-Rodgers Division of Emerson Electric Co.)

sensor. From terminal number 4, current flows to terminal number 3, through a closed set of contacts. From terminal number 3, current flows to the pilot valve, which will open the valve and allow gas to flow to the pilot.

2. The flow of gas to the pilot will cause the gas pressure switch to close and the ignitor to light the pilot gas.
3. The flame from the pilot heats the sensor and causes the mercury to vaporize. This will apply pressure on the diaphragm of the sensor causing the normally open (hot) contacts to close, energizing the main gas valve. The normally closed (cold) contacts will open, breaking the circuit to the pilot valve coil. The gas pressure switch is in parallel with the normally closed (cold) contacts, which will keep the pilot valve energized during burner operation.
4. When the thermostat is satisfied, terminals R and W will open, which will de-energize the pilot valve, the main gas valve, and the ignition transformer, ending the burner's cycle.

STUDY QUESTIONS

Answers to the study questions may be found in the sections noted in brackets.

11–1. What power supply should be used on a standard gas furnace? *[Power Supply]*

11–2. How many circuits are required to operate a two-speed fan? *[Fan]*

11–3. What two thermostat terminals must close to provide a call for heating? *[Gas Valve]*

11–4. What is the usual cut-out temperature of a secondary limit control? *[Gas Valve]*

11–5. What are the two terminals that close on the thermostat to call for cooling? *[Accessories]*

11–6. What type of furnace uses an auxiliary limit (LA) control? *[Gas Valve]*

11–7. In testing a fan relay, what voltage should be applied to the fan relay coil? *[Typical Wiring Diagrams]*

11–8. Describe the three types of gas burner ignition systems. *[Burner Ignition]*

12

High-Efficiency Furnaces

OBJECTIVES

After studying this chapter, the student will be able to:

- Select a furnace based on its energy requirements
- Read a wiring diagram for a high-efficiency furnace and determine the sequence of operation
- Install and service furnaces with energy-saving components
- Troubleshoot a solid-state control system

78 TO 80% AFUE FURNACES

The minimum requirement for an energy-saving furnace is 78% AFUE (annual fuel utilization efficiency). The testing procedure was developed by the U.S. Department of Energy (DOE). All furnace manufacturers make units in the 78 to 80% AFUE category. Furnaces with efficiencies as high as 96 to 97% AFUE, known as *high-efficiency furnaces* (HEFs), are also available. In many areas the increased cost of an HEF can be justified in view of the additional fuel saving.

In this chapter we study both the "78–80s" and the HEF units to see how these efficiencies are achieved. One of the important functions of the heating-cooling technician is to assure that these ratings are maintained not only in the original installation, but also throughout the life of the equipment.

Design Characteristics

There is considerable similarity in various manufacturer's models, although there are individual differences that may be important to the customer. A typical unit is shown in Figure 12–1. Some of the principal components are identified:

> Induced draft blower (Figure 12–2)
>
> Tubular heat exchanger (Figure 12–3)
>
> Hot surface ignitor (Figure 12–4)
>
> In-shot gas burner (Figure 12–5)
>
> Solid-state control board (Figure 12–6)

Components

A description of the essential parts of these units, as supplied by various manufacturers, is given below.

Heat exchangers   The heat exchangers (HXs) are all single pass, with a separate HX for each burner, assembled together into a single part. These units carry an extended warranty all the way from 10 years to the lifetime of the original purchaser. One manufacturer indicates that their HX units have more space between sections than those of their competitors, thus offering less air resistance to the blower.

Gas burner lighting arrangement   There are basically five types: standing pilot, pilot spark ignition, pilot hot surface ignition, direct spark ignition, and direct hot surface ignition.

Controls   Most units are equipped with solid-state control boards, which when defective are replaced as a single unit. These units can also be diagnostic, to assist in troubleshooting. There are various ways to control the blower. Continuous blower operation is always an option. For heating, a timed fan start is the usual arrangement. Termination is generally by temperature. A limit control is always provided to protect against overheating in case the fan does not start.

Gas valves   Some units have slow-opening gas valves to prevent noisy startup, while others are fast opening.

Draft arrangements   The majority of units are equipped with induced draft fans which require a differential pressure switch to prove that the fan is running. One manufacturer does not use an induced draft fan, but their units are equipped with a draft diverter.

Gas burners   The in-shot burner is the most popular type, although there are a number of manufacturers that use the multiple port type. A roll-out safety switch is provided to close off the gas supply in case the flue is blocked.

FIGURE 12–1 Cutaway view of typical 78% AFUE furnace. (Courtesy of Rheem Air Conditioning Co.)

FIGURE 12–2   Induced draft blower. (Courtesy of Rheem Air Conditioning Co.)

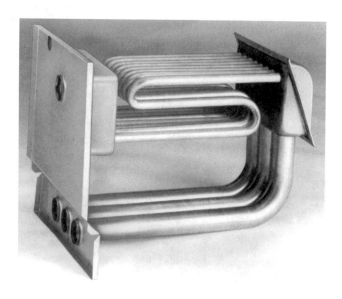

FIGURE 12–3   Tubular heat exchanger. (Courtesy of Rheem Air Conditioning Co.)

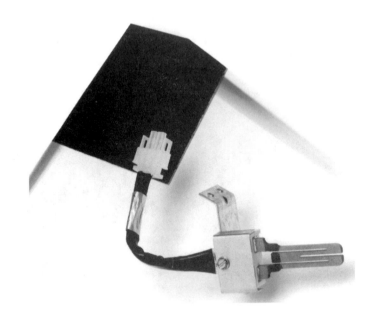

FIGURE 12–4 Hot surface ignitor. (Courtesy of Rheem Air Conditioning Co.)

FIGURE 12–5 In-shot gas burner. (Courtesy of Rheem Air Conditioning Co.)

FIGURE 12–6   Solid-state control board. (Courtesy of Rheem Air Conditioning Co.)

CONTROL SEQUENCE

A typical control sequence is shown in Figures 12–7 to 12–13. The wiring diagrams have been simplified for easier understanding. The legend for the wiring diagrams is as follows:

ALS	Auxiliary limit switch
BLWM	Blower motor
CFR	Cooling blower relay
DSS	Draft safeguard switch
F	Fuse
FL	Fusible link
GV	Gas valve
HFR	Heating blower relay
IDM	Induced draft motor
IDR	Induced draft relay
LS	Limit switch
PRS	Pressure switch
TRAN	24-V transformer

The various stages of operation are illustrated in the following diagrams. The descriptions of the action can be traced on the diagrams.

Ready to start (Figure 12–7) The unit is in the ready-to-start mode. The door interlock switch is closed and power is available at three electrical devices:

1. L_1 and L_2 are connected to the line side of the transformer which is energized.
2. One side of the low-voltage power is connected to the heating blower relay.
3. One side of the low-voltage power is connected to the induced draft relay through the fusible link and limit switches.

Call for heat, IDR energized (Figure 12–8) On a call for heat: (1) the R and W contacts on the thermostat close, (2) connecting the other side of the low-voltage power to the induced draft relay, (3) through the normally closed pressure switch contacts.

Call for heat, IDM energized (Figure 12–9) Note that the induced draft relay has two sets of normally open contacts:

1. One set of contacts close to form a holding circuit for the induced draft relay.
2. The other set of contacts close to start the induced draft motor.

Call for heat, gas valve energized (Figure 12–10) Assuming that the vent system is free from blockage or restriction and that the inducer fan is operating satisfactorily:

1. The pressure switch will sense the required difference in pressure and switch positions.
2. The induced draft relay stays energized through its holding circuit.
3. With the pressure switch in its new position, power is supplied to the gas valve

FIGURE 12–7 Wiring diagram for furnace in ready-to-start mode. (Courtesy of Carrier Corporation.)

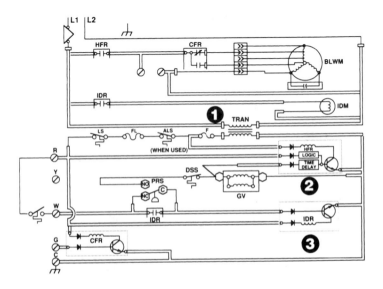

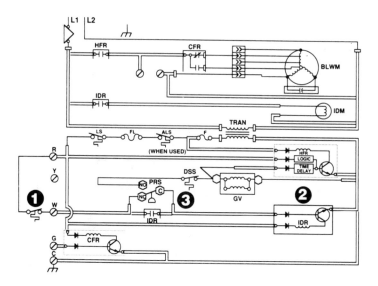

FIGURE 12–8   Wiring diagram on call for heat with IDR energized. (Courtesy of Carrier Corporation.)

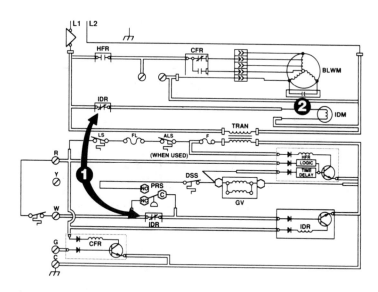

FIGURE 12–9   Wiring diagram on call for heat with IDM energized. (Courtesy of Carrier Corporation.)

FIGURE 12–10 Wiring diagram on call for heat, gas valve energized. (Courtesy of Carrier Corporation.)

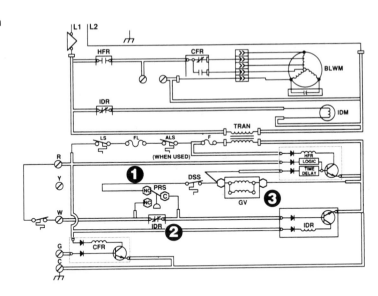

through the closed draft safeguard switch. Assuming that the pilot is burning satisfactorily, the gas valve will open and the burners will light.

Call for heat, fan motor energized (Figure 12–11)

1. At the same time the power is supplied to the gas valve, power is also applied to the time-delay circuit of the heating blower relay. After 45 seconds the contacts of the heating relay close.

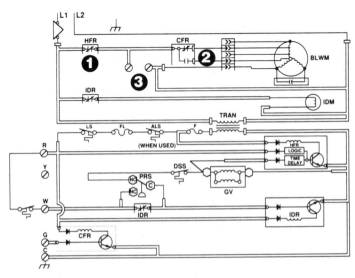

FIGURE 12–11 Wiring diagram on call for heat, fan motor energized. (Courtesy of Carrier Corporation.)

2. This applies power to the selected winding of the blower motor through the normally closed cooling blower relay contacts, and the blower is started.
3. If an electronic air filter is installed, power is available at the screw terminals. It is energized at the same time as the blower motor. Its load cannot exceed 1 A at 115 V.

Thermostat satisfied (Figure 12–12)   The furnace will continue to run until the thermostat is satisfied. When this occurs the gas valve is immediately de-energized, shutting off the burners. The blower motor continues to run for 120 seconds before shutting off. The blower off-delay resistor on the circuit board can be clipped off to provide a 180-second run time.

Call for Cooling (Figure 12–13)   On a call for cooling, the R-Y and R-G circuits are energized. The Y terminal is not used. It could be used, however, as a connection point for the outdoor condensing unit relay. The action that takes place when these circuits are energized is as follows:

1. The cooling blower relay is energized, closing the relay contacts that supply power to the blower motor speed circuit for cooling. The electronic air filter could also be activated at the same time.
2. The heating blower relay is also energized closing its contacts, which provide a power path to the cooling blower relay.
3. Power is supplied to the condensing unit relay, which starts the compressor.

Continuous Blower Operation   If continuous blower operation is used, the furnace will operate as follows:

1. On cooling, the fan will run continuously at the higher cooling speed.
2. On heating, the fan will run continuously at the higher cooling speed. Then on a call for heat, the blower will shut off for 45 seconds to allow the heat exchangers

THERMOSTAT SATISFIED

- **GAS VALVE DE-ENERGIZED**
- **BLOWER RUNS 120 SECONDS***

* 180 SECONDS IF RESISTOR CLIPPED

FIGURE 12–12   Thermostat satisfied. (Courtesy of Carrier Corporation.)

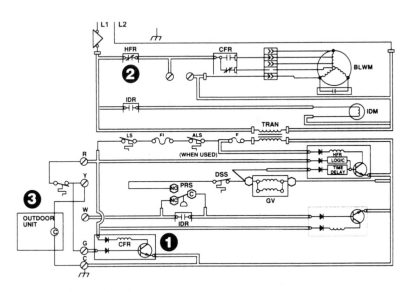

FIGURE 12–13   Wiring diagram on a call for cooling. (Courtesy of Carrier Corporation.)

to warm up. After the warm-up period the blower will run at the speed selected for heating. When the thermostat is satisfied, the blower will continue to run for 120 or 180 seconds at the heating speed. Then it will resume continuous operation at the higher cooling speed.

CHARACTERISTICS OF HIGH-EFFICIENCY FURNACES

The energy crisis has encouraged manufacturers of gas furnaces to design equipment that exceeds the usual 80% efficiency. The ability of high-efficiency furnaces (HEFs) to achieve better performance is based on two qualities:

1. *Lower flue gas temperature.* The furnaces extract more heat from the flue gas by lowering its temperature and bringing it nearer to ambient temperature before exhausting the flue gas.
2. *Condensation of the water vapor in the flue gas.* Condensation results in the recovery of the latent heat of vaporization. Almost 1000 Btu is released per pound of water condensed.

Components common to the various designs include the following:

1. *Induced draft fan.* This fan propels the flue gas mechanically through the heat exchanger passages. On the pulse furnace, the induced draft fan serves only as a purge device and is used only in the precombustion and postcombustion cycles.
2. *Secondary heat-exchanger surface.* Such a surface permits removing more heat from the flue gases than the normal primary heat exchanger. The basic heating

surface reduces the flue gas temperature to around 500°F, and the secondary surface brings it down to around 150°F or lower.

3. *Condensate drain.* This drain is required to remove the products of combustion that condense at the lower flue gas temperatures. This condensate consists mainly of water vapor, but can contain other substances, due to impurities in the gas, and can be corrosive. Therefore, it must be handled properly to prevent damage caused by improper piping or an inadequate disposal arrangement.

4. *Flue pipe design.* Due to the lower temperature and the reduced volume of flue gas, such materials as PVC plastic piping can be used for the vent stack. This feature has an advantage in the application of the equipment, simplifying the structural requirements.

One possible disadvantage of HEFs may be their limited capacities. Most of these units do not exceed 115,000 Btuh output. Due to the improved construction of most homes and the practice of more accurate furnace sizing, however, the smaller-capacity furnaces are adequate for many larger homes. The use of two furnaces is usually a good solution where more capacity is required.

TYPES OF DESIGNS

Generally speaking, the industry has created three distinctive HEF designs. All these designs have AFUE ratings in excess of 80%, meaning that the ratio of output to input is in the range 80 to 97%. These designs include the following:

1. Recuperative design
2. Condensing design
3. Pulse design

Recuperative Design

The typical recuperative design operates in the range of 80 to 85% AFUE and is so called because it recoups some of the heat used for venting by employing a mechanical vent fan. The additional heat is often removed in an extra heat exchanger section that does not have a burner in it. All vent gases from the other sections must pass through the extra section before being vented out of the furnace. Some manufacturers do not use an extra section, but instead, have a special design, causing the vent gases to remain longer in the heat exchanger. This will again extract more heat and lower the temperature of the vent gases. Figure 12–14 shows a typical recuperative design. Operation of this furnace is similar to that of the condensing design, described in the following pages.

Condensing Design

An illustration of a typical condensing design is shown in Figure 12–15. The figure lists the various components. With reference to the figure, this furnace operates as

1. **HOT SURFACE IGNITION**
   Eliminated pilot light to save gas and add reliablity to furnace operation.

2. **ELECTRICAL CONTROL BOARD**
   Provides accurate furnace control and trusted performance. A self-test function helps ensure proper installation. It's backed by a three-year limited warranty.

3. **FOUR-PASS™ HEAT EXCHANGER**
   Provides excellent heat transfer through serpentine shape. Aluminized steel, crimped seam construction is backed by a twenty-year limited warranty.

4. **INDUCER ASSEMBLY**
   Features a new design that reduces noise and pulls the exact amount of air needed for superior heat transfer.

5. **SLOW OPENING GAS VALVE**
   Starts the heating process smoothly, quietly and reliably.

6. **CABINET INSULATION**
   Reduces sound output and minimizes heat loss from furnace.

7. **PRE-PAINTED CABINET**
   Scratch-resistant finish on a one piece wrap-around cabinet for a tough, long-lasting finish.

FIGURE 12–14 Typical recuperative design. (Courtesy of Carrier Corporation.)

follows: Natural gas (or LP) is metered through a redundant gas valve (1) and is burned using monoport in-shot burners (2), and combustion takes place in the lower portion of the primary heat exchangers (3). The hot gases then pass into a collection chamber and through a stainless steel duct into a secondary heat exchanger (4). This heat exchanger has stainless steel tubes with turbulators and exterior aluminum fins. Combustion gases are drawn through the secondary heat exchanger by an induced draft fan (5) and exhausted to the vent stack (6). Moisture that condenses out of the flue gas, is collected in the drain assembly (7), and is directed to the floor drain.

The multispeed direct-drive fan (8) delivers return air first over the secondary heating surface (4) and then over the primary surface (3) to the plenum outlet. Electronic ignition eliminates the need for a continuous pilot. The cabinet is insulated with fiberglass. Another illustration of a condensing design is shown in Figure 12–16.

Theory of operation (combustion) The efficiency of this furnace is obtained through three basic processes that are not found on standard-efficiency gas furnaces:

1. Very accurate control of the combustion process by metering the volume of gas and fresh air entering the combustion chamber
2. The use of a secondary heat exchanger to absorb the residual heat from the flue gases that are leaving the primary exchanger
3. The introduction of air from outdoors to the combustion area of the furnace rather than from the immediate area of the furnace installation

Let's look closely at each of these processes and see how they work closely in unison to achieve the highest possible efficiencies.

1. REDUNDANT GAS VALVE

2. MONOPORT INSHOT BURNERS

3. ALUMINIZED, PRIMARY HEAT
   EXCHANGER

4. SECONDARY CONDENSING
   HEAT EXCHANGER

5. INDUCED DRAFT FAN

6. PVC VENT OUTLET

7. CONDENSATE DRAIN TRAP

8. MULTISPEED DIRECT-DRIVE
   MOTOR

FIGURE 12–15   Exposed view of condensing-type H.E. gas-fired furnace. (Courtesy of Bryant Air Conditioning.)

Sequence of operation (combustion)   Refer to Figure 12–17. As the furnace is firing, air is drawn through the combustion supply air tube (A) into the combustion chamber. The chamber is sealed (in fact, must be sealed) and operates at a slight negative pressure. A baffle ensures that each burner receives an adequate share of both primary and secondary combustion air. The ratio of gas to primary air is controlled by the conventional method of slotted shutters (B) between the gas orifice and burner tube venturi. The wider the shutter is opened, the greater the proportion of the mixture will be air. Each burner fires into a cell of the heat exchanger at an input of 20,000 or 25,000 Btuh, depending on the capacity of the furnace. This is the primary heat exchanger (C) and is fabricated of aluminized steel, utilizing the weldless, one-piece process of construction. The operation of the furnace at this point is essentially the same as that of a conventional furnace. Airflow across the exchanger takes heat to the conditioned space, and the combustion products exit the main exchanger into the collector (D) through a series of baffles. These baffles

FIGURE 12–16   Cutaway view of condensing-type H.E. gas-fired furnace. (Courtesy of The Trane Company Unitary Products Group.)

slow the exit of the combustion gases so that more heat is drawn from them before they leave the primary heat exchanger.

The similarity in operation between a standard furnace and a condensing furnace ends here. The exiting flue gases would leave the conventional furnace and go up the flue at a temperature of 350 to 550°F, wasting a significant amount of heat. The condensing gas furnace utilizes this heat by routing the combustion gases to the secondary heat exchanger.

This secondary exchanger (E) removes heat from the gases, but also takes latent heat from the water vapor in the combustion products. This causes the water vapor to condense, hence the term *condensing furnace* and the need for a drainage system. The liquids that condense in the secondary exchanger are not all as harmless as water. Several dilute, but powerful acids are also produced. This is the reason for the use of 29–4C stainless and high-temperature plastics in all areas of the furnace that are exposed to condensed combustion products. Even though these materials are expensive to buy and manufacture, they are essential to long product life and to the furnace's safety and reliability.

The combustion products now have little heat left in them. The remaining liquids from condensation are drained from the secondary exchanger to the drain

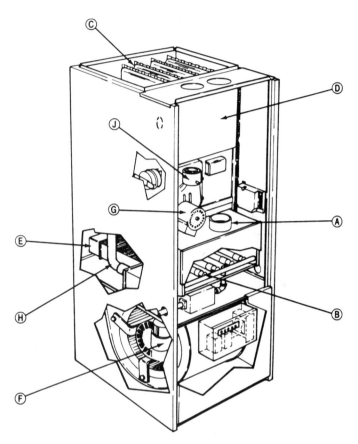

FIGURE 12–17 Cutaway view of condensing high efficiency gas-fired furnace. (Courtesy of ARCOAIRE, Inter-City Products Corporation, USA.)

trap/collector (F). The cooled (140 to 200°F) gases are drawn to the induced draft combustion blower (Power Ventor) (G) via a discharge tube (H) and through a restrictor. The restrictor controls the volume of gases drawn through the entire combustion system. Any remaining liquids are routed from the combustion blower to the drain trap/collector and drained from there to an external drain. The remaining gases exit the furnace through the vent pipe (J) to the outdoors.

Burners and burner orifices   A slotted-tube burner is used in this furnace. These burners have certain flame requirements. Burner flame should run the length of the tube and be 3 to 4 in. in height. If the flame should lift from the burner, turn orange in color, or start rolling out from under the flash burner access shield after ignition, an adjustment is necessary or the heat exchanger needs to be inspected and possibly cleaned. Checking the burner flame should give an indication of the need for further inspection (see Figures 12–18 and 12–19).

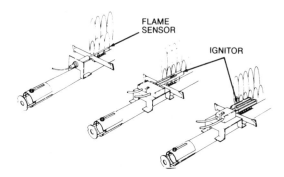

FiGURE 12–18   Slotted burners. (Courtesy of Carrier Corporation.)

Gas valve   The control used on this furnace is a redundant combination gas valve. This design provides a manual main valve, servo-regulated automatic main diaphragm valve, plus the added safety of an additional in-line electromechanical operated redundant valve (see Figure 12–20).

Pressure regulator   A pressure tap has been provided on the gas valve (see Figure 12–20). Attach a pressure gauge fitting to this tap and check the outlet pressure. The pressure should be set as indicated on the rating plate. To adjust the pressure regulator, remove the cap covering the pressure-regulator-adjusting screw. On valves with more than one adjusting screw, adjust only the screw marked "HI." Turn the adjusting screw out (counterclockwise) to decrease the pressure, and in (clockwise) to increase the pressure. Reinstall the cap securely.

Sequence of operation (general)   Let's follow the operation of the furnace through a demand for heat (refer to Figures 12–21 and 12–22). The room thermostat calls for heat, closing a circuit between terminals R and W. Inside the control center, voltage is applied to the heat relay coil (P), completing the W and C low-voltage circuit. The contacts close and supply line voltage to the induced draft motor.

FIGURE 12–19   Burner assembly. (Courtesy of ARCOAIRE, Inter-City Products Corporation, USA.)

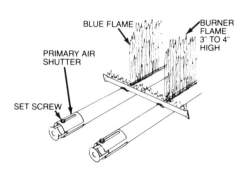

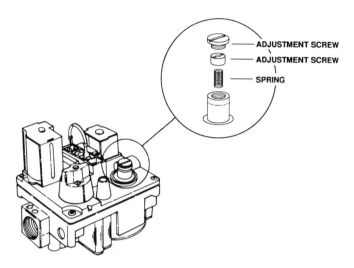

FIGURE 12–20   Redundant gas valve. (Courtesy of ARCOAIRE Inter-City Products Corporation, USA.)

The pressure switch (D) proves that the combustion blower is operating and closes on a rise in pressure differential across the combustion blower. This sends 24 V to the normally closed limit switch of the combination fan and limit control (E). If the limit is closed, voltage becomes available to a condensate safety sensor (G). This sensor ensures that the secondary heat exchanger is not filled with condensate and that the fresh air intake and vent pipes are not blocked. In effect, it verifies airflow through the entire combustion system of the furnace.

Sequence of operation (electrical)   Refer to Figures 12–21 and 12–22. The furnace requires an external 115-V power source of the ampacity stated on the nameplate. A junction box (F) for connection to line voltage is located at the upper left-hand front corner of the furnace. Line voltage is converted to 24-V control voltage by the furnace's transformer (A), located in the control center in the blower compartment. Neither line or control voltage will be available unless the door interlock switch (B) is closed.

To operate the furnace as a heating unit only, a 24-V thermostat is the only external control required. This thermostat would be connected to the R and W terminals of the terminal strip (C). For operation with a heating and cooling unit or if continuous indoor blower operation is required, a combination heating/cooling thermostat will be required. In this application R to G will energize the blower at high speed.

Terminal C is 24-V common; clock-type thermostats and an air-conditioning unit would require use of terminal C. Terminal Y is simply a binding post to connect the Y lead from the thermostat to the Y lead of the condensing unit and is not electrically connected to the furnace controls in any way. Under no circumstances

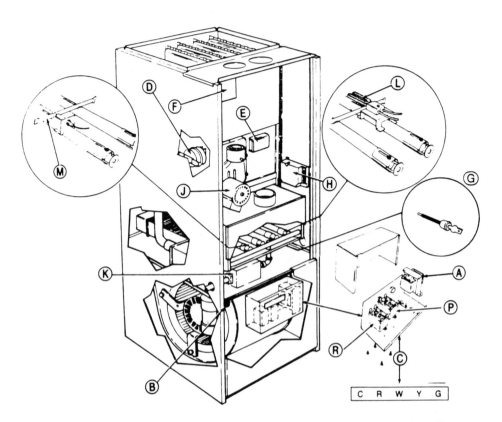

FIGURE 12–21 Exploded view of HEF. (Courtesy of ARCOAIRE, Inter-City Products Corporation, USA.)

should the R and C terminals be connected. Such action constitutes abuse and will damage the furnace controls. This damage will render the furnace transformer inoperable and will not be covered under warranty. The furnace transformer is capable of handling all internal furnace functions, any recommended thermostat and any control voltage requirements of any matching approved split system air-conditioning unit or heat pump. Heat pumps require the application of an "add-on" kit to interlock controls.

When this series of controls are all closed (the entire sequence occurs in a few seconds), 24 V is available to the ignition module (H). At this time the module will start the ignition sequence. The module will require a 30-second prepurge from the time it receives power. This means that the combustion blower (J) will clear both heat exchangers and vent pipes of all gases (other than fresh air) before ignition can take place. This is extremely important. Igniting residual combustible vapors in a sealed combustion system can cause severe equipment damage.

When the prepurge cycle is complete, the ignition module (H) closes a 115-V circuit to the ignitor (L). The module will allow approximately 15 seconds for the

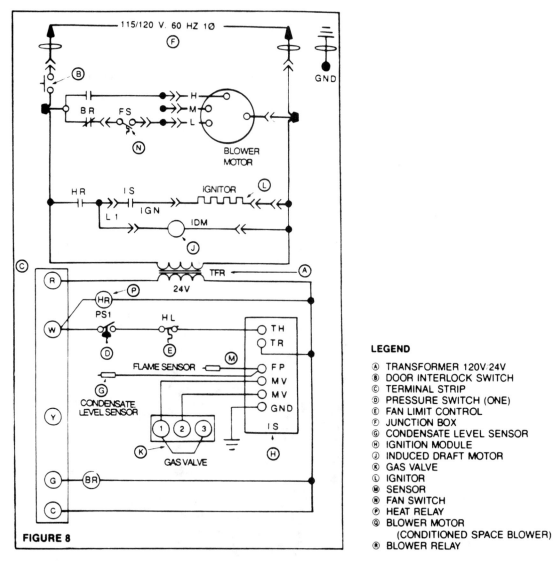

FIGURE 12–22   HEF wiring diagram, with legend. (Courtesy of ARCOAIRE, Inter-City Products Corporation, USA.)

ignitor to warm up. The ignitor will now be glowing almost white-hot over the right-hand burner. The gas valve (K) will receive 24 V from the module.

Ignition occurs   The sensor M, located over the left-hand burner, must sense flame in 7 seconds or less; if it does not, the module will shut the gas valve off and retry the ignition sequence twice more before locking out. As the heat exchangers begin to heat up, the fan switch of the fan and limit control (N) will close, causing the main blower to run at heating speed (selected by the normally closed contacts of the blower relay), bringing air from the conditioned space across the secondary heat exchanger and the primary heat exchanger, then returning it to the conditioned space.

When the space thermostat is satisfied and the call for heat ends, the 24-V supply will be interrupted to terminal W. The combustion blower will stop and the gas valve closes. The burner will extinguish. The main blower will continue to run until the heat exchangers cool off and the fan switch of the fan and limit control opens. The furnace remains in this condition until there is another demand for heat.

Pulse Design

The essential parts of the pulse combustion unit and its sequence of operation are shown in Figures 12–23 and 12–24. Combustion takes place in a finned, cast-iron chamber. Note in the lower part of this chamber the gas intake, the air intake, the spark plug ignition, and the flame sensor. At the time of initial combustion the spark plug ignites the gas-air mixture. The pressure in the chamber following combustion closes the

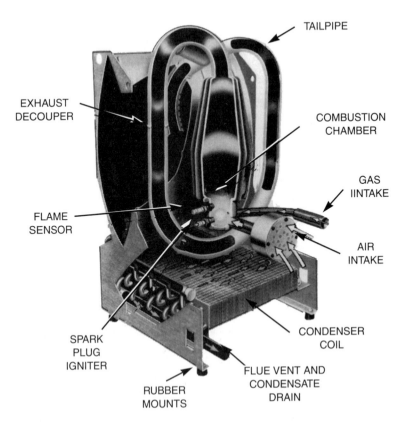

FIGURE 12–23   Cutaway view of the pulse heat exchanger. (Courtesy of Lennox Industries, Inc.)

HOW A PULSE FURNACE WORKS:

1 The heating process begins as air and gas enter the combustion chamber and mix near the spark igniter.

2 A spark creates initial combustion, similar to the way a spark plug works in your car. This causes a pressure build-up inside the combustion chamber.

3 The internal pressure relieves itself by forcing the products of combustion down a tailpipe and venting them outdoors.

4 As the combustion chamber empties, it creates a vacuum that prepares it for the next ignition. At the same instant, pressure "pulses" back from the end of the tailpipe.

5 The "pulse" returning from the tailpipe re-enters the combustion chamber, causing the new gas/air mixture in the chamber to ignite. As a result, the heating cycle is repeated at a rate of 60 to 70 times per second.

FIGURE 12–24   Sequence of pulse ignition cycle. (Courtesy of Lennox Industries, Inc.)

229

gas and air intakes. The pressure buildup also forces the hot gases out of the combustion chamber, through the tailpipe, into the heat-exchanger exhaust decoupler, and into the heat exchanger coil. As the chamber empties after combustion, its pressure becomes negative, drawing in a new supply of gas and air for the next pulse of combustion. The flame remnants of the previous combustion ignite the new gas-air mixtures and the cycle continues. Once combustion is started the purge fan and the spark ignitor are shut off. These pulse cycles occur about 60 to 70 times a second.

The sequence of operation of the pulse furnace is as follows. When the room thermostat calls for heat it initiates the operation of the purge fan, which runs for 34 seconds. This is followed by the turning on of the ignition and the opening of the gas valve. The flame sensor provides proof of ignition and de-energizes the purge fan and spark ignition.

When the thermostat is satisfied, the gas valve closes and the purge fan is turned on for 34 seconds. The furnace continues to operate until the temperature in the plenum reaches 90°F. In case the flame is lost before the thermostat is satisfied, the flame sensor will try to reignite the gas-air mixture three or five times before locking out. Should there be either a loss of intake gas or air, the furnace will shut down automatically.

Note that combustion air is piped with the same PVC pipe as used for the exhaust gases. The range of the condensate liquids is from a pH of 4.0 to 6.0, which permits it to be drained into city sewers or septic tanks. The combustion mixture of gas and air are preset at the factory. No field adjustments are necessary.

COMPUTERIZED CONTROL OF HIGH-EFFICIENCY FURNACES

Many features have been added to available furnaces as a result of the application of high technology. Here we describe the use of a computerized control system for the high-efficiency furnace. It is attractive from the standpoint of saving energy, improving occupant comfort level and lowering the noise level of the installed equipment.

The furnace described has a 93.5 annual fuel utilization efficiency (AFUE). As an example of the energy it saves, assuming that it is installed in Cleveland, Ohio, the saving in a single heating season would be $230 on the gas bill and $90 on the electric bill as compared to a standard 78% AFUE furnace.

Primarily, we will review the control system, but let us first take a look at the major components, particularly those that differ from other high-efficiency furnaces. Figure 12–25 is a cutaway view of this furnace, showing the major components. Figure 12–26 shows the variable-speed inducer fan at (2) and its speed controller (3). Figure 12–27 shows the high-pressure switch at (1) and the low-pressure switch at (2), which monitor combustion air flow during high and low fire operation, respectively.

Figure 12–28 shows the exterior of the miniature computer or microprocessor. It adjusts the burner input and the furnace blower speed to match the load. Figure 12–29 shows a view of the circuit board, with the cover removed. Figure 12–30 shows the LED indicator lights that signal fault codes to guide the service technician.

Figure 12–31 shows the Personality Plug, which lets the microprocessor know the size of the furnace to which it is connected. Figure 12–32 shows a series of switches

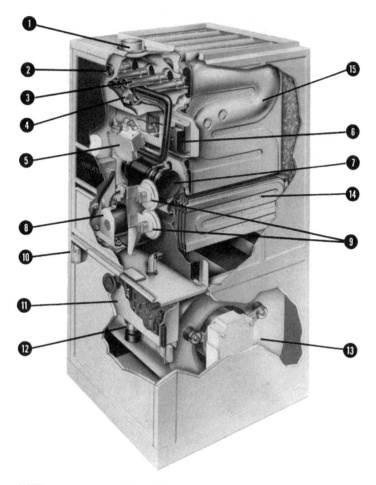

NOTE: The 58SXB Furnace is factory built for use with natural gas. The furnace can be field-conve
for propane gas with a factory-authorized and listed accessory conversion kit.

NOTE: Control location and actual controls may be different than shown above.

1	Combustion-Air Pipe Connection	**9**	Pressure Switches
2	Sight Glass	**10**	Blower Door Safety Switch
3	Burner Assembly	**11**	Control Box
4	Pilot	**12**	Condensate Trap
5	Two-Stage Gas Valve	**13**	Blower Assembly With Variable-Spe Motor
6	Electronic Spark Ignition System		
7	Vent Pipe Connection	**14**	Secondary Heat Exchanger
8	Variable Speed Inducer Motor	**15**	Primary Heat Exchanger

FIGURE 12–25   Cutaway view of typical HEF with computerized control. (Courtesy of Carrier Corporation.)

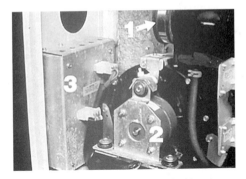

FIGURE 12–26 Variable-speed condenser fan. (Courtesy of Carrier Corporation.)

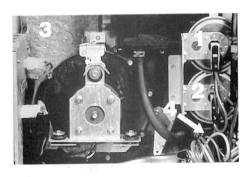

FIGURE 12–27 High/low pressure switch. (Courtesy of Carrier Corporation.)

FIGURE 12–28 Computer or microprocessor. (Courtesy of Carrier Corporation.)

FIGURE 12–29 Circuit board. (Courtesy of Carrier Corporation.)

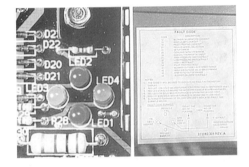

FIGURE 12–30 LED indicator lights. (Courtesy of Carrier Corporation.)

FIGURE 12–31 Personality Plug. (Courtesy of Carrier Corporation.)

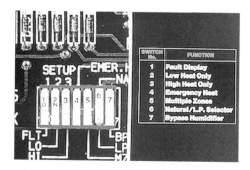

FIGURE 12–32   Computer switches. (Courtesy of Carrier Corporation.)

FIGURE 12–33   Air flow switch. (Courtesy of Carrier Corporation.)

that permit the service technician to supply input to the computer to check system operation. Figure 12–33 shows the rotary switch used in adjusting the airflow on cooling. At 400 cfm per ton, a 2-ton system requires 800 cfm. This would be accomplished by setting the switch on "2." Figure 12–34 shows the rotary control switch that is used to adjust the delay in the shutdown of the blower when there is a call for the heating mode. The information that follows shows various diagrams of the control arrangement and the sequence of operation.

Power supplied (Figure 12–35)   On a call for heat, the blower door switch must be closed (1). Line voltage power is supplied to the inducer motor controller (PCB1) and the blower motor controller (PCB2). Power is also applied to the transformer (2), which supplies low-voltage power to the microprocessor board (PCB3) and to the R terminal of the thermostat connection.

Call for heat (Figures 12–36 and 12–37)   Flow sensing switches are energized (Figure 12–36). On a call for heat the R and W contacts on the thermostat close (1), supplying low-voltage power to the low- and high-flow sensing pressure switches (2), normally closed. The microprocessor signals the inducer motor to start (Figure 12–37), gradually bringing it up to speed.

FIGURE 12–34   Blower control switch. (Courtesy of Carrier Corporation.)

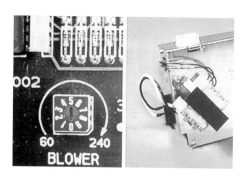

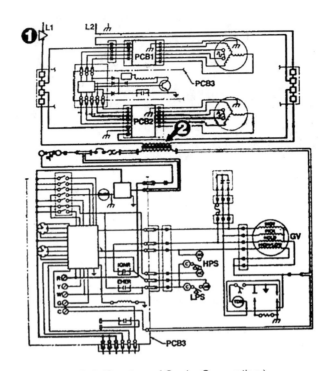

FIGURE 12–35 Power supplied. (Courtesy of Carrier Corporation.)

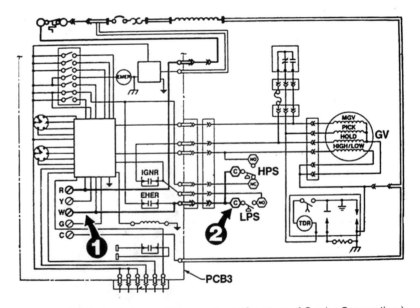

FIGURE 12–36 Call for heat, flow switch energized. (Courtesy of Carrier Corporation.)

FIGURE 12–37 Microprocessor signals inducer motor to start. (Courtesy of Carrier Corporation.)

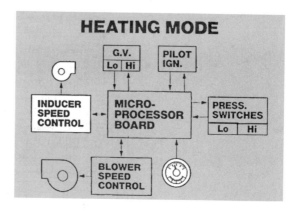

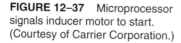

Inducer fan in operation (Figure 12–38) With the inducer fan in operation, the normally open contacts on the flow sensing switches close (1), supplying power to the ignition relay contacts (2) and the high-fire solenoid in the gas valve (3). A signal is also sent to the microprocessor (4) to indicate that these actions have taken place.

Ignition relay energized (Figure 12–39) After the flow sensing switch is made for 10 seconds, the microprocessor energizes the ignition relay (1). This supplies power to the holding coil of the gas valve. At the same time, the pick coil of the gas valve and the time delay circuit of the spark generator are energized (2), through the normally closed contacts of the pilot assembly (3).

Gas flows to pilot (Figure 12–40) With the pick coil energized, gas flows to the pilot. After 10 seconds the time delay circuit in the spark generator is energized (1), causing the pilot to be lighted by a spark.

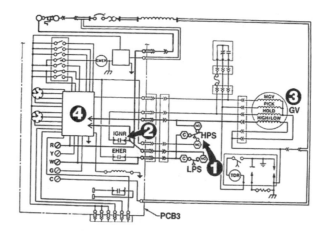

FIGURE 12–38 Inducer fan operation. (Courtesy of Carrier Corporation.)

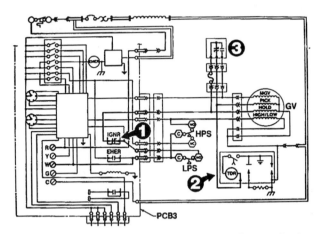

FIGURE 12–39   Ignition relay energized. (Courtesy of Carrier Corporation.)

Main gas valve energized (Figure 12–41)   Heat from the pilot flame will cause the normally open contacts to close and the normally closed contacts to open on the pilot assembly (1). This de-energizes the pick coil on the gas valve (2), energizes the main gas valve, and sends a flame-proving signal to the microprocessor (3). The pilot flame then ignites the main burners in the high-fire mode.

Heating mode (Figures 12–42 to 12–44)   For the first 35 seconds of high-fire operation the blower does not run (Figure 12–42). This allows the heat exchanger to increase rapidly in temperature. This is controlled by the computer. At the end of the 35–second period, the blower is started at low speed for 20 seconds (Figure 12–43).

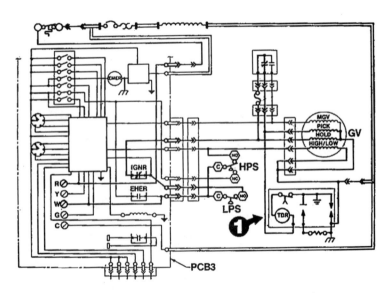

FIGURE 12–40   Gas flowing to pilot. (Courtesy of Carrier Corporation.)

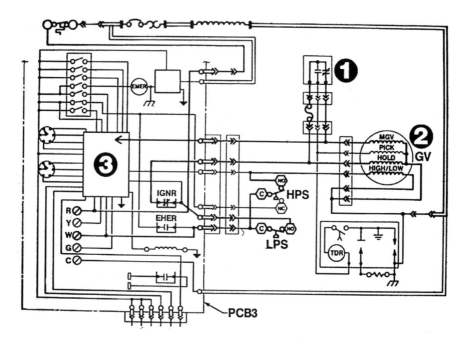

FIGURE 12–41   Main gas valve energized. (Courtesy of Carrier Corporation.)

The computer then goes through a brief calibration procedure. It senses the condition of the air supply system, calculates the rev/min value of the blower that is necessary to produce the required temperature rise across the heat exchangers, and adjusts the blower speed accordingly.

After 1 min., which includes the high-fire operation and the calculation period, the burner switches to low fire (Figure 12–44). In this initial cycle the unit will operate for 6 min. Then, if the thermostat is not satisfied, the system will switch to high fire until the thermostat is satisfied. Any time there is an interruption of power the system will restart in the initial cycle condition. After the initial cycle the operation of the unit will be controlled by the computer in accordance with inside and outside conditions.

Emergency heat (Figures 12–45 and 12–46)   In the emergency heat mode the burner always operates at high fire. The blower operates at a high speed, higher than the air-conditioning speed (Figure 12–45). The setup switch (1) is closed when emergency heat is selected. On a call for heat the R-W circuit is energized, which causes the emergency heat relay (2) to energize. The emergency heat relay contacts close, starting the inducer motor and the blower motor. When the burners are lighted (Figure 12–46), low- and high-flow sensing switches close (1). Power is supplied to the ignition relay (2), gas valve, and time delay of the spark generator. A holding path for the emergency heat relay is established (3). The sequence of operation that follows is similar to normal operation except that the burner operates only in the high-fire mode and the blower only at high

FIGURE 12–42   Heating mode, first 35 seconds. (Courtesy of Carrier Corporation.)

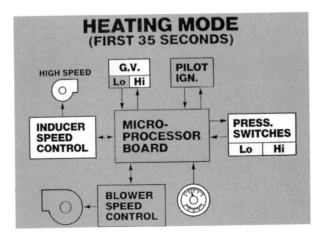

FIGURE 12–43   Heating mode, blower energized. (Courtesy of Carrier Corporation.)

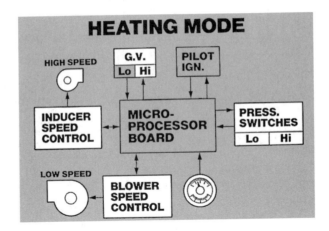

FIGURE 12–44   Heating mode, burner switches to low fire. (Courtesy of Carrier Corporation.)

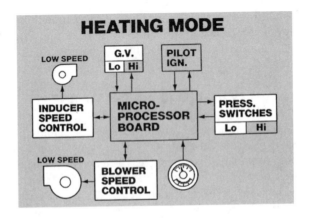

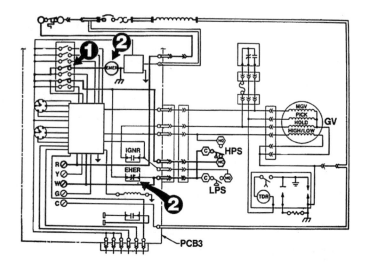

FIGURE 12–45   Emergency heat relay energized. (Courtesy of Carrier Corporation.)

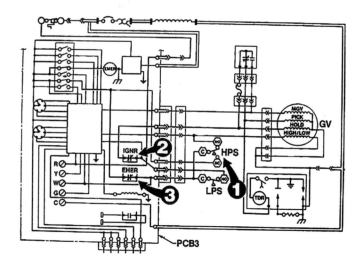

FIGURE 12–46   Emergency heat, burners energized. (Courtesy of Carrier Corporation.)

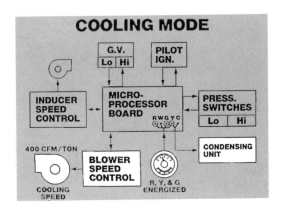

FIGURE 12–47 Microprocessor in cooling mode. (Courtesy of Carrier Corporation.)

speed. The unit should be operated in the emergency heat mode only for relatively short periods of time.

Cooling mode (Figure 12–47) On a call for cooling, the R-Y circuit is energized, starting the outdoor condensing unit. The computer starts the blower at low speed for 20 seconds and then goes through a brief calculation period and sets the rev/min value of the blower at a speed equivalent to 400 cfm per ton.

Sequence of operation of a White Rodgers 50A50 furnace control (Figures 12–48 and 12–49)

1. Line voltage feeds through the door switch when access panel is in place.
2. The transformer provides 24 volts across (TH) and (TR).
3. Twenty-four volts is brought to the (R) terminal on the thermostat.
4. On a call for heat the thermostat closes from (R) to (W) and completes a circuit on the 50A50 control causing the (K4) contacts to close.
5. 115 volts will energize the inducer motor from the (IND) and (IND/N) terminals.
6. The pressure switch will close, proving the operation of the inducer motor. This prepurge will last 30 seconds.
7. During the 30 seconds, the control does a self-test, making sure the flame roll out switch and the limit control are in the closed position.
8. Switch (K6), located inside of the control, will complete the circuit to the hot surface igniter across terminals (IGN) and (IGN/N) for 17 seconds.
9. After the 17 seconds of ignition, (K7) and (K8) will close energizing the main gas valve. The igniter will remain energized 4 seconds after the main gas valve is energized.
10. The main gas is proved by a flame rectification system that is built into the 50A50 control.
    (If the flame is not proven after 7 seconds, the main gas valve is de-energized and is returned to the prepurge/trial for ignition sequence for 6 times, before locking out completely.)
11. When the main valve is energized, this will start the "time on" delay for the blower circuit. The position of the dip switches (see Figure 12-50), located on the

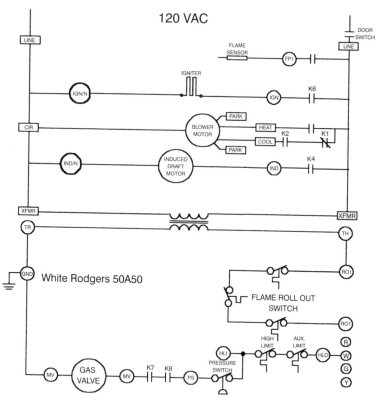

FIGURE 12–48   Schematic of the White Rodgers (50A50) furnace control. (Courtesy of White Rodgers Division of Emerson Electric Co.)

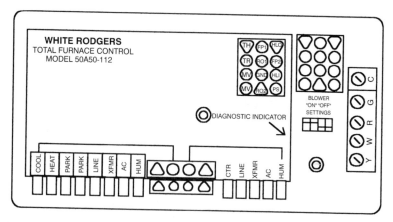

FIGURE 12–49   A White Rodgers (50A50) furnace control. (Courtesy of White Rodgers Division of Emerson Electric Co.)

HEAT "ON" DELAY		
SW1	SW2	(SEC)
OFF	OFF	15
OFF	ON	30
ON	OFF	45
ON	ON	60

HEAT "OFF" DELAY		
SW3	SW4	(SEC)
ON	ON	60
OFF	ON	90
ON	OFF	120
OFF	OFF	180

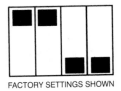

FACTORY SETTINGS SHOWN

FIGURE 12–50   Fan "On/Off" delay settings for the 50A50 control. (Courtesy of White Rodgers Division of Emerson Electric Co.)

50A50 control, will determine the time that the fan is energized. Time on settings are 15, 30, 45, or 60 seconds.

12. When the blower is energized the (EAC) and the (HUM) terminals bring 115 volts to the electronic air cleaner and the humidifier circuits.

13. When the thermostat is satisfied, 24-volt supply is interrupted to the gas valve circuit. This causes the gas valve to close and (K4) contacts to open, de-energizing the inducer motor.

14. The "time off" delay begins on the blower motor circuit to de-energize the motor for the off cycle. The position of the dip switches, located on the 50A50 control, will determine the time that the fan is de-energized. Time off settings are 60, 90, 120, and 180 seconds.

SEQUENCE OF OPERATION OF A HONEYWELL SV9500/SV9600 SMART VALVE SYSTEM (Figure 12–51)

1. Line voltage is brought to terminals (S1) and (N1) on the circuit board. This will energize the 120-volt primary side of the transformer from terminals (S2) and (N4).

2. Twenty-four volts is brought from the transformer's secondary side to terminals (X) and (C) on the ST9120 circuit board and to the circuit board located in the SV9500/SV9600 gas valve.

3. Twenty-four volts is brought from the (R) terminal on the ST9120 circuit board to the (R) terminal on the thermostat.

4. On a call for heat the thermostat closes from (R) to (W). This will cause the combustion motor to be energized by 120 volts from terminals (D1) and (N3) on the ST9120 circuit board.

5. The pressure switch closes, completing a circuit to a terminal located on the SV9500/SV9600 gas valve. This will start a self-check to monitor the system for a flame signal for 2 seconds. If a pilot flame is detected, the ST9120 electronic fan circuit will energize, causing the indoor blower to cycle on. At the same time this will cause the pilot and igniter to remain de-energized.

6. If a pilot flame is not detected, the pilot igniter will be energized with 24 volts for 5 seconds and then the pilot valve will open.

7. The pilot will light and the SV9500/SV9600 gas valve will sense a .2 micro amp (minimum) signal from the flame sensor. If the pilot flame is not sensed, the igniter will stay on and the pilot valve will remain open until a flame is sensed or the thermostat is satisfied. This system does not lock out.

8. After the pilot flame is sensed, the igniter will de-energize, the SV9500/SV9600 main gas valve will open and the pilot will light the main burners. This will also energize an electronic fan timer output signal from the SV9500/SV9600 to the ST9120 circuit board.

9. This is the "ON" delay time. The blower will energize after a fixed 60 seconds or an adjustable 30 or 60 second delay time.

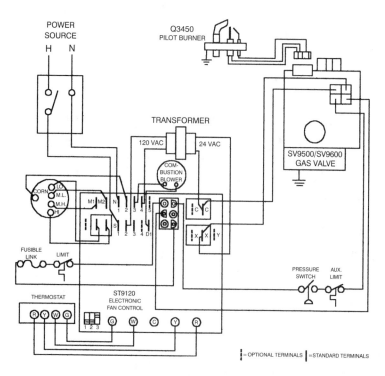

FIGURE 12–51   A diagram of the Honeywell Smart Value System. (Courtesy of Honeywell Inc.)

10. Once the thermostat is satisfied, the (R) and (W) contacts open, ending a call for heat. This will cause the main and pilot gas valves to close immediately and de-energize the electronic fan timer output signal. This is the "OFF" delay time and the blower will de-energize after a preselected time of 60, 90, 120, or 150 seconds.

UNIQUE CONTROL FUNCTIONS OF THE ST9120 FAN CONTROL BOARD

1. Energizing the (G) terminal by setting the thermostat to "Fan On" will cause the blower to run on the heating speed.
2. On the ST9120G fan control board, a continuous fan terminal is used if constant fan circulation is desired. A speed other than the "Heat" or "Cool" speed can be connected to this terminal. Only when the thermostat is in the "Off" position and the fan selector switch is in the "Auto" position, will the terminal be energized to operate the fan continuously on the selected speed. Do not mistake this feature for the "Fan On" feature used at the thermostat's subbase.
3. Energizing the (Y) and (G) terminals together will cause the blower to run in the cooling speed. It is important to connect the yellow wire from the thermostat to the (Y) terminal on the ST9120 circuit board or the blower will run in the heating speed when the system is in the cooling cycle.
4. The cooling speed will be delayed before and after each cycle for a fixed delay of 30 seconds.
5. If the system utilizes a humidifier, the HUM terminals are used in conjunction with the (D1) terminal to energize a humidifier when the combustion motor is energized.

STUDY QUESTIONS

Answers to the study questions may be found in the sections noted in brackets.

12–1. Describe the control components for a 78% AFUE furnace. *[Components]*

12–2. What parts are energized when a 78% AFUE furnace is ready to start? *[Ready to Start]*

12–3. When a 78% furnace calls for heat, what part is energized first? *[Call for Heat]*

12–4. What is the normal number of pulses per second for a pulse furnace? *[Pulse Design]*

12–5. What is the pH range for the condensing liquid on a HEF? *[Pulse Design]*

12–6. Name four characteristics of HEFs. *[Characteristics of HEFs]*

12–7. Describe the piping used for combustion air on a HEF. *[Air for Combustion]*

12–8. How many speeds has the inducer motor on a computerized HEF? *[Computerized Control]*

12–9. What is the function of the computer on a HEF? *[Computerized Control]*

12–10. Describe the action that takes place on a computerized HEF when calling for emergency heat. *[Computerized Control]*

13

Components of Oil-Burning Furnaces

OBJECTIVES

After studying this chapter, the student will be able to:

- Identify the components of an oil burner
- Adjust an oil burner for best performance
- Provide service and maintenance for an oil burner

OIL-BURNING UNITS

Oil must be vaporized to burn. There are two ways to vaporize oil:

1. *By heat alone.* For example, oil can be vaporized by heating an iron pot containing oil and igniting it with a flare or spark.
2. *By atomization and heating.* Oil is vaporized by forcing it under pressure through an orifice, causing it to break up into small droplets. The atomized oil is then ignited by an electric spark.

TYPES OF BURNERS

There are two types of atomizing oil burners:

1. Low pressure
2. High pressure

Low-Pressure Burner

In a low-pressure gun burner (Figure 13–1), oil and primary air are mixed prior to being forced through an orifice or nozzle. A pressure of 1 to 15 psig on the mixture, plus the action of the orifice, causes atomization of the oil. Secondary air is drawn into the spray mixture after it is released from the nozzle. Electric spark ignition is used to light the combustible mixture.

Although the low-pressure burner has achieved some success, it has been replaced to a great extent by the high-pressure burner. Higher pressure produces better atomization and high efficiencies.

High-Pressure Burner

A high-pressure gun burner (Figure 13–2), forces oil at 100 psig pressure through the nozzle, breaking the oil into fine, mistlike droplets. Some models require operating oil pump pressures in the 140–200 psig range. The atomized oil spray creates a low-pressure area into which the combustion air flows. Combustion air is supplied by a fan through vanes, creating turbulence and complete mixing action.

The high-pressure gun burner is the most popular domestic burner. It is simple in construction, relatively easy to maintain, and efficient in operation. Therefore, the balance of this unit concentrates exclusively on providing information relative to the high-pressure burner.

HIGH-PRESSURE BURNER COMPONENTS

The high-pressure oil burner is actually an assembled unit. The component parts are made by a few well-known manufacturers. The parts are mass-produced, low in cost, and readily available for servicing requirements.

FIGURE 13–1   Low-pressure gun-type oil burner. (Courtesy of Carrier Corporation.)

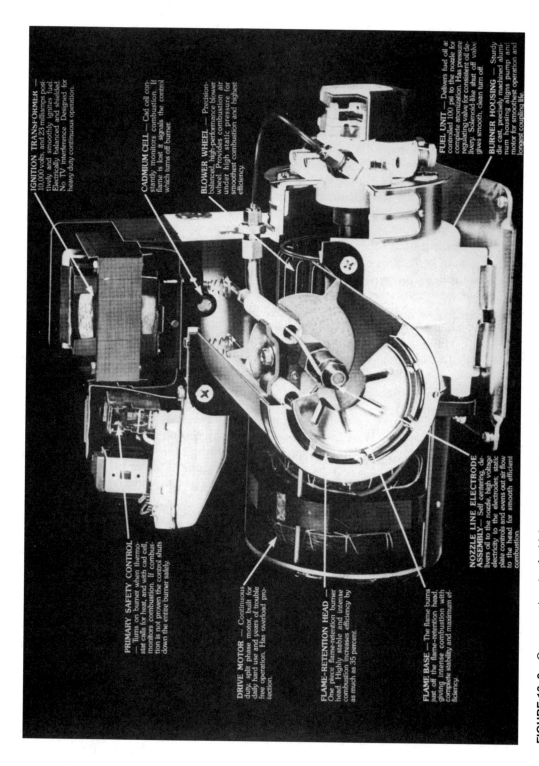

IGNITION TRANSFORMER — 10,000 volts, and 23 milliamps positively and smoothly ignites fuel. Electrically balanced and shielded. No TV interference. Designed for heavy duty continuous operation.

CADMIUM CELL — Cad cell constantly monitors combustion. If flame is lost it signals the control which turns off burner.

BLOWER WHEEL — Precision balanced, high-performance blower wheel. Provides combustion air under high static pressure for smoothest combustion and highest efficiency.

FUEL UNIT — Delivers fuel oil at controlled 100 psi to the nozzle for complete atomization. Has pressure regulating valve for consistent oil delivery. Solenoid-like shut off valve gives smooth, clean turn off.

BURNER HOUSING — Sturdy die cast, precisely machined aluminum housing aligns pump and motor for smoothest operation and longest coupling life.

PRIMARY SAFETY CONTROL — Turns on burner when thermostat calls for heat, and with cad cell, monitors combustion. If combustion is not proven the control shuts down the entire burner safely.

DRIVE MOTOR — Continuous duty, split phase motor, built for daily hard use and years of trouble free operation. Has overload protection.

FLAME-RETENTION HEAD — One piece flame-retention burner head. Highly stable and intense combustion increases efficiency by as much as 35 percent.

FLAME BASE — The flame burns just off the flame-retention head, giving intense combustion with complete stability and maximum efficiency.

NOZZLE LINE ELECTRODE ASSEMBLY — Self centering, delivers oil to the nozzle, high voltage electricity to the electrodes, static plate controls and evens out air flow to the head for smooth efficient combustion.

FIGURE 13–2 Component parts of a high-pressure oil burner. (Courtesy of R.W. Beckett Corporation.)

247

Power Assembly

The power assembly consists of the motor, fan, and fuel pump. The nozzle assembly consists of the nozzle, the electrodes, and parts related to the oil-air mixing action. The ignition system consists of the transformer and electrical parts. The motor drives the fan and fuel pump. The fan forces air through the blast tube to provide combustion air for the atomized oil. The fuel pump draws oil from the storage tank and delivers it to the nozzle.

The oil-air mixture is ignited by an electric spark formed between two properly positioned electrodes in the nozzle assembly. The spark is created by a transformer that increases the 120-V primary power supply to 10,000-V secondary supply to form a low-current spark arc.

Fuel pumps   All fuel pumps are of the rotary type, using cams, gears, or a combination of both. The principal parts of the fuel pump in addition to the gears are the shaft seal, the pressure-regulating valve, and the automatic cutoff valve. The shaft seal is necessary, since the pump is driven by an external source of power. The pressure-regulating valve has an adjustable spring that permits regulation of the oil pressure. The pump actually delivers more oil than the burner can use. The excess oil is dumped back into the supply line or returns to the tank. All pumps also have an adjustment screw for regulating the pressure of the oil delivered to the nozzle. The automatic cutoff valve stops the flow of oil as soon as the pressure drops. Thus, when the burner is stopped, the oil is quickly cut off to the nozzle to prevent oil dripping into the combustion chamber.

Fuel oil pumps are designed for single-stage or two-stage operation (Figure 13–3). The single-stage unit is used where the supply of oil is above the burner and the oil flows to the pump by gravity. The two-stage unit is used where the storage tank is below the burner. The first stage is used to draw the oil to the pump. The second stage is used to provide the pressure required by the nozzle. The suction on the pump should not exceed a 15-in. vacuum.

Piping connections to the fuel pump are of two types: single-pipe and two-pipe. Installation instructions for both are shown in Figure 13–4. Various pump models are made by a number of manufacturers. Some pumps have clockwise rotation; some have counterclockwise rotation. It is important when changing a pump to use an identical replacement, since oil pumps vary in the location of connections. Always refer to the manufacturer's information and specification sheets for connection details.

Test Procedure for Oil Pumps   A simplified test procedure for oil burner pumps is shown in Figure 13–5. Note that the connections shown are for a specific model pump. Similar connections can be made to other models by referring to the manufacturer's connection details on the specification sheets.

Motor   The motor supplies power to rotate the pump and fan. Usually, a split-phase motor (with a start and run winding) is used (Figure 13–6). This type of motor provides enough torque (starting power) to move the connected components. In the event

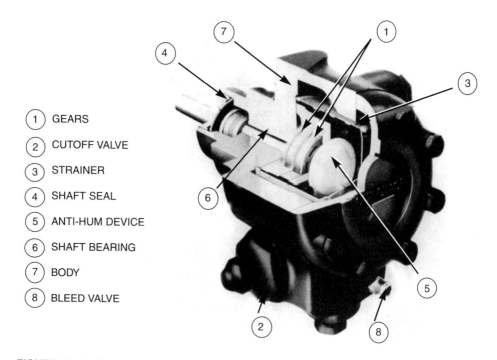

1. GEARS
2. CUTOFF VALVE
3. STRAINER
4. SHAFT SEAL
5. ANTI-HUM DEVICE
6. SHAFT BEARING
7. BODY
8. BLEED VALVE

FIGURE 13–3   Two-stage oil pump. (Courtesy of Sundstrand Hydraulics, Inc.)

that a motor fails, it must be replaced by substituting one with the same horsepower, direction of rotation, mounting dimension, revolutions per minute, shaft length, and shaft diameter.

Multiblade fan and air shutters   The multiblade (squirrel cage) centrifugal fan delivers air for combustion. It is enclosed within the fan housing. The inlet to the fan has an adjustable opening so that the amount of air volume handled by the fan can be manually controlled. The outlet of the fan delivers the combustion air through the blast tube of the burner (see Figure 13–2).

Shaft coupling   The shaft coupling connects the motor to the fuel pump (see Figure 13–7). This coupling:

- Provides alignment between the pump and motor shafts
- Absorbs noise that may be created by the rotating parts
- Is strongly constructed to endure the starting and stopping action of the motor

Static disk, choke and swirl vanes   As shown in Figure 13–8, the static disk, which is located in the center of the draft tube, causes the air from the fan to build up velocity at the inside surface of the tube. The choke is located at the end of the tube and restricts the area, thus further increasing the air velocity. The swirl vanes located near the choke give turbulence to the leaving air, which assists the mixing action.

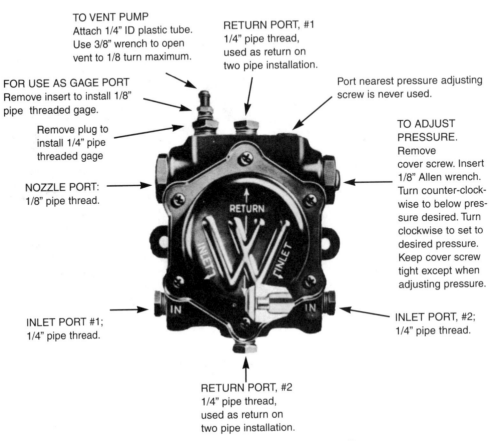

TO VENT PUMP
Attach 1/4" ID plastic tube.
Use 3/8" wrench to open
vent to 1/8 turn maximum.

RETURN PORT, #1
1/4" pipe thread,
used as return on
two pipe installation.

FOR USE AS GAGE PORT
Remove insert to install 1/8"
pipe threaded gage.

Port nearest pressure adjusting
screw is never used.

Remove plug to
install 1/4" pipe
threaded gage

TO ADJUST
PRESSURE.
Remove
cover screw. Insert
1/8" Allen wrench.
Turn counter-clock-
wise to below pres-
sure desired. Turn
clockwise to set to
desired pressure.
Keep cover screw
tight except when
adjusting pressure.

NOZZLE PORT:
1/8" pipe thread.

INLET PORT #1;
1/4" pipe thread.

INLET PORT, #2;
1/4" pipe thread.

RETURN PORT, #2
1/4" pipe thread,
used as return on
two pipe installation.

NOTE: For maximum performance INLET VACUUM,
when measured at unused INLET PORT, should not
exceed 10'' Hg on single stage pumps, and 15'' Hg
on two stage pumps.

SINGLE PIPE INSTALLATION

    Recommended only when bottom of tank is above
fuel unit, unless pump code ends in 15.
1. Remove BYPASS PLUG if installed, through IN-
LET PORT #2.
2. Connect inlet line to preferred INLET PORT.
3. Plug all unused ports securely.
4. Start burner and bleed all air from the system by
opening VENT PLUG. Close VENT securely when
oil flow in-tube is clear.

TWO-PIPE INSTALLATION

1. Insert BYPASS PLUG if not installed, through
INLET PORT #2.
2. Connect inlet line to preferred INLET PORT.
3. Connect return line to preferred RETURN PORT.
4. Plug all unused ports securely.
5. Start burner. Two stage pumps will self-vent. If
single stage and code ends in 3 or 4, bleed all
air from system by opening VENT PLUG. Close
VENT securely when oil flow in tube is clear.

FIGURE 13–4 Oil pump showing connection locations. (Courtesy of Webster Electric Company, Inc.)

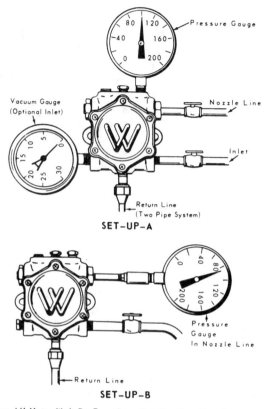

FIGURE 13–5   Test procedure for oil burner pump. (Courtesy of Webster Electric Company, Inc.)

Nozzle Assembly

The nozzle assembly consists of the oil feed line, the nozzle, electrodes, and transformer connections (Figure 13–9). The assembly serves to position the electrodes in respect to the nozzle opening and provides a mounting for the high-potential electrical leads from the transformer. The assembly is located near the end of the blast tube.

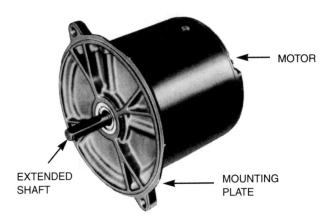

FIGURE 13–6   Oil burner motor. (Courtesy of Essex Group, Controls Division, Steveco Products, Inc.)

Electrode position   The correct position of the electrodes is shown in Figure 13–10. The electrodes must be located out of the oil spray but close enough for the spark to arc into the spray. The spark gap between the electrodes is important. If the electrodes are not centered on the nozzle orifice, the flame will be one-sided and cause carbon to form on the nozzle.

Nozzle   A nozzle construction is shown in Figure 13–11. The purpose of the nozzle is to prepare the oil for mixing with the air. The process is called atomization. Oil first enters the strainer. The strainer has a mesh that is finer in size than the nozzle orifice in order to catch solid particles that could clog the nozzle.

From the strainer, the oil enters slots that direct the oil to the swirl chamber. The swirl chamber gives the oil a rotary motion when it enters the nozzle orifice, thus shaping the spray pattern. The nozzle orifice increases the velocity of the oil. The oil leaves in the form of a mist or spray and mixes with the air from the blast tube. Because of the fine tolerances of the nozzle construction, servicing is usually impractical. A defective or dirty nozzle is normally replaced.

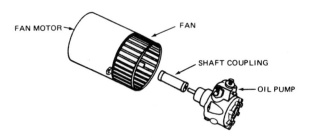

FIGURE 13–7   Shaft coupling. (Courtesy of Carrier Corporation.)

FIGURE 13–8 Static disk, choke, and swirl vanes. (Courtesy of Carrier Corporation.)

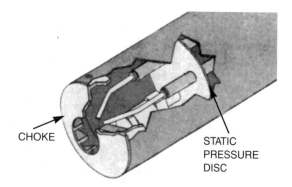

CHOKE

STATIC PRESSURE DISC

FIGURE 13–9 Nozzle assembly. (Courtesy of Carrier Corporation.)

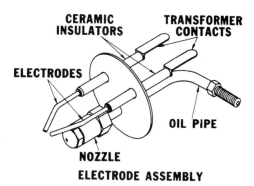

CERAMIC INSULATORS

TRANSFORMER CONTACTS

ELECTRODES

OIL PIPE

NOZZLE

ELECTRODE ASSEMBLY

FIGURE 13–10 Electrode positioning. (Courtesy of Delavan Corporation.)

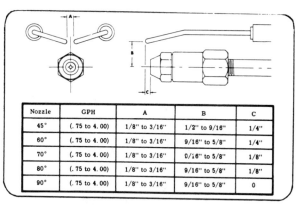

Nozzle	GPH	A	B	C
45°	(.75 to 4.00)	1/8" to 3/16"	1/2" to 9/16"	1/4"
60°	(.75 to 4.00)	1/8" to 3/16"	9/16" to 5/8"	1/4"
70°	(.75 to 4.00)	1/8" to 3/16"	9/16" to 5/8"	1/8"
80°	(.75 to 4.00)	1/8" to 3/16"	9/16" to 5/8"	1/8"
90°	(.75 to 4.00)	1/8" to 3/16"	9/16" to 5/8"	0

Recommended Electrode Settings. NOTE: Above 4.00 GPH, it may be advisable to increase dimension C by 1/8" to insure smooth starting. When using double adapters: (1) Twin ignition is the safest and is recommended, with settings same as above. (2) With single ignition, use the same A and B dimensions as above, but add 1/4" to dimension C. Locate the electrode gap on a line midway between the two nozzles.

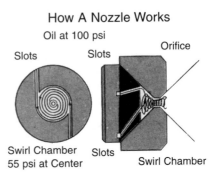

ORIFICE
SWIRL CHAMBER
STAINLESS STEEL
ORIFICE DISC
BRASS BODY
TANGENTIAL
SLOTS
STAINLESS STEEL
DISTRIBUTER
RETAINER
SINTERED FILTER

How A Nozzle Works
Oil at 100 psi
Slots   Slots   Orifice

Swirl Chamber   Slots
55 psi at Center   Swirl Chamber

FIGURE 13–11   Nozzle construction. (Courtesy of Delavan Corporation.)

Spray patterns   The requirements for nozzles vary with the type of application. Nozzles are supplied with two variations: the shape of the spray and the angle between the sides of the spray. There are three spray shapes, as shown in Figure 13–12: hollow (H), semi-hollow (SH), and solid (S). The hollow and the semi-hollow are most popular on domestic burners because they provide better efficiencies when used with modern combustion chambers.

The angle of the spray must correspond to the type of combustion chamber (Figure 13–13). An angle of 70 to 90 degrees is usually best for square or round chambers. An angle of 30 to 60 degrees is best for long, narrow chambers.

Ignition system   All high-pressure burners have electric ignition. The power is supplied by a step-up transformer connected to two electrodes. A transformer is shown in Figure 13–14. The transformer supplies high voltage, which causes a spark to jump between the two electrodes. The force of the air in the blast tube causes the spark to arc (or bend) into the oil-air mixture, igniting it. Ceramic insulators surround the electrodes where they are close to metal parts. Insulators also serve to position the electrodes. The transformer* increases the voltage from 120 V to 10,000 V but reduces the amperage (current flow) to about 20 mA. This low amperage is relatively harmless and reduces wear on the electrode tips.

Oil Storage and Piping

Most cities have rules and regulations governing the installation and piping of oil tanks to which the installation mechanic must adhere. There are two tank locations:

1. Outside (underground)
2. Inside (usually in the basement)

---

*Because of its high voltage, caution should be used in checking the transformer.

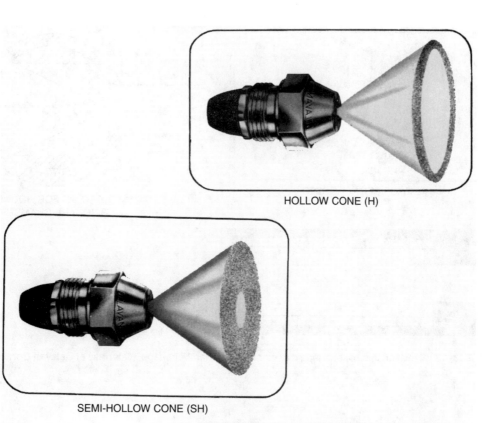

HOLLOW CONE (H)

SEMI-HOLLOW CONE (SH)

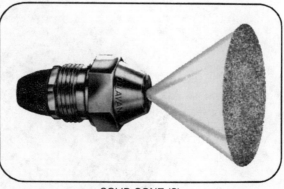

SOLID CONE (S)

FIGURE 13–12   Spray patterns. (Courtesy of Delavan Corporation.)

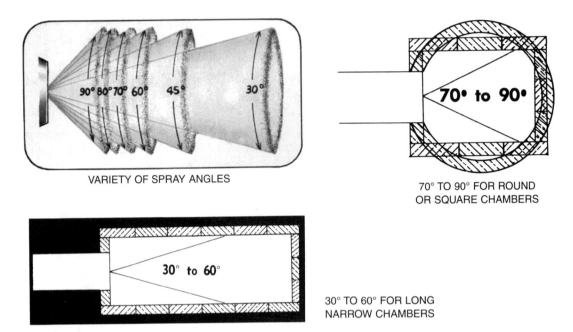

VARIETY OF SPRAY ANGLES

70° TO 90° FOR ROUND
OR SQUARE CHAMBERS

30° TO 60° FOR LONG
NARROW CHAMBERS

FIGURE 13–13   Relationship of spray angle to combustion chamber shape. (Courtesy of Delavan Corporation.)

FIGURE 13–14   Transformer. (Courtesy of Webster Electric Company, Inc.)

An outside tank can be 550, 1000, or 1500 gal in capacity. An inside tank usually has a capacity of 275 gal. Tanks must be approved by Underwriter's Laboratories (UL).

Outside underground tank   As shown in Figure 13–15, an outside underground tank should be installed at least 2 ft. below the surface. The fill pipe should be 2 in. iron pipe size (IPS) and the vent pipe $1^{1}/_{4}$ in. IPS. The vent pipe must be of a greater height than the fill pipe. The bottom of the tank should slope away from the end having the suction connection. A slope of 3 in. in its length is adequate. Piping connections to the tank should use swing connections to prevent breaking the pipe when movement occurs. Oil suction and return lines are usually made of $^{3}/_{8}$-in.-outside-diameter (OD) copper tubing, positioned within 3 in. of the bottom of the tank.

A UL-approved suction line filter should be used. A globe valve should be installed between the tank and the filter. A check valve should be installed in the suction line at the pump to keep the line filled at all times. A suitable oil level gauge should be installed. The tank should be painted with at least two coats of tar or asphaltum paint.

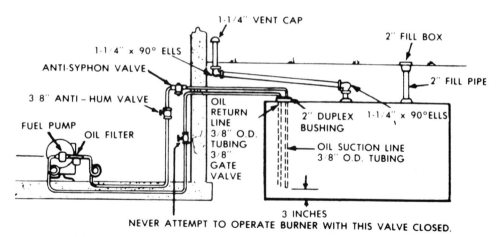

TWO STAGE PUMP (2 PIPE)

DISTANCE TANK BOTTOM BELOW PUMP (FEET)	MAX. RUN LENGTH (FT.) INCLUDES LIFT		DISTANCE TANK BOTTOM BELOW PUMP (FEET)	MAX. RUN LENGTH (FT.) INCLUDES LIFT	
	3/8" O.D. TUBING	1/2" O.D. TUBING		3/8" O.D. TUBING	1/2" O.D. TUBING
1	65	100	9	45	100
2	63	100	10	42	100
3	60	100	11	40	100
4	58	100	12	37	100
5	55	100	13	35	100
6	53	100	14	32	100
7	50	100	15	30	100
8	48	100	16	27	100

FIGURE 13–15   Outside underground tank installation. (Courtesy of Heil-Quaker.)

Inside tank   An inside tank installation is shown in Figure 13–16. Many of the regulations and installation conditions for inside tanks are the same as those for outside tanks. The fill pipe should be 2 in. IPS and the vent pipe, $1^1/4$ in. IPS. An oil level gauge should be installed. The oil piping is usually $^3/_8$-in.-OD copper tubing. A filter should be installed in the oil suction lines.

Inside tank installation varies in some ways from outside tank installation. The slope for the tank bottom should be about 1 in. and directed toward the oil suction connection. Two globe-type shutoff valves should be used, one at the tank and one at the burner. The valve at the tank should be a fuse type. The oil line between the tank and the burner should be buried in concrete. The tank should be at least 7 ft. from the burner.

ACCESSORIES

Two important accessories are the combustion chamber and the draft regulator. The combustion chamber is placed in the lower portion of the heat exchanger, surrounding the flame on all sides with the exception of the top. A barometric damper is used as a draft regulator. The draft regulator is placed in the flue pipe between the furnace and the chimney.

Combustion Chambers

The purpose of a combustion chamber is to protect the heat exchanger and to provide reflected heat to the burning oil. The reflected heat warms the tips of the flame, assuring complete combustion. No part of the flame should touch the surface of the

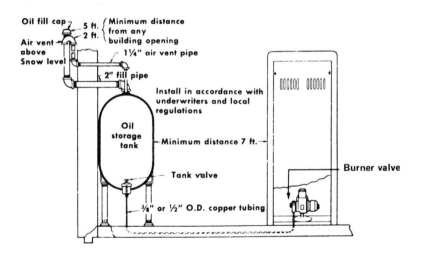

FIGURE 13–16   Inside tank installation. (Courtesy of Webster Electric Company, Inc.)

FIGURE 13–17 Molded ceramic combustion chamber. (Courtesy of Luxaire, Inc.)

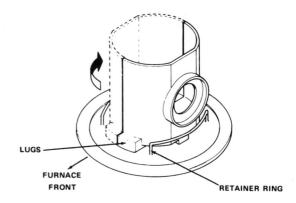

LUGS

FURNACE
FRONT

RETAINER RING

combustion chamber. If the combustible mixture does touch, the surface will be cooled and incomplete combustion will result. It is essential that the chamber fit the flame. The nozzle must be located at the proper height above the floor. The bottom area of the combustion chamber is usually 80 in.^{2}/gal for nozzles between 0.75 and 3.00 gpm, 90 in.^{2}/gal for nozzles between 3.50 and 6.00 gpm, and 100 in.^{2}/gal for nozzles 6.50 and higher.

Three types of material are generally used for combustion chambers:

1. Metal (usually stainless steel)
2. Insulating firebrick
3. Molded ceramic

Metal is used in factory-built, self-contained furnaces and is used without backfill (material in space between chamber and heat exchanger). Insulated firebrick is used for conversion burners to fit almost any type of heat-exchanger shape, and uses fiberglass backfill. The molded ceramic chamber is prefabricated to the proper shape and size and uses fiberglass backfill (Figure 13–17).

Draft Regulators

A draft regulator maintains a constant draft over the fire, usually –0.01 to –0.03 in. W.C. Too high a draft causes undue loss of heat through the chimney. Too little draft causes incomplete combustion. A draft regulator (Figure 13–18) consists of a small door in the side of the flue pipe. The door is hinged near the center and controlled by adjustable weights. Building air is admitted to the flue pipe as required to maintain a proper draft over the fire.

MAINTENANCE AND SERVICE

Annual maintenance of oil burner equipment is essential to good operation. Service procedures are outlined on the next page (see Figure 13–19).

FIGURE 13–18 Application of draft regulator. (Courtesy of Heil-Quaker.)

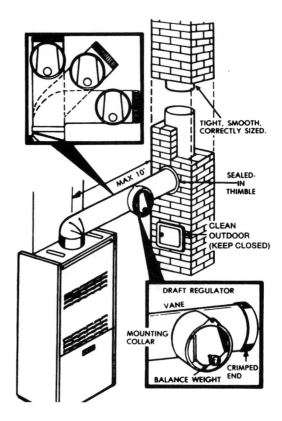

Burner Assembly

1. Clean fan blades, fan housing, and screen.
2. Oil motor with a few drops of SAE No. 10 oil.
3. Clean pump strainer.
4. Adjust oil pressure to 100 psig. (Some models require operating pressures in the 140–200 psig range.)
5. Check oil pressure cutoff.
6. Conduct combustion test and adjust air to burner for best efficiency.

Nozzle Assembly

See Figures 13–20 and 13–21.
1. Replace nozzle.
2. Clean nozzle assembly.
3. Check ceramic insulators for hairline cracks and replace, if necessary.
4. Check location of electrodes and adjust, if necessary.
5. Replace cartridges in oil line strainers.

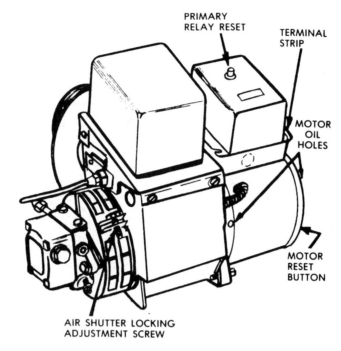

FIGURE 13–19   Oil burner. (Courtesy of Heil-Quaker.)

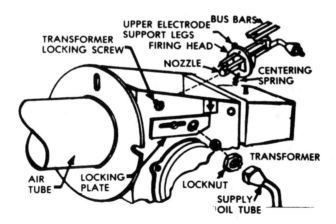

FIGURE 13–20   Removing oil burner nozzle assembly. (Courtesy of Heil-Quaker.)

Ignition System and Controls

1. Test transformer spark.
2. Clean thermostat contacts.

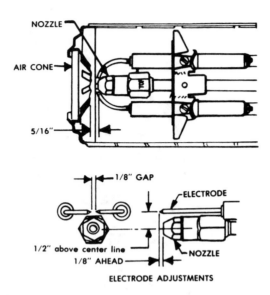

NOZZLE

AIR CONE

5/16"

1/8" GAP

ELECTRODE

1/2" above center line

1/8" AHEAD

NOZZLE

ELECTRODE ADJUSTMENTS

FIGURE 13–21 Nozzle position and electrode adjustment. (Courtesy of Heil-Quaker.) See Figure 13–10 for settings based on different nozzle angles.

3. Clean control elements that may become contaminated with soot, especially those that protrude into furnace or flue pipe.
4. Check system electrically.

Furnace

See Figure 13–22.

1. Clean combustion chamber and flue passages.
2. Clean furnace fan blades.
3. Oil fan motor.
4. Replace air filter.

After this work is completed, run the furnace through a complete cycle and check all safety controls (Chapter 14). Clean up the exterior of the furnace and the area around the furnace.

Caution: If the unit runs out of oil or if there is an air leak in the lines, the fuel pump can become air-bound and not pump oil. To correct this, the air must be bled from the pump and replaced with oil. On a one-pipe system, this is done by loosening or removing the plug on the port opposite the intake. Start the furnace and run until oil flows out of the opening; then turn it off and replace the plug. The system can then be put back into operation. A two-pipe pump is considered to be self-priming. If it does fail to prime, however, follow the procedure just described.

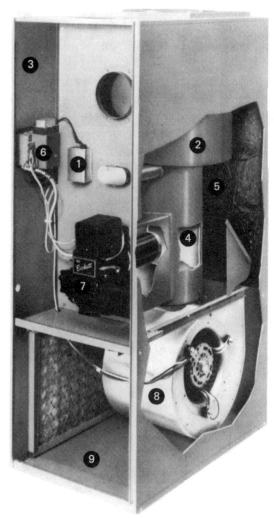

1. FAN SWITCH

2. HEAT EXCHANGER

3. CABINET

4. COMBUSTION CHAMBER

5. HEAVY INSULATION

6. RELAY

7. OIL BURNER

8. FAN

9. DUSTPROOF BASE PAN

FIGURE 13–22 Components of a typical forced warm air furnace, oil-fired. (Courtesy of Magic Chef Air Conditioning.)

STUDY QUESTIONS

Answers to the study questions may be found in the sections noted in brackets.

13–1. How is oil vaporized on a pressure-operated gun-type oil burner? *[Oil-Burning Units]*

13–2. Name and describe two types of oil burners. Which is the most popular? *[Types of Burners]*

13–3. On a high-pressure oil burner, is the air mixed with the oil before or after passing through the nozzle? *[High-Pressure Burner Components]*

13–4. Are the electrodes that ignite the oil located in or out of the oil spray? *[Electrode Position]*

13–5. Describe the application of single- and two-stage oil pumps. *[Fuel Pumps]*

13–6. What is the type of motor used on a gun-type oil burner? *[Motor]*

13–7. What is the purpose of the nozzle on an oil burner? *[Nozzle]*

13–8. What governs the shape of flame used on the oil burner? *[Spray Patterns]*

13–9. What is the normal capacity of an inside oil tank? *[Oil Storage and Piping]*

13–10. What size of copper tubing is used to connect the oil burner? *[Inside Tank]*

13–11. What are the maintenance and service requirements of an oil burner? *[Maintenance and Service]*

13–12. What action is necessary in case the burner runs out of oil and fails to start? *[Maintenance and Service]*

14

Oil Furnace Controls

OBJECTIVES

After studying this chapter, the student will be able to:

- Identify the various controls and circuits on an oil-fired furnace
- Determine the sequence of operation of the controls
- Service and troubleshoot the oil heating unit control system

USE OF OIL FURNACE CONTROLS

Many of the oil furnace controls are similar to those of gas furnaces. The main difference is in the control of the fuel-burning equipment. The major components controlled are:

- Oil burner (including ignition)
- Fan
- Accessories

As with gas furnaces, certain variations must be incorporated in the oil furnace control system to comply with various furnace models. A downflow furnace, for example, needs an auxiliary limit control and a timed fan start control, which are not required on an upflow furnace.

CIRCUITS

The control circuits for an oil-burning furnace consist of:

- Power circuit
- Fan circuit
- Ignition circuit
- Oil burner circuit
- Accessory circuits

Primary Control

Several of the control circuits are combined in a single primary control to simplify control construction and field wiring. The primary control is a type of central control assembly that supplies power for the ignition and oil burner circuits. The primary control actuates the oil burner and provides a safety device that stops the operation of the burner if the flame fails to ignite or is extinguished for any reason. This safety device prevents any sizable quantity of unburned oil from flowing into the furnace, thus reducing the possibility of an explosion. Two types of oil primary control sensors are commonly used:

1. Bimetallic sensor
2. Cad-cell sensor

Bimetallic sensor   The bimetallic sensor type of oil primary control is often called a *stack relay* because it is normally placed in the flue pipe between the heat exchanger and the barometric damper. It includes a relay that permits the low-voltage (24-V) thermostat to operate the line-voltage (120-V ac) oil burner. The internal wiring for a bimetallic sensor type of primary control is shown in Figure 14–1. The entry of the power supply (120-V ac) is shown at the top of the diagram. Line-voltage power is connected to the oil burner and to the transformer located in the primary control. The balance of the control operates on low voltage.

Figure 14–2 shows the installation of the bimetallic sensor (pyrotherm detector) in the furnace flue. Figure 14–3 shows the mechanical action that takes place when the bimetal expands as it senses heat from the flame. The normal position of the switches in this control are cold contacts NC, hot contacts NO. When the bimetal is heated, the cold contacts break and the hot contacts make.

Referring to Figure 14–1, when the thermostat calls for heat, the cold contacts are made and the safety switch heater is energized. If the flame fails to light and the cold contacts remain closed, the safety switch heater will "warp out" (open) the safety switch. The heaters and switch constitute a type of heat relay. With current flowing through this circuit, about 90 seconds are required to trip (open) the safety switch. If the burner produces flame and heats the bimetallic element, the switching occurs, opening the cold contacts and closing the hot contacts. This action causes the current to bypass the safety switch heater and the burner continues to run.

A stack relay type of primary control is shown in Figure 14–4. Line-voltage power is connected across terminals 1 and 2, and the oil burner motor is connected across 2 and 3. Constant ignition is also connected across terminals 2 and 3. Intermittent ignition is

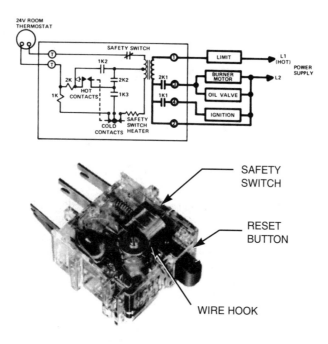

FIGURE 14–1   Internal wiring for a bimetallic sensor oil primary control with safety switch. (Courtesy of Honeywell Inc.)

connected across terminals 2 and 4. The thermostat is connected to terminals T and T (or W and B).

Two types of ignition are used in the field: constant and intermittent. With constant ignition the electrodes spark continuously. Intermittent ignition operates only when the burner is started. With constant ignition, both the oil burner motor and the ignition transformer are wired across terminals 2 and 3. Bimetallic stack relays are

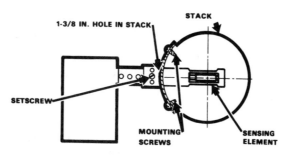

LOCATE DETECTOR

–DIRECTLY IN HOT STACK GASES.
–AHEAD AT ANY DRAFT REGULATOR.
–IN THE OUTSIDE CURVE OF AN ELBOW
  IF ELBOW LOCATION IS NECESSARY.

FIGURE 14–2   Pyrotherm flame detector. (Courtesy of Honeywell Inc.)

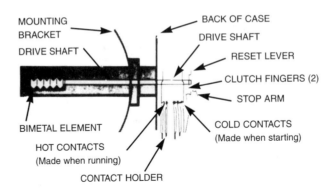

FIGURE 14–3 Pyrotherm flame detector operation. (Courtesy of Honeywell Inc.)

found on many furnaces now in the field. The new units, however, are usually equipped with a cad-cell type of primary control. *For the service technician's protection, it is important that the hot line of the power supply be brought to the number 1 terminal.* In accordance with good practice, the switching action of this control should be in the hot line.

If the thermostat is calling for heat, 120-V a.c. power must be available across terminals 2 and 3 on a constant ignition system. If intermittent ignition is used, though, 120-V a.c. power must also be available across terminals 2 and 4. After the thermostat has been removed, the thermostat terminals can be jumped to simulate the thermostat calling for heat.

The control should be tested without supplying heat to the bimetallic element. When this is done, the safety switch should shut off the power to the burner in about 90

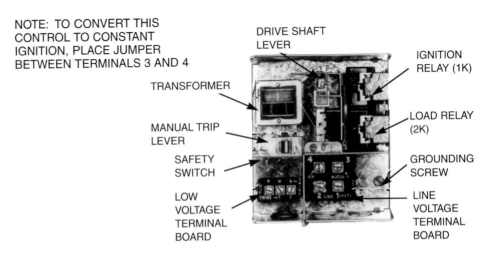

FIGURE 14–4 Typical primary control (pyrotherm-type) showing line-voltage and low-voltage electrical terminals. (Courtesy of Honeywell Inc.)

seconds. If heat is supplied to the bimetallic element, the burner should continue to run. Sometimes these controls get "out of step." That is, the cold contacts do not re-make when the bimetal cools down. This should be corrected by following the restepping procedure shown in Figure 14–5. To test the contact terminals, jumper across the cold contacts, as shown in Figure 14–6. If the bimetal is cold and contacts cannot be restepped, replace the primary control.

Stack relays have some built-in limitations. They are slow acting due to the thermal lag of the bimetal. Wiring must be completed in the field, so performance cannot be fully checked by the manufacturer. The bimetal element is exposed to the products of combustion and requires more maintenance than the cad-cell detector. Stack relays are no longer used in new installations. They are, however, used for the replacement of defective units. All new residential oil heating systems utilize cad-cell primary controls.

Cad-cell sensor   A cad cell is shown in Figure 14–7 and its location is shown in Figure 14–8. The cad-cell primary control has one feature that is not present in the bimetallic sensor. If the cad cell senses stray light (light not from the flame) before the thermostat calls for heat, the burner cannot be started by the thermostat. This is a protective arrangement. Therefore, when testing the operation of the cad-cell primary, block off all light that might reach the cad cell.

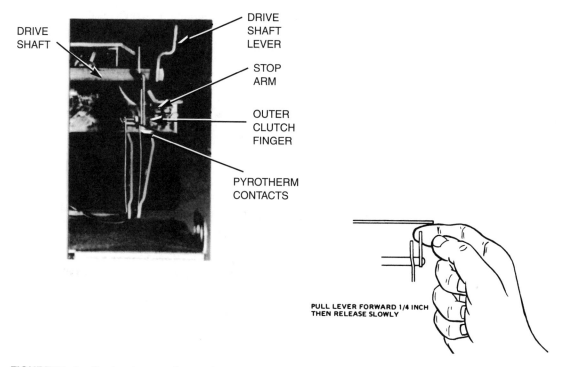

DRIVE SHAFT

DRIVE SHAFT LEVER

STOP ARM

OUTER CLUTCH FINGER

PYROTHERM CONTACTS

PULL LEVER FORWARD 1/4 INCH THEN RELEASE SLOWLY

FIGURE 14–5   Restepping pyrotherm relay control. (Courtesy of Honeywell, Inc.)

FIGURE 14–6 Use of jumper to test cold contacts on pyrotherm relay control. (Courtesy of Honeywell Inc.)

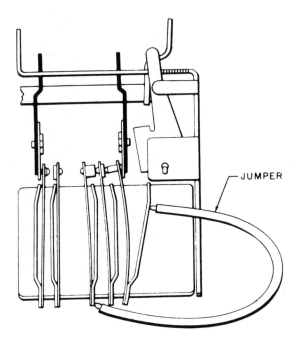

The cad cell itself can be tested with a suitable ohmmeter. The ohmmeter must be capable of reading up to 100,000 Ω. In the absence of light, the cad cell should have a resistance of about 100,000 Ω. In the presence of light, its resistance should not exceed 1500 Ω.

To test the primary control, start the burner and within 30 seconds jump the cad-cell-terminals with a 1000- to 1500-Ω resistor. If the burner continues to run, the cad-cell primary is operating correctly. In actual operation, a poor or inadequate oil burner flame can be a problem. The safety arrangement on a cad-cell primary control usually stops the burner in about 30 seconds if the cad-cell does not sense an adequate flame.

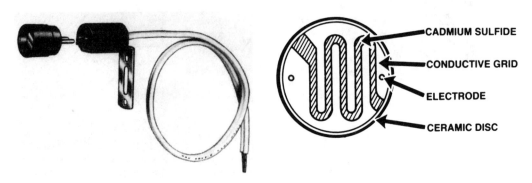

FIGURE 14–7 Cad-cell assembly and details of face. (Courtesy of Honeywell Inc.)

FIGURE 14–8 Cad-cell location
in oil burner assembly (Courtesy of
Honeywell Inc.)

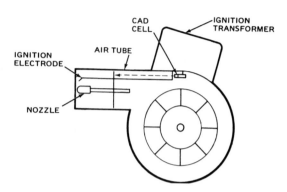

Electrical Response   The ability of the cad cell to change electrical resistance when exposed to different intensities of light makes possible the operation of a safety control circuit. Figure 14–9 shows the internal wiring connections for the primary cad-cell types of primary control as well as the internal circuiting. The power (120-V a.c.) connection to the burner and primary control transformer are shown at the top of the diagram. The balance of the control is low voltage (24-V a.c.). The thermostat and the cad cell are shown connected to the right side of the primary control (see Figure 14–10b).

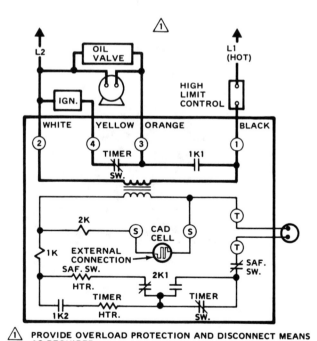

⚠ **PROVIDE OVERLOAD PROTECTION AND DISCONNECT MEANS
AS REQUIRED.**

FIGURE 14–9   Wiring for cad-cell oil primary control, with intermittent ignition. (Courtesy of Honeywell Inc.)

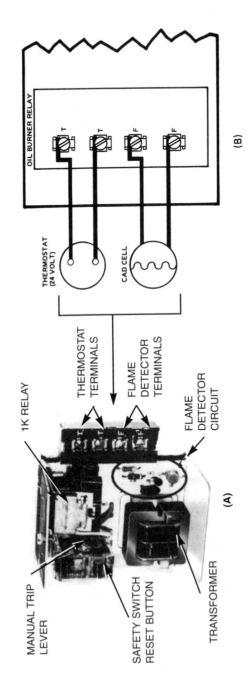

FIGURE 14-10 Cad-cell primary control showing thermostat and flame detector terminals. (Courtesy of Honeywell Inc.)

When the thermostat calls for heat, the oil burner starts and the safety switch heater is energized. If the flame fails to ignite, the heater warps out the safety switch in about 30 seconds, turning off the burner. If the flame is produced, it is sensed by the cad cell. This causes the safety switch heater to be bypassed and the burner stays on.

The cad-cell primary control power supply (120-V a.c.) is wired to the black (hot) and white (neutral) connections. The oil burner motor is wired to the white and orange connections. The thermostat is connected to terminals T and T. The cad cell is connected to terminals S and S (or F and F), as shown in Figure 14–10.

Options Available   There are two important options available on the cad-cell primary control:

1. Constant or intermittent ignition
2. Variations in motor control arrangement

On constant ignition, both the oil burner motor and the ignition transformer are wired across the white and orange connections. On intermittent ignition, the motor is wired across white and orange, and the ignition transformer is wired across white and yellow.

Solid-State Sensor   Solid-state technology is based on manipulating semiconductors to perform different functions in an electronic circuit. The solid-state circuit, which replaces the sensitive relay in cad-cell primaries, consists of two resistors, one capacitor, and two solid-state switches. One of these is a bilateral switch, and the other is a Triac, as shown in Figure 14–11.

The Triac acts as a NO switch. It will conduct current between terminals A and B after a triggering current is applied to the gate terminal. It will continue to conduct after the triggering current is removed until current between A and B drops to zero. At this time, it becomes nonconducting, and another triggering signal is required before it will conduct again.

The bilateral switch is frequently used to trigger a Triac. When only terminals 1 and 2 are used, it acts as a resistor until a certain voltage, called the *breakover voltage,*

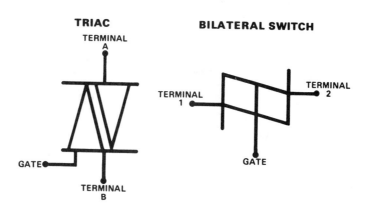

FIGURE 14–11   Solid-state switches. (Courtesy of Honeywell Inc.)

is reached. This voltage is very small, on the order of 8 V. When the breakover voltage is passed, the resistance of the switch collapses and current flows. When the bilateral switch is used as a three-terminal device, current is applied to the gate terminal to change the breakover voltage.

In Figure 14–12, which shows a solid-state flame-sensing circuit, the resistors and the capacitor in the cad-cell primary are not, strictly speaking, solid-state devices, but they are used extensively in solid-state circuits. A resistor simply opposes the flow of current. A capacitor, in a d.c. circuit, blocks the flow of current. In an a.c. circuit, the capacitor stores current on one half-cycle and releases it on the reverse half-cycle. Resistor R1 in Figure 14–12 determines the voltage drop across the F-F terminals, and resistor R2 protects the solid–state components from abnormally high voltages. The capacitor provides an extra burst of current each half-cycle to ensure that the Triac is triggered when necessary. The solid-state, flame-sensing circuit is less affected by ambient light hitting the cad cell than is a comparable sensitive relay.

Sequence of Operation   The schematic of an intermittent ignition model of a cad-cell primary control is shown in Figure 14–13. When the line switch is closed, the internal transformer is powered, whether or not the thermostat is calling for heat. A line-voltage thermostat can be used with this control if terminals T-T on the primary are jumpered. In this case, the primary and cad cell will not be powered until the thermostat calls for heat.

The solid-state flame-sensing circuit is designed so that the Triac will conduct current only when cad-cell resistance is high, indicating no flame. If cad-cell resistance is high, the voltage across the bilateral switch exceeds the breakover voltage, causing it to conduct and trigger the Triac. The capacitor provides a current pulse each half-cycle to make sure the breakover voltage is exceeded.

On flame failure, cad-cell resistance increases until the Triac is energized. The safety switch heats until the bimetal warps enough to break the circuit and stop the burner. The primary control must be reset before the burner can be restarted. If there is a power failure during a call for heat, the burner shuts down safely and automatically. The system automatically returns to normal operation when power is restored.

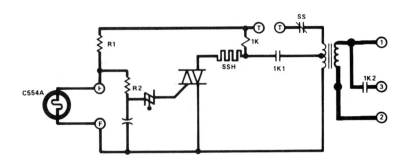

FIGURE 14–12   Solid-state flame-sensing circuit. (Courtesy of Honeywell Inc.)

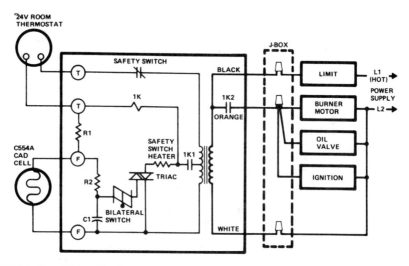

FIGURE 14–13   Wiring diagram for solid state, cad-cell primary. (Courtesy of Honeywell Inc.)

Cad-cell versus thermal detection   Regardless of the type of detector and primary control used to supervise the burner, there are basic similarities in the general operation of the primary control. In all systems, a call for heat energizes the burner and starts the safety switch heater. If flame is established, the flame detector (thermal or optical) acts to bypass the safety switch heater and allows the burner to run.

The steps taken by the cad cell to bypass the safety switch heater and allow the burner to run are comparable to the steps taken by the stack detector. The cad cell's sighting of the flame and lowering its resistance is matched by the thermal detector's bimetal element "feeling" the change in stack gas temperature and moving the drive shaft outward. The pull-in of the sensitive relay or electronic network is matched by the opening of the stack relay contacts. The actions of both detectors when flame is proved have the same result: the breaking of the safety switch heater circuit. Compare the parts of a thermal flame detector to the cad-cell detector. The electronic network replaces the pyrostat contacts, and the light-sensitive cell replaces the heat-sensitive bimetal element, as shown in Figure 14–14.

The cad cell has certain advantages over the thermal detector. Its response time is faster than the bimetal's. On exposure to light its resistance drops almost immediately, while the bimetal reacts slowly to a relatively slow change in stack temperature. Because of this faster response, the cell is better suited to modern installations. The cad cell is also well suited to the "package" concept, since the cad cell and its associated primary control can be completely installed and wired by the burner manufacturer.

Power Circuit

Following is the key to the schematic diagrams used in the study of the power circuit and other circuits described in this chapter:

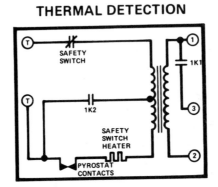

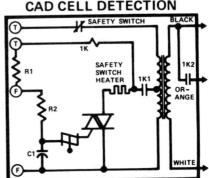

THERMAL DETECTION

CAD CELL DETECTION

1. 1K PULLS IN, ENERGIZES BURNER.
2. SS HEATS THROUGH PYROSTAT CONTACTS.
3. FLAME ESTABLISHED, PYROSTAT CONTACTS OPEN.
4. SS HEATER IS BYPASSED.

1. 1K PULLS IN, ENERGIZES BURNER.
2. SS HEATS THROUGH TRIAC.
3. FLAME ESTABLISHED, TRIAC STOPS CONDUCTING.
4. SS HEATER IS BYPASSED.

FIGURE 14–14 Basic primary control function. (Courtesy of Honeywell Inc.)

BK	Black-wire color	FC	Fan control
BL	Blue-wire color	FM	Fan motor
G	Green-wire color	FR	Fan relay
OR	Orange-wire color	L	Limit
R	Red-wire color	LA	Limit auxiliary
W	White-wire color	$L_1 L_2$	Line 1, line 2 of power supply
Y	Yellow-wire color	S	Cad-cell terminal
C	24-V common connection	T	Thermostat terminal
CC	Compressor relay	TFS	Timed fan start

Referring to the power circuit shown in Figure 14–15, 120-V a.c. power is supplied to the primary control. A fused disconnect is placed in the hot side of the line. A limit control is wired in series with the hot side of the power supply (L_1) and the black connection on the primary control. The transformer is a part of the primary control.

Fan Circuit

The simplest type of fan circuit consists of a fan control in series with a single-speed fan motor, as shown in Figure 14–16. Using a multiple-speed fan motor the switch on the subbase of the thermostat changes the fan speed, as shown in Figure 14–17.

On downflow and horizontal furnaces, a timed fan start (TFS) is used to start the fan and the fan control (FC) stops it, as shown in Figure 14–18. An auxiliary limit control is used in addition to the regular limit control and is wired in series with the primary control.

FIGURE 14–15   Power circuit.

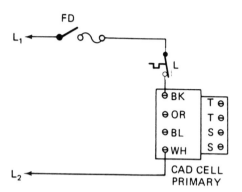

FIGURE 14–16   Fan circuit with single-speed fan motor.

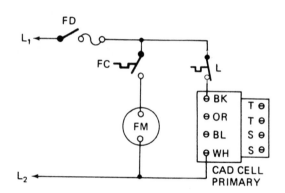

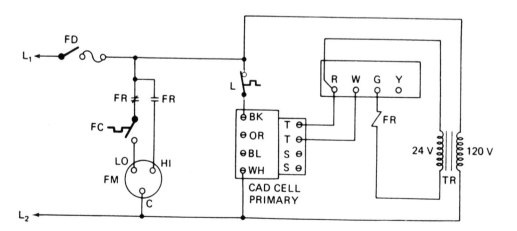

FIGURE 14–17   Fan circuit with multispeed fan motor.

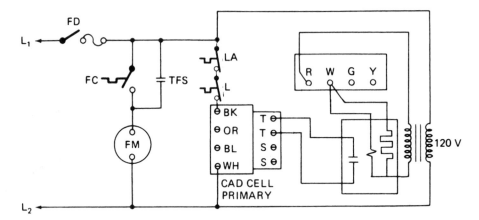

FIGURE 14–18 Fan circuit for downflow and horizontal furnaces.

Ignition and Oil Burner Circuits

Ignition and oil burner circuits are shown in Figure 14–19. The ignition transformer is wired in parallel with the oil burner motor on a constant ignition system. The burner is wired to the orange and white connections on the primary control.

Accessory Circuits

Accessories for oil furnaces can be added in a manner similar to those shown in Chapter 11 for gas furnaces. Since the transformer for heating is contained within the cad-cell primary, a separate transformer is usually required for control circuit power when cooling is added (see Figures 14–17 and 14–18).

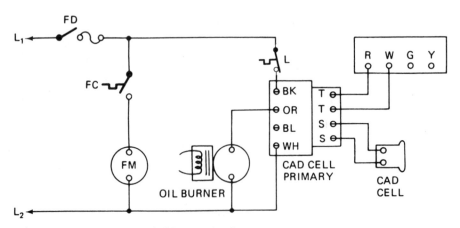

FIGURE 14–19 Ignition and oil burner circuits.

TYPICAL WIRING DIAGRAMS

Upflow

Figure 14–20 shows a typical connection diagram for an upflow oil furnace. Note that on this unit most of the wiring connections are brought to a common junction box. Since both the fan and limit controls are of line-voltage type, a jumper can be used between common terminals. The schematic wiring diagram for the upflow unit is shown in Figure 14–21.

Oil Furnace with Multispeed Fan Motor

Figure 14–22 shows a connection diagram for an oil furnace with multispeed fan motor. All wiring connections are made either in the primary control junction box or in a separate junction box that includes the indoor fan relay. The schematic wiring diagram for the oil furnace with multispeed fan motor is shown in Figure 14–23.

TROUBLESHOOTING AND SERVICE

In troubleshooting an oil-fired furnace, attention should be given to the electrical and fluid flows through the furnace, for the following reasons:

- Electrical power is required to operate the control system, ignite the fuel, and energize the loads.
- Fuel oil is required for combustion.
- Air is required for combustion and to convey heat from the furnace to the spaces being heated.

Electricity, oil, and air each have a circuit or path of movement through the furnace. Each must be supplied in the proper place, in the proper quantity, and at the proper time. Troubleshooting the fuel oil and air supply have been covered in other chapters. Therefore, the concern here is chiefly electrical power and control.

Use of Test Meters

Figure 14–24 shows the use of various test meters in measuring voltage and current in the electrical system of the furnace. The technique in electrical troubleshooting is to "start from power" and follow the availability of power through the control system to the load. If the power supply is stopped for any reason along the proper path, the reason for the stoppage should be determined and corrected. If power in the proper quantity is supplied to the load and it does not operate, the load device is at fault. Seven locations where meter readings are taken along the path of the electrical current are shown in Figure 14–24. Locations to be checked are:

1. Voltage supply to the unit
2. Voltage across the limit control to determine if this control switch is properly closed

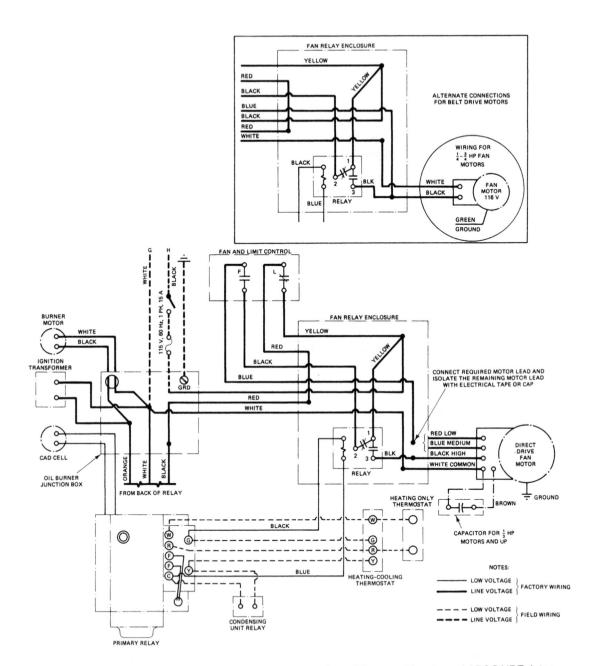

FIGURE 14–20 Heat-cool connection wiring diagram for upflow oil furnace. (Courtesy of ARCOAIRE, Inter-City Products Corporation, USA.)

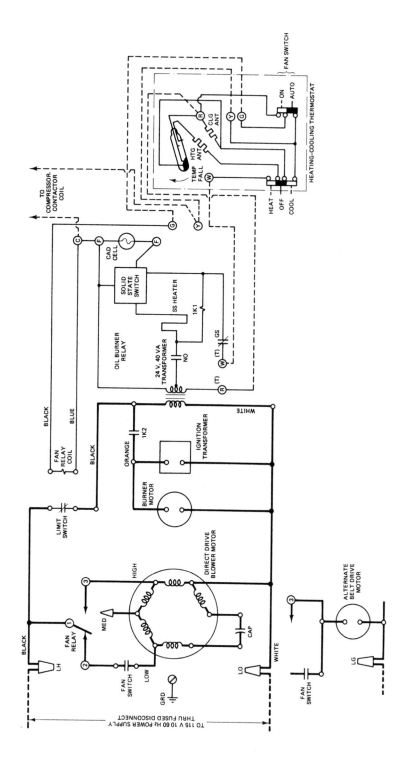

FIGURE 14-21 Heat-cool schematic wiring diagram for upflow oil furnace. (Courtesy of ARCOAIRE, Inter-City Products Corporation, USA.)

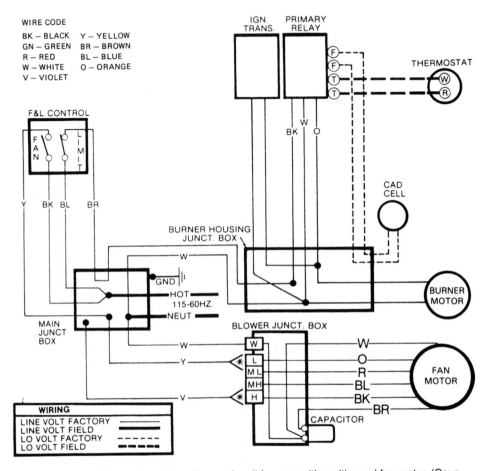

FIGURE 14–22 Connection wiring diagram for oil furnace with multispeed fan motor. (Courtesy of Heil-Quaker.)

3. Voltage across the thermostat to be certain that it is calling for heat
4. Voltage at the oil burner motor and ignition transformer to be certain that 120-V a.c. is being supplied
5. Voltage across the fan control to determine that it is calling for fan operation
6. Voltage at the fan motor to be certain that 120-V a.c. is being supplied
7. Amperage to the fan motor to measure the running amperes (should agree with the data on the motor nameplate)

In meter readings 2, 3, and 5, a voltmeter is used to test a switch. If the switch is open, a voltage shows on the meter. If the switch is closed, the voltmeter reads zero.

Testing Components

The most complex element in an oil-fired furnace control system is the primary control. Therefore, it is this element that has the greatest potential need for service.

FIGURE 14–23 Schematic wiring diagram for oil furnace with multi-speed fan motor. (Courtesy of Heil-Quaker.)

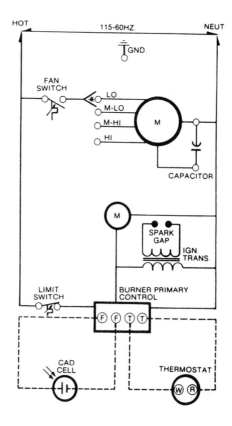

Specific testing procedures are necessary to determine if the primary control is functioning properly.

Other Servicing Techniques

Most oil-burning furnaces have a manual test overload on the oil burner motor and a reset-type safety switch on the primary control. After an overload, these devices must be manually reset. The tripping of an overload switch is an indicator of a problem that must be found and corrected. Resetting the overload switches may start the equipment, but unless the problem is resolved, nuisance tripout will continue to recur.

Regardless of the complaint, much time can often be saved at first by checking the following routine conditions:

- Does the tank contain fuel?
- Is power being delivered to the building?
- Are all hand-operated switches closed?
- Are all hand valves in the oil supply line open?
- Are all limit controls in their normal (closed) position?
- Is the thermostat calling for heat?
- Are all overload switches closed?

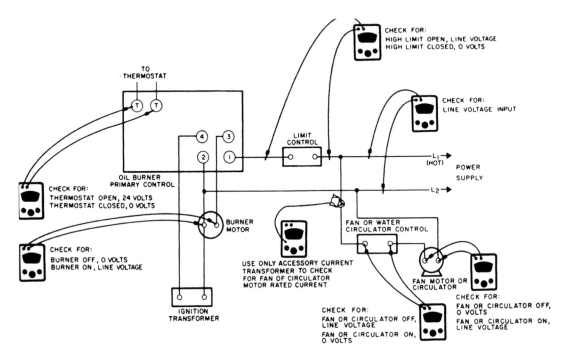

FIGURE 14–24 Use of various electrical meters in troubleshooting oil burner systems. (Courtesy of Honeywell Inc.)

Low voltage can cause problems, such as low oil pump speed, motor burnouts from overload, and burners that fail to operate because relays do not pull in. The power supply voltage should be checked while the greatest power usage is occurring. Low voltage should never be overlooked as a source of service problems. Where the service to the building is at fault, the local power company should be contacted. If the problem is within the building, the services of an electrician may be required to solve the problem.

STUDY QUESTIONS

Answers to the study questions may be found in the sections noted in brackets.

14–1. What are the various circuits in an oil burner control system? *[Circuits]*

14–2. What are the two types of primary controls? *[Primary Control]*

14–3. On the stack relay, are the cold contacts normally open or closed when starting? *[Bimetallic Sensor]*

14–4. What are the component materials on a cad cell? *[Cad-Cell Sensor]*

14–5. What is the resistance of a cad cell in the absence of light? *[Cad-Cell Sensor]*

14–6. To which terminals of the primary control is the cad cell connected? *[Cad-Cell Sensor]*

14–7. How many low-voltage terminals are on the cad-cell primary control? *[Cad-Cell Sensor]*

14–8. On the cad-cell primary control, which terminal is used for the hot side of the power supply? *[Cad-Cell Sensor]*

14–9. On the bimetal stack relay, which terminals are used for the power supply? *[Bimetallic Sensor]*

14–10. In testing a switch with a voltmeter, a reading of zero indicates what position of the switch? *[Use of Test Meters]*

14–11. On a stack relay, if the flame fails, how long before the burner will stop on safety? *[Bimetallic Sensor]*

14–12. What is the resistance of the cad cell when it senses light? *[Cad-Cell Sensor]*

14–13. Describe the solid-state cad-cell circuit. *[Solid-State Sensor]*

14–14. Which control requires the most service on an oil burner control system? *[Testing Components]*

15

Electric Heating

OBJECTIVES

After studying this chapter, the student will be able to:
- Identify the various types of controls and circuits used on an electric furnace
- Determine the sequence of operation of the controls
- Service and troubleshoot the electric furnace control system

CONVERSION OF ELECTRICITY TO HEAT

An electric heating furnace converts energy in the form of electricity to heat. The conversion takes place in resistance heaters. Electric furnaces differ from gas or oil furnaces in that no heat exchanger is required. Return air from the space being heated passes directly over the resistance heaters and into the supply air plenum. The amount of heat supplied depends on the number and size of the resistance heaters used. The conversion of electricity to heat (the heat equivalent for 1 W of electrical power) takes place in accordance with the following formula:

$$1 \text{ W} = 3.415 \text{ Btu}$$

ELECTRIC FURNACE COMPONENTS

Figure 15–1 shows an electric forced warm air furnace (upflow model). Return air is brought into the blower compartment through the filters, then passed over the heating elements and sent out into the distribution system. An electric furnace requires no flue. All of the heat produced is used in heating the building. Input is equal to output. Thus, it operates at 100% efficiency. Major components, excluding the controls, are:

- Heating elements
- Fan and motor assembly
- Furnace enclosure
- Accessories, such as filters, humidifier, and cooling (optional)

Following is the key to the schematic diagrams used in this chapter:

AC	Auxiliary contacts	L	Limit control
C	24-V common connection	$L_1 L_2$	Line 1, line 2 of power supply
FC	Fan control	OT	Outdoor thermostat
FD	Fused disconnect	R	Red wire, thermostat connection
FL	Fuse link	SQ	Sequencer
FM	Fan motor	TFS	Timed fan start
FU	Fuse	TR	Transformer
HR	Heat relay	W	White wire, thermostat connection

TYPICAL ELECTRIC FURNACE FEATURES

BUILT-IN COOLING COIL COMPARTMENT — Slide-in type for easier conversion to summer cooling. Accommodates 1½, 2, 2½, and 3 ton air conditioner cooling coils. See note on reverse side on heat pump installation.

CONTROLS — On demand from the wall thermostat, the heating elements are energized by electrical contactors. The 15 thru 30 KW versions have the blower motor interlocked with each stage for safety. Easily two staged.

LIMIT SWITCH — Thermal snap disc in each heating element shuts off power automatically if system air temperature becomes excessive.

BUILT-IN TRANSFORMER — Provides power supply for heating and optional cooling controls.

BLOWER RELAY — Provides automatic blower speed change-over to meet heating and cooling air delivery requirements.

BRANCH CIRCUIT FUSING — Factory installed in models rated over 48 amps.

HEATING ELEMENTS — Nickel-chrome wire with individual fusible links for long life. Entire assembly slides out for easy maintenance.

MOTOR — Multi-speed for both heating and cooling.

BLOWER — Heated air is quietly circulated by large volume centrifugal blower that is matched to the electrical heating system for efficiency. Slides out for easy maintenance.

FILTERS — Twin permanent type slide out from front for easy cleaning on all models except Models EFC5 and EFC10.

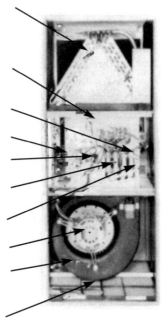

FIGURE 15–1   Electric forced warm air furnace, upflow model. (Courtesy of Bard Manufacturing Company.)

Heating Elements

The heating elements are made of Nichrome, a metal consisting chiefly of nickel and chromium. Heating elements are rated in kilowatts of electrical power consumed (1 kW = 1000 W). A typical heating element assembly is shown in Figure 15–2. The Nichrome wire is supported by insulating material placed to provide a minimum amount of air resistance and a maximum amount of contact between the air and the resistance heaters.

Each element assembly contains a thermal fuse and a safety limit switch (Figure 15–3). The safety limit switch is shown in schematic form in Figure 15–4. The limit switch is usually set to open at 160°F and close when the temperature drops to 125°F. The thermal fuse, a backup for the safety limit switch, is set to open at a temperature slightly higher than the limit switch. In addition to the safety controls in the element assembly, each assembly is fused where it connects to the power supply. Triple safety protection is thereby provided.

Electric furnaces have various individual numbers and sizes of heating element assemblies, depending on the total capacity of the equipment. Elements are placed on the line (power supply) in stages in order not to overload the electrical system on startup. In most units, the maximum size of an element energized or de-energized at one time is 5 kW (17,075 Btuh). Figure 15–4 shows how the heater sequencer operates.

Fan and Motor Assembly

The fan and motor assembly is similar to that used on a gas or oil furnace. Fans may be either direct-drive or belt-driven. There is a trend toward the use of multispeed direct-drive fans, since they facilitate adjustment of the airflow by changing the blower speed. This is usually necessary when cooling is added, since larger air quantities and, consequently, higher speeds are required.

FIGURE 15–2   Typical heating element.

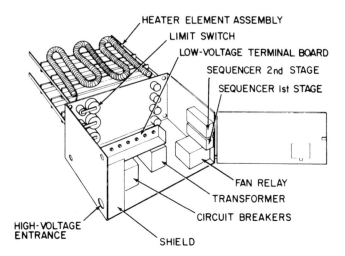

FIGURE 15-3   Heater element assembly with circuit breakers. (Courtesy of Bryant Air Conditioning.)

Enclosures

The exterior of the casing is similar to that of a gas or oil furnace but without the flue pipe connection. The interior is designed to permit the air to flow over the heating elements. The section supporting the heating elements is usually insulated from the exterior casing by an air space.

Accessories

Filters, humidifiers, and cooling are added to an electric heating furnace in a manner similar to gas and oil furnaces. Electric heating can therefore provide all of the related climate control features provided by other types of fuel.

POWER SUPPLY

The power supply for an electric furnace is 208/240-V, single-phase, 60-Hz. This power is supplied by three wires: two are hot and one is neutral. Fused disconnects are placed in the hot lines leading to the furnace. The National Electrical Code® limits to 48 A the amount of service in a single circuit. If the running current exceeds this amount, additional circuits and fused disconnects must be provided. The fuses for a 48-A service must not exceed 60 A. This is a National Electrical Code® requirement, specifying that fuses should not exceed 125% of full-load amperes ($48 \times 1.25 = 60$).

All wiring must be enclosed in conduit with proper connectors. Since 208/240 V is considerably more dangerous than lower voltages, every possible protection must be

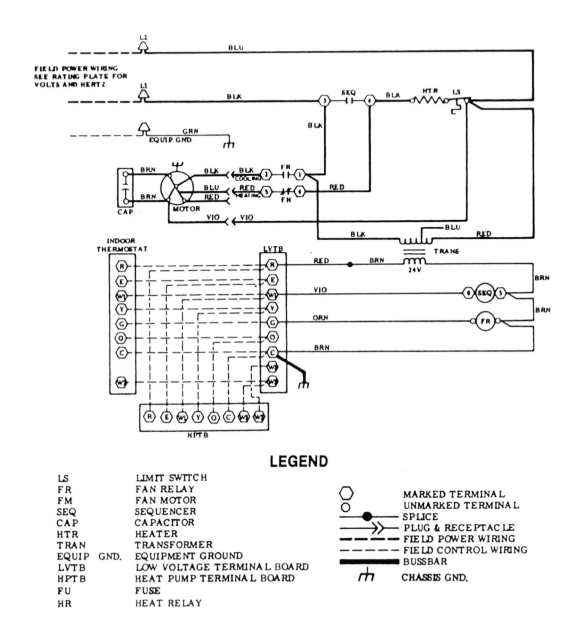

LEGEND

LS	LIMIT SWITCH
FR	FAN RELAY
FM	FAN MOTOR
SEQ	SEQUENCER
CAP	CAPACITOR
HTR	HEATER
TRAN	TRANSFORMER
EQUIP GND.	EQUIPMENT GROUND
LVTB	LOW VOLTAGE TERMINAL BOARD
HPTB	HEAT PUMP TERMINAL BOARD
FU	FUSE
HR	HEAT RELAY

- ⬡ MARKED TERMINAL
- ○ UNMARKED TERMINAL
- ● SPLICE
- ⟶⟫ PLUG & RECEPTACLE
- FIELD POWER WIRING
- FIELD CONTROL WIRING
- ▬ BUSSBAR
- ⊓ CHASSIS GND.

FIGURE 15–4   Schematic wiring diagram for electric heating-cooling unit. (Courtesy of Bryant Air Conditioning.)

provided. The National Electrical Code® also requires that the furnace be grounded. The ground wire in the power supply is provided for this purpose.

CONTROL SYSTEM

Since the control system for an electric furnace includes more electrical parts than a gas or oil furnace, the wiring is more involved. It is extremely important to use a schematic diagram to assist in troubleshooting. If a schematic is not available from the manufacturer, one should be drawn by the service technician. The control system consists of the following electrical circuits:

- Power circuit
- Fan circuit
- Heating element circuits
- Control circuits operated from the thermostat

Power Circuit

The power supply consists of one or more 208/240-V a.c. sources, directed through fused disconnects to the load circuits, including the 208/240-V/24-V transformer. The load lines are both hot, as shown in Figure 15–5.

Fan Circuit

The fan circuits on an electric furnace are similar to those used with gas or oil except for the following changes:

1. The fan motor is usually 208/240 V a.c.
2. A timed fan start is used to start the fan. This is usually a part of the sequencer (an electrical device for staging the loads).
3. The fan starts from the timed fan start but is stopped by the regular thermal fan control.

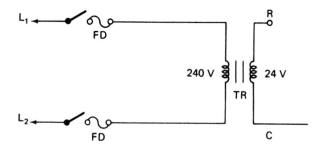

FIGURE 15–5   Power circuit showing hot load lines.

Details of the fan circuit arrangement are shown in Figure 15–6. When the thermostat calls for heating, R and W in the thermostat are made, energizing the low-voltage heater in the sequencer. After approximately 45 seconds, the fan operates. Just as soon as the temperature leaving the furnace rises to the fan control cut-in temperature, this control makes. It has no effect on the fan, however, since it is already running.

Approximately 45 seconds after the thermostat is satisfied, the timed fan start switch opens. It has no effect on the fan, though, since the fan control is made. When the leaving air temperature drops to the cut-out setting of the fan control, the fan stops.

Heating Element Circuits

The heating element assemblies are connected in parallel to the power supply. These assemblies are turned on by the sequencer or heat relays so that the load is gradually placed on the line. Each heating element has a sequencer switch wired in series with the element to start its operation. Figure 15–7 shows the fan and the heating elements operated by a sequencer.

Control Circuits

When the thermostat calls for heating, R and W make, energizing the low-voltage heater (SQ) in the sequencer. In approximately 45 seconds, the switch to the fan (SQ$_1$) and the first heating element (SQ$_2$) are made simultaneously. Approximately 30 seconds later, the switch to the second heater element (SQ$_3$) is made. If additional heating elements are used, there is a comparable 30-second delay before each succeeding element is operated.

A two-stage thermostat is used on some systems. This thermostat has two mercury bulb switches, one for each stage. The first stage is set to make at a temperature a few degrees higher than the second stage. The first stage controls the fan and some of the heating elements. The second stage controls the balance of the heating elements.

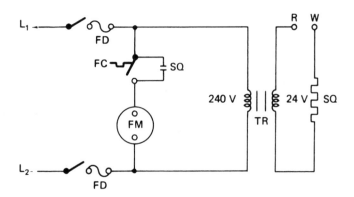

FIGURE 15–6   Typical fan circuit.

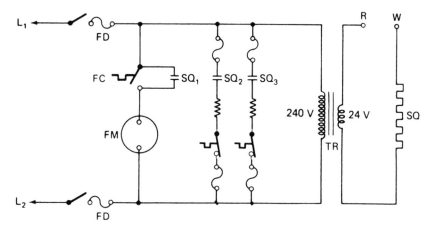

FIGURE 15–7   Fan and heating elements operated by a sequencer.

Referring to Figure 15–8, when the first stage of the thermostat calls for heat, R and W_1 make, energizing the heater SQ in the sequencer. This action switches on the first element and the fan. Then the second element will be energized in 30 seconds. If the room temperature continues to drop to the setting of the second stage of the thermostat, R and W_2 are made, energizing the heat relay heater (HR). In approximately 45 seconds the switch to the third heating element (HR_1) will be made, operating the final stage of heating.

The second-stage thermostat can also be an outdoor thermostat rather than a part of the first-stage thermostat assembly. The low-voltage control circuit for this type of installation is shown in Figure 15–9.

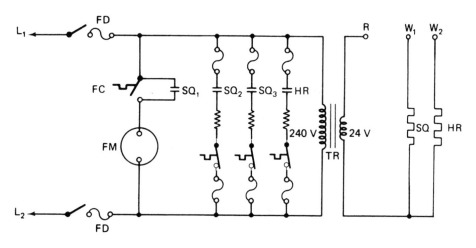

FIGURE 15–8   Thermostat assembly in two-stage heating.

FIGURE 15–9 Use of outdoor thermostat.

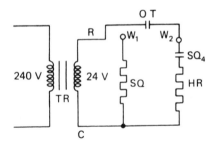

The first-stage (standard) thermostat operates the first-stage heating in the usual manner. A switch on the sequencer (SQ$_4$), an auxiliary switch, is also made in stage 1 to permit stage 2 to operate. When the outside temperature reaches the setting of the outdoor thermostat (OT), the second-stage heating is operated in a manner similar to that shown in Figure 15–8. Separate heat relays for each load can be used as an alternative to the use of the sequencer for staging the loads on an electric heating furnace. These relays function in a manner similar to the sequencer, as shown in Figure 15–10.

When R and W make, the heater on heat relay 1 (HR$_1$) is energized along with the fan relay (FR). In this arrangement the fan starts immediately and in about 30 seconds heat relay 1 switch (HR$_1$) closes, operating the first heater element. At the same time, the other HR$_1$ switch in the 24-V circuit closes, energizing the heater on heat relay 2. In approximately 30 seconds, the two switches (HR$_2$) in heat relay 2 close. One operates heating element 2 and the other energizes the heater in heat relay 3. In approximately 30 seconds the switch (HR$_3$) closes, operating heating element 3. The fan and all heating elements are thereby placed on the line in sequence, as shown in Figure 15–10.

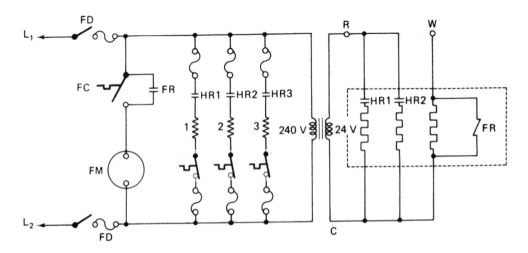

FIGURE 15–10 Use of heat relays (single-stage thermostat).

USE OF SEQUENCERS AND HEAT RELAYS

A typical example of the use of sequencer to stage the loads on an electric furnace is shown in Figures 15–11 and 15–12. The furnace shown in Figure 15–11 has two heating elements.

This unit uses a single-stage thermostat. When R and W are made in the thermostat, the fan immediately starts on low speed. At the same time, the heater in the sequencer is energized and the heater elements are operated in stages at approximately 30-second intervals.

Referring to Figure 15–12, the set of normally open contacts of energized sequencer SEQ (between 1 and 2) closes and completes the circuit through the set of NC contacts of indoor fan relay FR (between 5 and 4) to the low-speed tap of indoor fan motor FM. The fan motor starts instantly. The circuit to heater elements HTR 1 is also completed and these elements are energized.

After a short built-in time delay that prevents both heater elements from energizing simultaneously, the set of NO contacts of energized sequencer SEQ (between 3 and 4) closes and completes the circuit to heater elements HTR 2 and these elements are energized.

The fan motor and the energized heater elements remain on until the room temperature rises to a point above the heating control setting of the room thermostat. At this point, the electrical connection between thermostat terminal R to terminal W (or W 1) opens. This open circuit de-energizes sequencer coil SEQ. The electric heating cycle is now off until there is another demand for heating by the room thermostat.

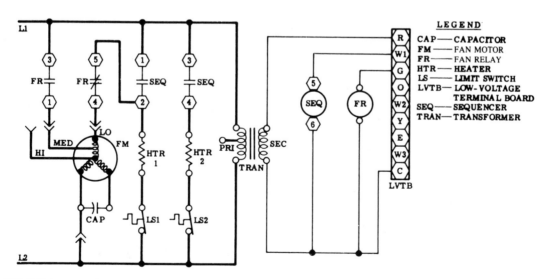

FIGURE 15–11   Typical schematic wiring diagram for electric heat sequencer. (Courtesy of Bryant Air Conditioning.)

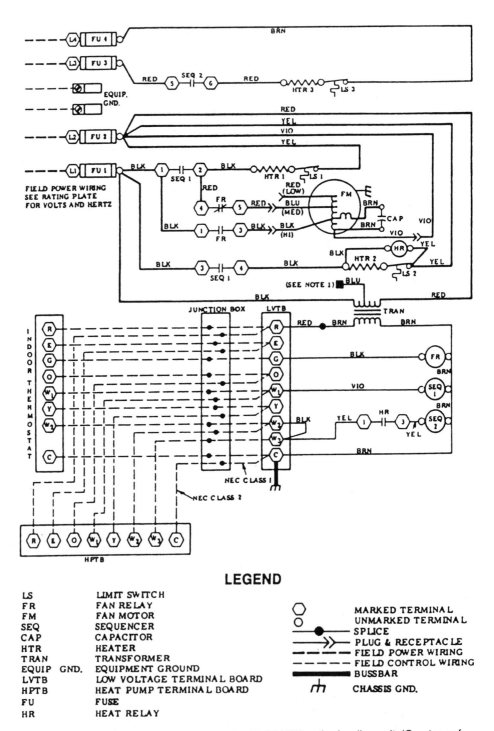

FIGURE 15–12 Schematic wiring diagram for 12–20 kW heating/cooling unit. (Courtesy of Bryant Air Conditioning.)

TROUBLESHOOTING AND SERVICE

In troubleshooting, it is good practice to use the nature of the complaint as a key to the area in which service is required. For example, if the complaint of a homeowner is that the fan will not run, troubleshooting should be confined to this area until the problem is found and corrected.

If the complaint is more general, such as no heat, then a thorough and systematic check of the electrical system must be made. This requires an electrical check, starting where power is available and tracing through the electrical system to determine where it is no longer available. Switches must be checked to be sure that they are in their proper positions. Loads must be checked to be certain that they operate when supplied with the proper power. A schematic wiring diagram is extremely helpful in determining the sequence in which power travels through the unit and for checking the correct operation of switches and loads.

Service Hints

Insufficient heat

1. *System or building incomplete.* Your new furnace will not produce proper comfort until all construction has been completed and all insulation is in place.
2. *Building not properly winterized.* If a drafty condition exists, we suggest installation of storm doors and windows, as needed. If walls or ceiling are excessively cold, proper insulation (if practical to install) will do much to reduce fuel bills and improve comfort.
3. *Furnace overloaded.* This can happen when a dwelling is enlarged (by adding on rooms or opening up previously unused attic space). Have a heating engineer check the required heat load against the furnace capacity, and make proper and economical recommendations for solving this problem.
4. *Power supply turned off.* Close switch.
5. *Low power supply voltage.* Contact power company.
6. *Main fuse blown.* Replace fuse with correct type.
7. *Incorrect thermostat anticipator setting.* Correct setting.
8. *Fan operating at too high a speed resulting in a low-temperature rise.* Reconnect fan motor to next lower speed.
9. *Unit cycling on limit controls because of inadequate air circulation.*
   (a) Dirty air filter—clean or replace filter.
   (b) Fan wheel blades dirty—clean blades.
   (c) Duct dampers closed—open dampers.
   (d) Registers closed or restricted—open registers.
   (e) Fan motor nonoperational—find reason and replace motor.

Other causes of insufficient heat could be open heater element or elements, blown element fuses, blown fan motor and transformer fuses, blown thermal link fuses, shorted contactor control, shorted wiring, shorted transformer, loose terminal connections, and so on. Any of these malfunctions requires the services of a technician or electrician.

Rooms too hot—or some too cold

1. *Thermostat located incorrectly.* Read the section in the thermostat installation instructions on locating the thermostat, and relocate it as necessary.
2. *System out of balance.* Readjust dampers.
3. *Registers blocked.* Check carefully to make sure that rugs or furniture are not covering or blocking discharge or return air registers.
4. *Air passages blocked.* Check to see that return air passages are not blocked. Remove obstructions such as fallen insulation.

Fan/motor noisy   Check fan assembly for loose bolts and then lubricate motor bearings.

Checking Power

It is essential that the proper power be supplied to the equipment and to the load devices in the furnace. Manufacturers' data on the nameplate indicate the proper voltage. Most equipment can be operated within a range of 10% above or below the rated voltage. If power is not available within these limits, the equipment will not operate properly.

Checking Switches

1. *Voltmeter.* This test can be used only when power is on and the voltmeter leads are placed across the two terminals of the switch. When the switch is closed, the voltmeter reads 0. When the switch is open, the voltmeter reads the voltage in the circuit.
2. *Ohmmeter. This test is used only when the power is* off. The leads of the ohmmeter are placed across the two terminals of the switch. The switch must be disconnected from the circuit. A 0 (zero) reading indicates that the switch is closed. An ∞ (infinity) reading indicates that the switch is open.
3. *Jumper.* This test is used with the power on. If a jumper across the two terminals of the switch operates the load, the switch is open.

Checking Loads

1. *Voltmeter.* Test with power on. Determine if proper voltage is available at the load. With proper voltage the load should operate.
2. *Ammeter.* This test is performed with power on.
   The ammeter test is used to check the current used by the total furnace or any one of its load components (Figure 15–13). The meter readings are compared with the data on the nameplate. This test offers an excellent means of checking the current through the sequencer to be certain that the elements are being staged on at the proper time. The jaws of the clamp-on ammeter are placed around one of the main power supply lines.

FIGURE 15–13   Ammeter used to read current draw of electric furnace.

STUDY QUESTIONS

Answers to the study questions may be found in the sections noted in brackets.

15–1. What is the principal difference between the electric heating furnace and other types? *[Conversion of Electricity to Heat]*

15–2. What is the heat equivalent of 1 W? *[Conversion of Electricity to Heat]*

15–3. What is the efficiency of an electric furnace? *[Electric Furnace Components]*

15–4. What is the cut-out temperature on an electric furnace limit control? *[Heating Elements]*

15–5. What is the maximum-sized heating element? *[Heating Elements]*

15–6. What voltage is supplied to an electric furnace? *[Power Supply]*

15–7. What are the voltages on a control circuit transformer on an electric furnace? *[Power Circuit]*

15–8. Are the heating elements connected in series or parallel? *[Heating Element Circuits]*

15–9. What is the purpose of the sequencer? *[Heating Element Circuits]*

15–10. The outdoor thermostat is used in place of what type of room thermostat? *[Heating Element Circuits]*

15–11. What instrument is used to check the flow of current through the heating elements? *[Checking Loads]*

15–12. What are the causes of insufficient heat? *[Service Hints]*

15–13. What causes rooms to be too hot? *[Service Hints]*

15–14. Should the fan always operate when the heating elements are on? *[Fan Circuit]*

16

Estimating the Heating Load

OBJECTIVES

After studying this chapter, the student will be able to:

- Utilize heating load calculation procedures described in the Air Conditioning Contractors of America's *Manual J*

OVERVIEW OF HEATING LOADS

The primary purpose of a heating system is to provide comfort conditions with the expenditure of a minimum amount of energy. This process requires that the heating system be properly sized to fit the building requirements. Most heat load calculations are derived from ASHRAE information published by the Air Conditioning Contractors of America (ACCA) in *Manual J*, which has become the standard of the residential heating industry.

Manual J provides an orderly procedure for calculating the total load of a structure, which is then used as the basis for selecting furnace size. The *Manual J* calculation also provides the loads of the individual rooms, which can be used to design the duct system using ACCA's *Manual D*. This chapter deals only with the use of *Manual J*. Selecting the correct furnace size is very important, since an undersized unit will not handle the load, whereas an oversized unit with excess capacity can result in poor control, inefficiency, excessive operating costs, and other problems.

TYPICAL CALCULATION

To illustrate how to use *Manual J*, a typical calculation is shown. An abbreviated floor plan is given in Figure 16–1. For simplicity, the outside walls and partitions are shown

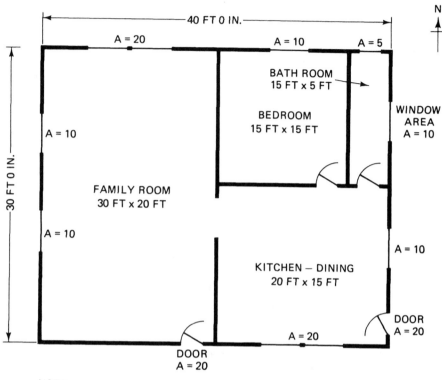

FIGURE 16–1   Floor plan.

as single lines. In actual practice the outside dimensions of the house would be used for the "entire house" calculation. The inside dimensions of the outside walls would be used in calculating the individual room loads.

Determining Outside Design Temperature

In the example shown, the city selected from Table 16–1* is Detroit, Michigan, which has a winter design temperature of +6°F. This is not the lowest temperature reached in the area, but 97^{1}/$_{2}$% of the time the temperature will be above the +6°F outdoor design temperature.

Selecting Inside Design Temperature

The recommended selection is 70°F.

---

*All tables used in this chapter are from ACCA's *Manual J*.

TABLE 16–1 Outdoor design conditions for representative cities in Georgia and Michigan.

| | | Winter | |
| | | | |
Location	Latitude (degrees)	97¹/₂% design (db)	Heating D.D. below 65°F
Georgia			
Atlanta	33	+22	2990
Augusta	33	+23	2410
Savannah	32	+27	1850
Michigan			
Detroit	42	(+6)	6290
Grand Rapids	42	+5	6890
Lansing	42	+1	6940

Source: Courtesy of Air Conditioning Contractors of America.

Determining Design Temperature Difference

Design temperature difference is the difference between the inside design temperature of 70°F and the outside design temperature of 6°F:

$$70°F - 6°F = 64°F$$

Rounding this figure to the nearest 5°F interval, the value used is 65°F. (This is done to comply with the 5°F temperature increments shown in the tables.)

Determining Construction Numbers

The construction numbers for windows, doors, walls, ceilings, and floors are given in Table 16–2. These numbers represent the materials used in construction of these various exposures. Referring to the excerpts from Table 16–2, note that each type of construction is represented by a number and a letter. A "double-pane window" with a "metal frame" is therefore identified as construction number "3C."

Determining Heat-Transfer Multipliers

The heat-transfer multiplier (HTM) for each construction number is based on the design temperature difference. For example, for a double-pane window, the construction number 3C has an HTM value of 47.1 at a winter temperature difference of 65°F. A summary of the construction numbers and HTM values for the example is shown in Figure 16–2.

Recording Construction Numbers

The construction numbers and the HTM values are recorded in the appropriate locations on the data sheet (see Figure 16–3).

TABLE 16–2 Heat-transfer multipliers (heating)

		Winter T.D.	
	60	65	70
		–HTM–	
No. 3 double-pane window			
Clear Glass			
A. Wood frame	33.1	35.8	38.6
B. T.I.M. frame*	36.5	39.6	42.6
C. Metal frame	43.5	(47.1)	50.8
No. 11 metal doors			
A. Fiberglass core	35.4	(38.4)	41.3
B. Fiberglass core and storm	22.0	23.9	25.7
C. Polystyrene core	28.2	30.6	32.9

No. 12 wood frame exterior walls with sheathing and siding or brick, or other exterior finish

	Cav. insul.	Sheathing			
A.	None	$1/2$ in. GYPSUM BRD. (R. 0.5)	16.3	17.6	19.0
B.	None	$1/2$ in. ASPHALT BRD. (R. 1.3)	13.0	14.1	15.2
C.	R-11	$1/2$ in. GYPSUM BRD. (R. 0.5)	5.4	5.8	6.3
D.	R-11	$1/2$ in. ASPHALT BRD. (R. 1.3)	4.8	(5.2)	5.6

No. 16 ceiling under ventilated attic space or unheated room			
A. No insulation	35.9	38.9	41.3
B. R-7 insulation	7.2	7.8	8.4
C. R-11 insulation	5.3	5.7	6.2
D. R-19 insulation	3.2	(3.4)	3.7

No. 19 floors over an unheated basement, enclosed crawl space			
A. Hardwood floor + no insul.	9.4	10.1	10.9
B. Hardwood floor + R11 insul.	2.4	(2.6)	2.8
C. Hardwood floor + R13 insul.	2.3	2.5	2.7

*T.I.M. Thermally improved metal frame.

Source: Courtesy of Air Conditioning Contractors of America

Determining Infiltration

For the sample calculation, referring to Table 16–3, the number of winter air changes per hour for this 1200-ft.^{2} residence of average construction is 1.0 air change per hour. Using procedure A in Table 16–3, the HTM value for infiltration is 84.7. This value is recorded on the data sheet.

	Const. no.	HTM
A. Determine outdoor design temperature + 6F db (Table 1) Detroit, Mich.		
B. Select inside design temperature + 70°F db		
C. Design temperature difference: 70° − 6° = 64°F (For convenience, use 65°F.)		
D. Windows: all rooms—clear glass, double pane, metal frame (no storm); Table 2	3C	47.1
E. Doors: Metal, fiberglass core, no storm; Table 2	11A	38.4
F. First-floor walls: basic frame construction, plastic vapor barrier, R-11 insulation, ½-in. asphalt brd. (R1.3) sheathing, and face brick; Table 2	12D	5.2
G. Ceiling: basic construction, under vented attic, with R-19 insulation; Table 2	16D	3.4
H. Floor: Hardwood plus R-11 insulation; over enclosed unheated crawl space; Table 2	19B	2.6

Note: Ceilings are 8 ft.; all duct work is located in the unheated crawl space and is covered with R-4 insulation (7A, multiplier 0.10).

FIGURE 16–2 Assumed design conditions and construction (heating). (Courtesy of Air Conditioning Contractors of America.)

Determining Duct-Loss Multiplier

For the example shown, refer to Table 16–4; based on supply air temperatures below 120°F and the duct with R-4 insulation located in the crawl space, the duct-loss multiplier is 0. 10 (10%). This is recorded on the data sheet (see Figure 16–3).

Recording Exposed Areas

The exposed areas for the entire house and individual rooms are recorded on the data sheet (see Figure 16–3).

Multiplying Exposed Areas by HTM Factors

The exposed areas are multiplied by the HTM factors to obtain the heat loss through each exposure. Add the individual exposure losses to obtain a subtotal. Add the duct loss to the subtotal. For the example shown, the total Btuh loss for the entire house is 32,745 Btuh (29,768 + 2977). For one individual room (the family room) the load is 15,327 Btuh (13,934 + 1393). The same procedure applies to the other rooms in the house.

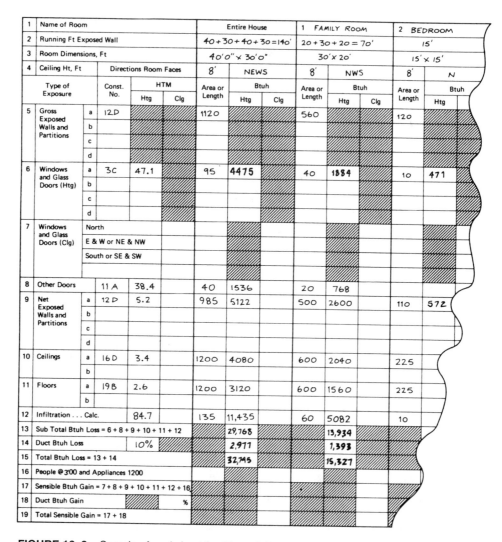

			HTM		Entire House	Btuh		1 FAMILY ROOM	Btuh		2 BEDROOM	Btuh
1	Name of Room				Entire House			FAMILY ROOM			BEDROOM	
2	Running Ft Exposed Wall				40+30+40+30=140'			20+30+20=70'			15'	
3	Room Dimensions, Ft				40'0" x 30'0"			30'x20'			15'x15'	
4	Ceiling Ht, Ft	Directions Room Faces			8'	NEWS		8' NWS			8' N	
	Type of Exposure	Const. No.	Htg	Clg	Area or Length	Htg	Clg	Area or Length	Htg	Clg	Area or Length	Btuh Htg
5	Gross Exposed Walls and Partitions a b c d	12D			1120			560			120	
6	Windows and Glass Doors (Htg) a b c d	3C	47.1		95	4475		40	1884		10	471
7	Windows and Glass Doors (Clg) North / E & W or NE & NW / South or SE & SW											
8	Other Doors	11 A	38.4		40	1536		20	768			
9	Net Exposed Walls and Partitions a b c d	12 D	5.2		985	5122		500	2600		110	572
10	Ceilings a b	16 D	3.4		1200	4080		600	2040		225	
11	Floors a b	19 B	2.6		1200	3120		600	1560		225	
12	Infiltration . . . Calc.		84.7		135	11,435		60	5082		10	
13	Sub Total Btuh Loss = 6 + 8 + 9 + 10 + 11 + 12					29,768			13,934			
14	Duct Btuh Loss		10%			2,971			1,393			
15	Total Btuh Loss = 13 + 14					32,745			15,327			
16	People @ 300 and Appliances 1200											
17	Sensible Btuh Gain = 7 + 8 + 9 + 10 + 11 + 12 + 16											
18	Duct Btuh Gain			%								
19	Total Sensible Gain = 17 + 18											

FIGURE 16–3 Sample of worksheet for *Manual J* load calculation. (Courtesy of Air Conditioning Contractors of America.)

COMPUTER PROGRAMS

A number of computer programs are available for calculating heating and cooling loads. Generally speaking, there are two types:

1. Those that relate directly to the information published by ASHRAE
2. The Right-J Program, which relates directly to *Manual J*, published by ACCA

When using the Right-J Program, it should be determined that the program follows the most recent edition of *Manual J*. A number of important changes have been

TABLE 16–3   Infiltration evaluation of winter air changes per hour

Floor Area	900 or less	900–1500
Best	0.4	0.4
Average	1.2	(1.0)
Poor	2.2	1.6

Best, average, and poor categories are based on the quality of the structure. *For example, Average* would include a plastic vapor barrier, caulking, weather-stripping, exhaust fans dampered, combustion air from inside, intermittent ignition, and a flue damper.

Procedure A—winter infiltration, HTM calculation.

1. Winter infiltration CFM
   1.0 AC/H × 9600 ft.^{3} volume × 0.0167
   $$= 160 \text{ ft.}^3/\text{min}$$

2. Winter infiltration Btuh
   1.1 × 160 ft.^{3}/min × 65°Winter TD
   $$= 11,440 \text{ Btuh}$$

3. Winter infiltration HTM
   11,440 Btuh ÷ 135 total window and door area
   $$= 84.7 \text{ HTM}$$

Cubic volume of house = floor area × ceiling height In example: 1200 × 8 = 9600 ft.^{3}

Source: Courtesy of Air Conditioning Contractors of America.

made in the calculation procedures in recent years. Of primary importance is the calculation of infiltration. Tests have shown that when compared to newer structures, some older types of construction have high infiltration factors, which can practically double the total load.

The computer programs are fast and accurate, provided that good data are supplied and the operator has sufficient training in operating the computer. It is advisable to compare computer results with manual calculations when using the computer programs initially as a check for possible errors.

TABLE 16–4   Duct loss multipliers

Supply air temperatures below 120°F	Duct loss multipliers	
Duct location and insulation value	Winter design below 15°F	Winter design above 15°F
Enclosed in unheated space		
Crawl space or basement–none	0.20	0.15
Crawl space or basement–R2	0.15	0.10
Crawl space or basement–R4	(0.10)	0.05
Crawl space or basement–R6	0.05	0.00

Source: Courtesy of Air Conditioning Contractors of America.

The printouts from the computer programs are useful in making presentations or submitting information to building authorities. The summaries indicate not only the final load calculations but also the construction factors used. Another feature of the computer programs is the ease in making "what-if" (prediction) calculations. For example, it might be of interest to compare various amounts of insulation to determine the most cost-effective thickness to use. This would confirm that the extra first cost is justified based on the savings in operating costs. It is then a simple matter to recalculate the load based on assumed changes in construction factors.

STUDY QUESTIONS

Answers to the study questions may be found in the sections noted in brackets.

16–1. What is the primary purpose of the heating system? *[Overview of Heating Loads]*

16–2. Why *is Manual J* considered a standard of the industry for calculating residential heating loads? *[Overview of Heating Loads]*

16–3. Are the outside or inside dimensions of a house used in calculating a heating load? *[Typical Calculation]*

16–4. Which table is used to determine the outside design temperature? *[Typical Calculation]*

16–5. Which table is used to select the construction factors? *[Typical Calculation]*

16–6. Give an example of determining the design temperature difference. *[Typical Calculation]*

16–7. Give an example of selecting the heat-transfer multiplier (HTM). How is it used? *[Typical Calculation]*

16–8. What is infiltration, and what is its unit of measurement? *[Typical Calculation]*

16–9. What factors are multiplied to determine the heat loss through an exposure? *[Typical Calculation]*

16–10. What is the construction number for hardwood floors with no insulation over an unheated basement? Also, what is the HTM factor for a winter design temperature difference of 65°F? *[Determining Heat Transfer Multipliers]*

17

Evaluating a Heating System

OBJECTIVES

After studying this chapter, the student will be able to:

- Evaluate the furnace selection and the air distribution system for an existing residence
- Determine the input value of fuel used for a heating system
- Measure the air quantity actually being circulated in a forced warm air heating system

DIAGNOSING THE PROBLEM

To diagnose a problem and then decide what is needed to correct it, a service technician must first determine whether the difficulty is a system problem or a mechanical problem. Some typical system problems are:

- Drafts
- Uneven temperature
- Not enough heat

Drafts are currents of relatively cold air that cause discomfort when they come in contact with the body. Drafts may be caused by a downflow of cold air from an outside wall or window. Uneven temperatures can cause discomfort and are generally due to the following:

1. Different temperatures in a room near the floor and near the ceiling (sometimes called *stratification*) (Figure 17–1)
2. Different temperatures in one room compared to another
3. Different temperatures on one floor level compared to another

FIGURE 17–1 Stratification of room air.

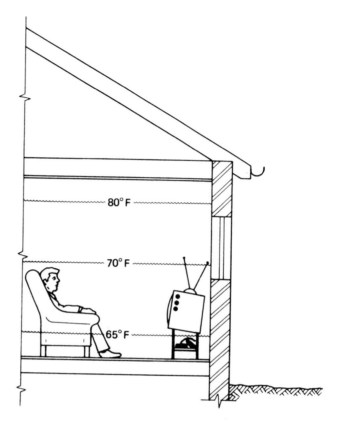

Uneven room temperatures may be caused by incorrect supply diffuser locations. Cold outside surfaces of a room should be warmed by properly located supply air outlets. Temperature differences between rooms may be caused by improper balancing of the system due to the lack of duct dampers in the branch run to each outlet. Balancing is the process of regulating the flow of air into each room to produce even temperatures. Not enough heat may be caused by too small a furnace or improper fuel input to the unit to match the heating load of the house.

Some system problems can be solved or improved by the service technician. Some problems, however, are built into the design of the system and can only be corrected by redesign or replacement of major components.

EVALUATING THE SYSTEM

Three items should be considered:

1. Furnace (energy source and efficiency)
2. Fan
3. Air distribution systems (supply and return)

Two questions relate to the furnace:

1. Has the proper size been selected?
2. Is the furnace adjusted to produce its rated output?

In Chapter 16 a method was given for determining the heating load of a building. Any losses that occur, such as duct loss or ventilation air, are added to the total room loss to determine the total required heating load. The furnace output rating should be equal to, but not greater than 15% higher, than the total required heating load. If the furnace is too small, it will not heat properly in extreme weather. If it is too large, the "off" cycles will be too long, and the result will be uneven heating.

To determine if a furnace is producing its rated capacity, it is necessary to check:

1. Fuel input
2. Combustion efficiency

Energy Source

Gas   Many manufacturers void their warranty if the gas input is not adjusted to within 2% of the rated input of the furnace, as shown on the furnace nameplate (see Figure 17–2). To determine input, proceed as follows:

1. Obtain the BTU/ft.^{3} rating of the gas from the local utility.*
2. Turn off all other appliances and operate the furnace continuously during the test.
3. Measure the length of time it takes for the furnace to consume 1 ft.^{3} of gas.

For example, if it takes 36 seconds to use 1 ft.^{3} of gas (using the 1-ft.^{3} dial on the meter) and the gas rating is 1000 Btu/ft.^{3}, the input is 1000 Btu/ft.^{3} × 100 ft.^{3} = 100,000 Btuh. The 100 is found on the "36 seconds" line in the 1-ft.^{3} dial column in Figure 17–3. If the furnace is rated at 100,000 Btuh input, the usage would be within requirements.†

Another method of computing the gas flow to a furnace or other appliances is by utilizing the following formula:

$$cubic\ feet\ of\ gas = \frac{3600 \times dial\ on\ the\ gas\ meter}{number\ of\ seconds\ for\ one\ revolution}$$

$$= \frac{3600 \times 1\ ft.^3\ dial}{36\ seconds/revolution} = 100\ ft.^3$$

$$furnace\ input = 100\ ft.^3 \times 1000\ Btu/ft.^3 = 100,000\ Btuh$$

Some meters have low input dials other than 1 ft.^{3}. Using the table shown in Figure 17–3 and the method described, a similar check on the gas input can be made. If the input is not correct, it should be changed to the furnace input rating by adjusting the gas-pressure regulating valve or by changing the size of the burner orifices (see the manufacturer's instructions for details).

---

*Consult the local gas company for this information.

†Input rating for a gas furnace is given on the furnace nameplate.

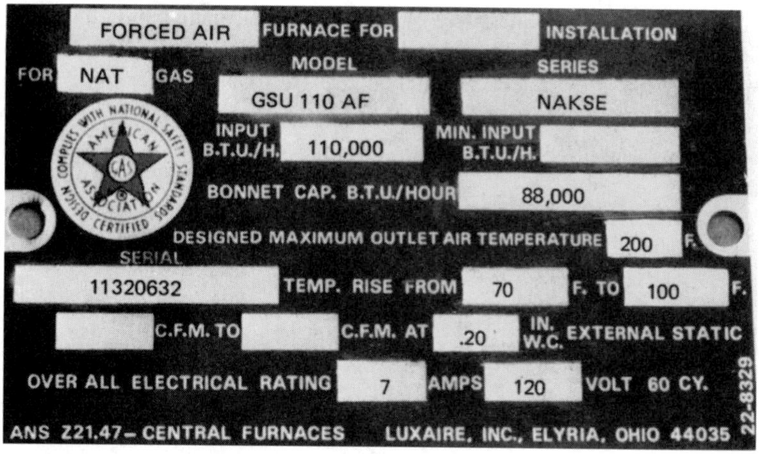

FIGURE 17–2 Typical gas furnace nameplate.

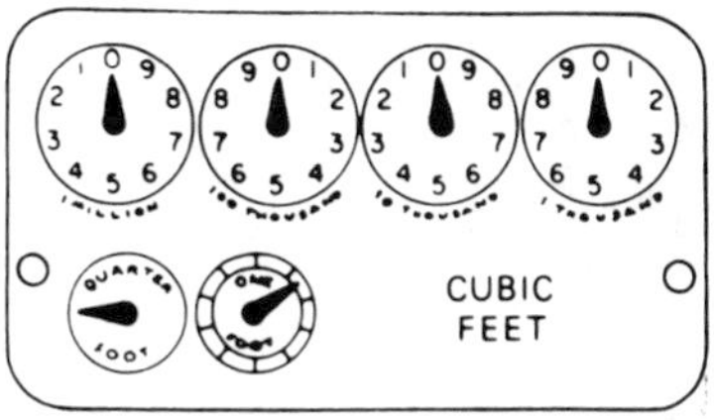

THE DIAL IS MARKED AS TO HOW MUCH GAS IS MEASURED FOR EACH REVOLUTION. USING THE NUMBER OF SECONDS FOR ONE REVOLUTION, AND THE SIZE OF THE TEST DIAL, FIND THE CUBIC FEET OF GAS CONSUMED PER HOUR FROM THE TABLE

SECONDS FOR ONE REV.	SIZE OF TEST DIAL ¼ CU.FT.	½ CU.FT.	1 CU.FT.	2 CU.FT.	5 CU.FT.	SECONDS FOR ONE REV.	SIZE OF TEST DIAL ¼ CU.FT.	½ CU.FT.	1 CU.FT.	2 CU.FT.	5 CU.FT.
10	90	180	360	720	1800						
11	82	164	327	655	1636	→ 36	25	50	→ 100	200	500
12	75	150	300	600	1500	37	–	–	97	195	486
13	69	138	277	555	1385	38	23	47	95	189	474
14	64	129	257	514	1286	39	–	–	92	185	462
15	60	120	240	480	1200	40	22	45	90	180	450
16	56	113	225	450	1125	41	–	–	–	176	439
17	53	106	212	424	1059	42	21	43	86	172	429
18	50	100	200	400	1000	43	–	–	–	167	419
19	47	95	189	379	947	44	–	41	82	164	409
20	45	90	180	360	900	45	20	40	80	160	400
21	43	86	171	343	857	46	–	–	78	157	391
22	41	82	164	327	818	47	19	38	76	153	383
23	39	78	157	313	783	48	–	–	75	150	375
24	37	75	150	300	750	49	–	–	–	147	367
25	36	72	144	288	720	50	18	36	72	144	360
26	34	69	138	277	692	51	–	–	–	141	355
27	33	67	133	267	667	52	–	–	69	138	346
28	32	64	129	257	643	53	17	34	–	136	240
29	31	62	124	248	621	54	–	–	67	133	333
30	30	60	120	240	600	55	–	–	–	131	327
31	–	–	116	232	581	56	16	32	64	129	321
32	28	56	113	225	563	57	–	–	–	126	316
33	–	–	109	218	545	58	–	31	62	124	310
34	26	53	106	212	529	59	–	–	–	122	305
35	–	–	103	206	514	60	15	30	60	120	300

FIGURE 17–3 Gas meter measuring dials and table for determining gas input based on dial readings. (Courtesy of Bard Manufacturing Company.)

Oil   The input rating to an oil furnace can be checked by determining the oil burner nozzle size and measuring the oil pressure. Nozzles are rated for a given amount of oil flow at 100 pounds per square inch gauge (psig) oil pressure. One gallon of grade No. 2 oil contains 140,000 Btu. The oil burner nozzle is examined and the input flow is read on the nozzle in gallons per hour (gal/h). Thus a nozzle rated at 0.75 gal/h operating with an oil pressure of 100 psi would produce an input rating of 105,000 Btu (0.75 gal/h x 140,000 Btu). The oil pressure is measured and adjusted, if necessary, to 100 psig within 3%. Figure 17–4 illustrates a typical oil furnace nameplate and oil burner nozzle.

Electricity   For an electric furnace the input is usually rated in watt-hours (Wh) or kilowatt-hours (kWh) (1000 Wh = 1 kWh of electricity consumed). Watts (W) can be converted to Btu by multiplying by 3.4131 (1 W = 3.4131 Btu). For example, if an electric furnace is rated at 30 kWh, the input is 102,393 Btuh (30 kWh $\times$ 1000 h/kWh $\times$ 3.4131 Btu). Figure 17–5 illustrates a typical electric furnace nameplate.

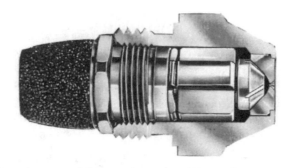

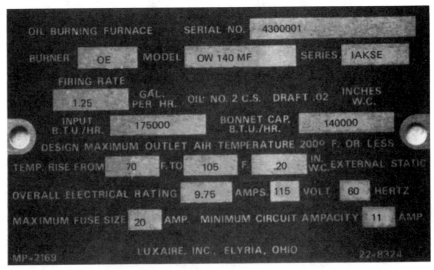

FIGURE 17–4   Typical oil burner nozzle and oil furnace nameplate. (Courtesy of Delavan Corporation.)

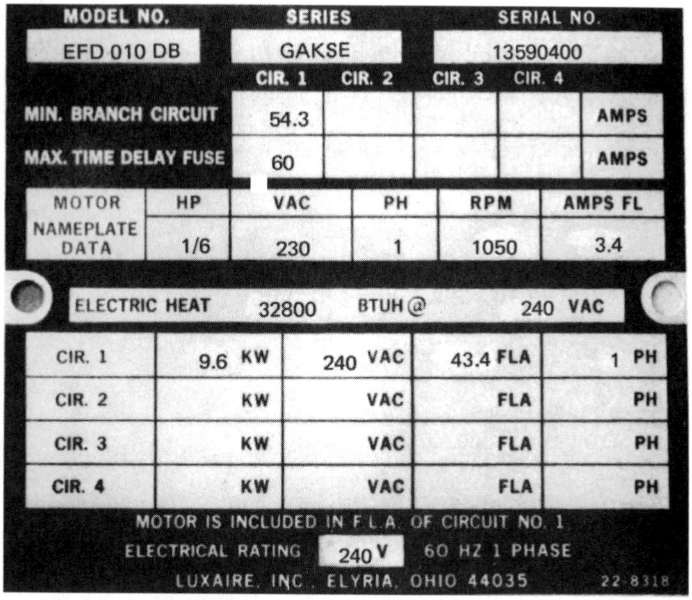

MODEL NO.		SERIES		SERIAL NO.		
EFD 010 DB		GAKSE		13590400		

	CIR. 1	CIR. 2	CIR. 3	CIR. 4	
MIN. BRANCH CIRCUIT	54.3				AMPS
MAX. TIME DELAY FUSE	60				AMPS

MOTOR NAMEPLATE DATA	HP	VAC	PH	RPM	AMPS FL
	1/6	230	1	1050	3.4

ELECTRIC HEAT 32800 BTUH @ 240 VAC

	KW	VAC	FLA	PH
CIR. 1	9.6 KW	240 VAC	43.4 FLA	1 PH
CIR. 2	KW	VAC	FLA	PH
CIR. 3	KW	VAC	FLA	PH
CIR. 4	KW	VAC	FLA	PH

MOTOR IS INCLUDED IN F.L.A. OF CIRCUIT NO. 1

ELECTRICAL RATING 240 V 60 HZ 1 PHASE

LUXAIRE, INC. ELYRIA, OHIO 44035   22-8318

FIGURE 17–5 Typical electrical furnace nameplate.

Efficiency

For both gas and oil furnaces, the output rating is reduced from the input rating by an efficiency factor. For an electric furnace, though, the input is equal to the output since there is no heat loss up the chimney. The general formula is

$$Btuh\ output = Btuh\ input \times efficiency\ factor$$

The output rating of both gas and oil furnaces is shown on the nameplate as a percentage of input. The efficiency of the installed furnace is usually lower, however. A service technician should perform an efficiency test to determine if the rated efficiency is actually being maintained. The method of determining and adjusting combustion efficiency for oil furnaces is covered in Chapter 13. Gas furnace adjustments are covered in Chapter 5. In most cases where the combustion efficiency is low, the technician can adjust the fuel burner so that the furnace might again approach the design efficiency. Having measured the efficiency of the furnace, the actual output can be calculated from the formula given. For example, if a gas furnace is operating at 80% efficiency* and has an input of 100,000 Btuh, the output (bonnet capacity) is 80,000 Btuh (100,000 Btuh × 0.80 efficiency). An electric furnace with 30 (kWh) (102,393 Btuh) input operates at 100% efficiency and has an output of 102,393 Btuh (102,393 Btuh × 1.00 efficiency).

It is seldom desirable to select a furnace with a rated output equal to the heat loss of the house. If this were done, the furnace could be too small due to system

*Manufacturer's rating.

losses or system inefficiency. Other losses can occur that are not accounted for in the heat-loss calculations, and combustion efficiencies may not always be achieved. For these reasons it is good practice to add 10 or 15% to the calculated heat loss to determine the required furnace output.

Fans

The fan produces the movement of air through the furnace, absorbing heat from the heat exchanger surface and carrying it through the distribution system to the areas to be heated. Discussion of the fan involves:

- Air volume
- Static pressure
- Causes of poor air distribution

Air volume   For the system to operate satisfactorily, the fan must deliver the proper air volume. Most furnaces permit some flexibility (variation) in the air volume capacity of the furnace. A furnace having an output of 80,000 Btuh may be able to produce 800, 1200, and 1600 cfm of air volume, depending on the requirements. Systems designed for heating only usually require less air than systems designed for both heating and cooling. The proper air volume for heating is usually determined by the required temperature rise. The temperature rise is the supply air temperature minus the return air temperature at the furnace. Systems used for heating only should be capable of a temperature rise of 85°F. Systems designed for heating and cooling should be capable of a minimum temperature rise of 70°F.

To find the quantity of air the furnace is actually circulating, a service technician measures the temperature rise. One thermometer is placed in the return air plenum and the other is placed in the supply air duct. While the furnace is operating continuously the readings are taken and the temperature rise (difference) computed. Thermometer locations for checking temperature rise are shown in Figure 17–6.

For a typical heating-only application, the return air temperature is 65°F and supply air temperature 150°F, indicating an 85°F temperature rise (150°F − 65°F = 85°F). For a typical heating-cooling system, the return air temperature is 65°F and the supply air temperature is 135°F, indicating a temperature rise of 70°F (135°F − 65°F = 70°F). The air volume circulated is proportionately different for the two types of systems. To determine air volume the following formula is used:

$$cfm = \frac{Btuh\ output\ of\ furnace}{temperature\ rise\ (°F) \times 1.08}$$

Thus if the temperature rise on an 80,000-Btu output furnace is 85°F, the air volume is

$$cfm = \frac{80,000\ Btuh}{80°F \times 1.08} = 870$$

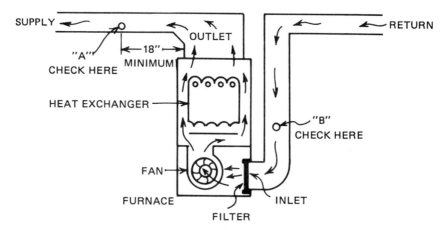

*CHECK POINT "A" MUST BE FAR ENOUGH DOWNSTREAM
THAT THE THERMOMETER IS NOT EXPOSED TO
RADIANT HEAT FROM THE HEAT EXCHANGER.

FIGURE 17–6   Thermometer locations for checking temperature

If the temperature rise on an 80,000-Btuh output furnace is 70°F, the air volume is

$$cfm = \frac{80,000 \text{ Btuh}}{70°F \times 1.08} = 1058$$

Many furnaces have two-speed fans, with the low speed used for heating and the high speed for cooling. Adjustments in the fan speed can be made on most furnaces to regulate the air volume to meet the requirements of the heating system. This is discussed further in Chapter 4.

Static pressure   A manufacturer rates the fan air volume of a furnace to produce each quantity of air at a certain external static pressure. *Static pressure* is the resistance to airflow offered by any component through which the air passes. *External static pressure is* the resistance of all components outside the furnace itself. Thus if a unit is rated to supply 600 cfm at an external static pressure of 0.20 in., it means that the total resistance offered by supply ducts + return ducts + supply diffusers + return grilles must not exceed 0.20 in. of static pressure. A system external and internal static pressure diagram is shown in Figure 17–7.

Static pressure is measured in inches of water column (W.C.) that the pressure of the fan is capable of raising on a water gauge *manometer* (Figure 17–8). A manometer is an instrument for measuring pressure of gases and vapors. The pressures in residential systems are small, so an inclined tube manometer is used to increase the accuracy of the readings taken. A manometer indicates the air pressure delivered by the fan above atmospheric pressure. To illustrate how small these fan readings are, 1 atmosphere 14.7 psi is equal to 408 in. W.C. Two-tenths of an inch (0.20 in. W.C.) of pressure is 1/2040 atmosphere.

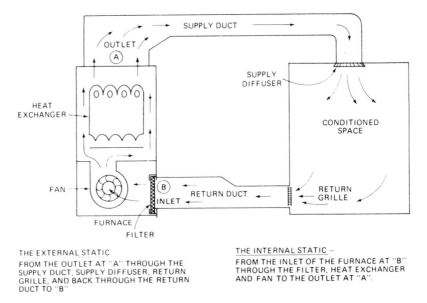

THE EXTERNAL STATIC
FROM THE OUTLET AT "A" THROUGH THE
SUPPLY DUCT, SUPPLY DIFFUSER, RETURN
GRILLE, AND BACK THROUGH THE RETURN
DUCT TO "B"

THE INTERNAL STATIC –
FROM THE INLET OF THE FURNACE AT "B"
THROUGH THE FILTER, HEAT EXCHANGER
AND FAN TO THE OUTLET AT "A".

FIGURE 17–7 System external and internal static pressure diagram.

    A great deal of care must be taken in designing an air distribution system to stay within the rated external static pressure of the furnace. If the system resistances are too high, the amount of airflow of the furnace is reduced. All manufacturers' ratings of external static pressure are based on clean filters. Dirty filters can cause reduced air volume and poor heating. A table showing the relationship between increased external static pressure and decreased air volume (cfm) is given in Figure 17–9.

    The greater the air volume and static pressure of a furnace, the larger the horsepower of the motor required to deliver the air. Therefore, units used for heat pumps, operating at higher air volumes and higher static pressures, require higher horsepower motors than do units used for heating only. The speed or revolutions per minute (rev/min) of the fan wheel must often be increased for cooling. The wet cooling coil installed external to the basic furnace has a resistance to the airflow in addition to ductwork and grilles. The total external static pressure of a cooling system may be as high as 0.50 in. W.C. static pressure. Following are two typical performance ratings for a unit that can be applied to either heating only or heating and cooling:

Use	Air Volume (CFM)	External Static (in. W.C.)	Motor HP
Heating only	700	0.20	$\frac{1}{8}$
Heating and cooling	800	0.50	$\frac{1}{4}$

MODEL 170 INCLINED-TYPE PORTABLE
MANOMETER, WITH BUILT-IN LEVELING
AND MAGNETIC CLIPS. RANGE: 0-0.50 IN.
WATER (COURTESY, DWYER INSTRUMENTS, INC.)

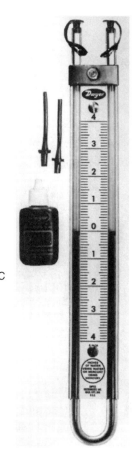

SERIES 1222-8-D FLEX-TUBE
U-TUBE MANOMETER, MAGNETIC
MOUNTING CLIPS AND RED
GAUGE OIL INCLUDED.
RANGE: 8-IN. WATER (4-0-4)
(COURTESY, DWYER
INSTRUMENTS, INC.)

MODEL MZF, DRY-TYPE.
SUPPLIED WITH 5-IN. DRAFT
TUBE AND 9 FT OF RUBBER
TUBING. RANGE +0.05 TO 0.25 IN.
WATER (COURTESY, BACHARACH
INSTRUMENT COMPANY.)

FIGURE 17–8   Types of manometers.

Causes of poor air distribution   One of the first jobs of a service technician in evaluating the distribution system is to determine whether it has been designed for heating only or for heating and cooling. If the air volume is found to be too low, it can be caused by one or more of the following:

1. Incorrect fan speed
2. Closed or partially closed dampers
3. Dirty filters
4. Incorrectly sized ducts
5. High-pressure-drop duct fittings

If improper fan speed is the problem, the technician can check on the possibility of speeding it up. This may require a larger motor. The increased speed must be kept within permissible noise levels. If closed dampers are the problem, adjustments can be made. Dampers are installed for balancing the system (regulating the

AIR DELIVERY—(CFM) FOR DIRECT DRIVE BLOWERS

MODEL NUMBER	BLOWER SIZE	MOTOR H.P.	BLOWER SPEED	EXTERNAL STATIC PRESSURE—INCHES WATER COLUMN													
				0.1		0.2		0.3		0.4		0.5		0.6		0.7	
				CFM	TEMP. RISE	CFM	TEMP. RISE	CFM	TEMP. RISE	CFM	TEMP. RISE	CFM	TEMP. RISE	CFM	TEMP. RISE	CFM	TEMP. RISE
GUH060A012	11.8x8	½	HIGH	1609	32.4	1550	33.6	1491	35.0	1431	36.4	1365	38.2	1280	40.7	1202	43.4
			MED.	1294	40.3	1268	41.1	1231	42.4	1188	43.9	1131	46.1	1070	48.9	992	52.6
			LOW	1045	49.9	1021	51.1	995	52.4	960	54.3	924	56.5	875	59.6	820	63.6
GUH075A012	11.8x8	½	HIGH	1609	40.1	1550	41.6	1491	43.3	1431	45.1	1365	47.3	1280	50.4	1202	53.7
			MED.	1294	49.9	1268	50.9	1231	52.4	1188	54.3	1131	57.1	1070	60.3	992	65.1
			LOW	1045	61.8	1021	63.2	995	64.9	960	67.2	924	69.8	875	73.8	820	78.7
GUH100A016	11.8x10.6	¾	HIGH	1642	52.4	1568	54.9	1505	57.2	1441	59.7	1359	63.3	1270	67.8	1170	78.5
			MED. HI	1621	53.1	1557	55.3	1487	57.9	1415	60.8	1357	63.4	1252	68.7	1152	74.7
			MED. LOW	1465	58.7	1399	61.5	1343	64.1	1285	67.0	1197	71.9	1122	76.7	1030	83.6
			LOW	1335	64.5	1295	66.4	1249	68.9	1207	71.3	1152	74.7	1084	79.4	1010	85.2
GUH125A016	11.8x10.6	¾	HIGH	1810	58.8	1750	60.8	1675	63.5	1628	65.4	1577	67.5	1470	72.4	1371	77.6
			MED. HIGH	1802	59.0	1730	61.5	1655	64.3	1575	67.6	1478	72.0	1380	77.1	1262	84.3
			MED. LOW	1685	63.1	1625	65.5	1565	68.0	1490	71.4	1403	75.8	1308	81.4	1188	89.6
			LOW	1562	68.1	1515	70.2	1460	72.9	1390	76.6	1313	81.0	1220	87.2	1103	96.5
GUH125A020	11.8x10.6	¾	HIGH	2160	48.5	2085	50.0	2010	52.1	1955	53.6	1890	55.4	1820	57.6	1680	62.4
			MED. HIGH	1891	55.4	1837	57.0	1784	58.7	1729	60.6	1675	62.6	1582	66.2	1490	70.3
			MED. LOW	1777	59.0	1728	60.6	1680	62.4	1614	64.9	1549	67.6	1495	70.1	1441	72.7
			LOW	1631	64.2	1596	65.7	1562	67.1	1505	69.6	1448	72.4	1389	75.4	1330	78.8

FIGURE 17–9 Manufacturer's data showing external static pressures. (Courtesy of ARCOAIRE, Inter-City Products Corporation, USA).

airflow to each room) (Figure 17–10). Misadjustments should be corrected and, if necessary, the system rebalanced. If dirty filters are the problem, the owner should be advised of proper preventive maintenance measures. If duct sizes are the problem, some improvement can be made by speeding up the fan. There are limitations to improving this condition without a major redesign, however.

High-pressure-drop duct fittings are a problem that can often be corrected by minor changes in the ductwork. The pressure drop in duct fittings is usually given in terms of the equivalent length of straight duct of the same size having an equal pressure drop.

Figure 17–11 shows pressure drops in terms of equivalent lengths for various duct fittings. Abrupt turns and restrictions should be avoided whenever possible. Where duct work is placed in an unheated attic, crawl space, or garage, insulated

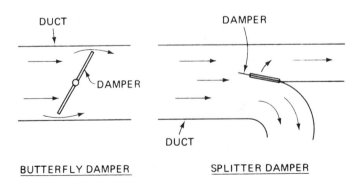

FIGURE 17–10 Balancing dampers.

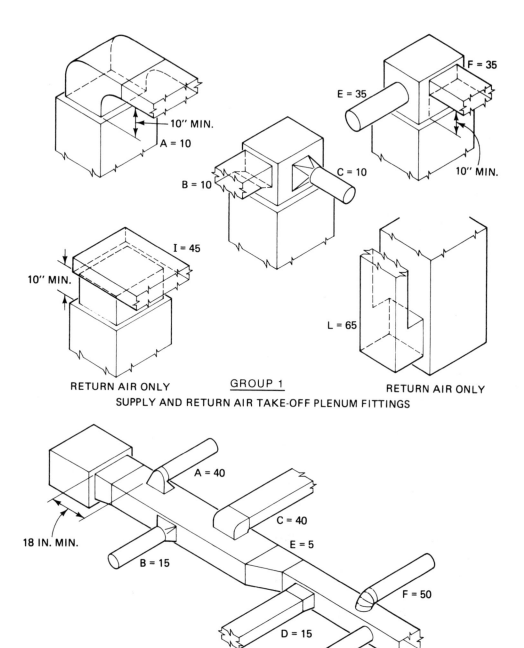

RETURN AIR ONLY

GROUP 1

RETURN AIR ONLY

SUPPLY AND RETURN AIR TAKE-OFF PLENUM FITTINGS

GROUP 3

EQUIVALENT LENGTH OF EXTENDED PLENUM FITTINGS

FIGURE 17–11 Supply and return fittings. (Courtesy of Air Conditioning Contractors of America.)

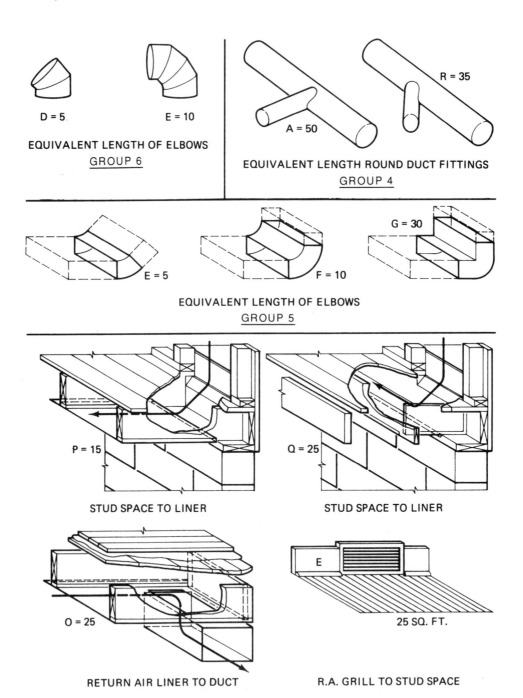

D = 5.

E = 10

EQUIVALENT LENGTH OF ELBOWS
GROUP 6

R = 35

A = 50

EQUIVALENT LENGTH ROUND DUCT FITTINGS
GROUP 4

G = 30

E = 5

F = 10

EQUIVALENT LENGTH OF ELBOWS
GROUP 5

P = 15

Q = 25

STUD SPACE TO LINER

STUD SPACE TO LINER

O = 25

E

RETURN AIR LINER TO DUCT

25 SQ. FT.

R.A. GRILL TO STUD SPACE

EQUIVALENT LENGTH OF RETURN SYSTEM COMPONENTS
GROUP 6

FIGURE 17–11   Continued.

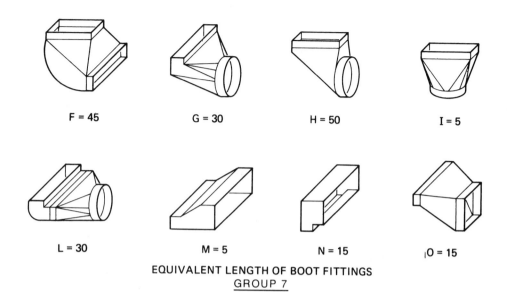

F = 45   G = 30   H = 50   I = 5

L = 30   M = 5   N = 15   ₁O = 15

EQUIVALENT LENGTH OF BOOT FITTINGS
GROUP 7

FIGURE 17–11   Continued.

ductwork should be used. Various types of flexible ducts and methods of insulating ducts are illustrated in Figure 17–12.

Supply Air Distribution Systems

In general, there are three types of supply air distribution systems:

1. Radial
2. Perimeter loop
3. Trunk duct and branch

Selection of a system depends on the house construction and room arrangement. Each system has its advantages for certain types of applications.

FIGURE 17–12   Various types of flexible ducts. (Courtesy of Anco Products, Inc.)

Radial   A radial system consists of a number of single pipes running from the furnace to the supply air outlets. In these systems the furnace is located near the center of the house so that the various runouts (supply air ducts) will be as nearly equal in length as possible. This system helps to provide warm floors and is used with both crawl-space construction and concrete slab floors.

Perimeter loop   The perimeter loop system (Figure 17–13) is a modification of the radial system. A single duct running along the perimeter (outer edge) of the house supplies air to each supply air diffuser located on the floor above. Radial ducts connect the perimeter loop to the furnace. The runout ducts from the furnace to the loop are larger and fewer than those in the radial system. This system lends itself for use with slab floor construction. The perimeter loop supplies extra heat along the perimeter of the house, warming the floor and heating the exterior walls of the house. The greatest heat loss in a slab floor is near its perimeter.

Extended plenum   The trunk-and-branch system is the most versatile system. It permits the furnace to be located in any convenient location in the house. Large ducts carry the air from the furnace to branches or runouts going to individual air outlets. The trunk duct (large duct from furnace) may be the same size throughout its entire length if the length does not exceed 25 ft. This is called an extended plenum (Figure 17–14). On large systems the trunk duct should be reduced in size, after branches remove a portion

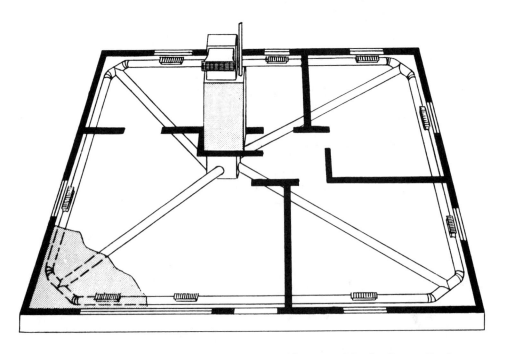

FIGURE 17–13   Perimeter loop supply air distribution system. (Courtesy of Carrier Corporation.)

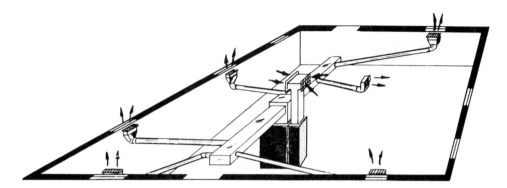

FIGURE 17–14   Extended plenum air supply distribution system. (Courtesy of Carrier Corporation.)

of the air, so that it tapers toward the end (Figure 17–15). A trunk duct can be used for basement installations or overhead installations of ductwork. It can be used for both supply and return systems.

Diffuser placement   The placement of supply air diffusers, or registers, depends to some extent on the climate of the area in which the house is located. In northern climates, where cold floors can be a problem and where outside exposures must be thoroughly heated, a perimeter location of the supply air diffusers is best. The register can be located in the floor adjacent to each exposed wall or in the baseboard. In many southern climates, where cooling air distribution is more important than heating air distribution, diffusers can be located on an inside wall as high as 6 ft. above the floor. In extremely warm climates, the supply air outlet can be placed in the ceiling. Figures 17–16 and 17–17 show and describe various locations for the placement of air supply distribution outlets. Figure 17–18 shows various types of diffusers, registers, and grilles, some of which are used for supply outlets and some for return inlets.

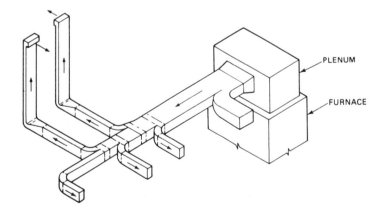

FIGURE 17–15   Reducing trunk duct used in supply or return air distribution systems.

FIGURE 17–16 Placement of air supply distribution outlets. (By permission from the ASHRAE Handbook.)

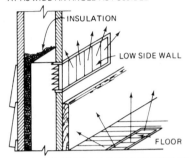

ᴬ REGISTERS SET TO DIRECT AIR UPWARD ALONG THE WALL AT AS WIDE AN ANGLE AS POSSIBLE

INSULATION

LOW SIDE WALL

FLOOR

FLOOR OR LOW SIDEWALL PERIMETER OUTLETSᴬ

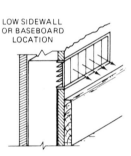

LOW SIDEWALL OR BASEBOARD LOCATION

ᴬ VERTICAL BARS WITH ADJUSTABLE DEFLECTION, OR FIXED VERTICAL BARS WITH DEFLECTION TO RIGHT AND LEFT NOT EXCEEDING ABOUT 22 DEG. FOR LOW SIDEWALL LOCATION, THE DEFLECTION FOR HORIZONTAL, MULTIPLE VANE REGISTERS SHOULD NOT EXCEED 22 DEG. FOR BASEBOARD LOCATIONS, THE DEFLECTION FOR HORIZONTAL, MULTIPLE VANE REGISTERS SHOULD NOT EXCEED ABOUT 10 DEG.

RECOMMENDED TYPE OF BASEBOARD AND LOW SIDEWALL INSTALLATION ON WARM WALLᴬ

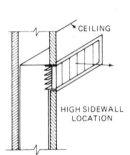

CEILING

HIGH SIDEWALL LOCATION

ᴬ HORIZONTAL VANES, IN BACK OR FRONT, TO GIVE DOWNWARD DEFLECTIONS NOT TO EXCEED 15 TO 22 DEG.

RECOMMENDED TYPE OF HIGH SIDEWALL INSTALLATION ON WARM WALLᴬ

Return Air Distribution Systems

The return air distribution system is usually of simple construction, having less pressure drop than the supply system. The radial system or the extended plenum system can be used. Where possible, return air is carried in boxed-in (enclosed) joist spaces (Figure 17–19).

Grille placement   In northern climates, where supply air diffusers are located along the perimeter, return air grilles (returns) are usually placed near the baseboard on inside walls. Since the room temperature is not affected by the location of returns,

GENERAL CHARACTERISTICS OF OUTLETS

GROUP	OUTLET TYPE	OUTLET FLOW PATTERN	SIZE DETERMINED BY
1	CEILING AND HIGH SIDEWALL	HORIZONTAL	MAJOR APPLICATION – HEATING OR COOLING
2	FLOOR REGISTERS, BASEBOARD AND LOW SIDEWALL	VERTICAL, NONSPREADING	MAXIMUM ACCEPTABLE HEATING TEMPERATURE DIFFERENTIAL
3	FLOOR REGISTERS, BASEBOARD AND LOW SIDEWALL	VERTICAL, SPREADING	MINIMUM SUPPLY VELOCITY DIFFERS WITH TYPE AND ACCEPTABLE TEMPERATURE DIFFERENTIAL
4	BASEBOARD AND LOW SIDEWALL	HORIZONTAL	MAXIMUM SUPPLY VELOCITY SHOULD BE LESS THAN 300 FPM

GROUP	MOST EFFECTIVE APPLICATION	PREFERRED LOCATION
1	COOLING	NOT CRITICAL
2	COOLING AND HEATING	NOT CRITICAL
3	HEATING AND COOLING	ALONG EXPOSED PERIMETER
4	HEATING ONLY	LONG OUTLET – PERIMETER, SHORT OUTLET – NOT CRITICAL

FIGURE 17–17   General characteristics of air supply distribution outlets. (By permission from the *ASHRAE Handbook.*)

though, they may be placed high on the inside walls to prevent drafts. In southern climates, where high inside wall outlets or ceiling diffusers are used, returns can be placed in any convenient location on inside walls. Short-circuiting of the supply air directly into the return, however, must be avoided. Whereas supply air outlets (one or more) are placed in every room to be heated, connecting rooms with open doorways can share a common return. Returns are not placed in bathrooms, kitchens, or garages. Air for these rooms must be taken from some other area. The general rule is that the total duct area for the return air system must be equal to the total duct area for the supply air system. Figure 17–20 shows possible locations for the placement of air return grilles in the return air system.

Provision for Cooling

Where cooling as well as heating is supplied from the same outlets, it is necessary to direct the supply air upward for cooling. Cold air is heavier than warm air and tends to puddle (collect near the floor). To raise cold air, baseboard diffusers should have adjustable vanes or baffles. This upward movement can be accomplished by using air deflectors (Figure 17–21).

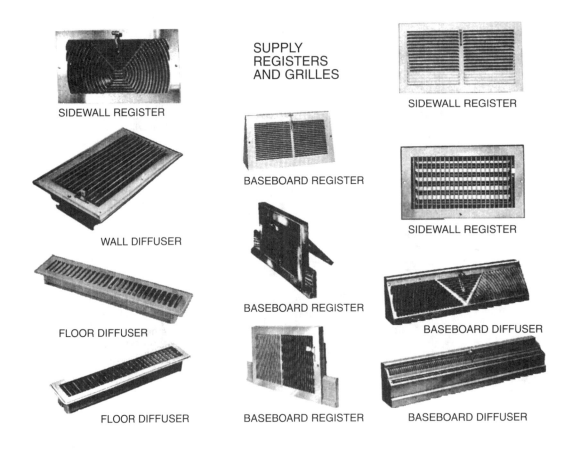

SIDEWALL REGISTER

SUPPLY
REGISTERS
AND GRILLES

SIDEWALL REGISTER

WALL DIFFUSER

BASEBOARD REGISTER

SIDEWALL REGISTER

FLOOR DIFFUSER

BASEBOARD REGISTER

BASEBOARD DIFFUSER

FLOOR DIFFUSER

BASEBOARD REGISTER

BASEBOARD DIFFUSER

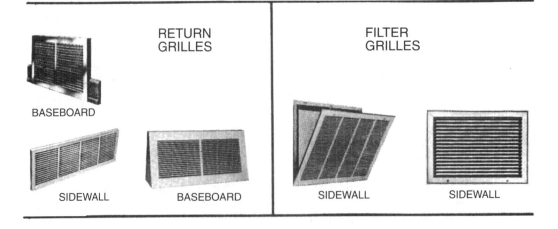

RETURN
GRILLES

FILTER
GRILLES

BASEBOARD

SIDEWALL

BASEBOARD

SIDEWALL

SIDEWALL

FIGURE 17–18 Various types of diffusers, grilles, and registers. (Courtesy of Hart & Cooley, Inc.)

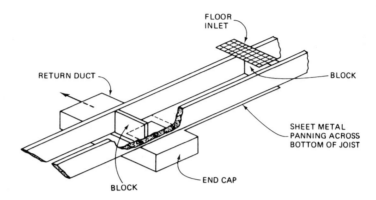

FIGURE 17–19   Boxed-in joist spaces in return air distribution system.

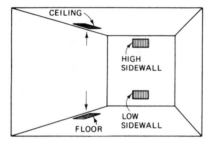

FIGURE 17–20   Placement of air return grilles in return air distribution system.

- FITS REGISTERS 9 TO 17 IN.
- SUPER HOLDING POWER MAGNETS
- CLEAR PLASTIC (BLENDS IN)
- HELPS ELIMINATE DRAFTS

FIGURE 17–21   Air deflector. (Courtesy of Skuttle Manufacturing Company.)

BAROMETRIC

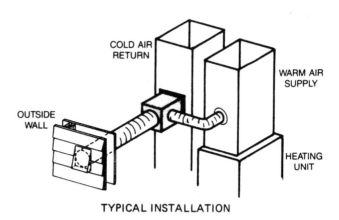

TYPICAL INSTALLATION

THERMAL

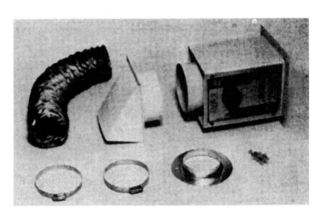

FIGURE 17–22   Barometric and thermal makeup air controls. (Courtesy of Skuttle Manufacturing Company.)

Other Provisions

- Dampers must be provided in each branch supply run from the furnace to balance the system.
- All ducts running in unconditioned areas such as attics or garages must be insulated.
- Ventilation air should be connected directly to the furnace or return air plenum, not to the intermediate return air ductwork.
- Ducted outside air can be made available to the furnace for ventilation air and/or combustion air (see Figure 17–22).

STUDY QUESTIONS

Answers to the study questions may be found in the sections noted in brackets.

17–1. What are some common problems of residential heating systems from a comfort standpoint? *[Diagnosing the Problem]*

17–2. Name three types of uneven temperatures that cause discomfort. *[Diagnosing the Problem]*

17–3. Name three parts of the system in which to look for comfort problems. *[Diagnosing the Problem]*

17–4. What is the method of determining whether or not a gas furnace is operating at its rated input? *[Energy Source: Gas]*

17–5. Which dial on the gas meter is used for timing the rated input of a furnace? *[Energy Source: Gas]*

17–6. What is the method of rating the flow of oil burner nozzles? *[Energy Source: Oil]*

17–7. What is the Btu equivalent for 1 W of electricity? *[Energy Source: Electricity]*

17–8. Give the formula for determining the efficiency of a furnace. *[Efficiency]*

17–9. Give the formula for determining the cubic feet per minute of air circulated. *[Air Volume]*

17–10. Define external static pressure in terms of system resistance to the flow of air. *[Static Pressure]*

17–11. How is static pressure measured? What units are used? *[Static Pressure]*

17–12. How does external static pressure affect the flow of air? *[Static Pressure]*

17–13. Is the volume of air required for cooling less than, equal to, or greater than the volume or air required for heating? *[Static Pressure]*

17–14. What are the five principal causes of poor air distribution? *[Causes of Poor Air Distribution]*

17–15. Describe the three types of supply air distribution systems. *[Supply Air Distribution Systems]*

17–16. Define the equivalent length rating of a duct fitting. *[Supply Air Distribution Systems]*

17–17. What is the best location for return air grilles? *[Supply Air Distribution Systems]*

18

Installation Practice

OBJECTIVES

After studying this chapter, the student will be able to:

- Evaluate the quality of a heating installation in a residence
- Determine the proper wire size and fuse size for electrical circuits
- Determine the proper gas pipe size for a residential gas furnace installation
- Evaluate the venting requirements for a residential gas furnace installation

EVALUATING CONSTRUCTION AND INSTALLATION

When a service technician is called upon to correct a system complaint, there are two areas to be evaluated.

1. *Building construction.* Does the heating system conform to the building requirements?
2. *Furnace installation.* Is the equipment installed properly?

System complaints involve such conditions as drafts, uneven temperatures, cold floors, and other conditions that cause discomfort, even when the equipment may be operating well mechanically. Some of these complaints are due to the design of the system, which cannot be modified without considerable expense. Other system problems can be improved, if not fully corrected, when a service technician understands the cause.

Building Construction

The types of building construction that require special treatment for best heating results include:

- Structures with basements
- Structures over crawl spaces
- Concrete slab construction
- Split-level structures

Structures with basements   These structures should have some heat in the basement to produce warm floors on the level above. This practice should be followed whether or not the basement is finished for a recreation room. The structure should also be designed so that the basement can be properly heated at reasonable cost. The recommended construction for a properly heated basement is shown in Figures 18–1 and 18–2.

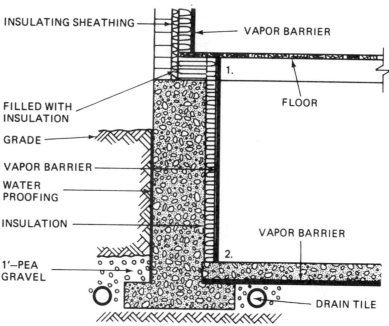

1. CONTINUE VAPOR BARRIER, LAP AND FASTEN, TO MAKE COMPLETE WARM-SIDE VAPOR BARRIER

2. CONTINUE VAPOR BARRIER DOWN WALL AND FOLD UNDER TO MAKE COMPLETE WARM-SIDE VAPOR BARRIER

FIGURE 18–1   Application of insulation in basement of existing structure. (Courtesy of the Detroit Edison Company.)

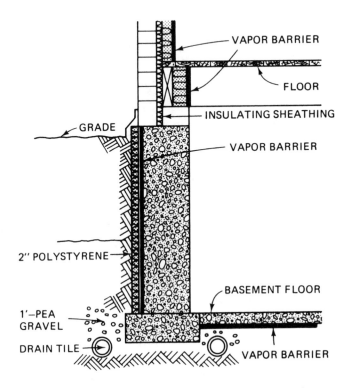

FIGURE 18–2   Application of insulation in basement of new structure. (Courtesy of the Detroit Edison Company.)

The following are desirable construction features of structures with basements:

- Subsoil below floor is well drained.
- A moisture barrier is placed below the floor and between the outside walls and the ground.
- Insulation is placed in the joist around the perimeter of the structure.
- Vaporproof insulating board is applied to the inside basement walls of existing structures and on the outside of new structures.
- Any piping that pierces the vapor barrier should be properly sealed.

Structures over crawl spaces   It is important that the crawl space be heated in this type of structure. Heating produces warm floors on the level above. The best construction is similar in many ways to basement construction. Where crawl spaces are built above the bare ground a moisture barrier should be used (see Figure 18–3). The following are features of crawl-space construction:

- A moisture barrier is placed over the ground and extended upward a minimum of 6 in. on the sidewalls.
- The walls are waterproofed on the outside below grade.
- Perimeter joist spaces should be insulated.

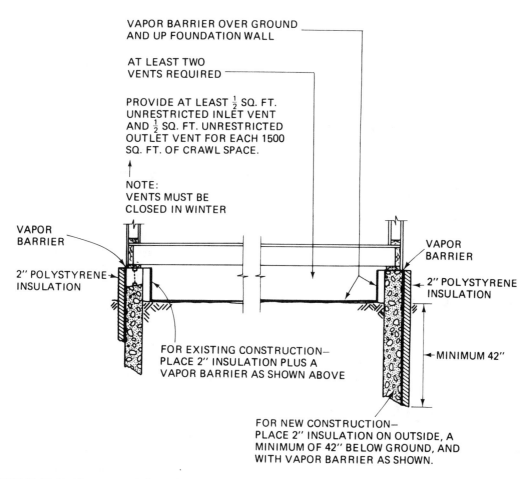

VAPOR BARRIER OVER GROUND AND UP FOUNDATION WALL

AT LEAST TWO VENTS REQUIRED

PROVIDE AT LEAST $\frac{1}{2}$ SQ. FT. UNRESTRICTED INLET VENT AND $\frac{1}{2}$ SQ. FT. UNRESTRICTED OUTLET VENT FOR EACH 1500 SQ. FT. OF CRAWL SPACE.

NOTE: VENTS MUST BE CLOSED IN WINTER

VAPOR BARRIER

2" POLYSTYRENE INSULATION

VAPOR BARRIER

2" POLYSTYRENE INSULATION

MINIMUM 42"

FOR EXISTING CONSTRUCTION— PLACE 2" INSULATION PLUS A VAPOR BARRIER AS SHOWN ABOVE

FOR NEW CONSTRUCTION— PLACE 2" INSULATION ON OUTSIDE, A MINIMUM OF 42" BELOW GROUND, AND WITH VAPOR BARRIER AS SHOWN.

FIGURE 18–3   Recommended crawl-space construction and ventilation.

- On existing structures insulation should be applied to the inside of the crawl-space walls, while on new structures it should be applied to the outside of the walls.
- Ventilation of the crawl space is provided in summer only.
- Dampers permit adjusting the heat feeding the crawl-space area.

Concrete slab construction   It is important to warm the floor in concrete slab construction, particularly around the perimeter where greatest heat loss occurs. This can be done by placing the heat-distributing ducts in the concrete floor. Some of the items included in this construction and shown in the illustrations are as follows:

- Edge insulation is installed around the perimeter of the slab, as shown in Figure 18–4.
- Ducts, embedded in the floor, supply perimeter heating (Figure 18–5).
- A concrete pit of proper size is poured below the furnace for the supply air plenum chamber (Figure 18–6).

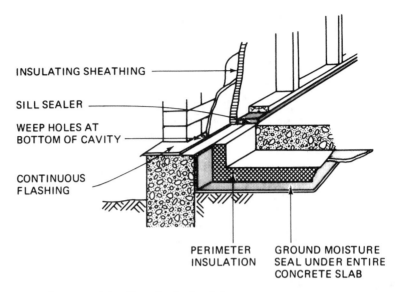

INSULATING SHEATHING

SILL SEALER

WEEP HOLES AT
BOTTOM OF CAVITY

CONTINUOUS
FLASHING

PERIMETER
INSULATION

GROUND MOISTURE
SEAL UNDER ENTIRE
CONCRETE SLAB

FIGURE 18–4   Concrete slab with perimeter insulation.

- A moisture barrier is placed over the ground before the concrete slab is poured.
- Feeder ducts slope downward from the perimeter to the plenum pit.
- Ducts are constructed of waterproof materials with waterproof joints.
- Dampering of individual outlets is provided at the register location.

Split-level structures   This type of construction presents a problem in balancing the heat distribution to provide even heating because each level has its own heat-loss characteristics. Each level must be treated separately from an air distribution and bal-

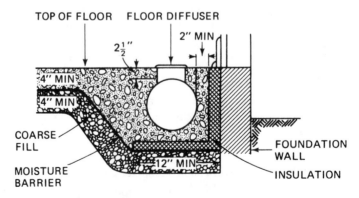

TOP OF FLOOR   FLOOR DIFFUSER

2" MIN

$2\frac{1}{2}$"

4" MIN

4" MIN

COARSE
FILL

MOISTURE
BARRIER

12" MIN

FOUNDATION
WALL

INSULATION

FIGURE 18–5   Cross section of slab construction containing perimeter duct made of one type of material. (By permission from the ASHRAE Handbook.)

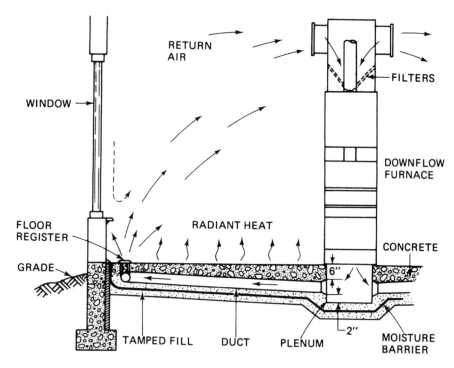

FIGURE 18–6   Construction of feeder ducts to plenum pit. (Courtesy of Carrier Corporation.)

ancing standpoint. Continuous fan operation is strongly recommended. In large structures of this type, a separate unit can be installed for each section.

Furnace Installation

When a furnace installation is inspected for the first time, the service technician should determine if minimum standards have been met in the original installation. The owner should be advised of any serious faults that may affect safety and performance. Some installation conditions of importance are

- Clearances from combustible materials
- Circulating air supply
- Air for combustion, draft hood dilution, and ventilation
- Vent connections
- Electrical connections
- Gas piping

A service technician should comply with the local codes and regulations that govern installations. If there are no local codes, the equipment should be installed in accordance with the recommendation made by the National Board of Fire Underwriters, the American National Standards Institute (ANSI 2223.1), and the American Standards Association (ASA 221.30).

Clearances from combustible materials   Clearances between the furnace and combustible construction should not be less than standard unless permissible clearances are indicated on the attached furnace nameplate. Standard clearances are as follows:

1. Keep 1 in. between combustible material and the top of plenum chamber, 0 to 6 in. at sides and rear of unit.
2. Keep 9 in. between combustible material and the draft hood and vent pipe in any direction.
3. Keep 18 in. between combustible material and the front of the unit.

Accessibility clearances take precedence over fire protection clearances (minimum clearances). Figure 18–7 shows recommended minimum clearances in a confined space. Allow at least 24 in. at the front of the furnace if all parts are accessible from the front. Otherwise, allow 24 in. on three sides of the furnace if back must be reached for servicing. When installation is made in a utility room, the door must be of sufficient size to allow replacement of the unit.

Circulating air supply   Circulating air supply may be 100% return air or any combination of fresh outside air and return air. It is recommended that return air plenums be lined with an acoustical duct liner to reduce any possible fan noise. This is particularly important when the distance from the return air grille to the furnace is close.

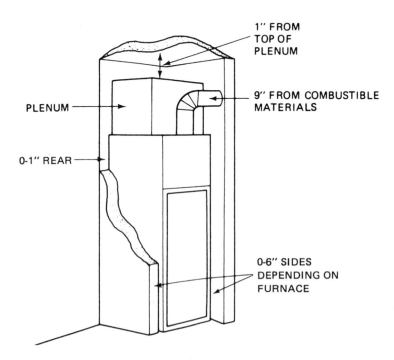

FIGURE 18–7   Recommended minimum clearances in a confined space.

All duct connections to the furnace must extend outside the furnace closet. Return air must not be taken from the furnace room or closet. Adequate return air duct height must be provided to allow filters to be removed and replaced. All return air must pass through the filter after it enters the return air plenum.

Air for combustion, draft hood dilution, and ventilation   Air for combustion, draft hood dilution, and ventilation differ somewhat for two types of conditions:

1. Furnace in a confined space
2. Furnace in an unconfined space

Confined Space   If the furnace is located in a confined space, such as a closet or small room, provisions must be made for supplying combustion and ventilation air (Figure 18–8 and 18–9). Two properly located openings of equal area are required. One opening should be located in the wall, door, or ceiling above the relief opening of the draft diverter. The other opening should be installed in the wall, door, or floor below the combustion air inlet of the furnace. The total free area* of each opening must be at least 1 in.^{2} for each 1000 Btuh input. It is recommended that the two permanent openings communicate directly with an additional room(s) of sufficient volume so that the combined volume of all spaces meets the criteria.

In closet installations where space is restricted, it is important to separate properly the incoming air to the furnace used for heating from that which is used for combustion. The openings must communicate directly or by ducts with the outdoors or spaces (crawl or attic) that are open to the outside. A schematic diagram of the air separation is shown in Figure 18–9.

Unconfined Space   Air for combustion, draft hood dilution, and ventilation must be obtained from the outside or from spaces connected with the outside. If the unconfined space is within a building of unusually tight construction, a permanent opening or openings, having a total free area of not less than 1 in.^{2} per 4000 Btuh of total input rating of all appliances, must be provided as specified in ASIA 221.30. These standards are adopted and approved by both the National Fire Protection Association and the National Board of Fire Underwriters, NFPA No. 54.

A direct-vented space heating system vents directly through the outside wall, as shown in Figure 18–10. Directly vented systems draw their combustion air from the outdoors and exhaust the product of combustion in the same manner. In most cases, conditioned air is not used for combustion and makeup air is not required. Direct-vent systems may be mechanically controlled draft or natural draft. Most direct-vent furnaces will have a fan section that can be attached to the return air to aid in air circulation.

Installation in crawl space   Codes in most communities no longer allow the installation of horizontal furnaces in crawl spaces. When a replacement is necessary, a new location must be found for the furnace.

---

*The free area of a grille is the total area of the opening through which the air passes.

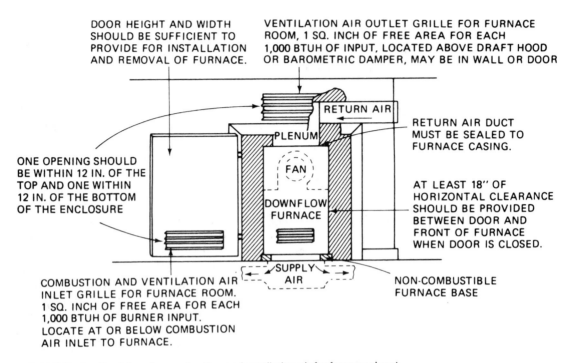

DOOR HEIGHT AND WIDTH SHOULD BE SUFFICIENT TO PROVIDE FOR INSTALLATION AND REMOVAL OF FURNACE.

VENTILATION AIR OUTLET GRILLE FOR FURNACE ROOM, 1 SQ. INCH OF FREE AREA FOR EACH 1,000 BTUH OF INPUT, LOCATED ABOVE DRAFT HOOD OR BAROMETRIC DAMPER, MAY BE IN WALL OR DOOR

RETURN AIR

RETURN AIR DUCT MUST BE SEALED TO FURNACE CASING.

PLENUM

FAN

ONE OPENING SHOULD BE WITHIN 12 IN. OF THE TOP AND ONE WITHIN 12 IN. OF THE BOTTOM OF THE ENCLOSURE

DOWNFLOW FURNACE

AT LEAST 18" OF HORIZONTAL CLEARANCE SHOULD BE PROVIDED BETWEEN DOOR AND FRONT OF FURNACE WHEN DOOR IS CLOSED.

SUPPLY AIR

COMBUSTION AND VENTILATION AIR INLET GRILLE FOR FURNACE ROOM. 1 SQ. INCH OF FREE AREA FOR EACH 1,000 BTUH OF BURNER INPUT. LOCATE AT OR BELOW COMBUSTION AIR INLET TO FURNACE.

NON-COMBUSTIBLE FURNACE BASE

FIGURE 18–8 Provisions for combustion and ventilation air for furnace closet.

Electrical wiring service   All electrical wiring and connections should be made in accordance with the National Electrical Code® and with any local ordinances that may apply. Some of the important items to be observed in providing electrical service are as follows:

1. A separate 120-V power circuit properly fused should be provided, with a disconnect service readily accessible at the furnace.
2. The fuse size and the wire size is determined by the National Electrical Code®. The wire size and fuse size are based on 125% of the nameplate-rating, full-load amperes (FLA). FLA is the manufacturer's running current rating when the motor is operated at peak load. The minimum branch circuit from the building service to the furnace should be AWG No. 14 wire protected by a 15-A circuit breaker or fuse.
3. All replacement wire used within the combustion area of a furnace should be of the same type and size as the original wire and rated 105°C.
4. Unless a circuit breaker is used, the fuse should be of the time-delay type.
5. Strain-relief connectors should be used at the entrance and exits of junction boxes.
6. Control circuit wire (for 24 V) should be AWG No. 18 wire with 105°C temperature rating. Low-voltage circuits (24 V) shall not be placed in any enclosure, compartment, or outlet box with line-voltage circuits.
7. Furnace shall be provided with a nameplate, voltage, and amperage ratings. Figure 18–11 shows typical furnace specifications.

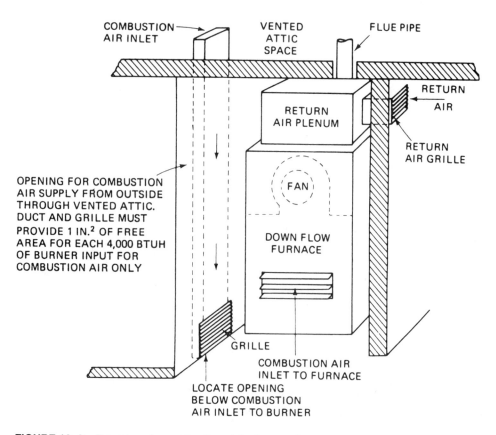

COMBUSTION AIR INLET

VENTED ATTIC SPACE

FLUE PIPE

RETURN AIR

RETURN AIR PLENUM

RETURN AIR GRILLE

FAN

OPENING FOR COMBUSTION AIR SUPPLY FROM OUTSIDE THROUGH VENTED ATTIC. DUCT AND GRILLE MUST PROVIDE 1 IN.^{2} OF FREE AREA FOR EACH 4,000 BTUH OF BURNER INPUT FOR COMBUSTION AIR ONLY

DOWN FLOW FURNACE

GRILLE

COMBUSTION AIR INLET TO FURNACE

LOCATE OPENING BELOW COMBUSTION AIR INLET TO BURNER

FIGURE 18–9   Provisions for combustion air for furnace from vented attic space.

FIGURE 18–10   Installation of direct-vented room heater. (Used by permission of the copyright holder, American Gas Association.)

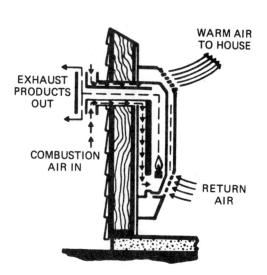

WARM AIR TO HOUSE

EXHAUST PRODUCTS OUT

COMBUSTION AIR IN

RETURN AIR

		NATURAL GAS				
	Model No.	NDGK040CF	NDGK050AF	NDGK075AF NDGK075CF	NDGK100AG NDGK100CG	NDGK125AK NDGK125CK
Capacity:	Input (Btuh)	40,000	50,000	75,000	100,000	125,000
	Heating capacity (Btuh)	38,000	48,000	70,000	91,000	114,000
	Heating capacity (Btuh) (Ca.)	37,154	46,034	67,648	88,174	108,937
	D.O.E. A.F.U.E.%	94.7	94.8	93.2	91.4	91.1
	C.A. seasonal eff.%	81.8	83.5	84.2	83.4	81.0
	Temp. rise (°F)	20–50	20–50	40–70	50–80	35–65
Flue size/type		2 in./PVC	2 in./PVC	2 in./PVC	2 in./PVC	2 in./PVC
Gas piping size		$1/2$ in.	$1/2$ in.	$1/2$ in.	$1/2$ in.	$1/2$ in.
Burners (number)		2	2	3	4	5
Electrical data	Volts-Ph-Hz.			115/60/1		
	(F.L.A.)	8.0 A	8.0 A	8.0 A	10.8 A	11.1 A
Transformer size (VA)				40		
Filter Data	Size (in.)			(2) 15 × 20 × 1		
	Type			Washable		
Cooling Capacity	Max. CFM @ .5 ESP	1300	1200	1230	1380	1965
	Nominal Tons	3	3	3	$3^{1}/_{2}$	5
Weight	Net (Lbs.)	180	180	190	215	242
	Shipping (Lbs.)	202	200	210	240	265

FIGURE 18–11 Typical furnace specifications.

Gas piping   A recommended gas piping arrangement at the furnace is shown in Figure 18–12. Some of the characteristics of good gas piping are as follows:

1. Piping should include a vertical section to collect scale and dirt.
2. A ground joint union should be placed at the connection to the furnace.
3. A drip leg should be installed at the bottom of the vertical riser.
4. The manual shutoff valve must be located external to the furnace casing.
5. Natural gas service pressure from the meter to the furnace is 7 in. W.C. (4.0 oz). At the furnace regulator it is then reduced to 3.5 in. (2.0 oz) to the burners. Liquid petroleum (LP) gas is furnished with a tank pressure regulator to provide 11 in. W.C. (6.3 oz) to the furnace burner.

Natural Gas Pipe Sizing   Adequate gas supply must be provided to the gas furnace. The installation contractor is usually responsible for providing piping from the gas source to the equipment. Therefore, if other gas appliances are used in the building, the entire gas piping layout must be examined from the gas meter to each piece of equipment to determine the proper gas piping sizes for the systems.

If additional gas requirements are being added to an existing building, it may also be advisable to be certain that the gas meter supplied is adequate. This can be done by advising the gas company of the total connected load. The utility company will provide the necessary service at the meter.

General Procedures   The procedure for determining the proper gas piping sizes from the meter is as follows:

1. Sketch a layout of the actual location of the gas piping from the meter to each gas appliance. Indicate on the sketch the length of each section of the piping diagram.

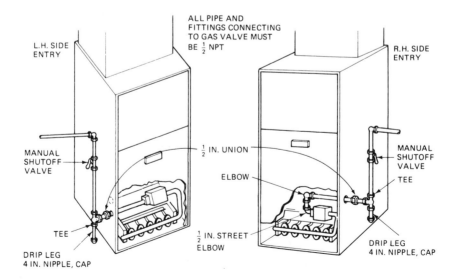

FIGURE 18–12   Recommended gas piping arrangement at the furnace.

Indicate on the sketch the Btuh input required for each gas appliance. See Figure 18–13 for an example. Note in this diagram that there are three appliances on the system.

2. Convert the Btuh input of each gas appliance to cubic feet per hour by dividing the Btuh input by the Btu/ft.^{3} rating of the gas used. The example shown uses natural gas with a rating of 1000 Btu/ft.^{3}. Thus, for the appliances shown in Figure 18–13, the cubic feet of gas used for each appliance is as follows:

Outlet	Appliance	Input (Btuh)	Natural Gas (ft.^{3}/h)
A	Water heater	30,000	30
B	Range	75,000	75
C	Furnace	136,000	136

3. Determine the amount of gas required in cubic feet per hour for each section of the piping system, as shown on the layout.
4. Using the appropriate figure (Figures 18–14, 18–15, 18–18, 18–20, and 18–21), select and record the proper pipe sizes.

Most residential gas piping systems are sized using Figure 18–14 because most natural gas is delivered from the meter at a pressure of 0.5 psig and a specific gravity of $^6/_{10}$ (0.6). The specific gravity refers to the relative weight of 1 ft.^{3} of the gas as compared to an equal quantity of air.

In using Figure 18–14, the maximum length of pipe to the appliance or the greatest distance from the meter is used for sizing the entire piping system. Thus, in Figure 18–13 the length of pipe to outlet (A) is 60 ft., and this number is used for all

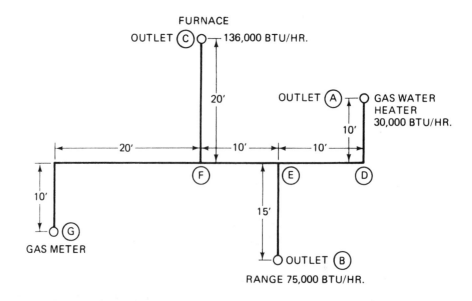

FIGURE 18–13   Typical gas piping layout.

SAMPLE PROBLEM STEPS

Nominal Iron Pipe Size, Inches	Length of Pipe, Feet													
	10	20	30	40	50	60	70	80	90	100	125	150	175	200
1/4	32	22	18	15	14	12	11	11	10	9	8	8	7	6
3/8	72	49	40	34	30	27	25	23	22	21	18	17	15	14
1/2	132	92	73	63	56	50	46	43	40	38	34	31	28	26
3/4	278	190	152	130	115	105	96	90	84	79	72	64	59	55
1	520	350	285	245	215	195	180	170	160	150	130	120	110	100
1 1/4	1050	730	590	500	440	400	370	350	320	305	275	250	225	210
1 1/2	1600	1100	890	760	670	610	560	530	490	460	410	380	350	320
2	3050	2100	1650	1450	1270	1150	1050	990	930	870	780	710	650	610
2 1/2	4800	3300	2700	2300	2000	1850	1700	1600	1500	1400	1250	1130	1050	980
3	8500	5900	4700	4100	3600	3250	3000	2800	2600	2500	2200	2000	1850	1700
4	17,500	12,000	9700	8300	7400	6800	6200	5800	5400	5100	4500	4100	3800	3500

For specific gravity figure, check your local utility company.

FIGURE 18–14 Maximum capacity of pipe in cubic feet of gas per hour for gas pressures of 0.5 psig or less and a pressure drop of 0.3 in. W.C. (based on 0.60 specific gravity gas). (Used by permission of the copyright holder, American Gas Association.)

pipe sizes. Using the data above with the piping layout in Figures 18–13 and 18–14, the pipe sizes are determined as follows:

1. Since 60 ft. is the greatest distance from the meter, point A to point G (10 ft. + 10 ft. + 10 ft. + 20 ft. + 10 ft.), the 60 "length of pipe" line is used in Figure 18–14.

Pipe section	Total-ft.³/h natural gas carried in section	Iron pipe size (in.)
AD	30	1/2
DE	30	1/2
BE	75	3/4
EF	105 (30 + 75)	3/4
CF	136	1
FG	241 (136 + 105)	1 1/4

2. Staying on the 60 "length of pipe" line, move down the column until the cubic feet per hour of the gas carried in AD (30) is covered. A 1/2-in. pipe, which can carry up to 50 ft.³/h, is used.
3. DE carries the same 30 ft.³/h, so it is also 1/2 in.
4. BE carries 75 ft.³/h, so it requires 3/4-in. pipe, which carries up to 105 ft.³/h.
5. EF carries 105 (30 + 75) ft.³/h, so it is also 3/4 in.
6. CF carries 136 ft.³/h, so it requires 1-in. pipe, which carries up to 195 ft.³/h.
7. FG carries 241 (136 + 105) ft.³/h, so it requires 1 1/4-in. pipe, which carries up to 400 ft.³/h.

When using specific gravities other than 0.60, use Figure 18–15. For example, assume that the natural gas has a specific gravity of 0.75. From Figure 18–15 the multiplier would be 0.90. This multiplier would be used to redetermine the cubic feet per hour of gas handled by each part of the piping system.

When the 0.90 multiplier is applied to the preceding example, the results are as follows:

Pipe section	ft.³/h determined in example	ft.³/h using multiplier of 0.90	Iron pipe size (in.)
AD	30	27 (0.90 × 30)	1/2
DE	30	27 (0.90 × 30)	1/2
BE	75	68 (0.90 × 75)	3/4
EF	105	94 (0.90 × 105)	3/4
CF	136	122 (0.90 × 136)	1
FG	241	217 (0.90 × 241)	1 1/4

Commercial/Industrial Sizing   The volume of gas to be provided must be determined directly from the manufacturer's input ratings for the equipment being installed. In industrial gas pipe sizing, the measured length and the equivalent length of fittings and valves are used to arrive at the total equivalent length (TEL), which is then used for sizing the pipe. See Figure 18–16 and the example given.

FIGURE 18–15 Multipliers to be used only with Figures 18–14 and 18–16 when applying different specific gravity factors. (Used by permission of the copyright holder, American Gas Association.)

Specific gravity	Multiplier	Specific gravity	Multiplier
.35	1.31	1.00	.78
.40	1.23	1.10	.74
.45	1.16	1.20	.71
.50	1.10	1.30	.68
.55	1.04	1.40	.66
.60	1.00	1.50	.63
.65	.96	1.60	.61
.70	.93	1.70	.59
(.75)	(.90)	1.80	.58
.80	.87	1.90	.56
.85	.84	2.00	.55
.90	.82	2.10	.54

Note: The "equivalent length" given for a fitting or gas cock is the resistance to flow that could be experienced in a section of straight pipe the same size. In the example the resistance to flow of the $^3/_4$-in. 90° ell is 2.06 ft., which is equal to the resistance to flow in 2.06 ft. of $^3/_4$-in. straight pipe (as shown in Figure 18–16).

Example 18–1

Using Figure 18–16 and the layout (Figure 18–17), the calculation for the TEL would be as follows, using the $^3/_4$-in. steel pipe.

$$Measured\ length = 38\ ft.$$
$$Fittings = 8.10\ ft.$$
$$Gas\ cock = \underline{0.48\ ft.}$$
$$TEL = 46.58\ ft.$$ □

The simplified method for sizing gas piping for commercial and industrial applications is described next.

1. Measure the length of pipe from the gas meter to the most remote outlet. This is the only measurement necessary. To find the TEL, simply add 50% to the measured length.

EQUIVALENT LENGTH OF STRAIGHT PIPE									
SCREWED FITTING		$^1/_2$	(3/4)	1	$1^1/_4$	$1^1/_2$	2	$2^1/_2$	3
90 ELL		1.55	2.06	2.62	3.45	4.02	5.17	6.16	7.67
45 ELL		0.73	0.96	1.22	1.61	1.88	2.41	2.88	3.58
TEE		3.10	4.12	5.24	6.90	8.04	10.3	12.3	15.3
GAS COCK		0.36	0.48	0.61	0.81	0.94	1.21	1.44	1.79

FIGURE 18–16 Equivalent lengths in feet, computed on the inside diameter of schedule 40 steel pipe.

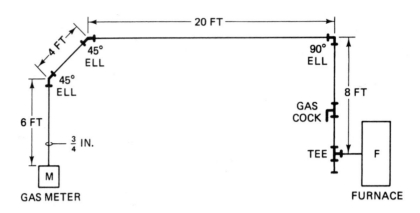

FIGURE 18-17 Sample piping layout, gas meter to furnace.

2. Determine the Btuh required for each piece of equipment. Divide these figures by the heating value of the gas. For example:

$$\frac{Btuh}{heating\ value} = ft.^3/h\ \frac{75,000}{1000} = 75\ ft.^3/h$$

3. Determine the volume (ft.³/h) of gas that each section of the piping will carry.
4. Use the measured length of pipe and volume of gas in each section and outlet. Use Figure 18–18 for sizing.

Nominal Iron Pipe Size Inches	Total Equivalent Length of Pipe in Feet										
	50	100	150	200	250	300	400	500	1000	1500	2000
1	284	195	157	134	119	108	92	82	56	45	39
1¼	583	400	322	275	244	221	189	168	115	93	79
1½	873	600	482	412	386	331	283	251	173	139	119
2	1681	1156	928	794	704	638	546	484	333	267	229
2½	2680	1842	1479	1266	1122	1017	870	771	530	426	364
3	4738	3256	2615	2238	1983	1797	1538	1363	937	752	644
3½	6937	4767	3828	3277	2904	2631	2252	1996	1372	1102	943
	9663	6641	5333	4565	4046	3666	3137	2780	1911	1535	1313
	17,482	12,015	9649	8258	7319	6632	5676	5030	3457	2776	2376
	28,308	19,456	15,624	13,372	11,851	10,738	9190	8145	5598	4496	3848
	58,161	39,974	52,100	27,474	24,350	22,062	18,883	16,735	11,502	9237	7905
	105,636	72,603	58,303	49,900	44,225	40,071	34,296	30,396	20,891	16,776	14,358
	167,236	114,940	92,301	78,998	70,014	63,438	54,295	48,120	33,073	26,559	22,731

FIGURE 18–18 Pipe sizing table for pressures under 1 lb. approximate capacity of pipes of different diameters and lengths in cubic feet per hour with pressure drop of 0.5 in. W.C. and 0.6 specific gravity. (Used by permission of the copyright holder, American Gas Association.)

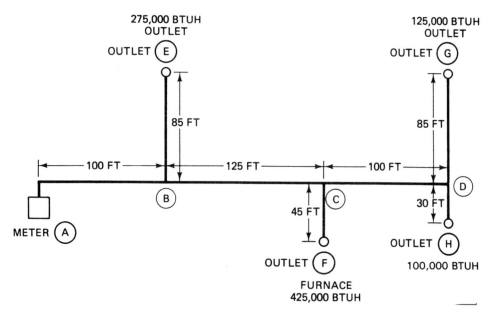

275,000 BTUH
OUTLET

OUTLET (E)

125,000 BTUH
OUTLET

OUTLET (G)

85 FT   85 FT

|← 100 FT →|← 125 FT →|← 100 FT →|

(B)   (C)   (D)

45 FT   30 FT

METER (A)

OUTLET (F)   OUTLET (H)

FURNACE   100,000 BTUH
425,000 BTUH

FIGURE 18–19   Sample piping layout of a commercial-industrial gas piping system.

Example
18–2

Determine the necessary pipe size for each section and outlet of Figure 18–19. The natural gas has a specific gravity of 0.6 and a heating value of 1000 Btu/ft.^{3}. The gas pressure is 8 in. W.C. with a maximum allowable pressure drop of 0.5 in. W.C. in the piping.

Solution

1. The measured length of the piping from the meter (A) to the most remote outlet (G) is 100 ft. + 125 ft. + 100 ft. + 85 ft. = 410 ft.
2. Increase the measured length by 50%: 410 ft. + 205 ft. = 615 ft. The value 615 ft. is then the TEL that is used to determine the pipe sizes from Figure 18–17.
3. When the calculated TEL falls between two columns in Figure 18–18, the larger TEL is used. In this case 615 ft. falls between 500 and 1000; therefore, the 1000 column is used.

Main sections	Btuh	Flow in section ft.^{3}/h	Nominal iron pipe size (in.)
AB	925,000	925	3
BC		925 – 275 = 650	3
CD		650 – 425 = 225	2

Branches	Btuh	Flow in branch ft.^{3}/h	Nominal iron pipe size (in.)
BE	275,000	275	2
CF	425,000	425	$2^1/_2$
DH	100,000	100	$1^1/_4$
DG	125,000	125	$1^1/_2$

Nominal (I.D.) Iron Pipe Size, Inches	Length of Pipe, Feet											
	10	20	30	40	50	60	70	80	90	100	125	150
1/2	275	189	152	129	114	103	96	89	83	78	69	63
3/4	567	393	315	267	237	217	196	185	173	162	146	132
1	1071	732	590	504	448	409	378	346	322	307	275	252
1 1/4	2205	1496	1212	1039	913	834	771	724	677	630	567	511
1 1/2	3307	2299	1858	1559	1417	1275	1181	1086	1023	976	866	787
2	6221	4331	3465	2992	2646	2394	2205	2047	1921	1811	1606	1496

FIGURE 18–20   Maximum capacity of pipe in thousands of Btuh of undiluted liquefied petroleum gases (at 11 in. W.C. inlet pressure, based on a pressure drop of 0.5 in. WC.). (Used by permission of the copyright holder, American Gas Association.)

Outside Diameter, Inch	Length of Tubing, Feet									
	10	20	30	40	50	60	70	80	90	100
3/8	39	26	21	19	—	—	—	—	—	—
1/2	92	62	50	41	37	35	31	29	27	26
5/8	199	131	107	90	79	72	67	62	59	55
3/4	329	216	181	145	131	121	112	104	95	90
7/8	501	346	277	233	198	187	164	155	146	138

FIGURE 18–21   Maximum capacity of semi-rigid tubing in thousands of Btuh of undiluted liquefied petroleum gases (at 11 in. W.C. inlet pressure, based on a pressure drop of 0.5 in. W.C.). (Used by permission of the copyright holder, American Gas Association.)

Liquid Petroleum Gas Pipe Sizing   Liquid petroleum gas is popular in areas where natural gas is in short supply. Trailers and recreation vehicles (RVs) use liquid petroleum (LP) gas for refrigeration as well as heating. Figures 18–20 and 18–21 are used to calculate the pipe or tubing sizes necessary to supply LP gas to the furnace.

VENTING

Venting of natural draft furnaces is accomplished with the temperature difference between the vent gases inside the flue and the surrounding air. The greater this temperature difference, the greater the push up the chimney. Sufficient draft is required also to move the moisture that is produced in the combustion process. This moisture is normally in the vapor state, but can condense and form liquid water while in the chimney. This condensate can be very corrosive. It can attack mortar, vent connectors, and heat exchangers. Condensation can be avoided by maintaining the vent gases at temperatures high enough to keep the chimney warm.

Temperatures of Various Furnaces

Conventional furnaces are designed to maintain the vent gas temperature above 400°F. Since most vent condensation will occur at approximately 126°F, the gases will not condense in a properly constructed and sized chimney. Standard furnaces with electric pilot ignition, forced draft, or induced draft still operate at above 400°F.

Recuperative furnaces with a seasonal efficiency of 80%+ reach this efficiency by removing additional heat from the flue gases. This brings the vent gas temperature down to approximately 180°F. Oversized or poorly constructed chimneys may reduce that temperature to 126°F and cause condensation.

Condensing furnaces with a seasonal efficiency of 90%+ operate with a vent temperature of approximately 120°F. Condensate removal is designed into this furnace. Therefore, conventional vent piping and chimneys are not used.

Masonry Venting

When used for flue gas venting, masonry chimneys must be lined with a fireclay tile. The tile liner must be installed with tight joints. By not touching the brick or block of the chimney, it produces a vacuum bottle insulating effect. The lining is designed to heat up quickly and remove very few Btu from the flue gases. If the tile is not installed correctly, gases will escape to the brick or block, cool rapidly, and condense. The remaining gases within the liner will not be able to keep the liner warm and will also condense. At the cooler temperature they will not maintain a sufficient push up the chimney and will spill into the building through the diverter. An oversized chimney requires more heat to keep the liner warm than is available in the flue gas, which causes the same problem.

Type B Venting

The type B vent consists of an outer galvanized steel pipe and an inner aluminum pipe with an airspace between the two pipes (Figure 18–22). Each manufacturer of type B

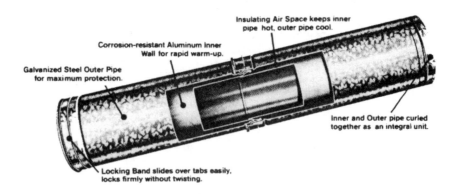

FIGURE 18–22 MetIvent type B double-wall insulated gas vent. (Courtesy of Hart & Cooley, Inc.)

vents produces a system that is unique, and various manufacturers' components must not be interchanged. Installation instructions must be followed with each system as to joint connections, securing, and vent termination height. Generally, sheet metal screws should not be used.

The ideal installation is to have a correctly sized type B vent for each appliance. Usually, though, a furnace and water heater are combined to be vented through one stack. If the water heater has a low Btu rating and operates frequently while the furnace is not operating, there may be insufficient heat in the vent gas to avoid condensation. This is the reason to size a common vent with great accuracy.

Plastic Venting

Furnaces which operate with flue gases that do or may condense require a noncorrosive vent system. Condensing furnaces, with flue gas temperatures at 120°F, generally are vented with low-temperature polyvinyl chloride (PVC) or chlorinated polyvinyl chloride (CPVC) plastic pipe and fittings.

As shown in Figure 18–23, horizontal pipe should be supported every 3 ft. with the first support as close to the furnace as possible. The induced draft fan and/or furnace cabinet should not support the weight of the flue pipes. The piping should be pitched upward from the furnace $1/4$-in. per foot to allow condensate to drain back into the furnace condensate removal system. Vertical pipe should not extend more than 30 ft. above the appliance.

All PVC piping must be prepared for gluing by using a purple cleaner-primer. Any other pipe preparation will not hold the pipe together in the long run and is not allowed by code.

Roof vent outlets are installed through a rubber flashing such as is used for plumbing stacks (Figure 18–24). Care should be taken to avoid locations where the wind can cause downdrafts. Any vent piping passing through unconditioned areas, such as an attic, garage, or crawl space, must be insulated to prevent excess condensation in the pipe.

Sidewall venting requires vent termination kits as designed by the manufacturer. Do not allow an open pipe to face into the prevailing winds (Figure 18–25). Sidewall vents may not terminate within 10 ft. of the property line.

The manufacturer's installation instructions must be followed for installation with reference to air intakes. If the furnace is operated without outside combustion air, the vent termination must not be any closer than 4 ft. from any opening into the building. When outside combustion air is used, the manufacturer's instructions must be followed. Figure 18–26 shows a typical installation.

Condensate Removal System

To remove the condensate on 90+ furnaces, the individual manufacturer's drain kits must be used (Figure 18–26). All kits provide a means of trapping the condensate to assure that no vent gases pass into the building or into the circulating airstream. It is

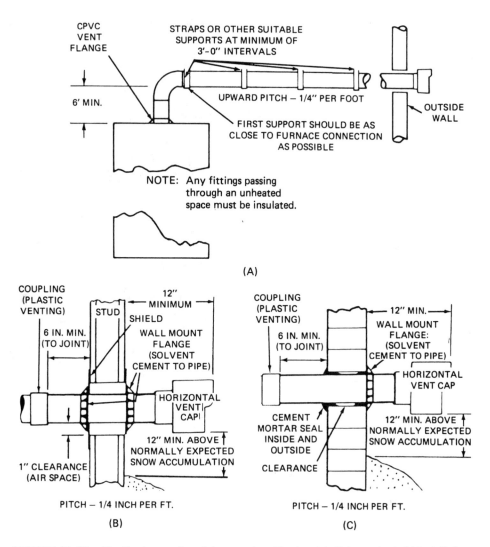

FIGURE 18–23   Plastic pipe venting: (a) support and horizontal pitch required; (b) installation through combustible walls; (c) installation through noncombustible walls. (Courtesy of the Trane Company Unitary Products Group.)

imperative that no additional or substitute traps be installed. Some kits also include a switch which will open the heating control circuit if the trap should become overfilled with condensate.

Condensate Neutralizer

Some communities will not allow the acidic condensate to enter the sewer system unless it is first neutralized. Neutralizer kits are available as an option from many manufacturers. Installation of a condensate neutralizer kit is shown in Figure 18–27.

FIGURE 18–24 Rubber roof flashing.

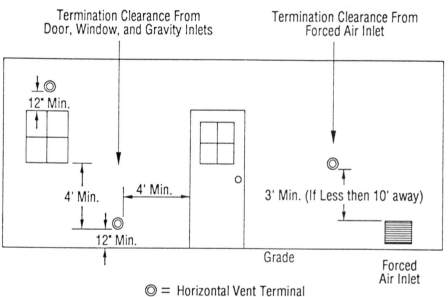

Termination Clearance From
Door, Window, and Gravity Inlets

Termination Clearance From
Forced Air Inlet

12" Min.

4' Min.

4' Min.

3' Min. (If Less then 10' away)

12" Min.

Grade

Forced
Air Inlet

◎ = Horizontal Vent Terminal

FIGURE 18–25 Vent termination clearances to openings in buildings. (Courtesy of
ARCOAIRE, Inter-City Products Corporation, USA.)

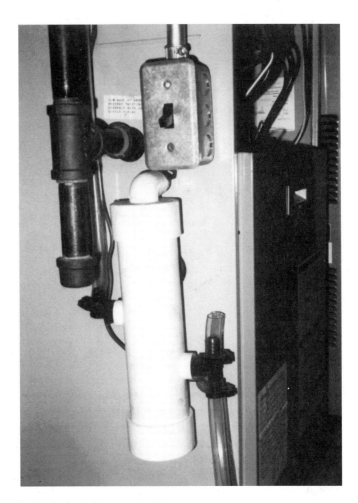

FIGURE 18–26   Typical condensate trap kit.

Vent Sizing Categories

Gas appliances are separated into four categories for venting purposes.

1. Category 1 appliances do not produce positive vent static pressure, operate at over 275°F vent gas temperatures, and rely on the heat content of combustion products to vent. Even if these furnaces are equipped with an induced draft blower, the blower is not strong enough to pressurize the vent. The new 78–80% furnaces and the midefficiency 80–90% furnaces fall into this category.

2. Category 2 is for natural draft appliances with a flue gas temperature of less than 275°F. At the time of this writing, furnaces of this type are not being manufactured.

3. Category 3 appliances rely on the heat content of the combustion products and mechanical or other means to vent. Recuperative furnaces fall into this category.

FIGURE 18–27 Installation of condensate neutralizer kit. (Courtesy of ARCOAIRE, Inter-City Products Corporation, USA.)

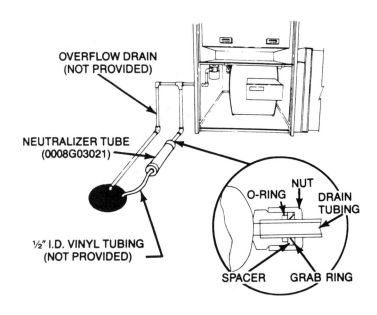

OVERFLOW DRAIN (NOT PROVIDED)

NEUTRALIZER TUBE (0008G03021)

½" I.D. VINYL TUBING (NOT PROVIDED)

O-RING   NUT   DRAIN TUBING

SPACER   GRAB RING

4. Category 4 includes the highest-efficiency furnaces that are designed to produce condensation in the heat exchanger.

General considerations for category 1 appliances   Correct sizing of the furnace, based on calculated load, will extend the running time, thereby decreasing the potential for condensation in the vent pipe. If the vent is oversized, the flue gases will move too slowly and condensation will result. When the vent is too small, it will not carry the total volume of the flue gases.

Two or more category 1 appliances may be connected to a single vent or chimney. Do not connect a category 1 appliance to any portion of a vent system that operates under positive pressure. Positive pressure would result with category 3 and 4 appliances. Do not connect any appliance to a chimney flue serving a fireplace.

The pipe from the appliance to the chimney or vent is called the vent connector (see Figure 18–28). The vent connector must be the same size as the appliance vent collar and should be kept as short as possible. Adding an elbow creates resistance. For example, adding a 6-in. 90-degree elbow would be the equivalent of adding 20 ft. of horizontal pipe; 45-degree elbows have lower resistance and can be utilized in most vent runs.

To minimize the potential for condensation, the vent connector to the furnace should have at least as much or more resistance than the connector from the water heater. This can be accomplished by keeping the water heater vent connector shorter and with fewer elbows, and by connecting the water heater to the vertical vent at a point above the furnace connection (Figure 18–28).

The vent pipe (chimney) must be a minimum of 5 ft. in total height from the draft diverter of the highest appliance up to the cap of the vent. This is dimension H in Figure 18–28. The connecting tee fitting should always be the same size as the common vent, as shown in Figure 18–29. The vent pipe must extend at least 3 ft., by code, above the point where it passes through the roof. Unless the vent termination is approved by the manufacturer for reduced clearances, the vent must end 2 ft. above any portion of the building within 10 ft. (see Figure 18–30).

Category 3 appliance venting   Midefficiency furnaces and recuperative furnaces that produce a positive pressure in the vent must have vent connections that are gastight to prevent leakage into the conditioned spaces. Furnaces are usually vented separately, but special designs may allow some common venting with water heaters. Special venting materials or aluminum piping are required because of the potential for condensation in the vent. Category 3 furnaces cannot be vented through a B vent.

Category 4 condensing furnace venting   PVC plastic may be specified for venting systems that will not exceed 160°F. For higher-temperature conditions, up to 210°F, CPVC may be required. These furnaces may not be connected to a common vent and must have a properly sized single vent directly to the outdoors. For sizing purposes, strictly follow the manufacturer's required calculations regarding vent length and number of elbows. Most residential category 4 furnaces have vent sizes in the 2 to 3 in. range. Figure 18–31 shows typical installation requirements.

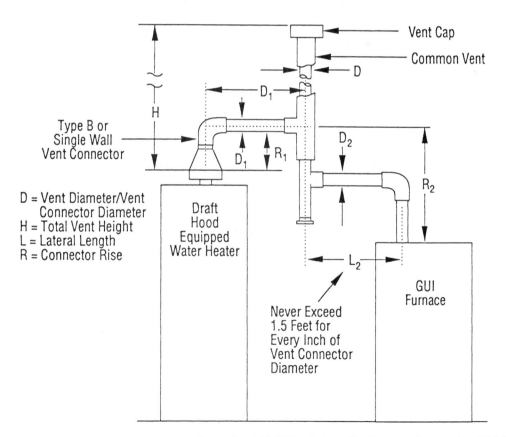

FIGURE 18–28   Common vertical venting. (Courtesy of ARCOAIRE, Inter-City Products Corporation, USA.)

FIGURE 18–29 Correct use of vent tee.

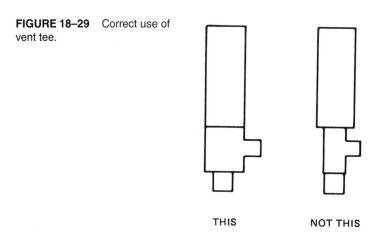

THIS   NOT THIS

Vent Sizing Tables

Category 1 appliance vent sizing is normally the responsibility of the installer. Category 3 and 4 sizing is the responsibility of the manufacturer. Vent systems can be divided into two basic types:

1. Single-appliance systems
2. Multiple-appliance systems

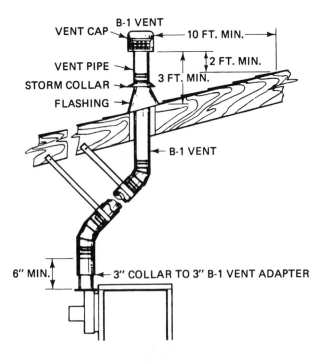

FIGURE 18–30 Recommendations for installation of type B vents.

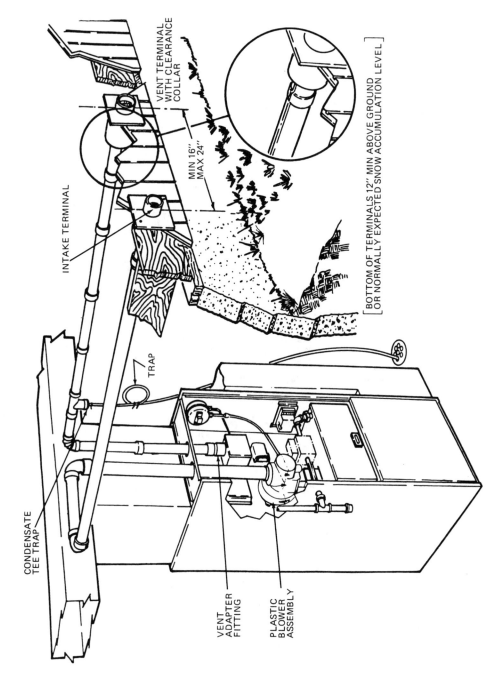

VENT TERMINAL WITH CLEARANCE COLLAR

INTAKE TERMINAL

MIN 16" MAX 24"

[BOTTOM OF TERMINALS 12" MIN ABOVE GROUND OR NORMALLY EXPECTED SNOW ACCUMULATION LEVEL]

CONDENSATE TEE TRAP

TRAP

VENT ADAPTER FITTING

PLASTIC BLOWER ASSEMBLY

FIGURE 18–31 Typical installation requirements. (Courtesy of ARCOAIRE, Inter-City Products Corporation, USA.)

Separate sizing tables must be used for single and multiple applications. In addition, separate sizing tables must be used for B vents and masonry chimneys.

Figure 18–32 shows a condensed sizing table for type B double-wall vents with single-wall metal vent connectors serving a single category 1 appliance. The first column is vent height from the appliance draft diverter to the top (cap) of the vent. The second column is any lateral (horizontal) dimension between the draft diverter and the cap. The numbers across the top represent the size of the vent connector and

Vent and Connector Diameter - D (inches)

Appliance Input Rating in Thousands of Btu Per Hour

Height H (ft)	Lateral L (ft)	3" FAN Min	3" FAN Max	3" NAT Max	4" FAN Min	4" FAN Max	4" NAT Max	5" FAN Min	5" FAN Max	5" NAT Max	6" FAN Min	6" FAN Max	6" NAT Max	7" FAN Min	7" FAN Max	7" NAT Max	8" FAN Min	8" FAN Max	8" NAT Max	9" FAN Min	9" FAN Max	9" NAT Max	10" FAN Min	10" FAN Max	10" NAT Max	12" FAN Min	12" FAN Max	12" NAT Max
6	0	38	77	45	59	151	85	85	249	140	126	373	204	165	522	284	211	695	369	267	894	469	371	1118	569	537	1639	849
	2	39	51	36	60	96	66	85	156	104	123	231	156	159	320	213	201	423	284	251	541	368	347	673	453	498	979	648
	4	NR	NR	33	74	92	63	102	152	102	146	225	152	187	313	208	237	416	277	295	533	360	409	664	443	584	971	638
	6	NR	NR	31	83	89	60	114	147	99	163	220	148	207	307	203	263	409	271	327	526	352	449	656	433	638	962	627
8	0	37	83	50	58	164	93	83	273	154	123	412	234	161	580	319	206	777	414	258	1002	536	360	1257	658	521	1852	967
	2	39	56	39	59	108	75	83	176	119	121	261	179	155	363	246	197	482	321	246	617	417	339	768	513	486	1120	743
	5	NR	NR	37	77	102	69	107	168	114	151	252	171	193	352	235	245	470	311	305	604	404	418	754	500	598	1104	730
	8	NR	NR	33	90	95	64	122	161	107	175	243	163	223	342	225	280	458	300	344	591	392	470	740	486	665	1089	715
10	0	37	87	53	57	174	99	82	293	165	120	444	254	158	628	344	202	844	449	253	1093	584	351	1373	718	507	2031	1057
	2	39	61	41	59	117	80	82	193	128	119	287	194	153	400	272	193	531	354	242	681	456	332	849	559	475	1242	848
	5	52	56	39	76	111	76	105	185	122	148	277	186	190	388	261	241	518	344	299	667	443	409	834	544	584	1224	825
	10	NR	NR	34	97	100	68	132	171	112	188	261	171	237	369	241	296	497	325	363	643	423	492	808	520	688	1194	788
15	0	36	93	57	56	190	111	80	325	186	116	499	283	153	713	388	195	966	523	244	1259	681	336	1591	838	488	2374	1237
	2	38	69	47	57	136	93	80	225	149	115	337	224	148	473	314	187	631	413	232	812	543	319	1015	673	457	1491	983
	5	51	63	44	75	128	86	102	216	140	144	326	217	182	459	298	231	616	400	287	795	526	392	997	657	562	1469	963
	10	NR	NR	39	95	116	79	128	201	131	182	308	203	228	438	284	284	592	381	349	768	501	470	966	628	664	1433	928
	15	NR	NR	NR	NR	NR	72	158	186	124	220	290	192	272	418	269	334	568	367	404	742	484	540	937	601	750	1399	894
20	0	35	96	60	54	200	118	78	346	201	114	537	306	149	772	428	190	1053	573	238	1379	750	326	1751	927	473	2631	1346
	2	37	74	50	56	148	99	78	248	165	113	375	248	144	528	344	182	708	468	227	914	611	309	1146	754	443	1689	1098
	5	50	68	47	73	140	94	100	239	158	141	363	239	178	514	334	224	692	457	279	896	596	381	1126	734	547	1665	1074
	10	NR	NR	41	93	129	86	125	223	146	177	344	224	222	491	316	277	666	437	339	866	570	457	1092	702	646	1626	1037
	15	NR	NR	NR	NR	NR	80	155	208	136	216	325	210	264	469	301	325	640	419	393	838	549	526	1060	677	730	1587	1005
	20	NR	NR	NR	NR	NR	NR	186	192	126	254	306	196	309	448	285	374	616	400	448	810	526	592	1028	651	808	1550	973
30	0	34	99	63	53	211	127	76	372	219	110	584	334	144	849	472	184	1168	647	229	1542	852	312	1971	1056	454	2996	1545
	2	37	80	56	55	164	111	76	281	183	109	429	279	139	610	392	175	823	533	219	1069	698	296	1346	863	424	1999	1308
	5	49	74	52	72	157	106	98	271	173	136	417	271	171	595	382	215	806	521	269	1049	684	366	1324	846	524	1971	1283
	10	NR	NR	NR	91	144	98	122	255	168	171	397	257	213	570	367	265	777	501	327	1017	662	440	1287	821	620	1927	1243
	15	NR	NR	NR	115	131	NR	151	239	157	208	377	242	255	547	349	312	750	481	379	985	638	507	1251	794	702	1884	1205
	20	NR	NR	NR	NR	NR	NR	181	223	NR	246	357	228	298	524	333	360	723	461	433	955	615	570	1216	768	780	1841	1166
	30	NR	NR	NR	NR	NR	NR	NR	NR	NR	NR	NR	NR	389	477	305	461	670	426	541	895	574	704	1147	720	937	1759	1101
50	0	33	99	66	51	213	133	73	394	230	105	629	361	138	928	515	176	1292	704	220	1724	948	295	2223	1189	428	3432	1818
	2	36	84	61	53	181	121	73	318	205	104	495	312	133	712	443	168	971	613	209	1273	811	280	1615	1007	401	2426	1509
	5	48	80	NR	70	174	117	94	308	198	131	482	305	164	696	435	204	953	602	257	1252	795	347	1591	991	496	2396	1490
	10	NR	NR	NR	89	160	NR	118	292	186	162	461	292	203	671	420	253	923	583	313	1217	765	418	1551	963	589	2347	1455
	15	NR	NR	NR	112	148	NR	145	275	174	199	441	280	244	646	405	299	894	562	363	1183	736	481	1512	934	668	2299	1421
	20	NR	NR	NR	NR	NR	NR	176	257	NR	236	420	267	285	622	389	345	866	543	415	1150	708	544	1473	906	741	2251	1387
	30	NR	NR	NR	NR	NR	NR	NR	NR	NR	315	376	NR	373	573	NR	442	809	502	521	1086	649	674	1399	848	892	2159	1318
100	0	NR	NR	NR	49	214	NR	69	403	NR	100	659	395	131	991	555	166	1404	765	207	1900	1033	273	2479	1300	395	3912	2042
	2	NR	NR	NR	51	192	NR	70	351	NR	98	563	373	125	828	508	158	1152	698	196	1532	933	259	1970	1168	371	3021	1817
	5	NR	NR	NR	67	186	NR	90	342	NR	125	551	366	156	813	501	194	1134	688	240	1511	921	322	1945	1153	460	2990	1796
	10	NR	NR	NR	85	175	NR	113	324	NR	153	532	354	191	789	486	238	1104	672	293	1477	902	389	1905	1133	547	2938	1763
	15	NR	NR	NR	132	162	NR	138	310	NR	188	511	343	230	764	473	281	1075	656	342	1443	884	447	1865	1110	618	2888	1730
	20	NR	NR	NR	NR	NR	NR	168	295	NR	224	487	NR	270	739	458	325	1046	639	391	1410	864	507	1825	1087	690	2838	1696
	30	NR	NR	NR	NR	NR	NR	231	264	NR	301	448	NR	355	685	NR	418	988	NR	491	1343	NR	631	1747	1041	834	2739	1627
	50	NR	NR	NR	NR	NR	NR	NR	NR	NR	540	584	NR	617	866	NR	711	1205	NR	895	1591	NR	1138	2547	1489			

FIGURE 18-32   Vent tables. Capacity of type B double-wall vents with single-wall metal connectors serving a single category 1 appliance. (Courtesy of Gas Appliance Manufacturers Association.)

the vent in inches diameter. This size must never be smaller than the vent collar on the furnace. The main body of the table represents the Btu input rating of the appliance in thousands (i.e., 38 = 38,000 Btu). Figures are shown for both natural draft and fan assisted draft appliances.

To use the table for a 120,000-Btuh natural draft appliance, first determine the height and any lateral offset for the vent system. Look for the appropriate row in columns 1 and 2. In that row move toward the right until you reach a number under a column "NAT-Max" that is 120 or larger. From that point, move up to establish the vent size.

For a fan-assisted induced draft appliance, follow the same instruction, but look for the input rating to fall between a set of minimum and maximum columns. The minimum is important to avoid condensation due to an oversized chimney.

Figure 18–33 shows a condensed common vent table for type B double-wall vents with single-wall connectors serving two or more category 1 appliances. To establish the common vent size, determine the vent height and the types of appliances connected (fan- assisted or natural draft) and their combined Btu input. In the row for the height, move to the right until you reach the combined Btuh input under the appropriate appliance combination column. Move to the top to establish the common vent size.

Figure 18–34 shows a condensed common vent table for a masonry chimney with single-wall metal connectors serving two or more category 1 appliances. Whenever a category 1 furnace is removed from a common venting system, particular attention must be paid to the sizing of the venting for the remaining appliance, such as a water heater. Without the larger appliance, the common vent is too large and may cause condensation and insufficient draft. Many codes require that the remaining appliance be vented through a chimney liner, which may be a type B vent or a flexible liner as shown in Figure 18–35.

	Common Vent Diameter - D (inches)																				
	4"			5"			6"			7"			8"			9"			10"		
Vent Height H (ft)	Combined Appliance Input Rating in Thousands of Btu Per Hour																				
	FAN +FAN	FAN +NAT	NAT +NAT	FAN +FAN	FAN +NAT	NAT +NAT	FAN +FAN	FAN +NAT	NAT +NAT	FAN +FAN	FAN +NAT	NAT +NAT	FAN +FAN	FAN +NAT	NAT +NAT	FAN +FAN	FAN +NAT	NAT +NAT	FAN +FAN	FAN +NAT	NAT +NAT
6	92	81	65	140	116	103	204	161	147	309	248	200	404	314	260	547	434	335	672	520	410
8	101	90	73	155	129	114	224	178	163	339	275	223	444	348	290	602	480	378	740	577	465
10	110	97	79	169	141	124	243	194	178	367	299	242	477	377	315	649	522	405	800	627	495
15	125	112	91	195	164	144	283	228	206	427	352	280	556	444	365	753	612	465	924	733	565
20	136	123	102	215	183	160	314	255	229	475	394	310	621	499	405	842	688	523	1035	826	640
30	152	138	118	244	210	185	361	297	266	547	459	360	720	585	470	979	808	605	1209	975	740
50	167	153	134	279	244	214	421	353	310	641	547	423	854	706	550	1164	977	705	1451	1188	860
100	175	163	NR	311	277	NR	489	421	NR	751	658	479	1025	873	625	1408	1215	800	1784	1502	975

FIGURE 18–33   Vent tables. Common vent capacity of type B double-wall vents with single-wall metal connectors serving two or more category 1 appliances. (Courtesy of Gas Appliance Manufacturers Association.)

Common Vent Capacity

Vent Height H (ft)	Minimum Internal Area of Chimney, Square Inches																							
	12			19			28			38			50			63			78			113		
	Combined Appliance Input Rating in Thousands of Btu Per Hour																							
	FAN +FAN	FAN +NAT	NAT +NAT	FAN +FAN	FAN +NAT	NAT +NAT	FAN +FAN	FAN +NAT	NAT +NAT	FAN +FAN	FAN +NAT	NAT +NAT	FAN +FAN	FAN +NAT	NAT +NAT	FAN +FAN	FAN +NAT	NAT +NAT	FAN +FAN	FAN +NAT	NAT +NAT	FAN +FAN	FAN +NAT	NAT +NAT
6	NR	74	25	NR	119	46	NR	178	71	NR	257	103	NR	351	143	NR	458	188	NR	582	246	NR	853	NR
8	NR	80	28	NR	130	53	NR	193	82	NR	279	119	NR	384	163	NR	501	218	NR	636	278	NR	937	408
10	NR	84	31	NR	138	56	NR	207	90	NR	299	131	NR	409	177	NR	538	236	NR	686	302	NR	1010	454
15	NR	90	36	NR	152	67	NR	233	106	NR	334	152	NR	467	212	NR	611	283	NR	781	365	NR	1156	546
20	NR	92	41	NR	159	75	NR	250	122	NR	368	172	NR	508	243	NR	668	323	NR	858	419	NR	1286	648
30	NR	NR	NR	NR	NR	NR	NR	270	137	NR	404	198	NR	564	278	NR	747	381	NR	969	496	NR	1473	749
50	NR	NR	NR	NR	NR	NR	NR	NR	NR	NR	NR	NR	NR	620	328	NR	831	461	NR	1089	606	NR	1692	922

FIGURE 18–34 Vent tables. Common vent capacity of masonry chimney flue with single-wall metal connectors serving two or more category 1 appliances. (Courtesy of Gas Appliance Manufacturers Association.)

Combustion Air

Many high-efficiency furnaces are specifically designed to use outside air for combustion, while others may have an accessory kit to convert for outside combustion air. Outside air is required when the furnace is installed in a closet, a small mechanical room, a tightly constructed building, or in a corrosive environment. Some manufacturing processes, chemical storage, stables, and beauty parlors are corrosive environments. With some manufacturers, installing the combustion air kit allows termination of the vent pipe closer to a window or other openings into the building.

Combustion air is normally provided through PVC piping. The manufacturer's instruction must be followed to obtain the correct size. Most pipe sizes are 1.5 to 3 in. in diameter. The outside termination of the combustion air piping must be weatherproof, since the piping is pitched down toward the furnace and there is no provision to eliminate water in the pipe. All piping must be secured as shown in Figure 18–36 to avoid any sagging, movement, or pressure on furnace components. The outdoor termination should be located within 24 in. of the vent termination, but be at least 14 in. away from it (see Figure 18–37).

CODES

There are various codes enforced for furnace, duct, piping, and venting installations, including the *BOCA* National Mechanical Code, the Uniform Mechanical Code (UMC), the National Fire Protection Association (NFPA), and others. Always determine which code is being enforced in your local community before doing any work. A person licensed to do mechanical work is not normally allowed to perform electrical and plumbing work.

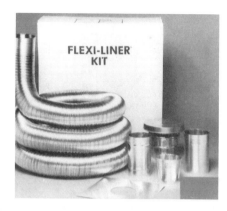

FIGURE 18–35   Flexi-Liner chimney liner components and typical installation. (Courtesy of Flex-L International, Inc.)

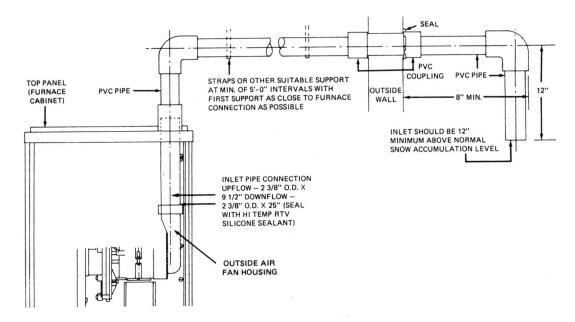

TOP PANEL
(FURNACE
CABINET)

PVC PIPE

STRAPS OR OTHER SUITABLE SUPPORT
AT MIN. OF 5'-0" INTERVALS WITH
FIRST SUPPORT AS CLOSE TO FURNACE
CONNECTION AS POSSIBLE

SEAL

PVC
COUPLING

OUTSIDE
WALL

PVC PIPE

8" MIN.

12"

INLET SHOULD BE 12"
MINIMUM ABOVE NORMAL
SNOW ACCUMULATION LEVEL

INLET PIPE CONNECTION
UPFLOW – 2 3/8" O.D. X
9 1/2" DOWNFLOW –
2 3/8" O.D. X 25" (SEAL
WITH HI TEMP RTV
SILICONE SEALANT)

OUTSIDE AIR
FAN HOUSING

FIGURE 18–36 Air piping for combustion. (Courtesy of the Trane Company Unitary Products Group.)

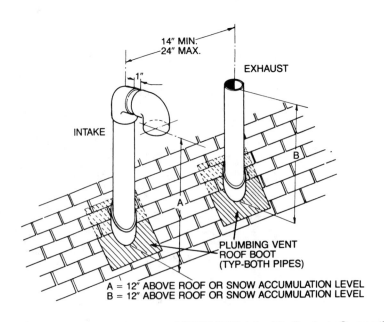

14" MIN.
24" MAX.

1"

EXHAUST

INTAKE

B

A

PLUMBING VENT
ROOF BOOT
(TYP-BOTH PIPES)

A = 12" ABOVE ROOF OR SNOW ACCUMULATION LEVEL
B = 12" ABOVE ROOF OR SNOW ACCUMULATION LEVEL

FIGURE 18–37 Roof vent termination. (Courtesy of ARCOAIRE, Inter-City Products Corporation. USA.)

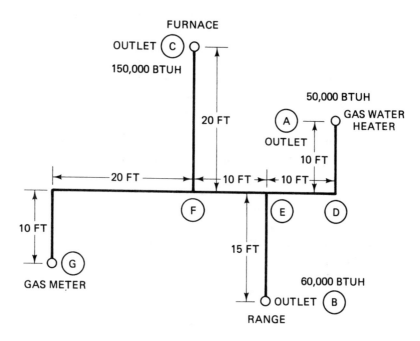

FIGURE 18–38   Gas piping layout from Figure 18–13 with new loads.

REVIEW PROBLEM

Using the sketch in Figure 18–38, assume the following loads:

Outlet A: 50,000
Outlet B: 60,000
Outlet C: 150,000

Determine the pipe sizes for natural gas using a pressure drop of 0.5 in. W.C. and 0.60 specific gravity gas.

STUDY QUESTIONS

Answers to the study questions may be found in the sections noted in brackets.

18–1. What are the desirable basement, crawl-space, and concrete slab construction features? *[Building Construction]*

18–2. Name three rules that apply to clearances from materials. *[Clearances from Combustible Materials]*

18–3. Name one important rule in supplying air for combustion. *[Air for Combustion, Draft Hood Dilution, and Ventilation]*

18–4. Name three (of the five) items of recommended practice for reconnecting gas to the furnace. *[Gas Piping]*

18–5. Briefly describe the procedure for determining the proper gas piping sizes from the meter to the various gas appliances. *[Gas Pipe Sizing]*

18–6. What is the natural gas pressure usually delivered from the meter? *[Natural Gas Pipe Sizing]*

18–7. What is the specific gravity of natural gas in most areas? *[Natural Gas Pipe Sizing]*

18–8. What design gas pipe pressure drop is considered good practice for residential gas piping? *[Natural Gas Pipe Sizing]*

18–9. What is the gas pressure delivered to the piping for LP gas? *[Liquid Petroleum Gas Pipe Sizing]*

18–10. What is the pressure drop used for sizing and piping using LP gas? *[Liquid Petroleum Gas Pipe Sizing]*

18–11. If the furnace is placed in a confined space, what special provisions need to be made? *[Air for Combustion, Draft Hood Dilution, and Ventilation]*

18–12. Why is vent sizing so important? *[Venting]*

18–13. Describe a type B vent. *[Type B Venting]*

18–14. List two types of plastic vent pipes and state the maximum temperature for which they are approved. *[Plastic Venting]*

18–15. List the types of furnaces in each category. *[Vent Sizing Categories]*

19

Heating System Maintenance and Customer Relations

OBJECTIVES

After studying this chapter, the student will be able to:

- Determine the maintenance requirements for a heating system
- Instruct the owner on proper care and operation of the system

IMPORTANCE OF PROPER MAINTENANCE

Any mechanical equipment requires proper maintenance to continue its original efficiency. Heating systems are no exception. With proper care, a heating system will provide good performance for many years. In addition to providing periodic maintenance, the service technician can often upgrade the system when new technology is available. The maintenance items that should receive attention include the following:

1. Testing and adjusting the fuel burning unit
2. Cleaning the air passages of the system
3. Servicing the fan-motor assembly
4. Rebalancing the system
5. Adjusting the thermostat anticipator and fan control
6. Testing the power and safety controls
7. Cleaning the heat exchangers
8. Changing air filters
9. Servicing accessories
10. Upgrading the equipment wherever possible

TESTING AND ADJUSTING

Information on combustion is covered in Chapter 3. The use of various types of combustion test instruments is supplied in Chapters 5, 8, and 13. It is important to adjust the fuel-burning unit to produce the highest efficiency that can be maintained continuously. The firing rate of the fuel and the supply of combustion air are the principal adjustments.

The firing rate of the fuel should be set to match the input requirements of the furnace indicated on the nameplate. For example, on a gas furnace, if the input rating is 100,000 Btuh and the heating value of the gas is 1000 Btu/ft.^{3}, the rate at which gas should be supplied is 100 ft.^{3}/hr. This can be tested by turning the thermostat up and timing the gas flow through the meter. If the input is incorrect, an adjustment can be made at the gas pressure regulator or to the size of the burner orifices. On an oil burner, the size of the nozzle and the oil pressure will determine the firing rate.

Gas Furnace

Observe the flame. It should be a soft blue color without yellow tips. Adjust the primary air if necessary. If the flame will not clean up when adjusted, remove the burners and clean them both inside and outside. Measure the gas pressure (Figure 19–1). It should be 3.5 in. W.C. for natural gas and 11.0 in. W.C. for liquid petroleum gas. Measurements are made at the manifold pressure tap with main burners operating and with other gas-burning appliances in operation. Check the thermocouple. The thermocouple, under no load, should generate 18 to 30 mV d.c. When under load, it should generate at least 7 mV d.c.

Oil Furnace

Clean the burner (Figure 19–2) and run a complete combustion test. Replace the oil burner nozzle if necessary. Adjust the air volume for maximum efficiency. Replace the

FIGURE 19–1 Measuring manifold gas pressure.

FIGURE 19–2   Typical oil burner assembly. (Courtesy of R. Beckett Company.)

oil line filter. Clean the bimetallic element on the stack relay (if used). Observe the flame after the burner is restarted. The flame should be yellow in color and centered in the combustion chamber.

At this point a final adjustment should be made using proper test instruments. Unless otherwise specified in the appliance manufacturer's instructions, the unit should be set as follows: After allowing 10 min. for warm-up, air should be set so that the smoke number is no greater than 1. Less than number 1 smoke is desired. *(Note:* Occasionally, a new heating unit requires more time than this to burn cleanly due to the oil film on heating surfaces.) Carbon dioxide measured in the stack (ahead of draft control) should be at least 8% for oil rates 1.0 gal/h or less and 9% for oil rates over 1.0 gal/h. The unit should be started and stopped several times to assure good operation.

Check the oil pressure (Figure 19–3). It should be 100 psig during operation and 85 psig immediately after shutdown. Some models require operating pressures in the 140–200 psig range. Motor life will be increased by proper oiling. Use a few drops of nondetergent oil at both motor oil holes twice each year. The line filter cartridge should be replaced every year to avoid contamination of the fuel unit and atomizing nozzle. Finally, the area around the heating unit should be kept clean and free of any combustible materials, especially papers and oil rags.

Electric Furnace

Set the thermostat to call for heat. Check by reading the incoming power amperage to make certain that all heater elements are operating. On the three- and four-element

FIGURE 19–3 Checking the oil pressure. (Courtesy of Sundstrand Hydraulics.)

furnaces that are equipped with a fused disconnect block, both legs of the heating elements are provided with cartridge fuses internal to the furnace. Two elements and the blower are grouped together on a 60-A fuse. On three-element furnaces, a single element is fused at 30 A.

Cleaning Air Passages

If construction work has taken place in the area or if the occupant is negligent in keeping the filters clean, there may be a layer of airborne dust on the outside surface of the heat exchangers. This surface needs to be kept clean. Particularly on high-efficiency furnaces, debris will collect on the external surface of the secondary heat exchanger. Stiff bristle brushes can be used to dislodge foreign material, and a commercial vacuum cleaner can be used to remove dirt and lint.

On high-efficiency furnaces it may be necessary to remove the blower to reach the secondary heat exchanger for cleaning, as shown in Figure 19–4. Brush strokes must be in the direction of the finned surface to avoid damage to the fins. Inspect and clean the blades of the fan wheel using a brush and vacuum. Care should be taken not to dislodge balance weights (clips) that may be on the fan wheel.

SERVICING FAN-MOTOR ASSEMBLY

The fan-motor assembly requires periodic attention. The unit may be belt-driven, as shown in Figure 4–13, or direct-driven, as shown in Figure 4–14. Most direct-drive units have multiple-speed arrangements. Some motors and bearings require lubrication, and some do not. Oil or grease should be applied in accordance with the manufacturer's instructions.

Clean out the blades of the fan wheel. Motors that require oil should be oiled twice a year. If there is more than $1/8$-in. end play on the shaft, move the thrust collar

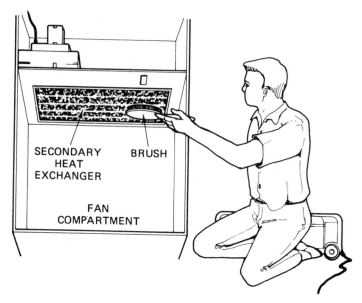

FIGURE 19–4   Cleaning secondary heat exchanger.

closer to the bearing. Furnace fans are designed to rotate in one direction. It is, therefore, important to determine proper rotation at the time of installation or when changing the fan motor (Figure 19–5). If it becomes necessary to reverse the rotation, follow the instructions on the motor terminal block for reversing the lead wires. The directions are usually found under the cover where the lead wires enter the motor.

It is important to determine if the proper amount of air is being supplied by the fan-motor assembly. The easiest way to determine the volume of air handled by the furnace is to measure the temperature rise through the furnace. The temperature rise plus the output rating of the furnace provides the information necessary for calculating the cubic feet per minute (cfm) handled by the fan:

$$cfm = \frac{output\ Btuh}{temperature\ rise \times 1.08}$$

FIGURE 19–5   Determining fan rotation.

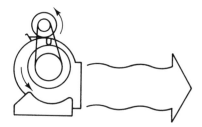

If the air volume handled by the fan does not comply with the manufacturer's requirement, the fan speed must be adjusted.

Belt-Driven Fans

If the unit is belt-driven, the speed of the fan can be changed by adjusting the variable pitch motor pulley, as shown in Figure 19–6. To adjust fan speed, loosen the setscrew in the outer flange outward to decrease fan speed or inward to increase speed. The outer flange must be rotated by half-turns to avoid damage to the threads, but the flange should not be rotated outward so that the belt is riding on the hub rather than on the flanges of the pulley. After each adjustment of the motor pulley, lock the outer flange in place by tightening the setscrew on the flat of the pulley hub. Line up the fan and motor pulleys by using a straightedge across two outer edges of the fan pulley, and adjust the pulley on the motor shaft so that the belt is parallel with the straightedge. Tighten the setscrew securely on the flat of the motor shaft.

Most fan motors rotate at 1725 rev/min. The following table shows how the revolutions per minute can be increased or decreased by changing either the diameter of the motor pulley or the fan pulley.

$$rev \,/\, min. \; of \; equipment = \frac{rev \,/\, min. \; of \; motor \times diameter \; of \; motor \; pulley}{diameter \; of \; equipment \; pulley}$$

For example, if the motor pulley is 2.00 in. in diameter and the fan pulley is 6 in., the fan would turn at 575 rev/min. If the motor pulley is increased in diameter to 3.00 in., the revolution per minute would increase to 862. It should be noted that an increase in fan revolutions per minute increases the amperage draw on the motor. Some procedures relating to belt installation, alignment, and adjustments of belt-driven fans are shown in Figure 19–7.

EQUIPMENT SPEED (REV/MIN) FOR MOTORS TURNING 1725 REV/MIN

Diameter of motor pulley (in.)	Diameter of pulley on equipment (in.)					
	5	6	7	8	9	10
1.25	431	359	308	270	240	216
1.50	518	431	370	323	288	259
1.75	604	503	431	377	335	302
2.00	690	575	493	431	383	345
2.25	776	646	554	485	431	388
2.50	862	719	616	539	479	431
2.75	949	791	678	593	527	474
3.00	1035	862	739	647	575	518
3.25	1121	934	801	701	623	561
3.50	1208	1006	862	755	671	604
3.75	1294	1078	924	809	719	647
4.00	1380	1150	986	862	767	690

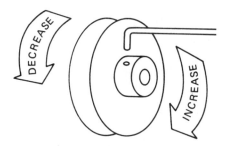

FIGURE 19–6   Adjustment of variable-speed pulley.

WIPE OFF PULLEYS AND BELT with a clean rag to get rid of all oil and dirt. Dirt and grease are tough abrasives that cause the belt to wear out faster, throwing it out of balance and shortening its life.

INSTALL V-BELT in pulley grooves by loosening the belt take-up or the adjusting screw on the motor. Do not "roll" or "snap" the belt on the pulleys; this causes much more strain than the pulleys should have. Be sure the belt doesn't "bottom" in the pulley grooves.

ALIGN BOTH PULLEYS AND SHAFTS by moving the motor on its motor mount. You can do this "by eye," but you're a lot safer if you hold a straight edge flush against the blower pulley, then move the motor until the belt is absolutely parallel to the straight edge.

HERE'S A SHORT-CUT WAY TO CHECK PULLEY ALIGNMENT: Sight down the top of the belt from slightly above it. If the belt is straight where it leaves the pulley and does not bend, you can bet that the alignment is reasonably good.

CHECK BELT TENSION before proceeding further. Remember that a V-belt "rides" the inside of the pulley faces. Since the sides of the belt wedge in the pulleys, the V-belt does not have to be tight. It should be as loose as possible without slipping in the pulley grooves.

USE THIS RULE-OF-THUMB FOR ADJUSTING BELT TENSION: Using the belt take-up or motor adjusting screw, tighten the belt until the slack side can be depressed about ¾" for each foot of span between the pulleys. WARNING: EXCESSIVE BELT TENSION IS THE MOST FREQUENT CAUSE OF BEARING WEAR AND RESULTING NOISE.

FIGURE 19–7   Removal, alignment, and adjustment of V-belts. (Courtesy of Lau Industries/Conaire Sales Division.)

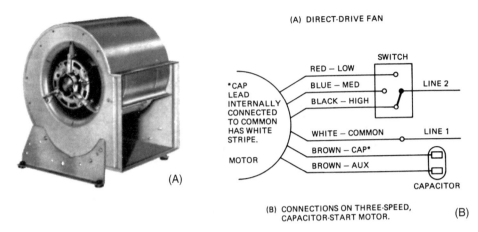

(A) DIRECT-DRIVE FAN

FIGURE 19–8   Direct-driven, multispeed fan with capacitor start motor. [(A) Courtesy of Conaire Division, Philips Industries, Inc.; (B) courtesy of Universal Electric.]

Direct-Driven Fans

Direct-driven fans (see Figure 19–8A) are more popular than the belt-driven type because they require less maintenance. Furnaces that are equipped for air conditioning are supplied with a multispeed motor. Multispeed motors have several connections in the motor windings, which allow the selection of different speeds. Most electric motors have a wiring diagram attached to the motor casing or to the underside of the plate that covers the motor terminals. The motor connections shown in Figure 19–8B are for a three-speed, capacitor-start motor.

FIGURE 19–9   Combination fan relay and transformer.

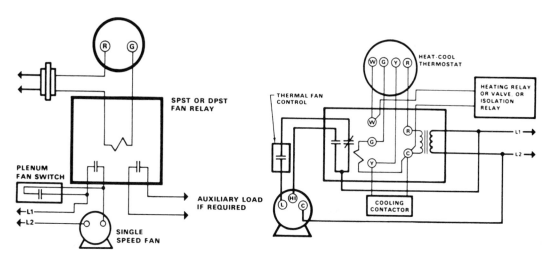

In the system shown, a call for cooling makes R-G in the thermostat and completes the circuit through the fan relay coil. The relay pulls in to energize the system fan. The plenum fan switch, for controlling the fan in the heating mode, is wired in parallel with the normally open fan relay contacts.

Low speed fan operation in heating mode is maintained through a normally closed contact in the fan relay. When the fan relay coil is energized on a call for cooling by the thermostat, this contact opens. This cuts off power to the low speed fan, and the normally open contacts close to energize the high speed windings of the fan motor.

(A) SINGLE SPEED FAN

(B) TWO SPEED FAN

FIGURE 19–10   Application of fan relay and transformer. (Courtesy of Honeywell Inc.)

When cooling is added to an existing furnace, the evaporator coil adds an additional pressure drop in the distribution system. In most cases, cooling also requires more air than heating. If the furnace does not already have a multispeed motor for the fan, it is advisable to install one. For heating, the fan speed is usually slower than that used for cooling. Some high efficiency furnaces, however, require a fan speed that is faster than a speed used for cooling. A combination fan relay and transformer (Figure 19–9) can be installed. This control provides a means of automatically changing the speed of the fan motor from heating to cooling.

The use of the fan relay and transformer as applied to single-speed fans is shown in Figure 19–10A, and that for two-speed fans is shown in Figure 19–10B.

REBALANCING THE SYSTEM

After a forced warm air system has been in use for a period of time, some rooms may be heating better than others. Rebalancing the system is therefore in order. Air balancing is performed by adjusting the branch-duct dampers to produce uniform temperatures throughout the building (Figure 17–10). The procedure is as follows:

1. Place a thermometer in each room at table height.
2. Open all supply and return air duct dampers.
3. Open all baffles and register dampers.
4. Set the thermostat to call for heat.
5. Adjust the dampers while the furnace is running to produce uniform temperatures in all the rooms.

The balancing should be done during weather cold enough to permit continuous operation of the heating equipment for a substantial period of time. Continuous fan operation with the furnace cycling at the rate of 8 to 10 times per hour provides good conditions for balancing.

ADJUSTING THE THERMOSTAT ANTICIPATOR AND FAN CONTROL

The thermostat anticipator is adjusted to control the length of the operating cycle. Raising the amperage setting of the anticipator lengthens the cycle. Lowering the amperage setting of the anticipator shortens the cycle. Refer to the section "Thermostat Anticipator Setting" in chapter 10 for detailed information for setting anticipators. Where continuous fan action is not used, the fan control on an upflow furnace starts the fan when the bonnet temperature reaches its cut-in point (Figure 19–11). If the fan is delivering air that is too cool for comfort, the cut-in point of the fan control can be raised. It is advantageous to have the longest possible fan-on time and still not blow cold air. The differential of the fan control (cut-in temperature minus cut-out temperature) should be great enough to prevent short cycling of the fan.

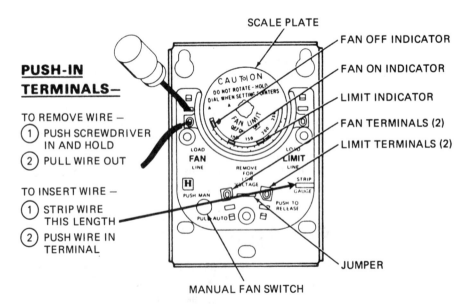

FIGURE 19–11   Fan control adjustment. (Courtesy of Honeywell Inc.)

TESTING THE POWER AND SAFETY CONTROLS

It is important to use a separately fused branch electrical circuit containing a properly sized fuse or circuit breaker for the furnace. A means for disconnecting the furnace must be located within sight and be readily accessible. Check the supply voltage to be certain that the proper power is being delivered to the furnace. To check the supply voltage to determine that it is adequate, the following procedure is recommended:

1. On a gas-fired forced air furnace, remove the transformer. Then check the power supply leads in the junction box (Figure 19–12).
2. On an oil-fired forced air furnace, remove the cad-cell control from the top of the oil burner assembly. Then check the power supply leads in the junction box (Figure 19–13).

Check to be sure that all wiring connections are tight and that wiring insulation is in good condition. With a thermometer, check the cut-out point of the limit control by shutting down the fan. The bonnet temperature must not exceed 200°F.

Safety Check of the Limit Control

The limit control shuts off the combustion control system and energizes the circulating-air fan motor if the furnace overheats. The recommended method of checking the limit control is gradually to block off the return air after the furnace has been operating for a period of at least 5 min. As soon as the limit has proven safe, the return air opening should be unblocked to permit normal air circulation. By using this method to check the limit control, it can be established that the limit is functioning properly and will provide a fail-safe if there is a motor failure. (The downflow or horizontal furnaces have a manual reset limit switch located on the fan housing.) On high-efficiency furnaces, there are many sensing switches and safeguard controls that must be checked to be certain that the equipment will run properly.

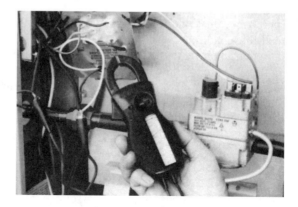

FIGURE 19–12   Checking the power supply on a gas-fired furnace.

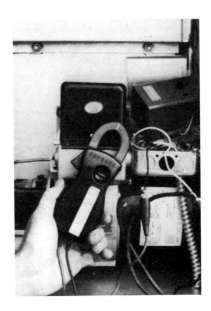

FIGURE 19–13 Checking the power supply on an oil-fired furnace.

Safety Check of the Flow-Sensing Switch

1. Turn off 115-V power to the furnace. Remove the control door and disconnect the inducer motor lead wires from the inducer printed-circuit board.
2. Turn on 115-V power to the furnace. Close the thermostat switch as if making a normal furnace start. The pilot should light and then cycle off and on. If the main burners do not light, the flow-sensing switch is functioning properly.
3. Turn off 115-V power to the furnace. Reconnect the inducer motor wires, replace the control door, and turn on 115-V power.

Safety Check of the Draft Safeguard Switch

The purpose of this control is to permit the safe shutdown of the furnace during certain blocked-flue conditions.
1. Disconnect power to the furnace and remove the vent pipe from the furnace outlet collar. Be sure to allow time for the vent pipe to cool down before removing.
2. Restore power to the furnace. Allow the furnace to operate for 2 min; then block (100%) the flue outlet. The furnace should cycle off within 2 min.
3. Reconnect the vent pipe. Wait 5 min. and then reset the draft safeguard switch.

CLEANING THE HEAT EXCHANGER

The only time that it is necessary to disassemble the furnace and clean the interior surface of the heat exchanger is when the fuel-burning device is out of adjustment and

FIGURE 19–14   Cleaning a heat exchanger.

sooting occurs in the flue passages. On some conventional furnaces, it is possible to use a brush to dislodge the soot (Figure 19–14) and a vacuum to remove it. On high-efficiency furnaces, two heat exchangers may require cleaning. A typical location of these heat exchangers is shown in Figure 19–15.

CHANGING AIR FILTERS

Clean or replace air filters as often as necessary to permit proper airflow. Replacement filters should be similar in material, thickness, and size to those removed. The air filters must be clean when testing any system for air volume. A dirty filter creates an unnecessary restriction, thereby reducing air volume.

SERVICING ACCESSORIES

Clean and service accessories in accordance with the manufacturer's instructions. Humidifiers may require cleaning more than once a year, depending on water conditions. The condenser surface on condensing units used for cooling must be kept clean. Condenser fans usually require lubrication.

UPGRADING THE FURNACE

The owner should be advised of any advanced technology that will improve efficiency and comfort. These items include programmable thermostats, electronic ignition, and so on.

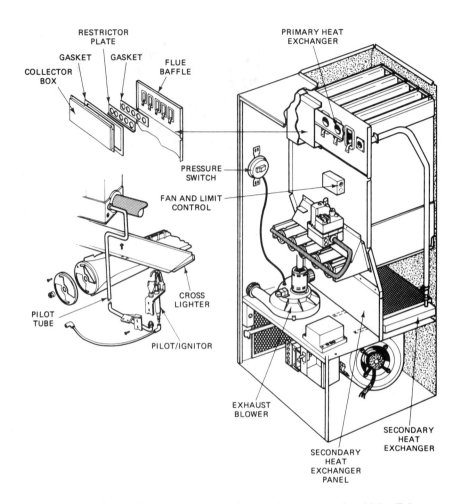

FIGURE 19–15   Location of primary and secondary heat exchangers in a high-efficiency furnace.

CUSTOMER RELATIONS

You can have a toolbox full of the latest tools, and if you cannot "get along" with your customers, what good are the tools? Treating the customer right is every bit as important as having the right tools.

Why are customer relations so important? Simply put, when you complete your service call, write out your service report, and present it to the customer, you expect payment. Gas valves do not write checks. Furnaces do not write checks. Motors do not write checks. People, customers, write checks. Creating a favorable attitude is as much a part of your job as repairing the equipment.

Consider the customer's frame of mind when you arrive. Perhaps they have been without heat for several hours. Perhaps they have heard horror stories about service people who make excessive charges. Perhaps an earlier service call had failed to solve the problem. When you come up the driveway, the customer may have already made a case against you.

Your first job is to make a favorable impression. Here are a few of the things you can do to get off to a good start:

1. Radiate value. Your truck should be clean and orderly. Your tools should be contained in a suitable box, easy to transport. Your instruments should be in proper cases, ready to use.
2. Polish up your self-image. Your appearance should be that of a professional. You should be confident of your ability and show it. Your smile should radiate success.
3. Develop good work habits. Plan your work. Use accurate information. Refer to the instruction manual whenever necessary. Seek the advice of the manufacturer if necessary. Exercise good time management. If you have undesirable work habits that hold you back, replace them. Make yourself more valuable to your customer as well as yourself.

Remember, sometimes customers appear to be difficult. For the most part, customers are not inherently rude. Something may be going on in their life that has them upset. Whatever it may be, it is part of your job as service person to show empathy and understanding and do the right thing for your customer. Becoming a service technician is one of the most exciting, rewarding careers you can choose. Put your heart into it. Develop your "people skills" and you will be rewarded.

Instructions for Equipment Service

Discuss with the owner the features of the installation, how the system operates, and the service necessary to maintain the equipment. It is important to leave a copy of the detailed service report with the customer. The proper instructions for maintenance and care shown in Figures 19–16 and 19–17 will be a helpful guide for the customer.

Warranty

The manufacturer's limited warranty (Figure 19–18) and the contractor's warranty should be supplied to the owner. Although the manufacturer does not include labor in replacing a defective part during the first year, usually the contractor's warranty does. Manufacturers often offer an extended warranty on parts such as heat exchangers.

MAINTENANCE AND CARE FOR THE OWNER OF
A GAS-FIRED FURNACE

Warning:

1. TURN OFF ELECTRICAL POWER SUPPLY TO YOUR FURNACE BEFORE REMOVING ACCESS DOORS TO SERVICE OR PERFORM MAINTENANCE.

2. When removing access doors or performing maintenance functions inside your furnace, be aware of sharp sheet metal parts and screws. BE EXTREMELY CAREFUL WHEN HANDLING PARTS OR REACHING INTO THE UNIT.

AIR FILTER

The air filter should be checked at least every 6 to 8 weeks and changed or cleaned whenever it becomes dirty.

The size of the air filter varies, depending on the furnace model and size. When replacing your furnace filter, always use the same size and type of filter that was originally supplied.

Warning: NEVER OPERATE YOUR FURNACE WITHOUT A FILTER IN PLACE.

Failure to heed this warning may result in damage to the furnace blower motor. An accumulation of dust and lint on internal parts of your furnace can cause a loss of efficiency and, in some cases, fire.

When inspecting, cleaning, or replacing the air filter in your furnace, refer to the appropriate following procedures that apply to your particular furnace.

1. Turn OFF the electrical supply to the furnace. Remove the control and fan access doors, respectively.

2. Gently remove the filter and carefully turn the dirty side up (if dirty) to avoid dislodging dirt from the filter.

3. If the filter is dirty, wash it in a sink or bathtub or outside with a garden hose. Always use cold water, and use a mild liquid detergent if necessary. Then, allow the filter to air dry.

4. Reinstall the clean filter with the crosshatch binding side facing the furnace fan. Be sure that the filter retainer is under the flange on the furnace casing.

5. Replace the fan and control access doors, and restore electrical power to your furnace.

COMBUSTION AREA AND VENT SYSTEM

The combustion area and vent system should be visually inspected before each heating season. An accumulation of dirt, soot, or rust can result in loss of efficiency and improper performance. Accumulations on the main burners can result in the burners firing out of normal time sequence. This delayed ignition is characterized by an especially loud sound that can be quite alarming.

Caution: If your furnace makes an especially loud noise when the main burners are ignited by the pilot, shut down your furnace and call your service person.

1. Turn OFF the electrical supply to your furnace and remove the access doors.

2. Carefully inspect the gas burner and pilot areas for dirt, rust, or scale. Then, inspect the flue connection area and flue pipe for rust.

Caution: If dirt, rust, soot, or scale accumulations are found, call your service person.

FIGURE 19–16 Typical gas-fired furnace maintenance and care instructions.

MAINTENANCE AND CARE FOR THE OWNER OF
AN OIL-FIRED FURNACE

SAFETY INFORMATION

Warning: These instructions are intended to aid you in the safe operation and proper maintenance of your oil furnace. Read these instructions thoroughly before attempting to operate the furnace. The purpose of WARNINGS and CAUTIONS in these instructions is to call attention to the possible danger of personal injury or equipment damage; they deserve careful attention and understanding. If you do not understand any part of these instructions, contact a qualified licensed service person for clarification.

1. Do not attempt to light the burner manually with a match or other flame.
2. Do not attempt to start the burner with oil or oil vapors in the combustion chamber.
3. Do not operate the furnace without all fan doors and compartment covers securely in place.
4. Do not attach any kind of device to the flue or vent.
5. Always shut off electrical power to the furnace before attempting any maintenance.

HOW YOUR SYSTEM OPERATES

As the flame from the oil burner warms the heat exchanger, the fan switch will start the fan operation. Warm air should now gently circulate from the supply diffusers throughout the dwelling and return to the furnace through return air grille(s).

When the temperature of the circulating air reaches the temperature setting of the thermostat, the oil burner will stop operation, the heat exchanger will cool, and the fan operation will soon be interrupted.

OPERATING INSTRUCTIONS

Burner operation

1. Set the room thermostat above room temperature.
2. Turn the electric switch on. The burner should start automatically.
3. After burner starts, reset the room thermostat for desired temperature.

If Burner Does Not Start

1. Check the fuse in the burner circuit.
2. Make sure the room thermostat is set above the room temperature.

Warning: An explosion or flash fire can occur if the combustion chamber is not free of oil when using the primary control reset button. Make sure the combustion chamber is free of oil before using the reset button.

3. Wait 5 minutes in order to allow the control to cool so that it will recycle. Reset the primary control.
4. If the burner still does not start, call your service person.

Note: CAD CELL MAY BE EXPOSED TO DIRECT ARTIFICIAL LIGHT OR SUNLIGHT, WHICH MAY ENTER THROUGH THE BURNER AIR-CONTROL BAND.

ANNUAL MAINTENANCE

1. Before the heating season, lubricate the burner motor using SAE No. 20 motor oil.

Caution: Do not oil more than necessary. Follow the instructions attached to the fan housing.

2. Have the burner, heating unit, and all controls checked by your service contractor to assure proper operation during the heating season.

TO CHANGE OIL FILTER

1. Turn electric switch off.
2. Close the oil-line valve at tank.
3. Carefully remove the lower section of the filter assembly containing the oil filter cartridge.
4. Drain excess oil from the oil line into a container; then dispose of the oil and the old cartridge.
5. Place a new filter cartridge in the filter assembly and screw it back into place.
6. Loosen the "bleed" screw on top of oil cartridge assembly, allowing air to be purged. Tighten the bleed screw.
7. Open valve in oil line at tank.

THINGS YOU MAY DO

1. **Warning:** Disconnect the main power to the unit before attempting any maintenance.
2. Keep the air filters clean.

Caution: DO NOT OPERATE YOUR SYSTEM FOR EXTENDED PERIODS WITHOUT FILTERS. ANY RECIRCULATED DUST PARTICLES WILL BE HEATED AND CHARRED BY CONTACT WITH THE FURNACE HEAT EXCHANGER. THIS RESIDUE WILL SOIL CEILINGS, WALLS, DRAPES, CARPETS, AND OTHER HOUSEHOLD ARTICLES.

LUBRICATION INSTRUCTIONS

Highboy Units

In order to oil the motor and fan, it is necessary to slide the fan out of the furnace. Remove the fan panel on the front of the furnace and slide the fan section out.

Counterflow Units

In order to oil the motor and fan, it is necessary to remove the upper inner panel of the fan compartment. Follow the instructions on the label.

Lowboy and Horizontal Units

In order to oil the motor and fan, it is necessary to remove only the fan compartment door. The fan is positioned within the compartment to make the fan bearings accessible for oiling.

Proper belt tension is important and may be checked by depressing the belt at a point halfway between the pulleys approximately 1 in. Belt tension may be adjusted by turning the adjustment screw attached to motor base to raise or lower motor.

FIGURE 19–17 Typical oil-fired furnace maintenance and care instructions.

LIMITED WARRANTY CERTIFICATE
Cooling & Heating Products For:

SAVE THIS CERTIFICATE. It gives you specific legal rights, and you may also have other rights which may vary from state to state and province to province.

In the event your unit needs servicing, contact your dealer or contractor who installed or services your unit. When requesting service, please have the model and serial number from each unit in your heating and/or cooling system readily available. If your dealer needs assistance, the distributor or factory branch is available for support and we, in turn, support their efforts.

Fill in the installation date and model and serial numbers of the unit in the space provided below and **retain this limited warranty for your files.**

GENERAL TERMS

This limited warranty applies only while the unit remains at the site of the original installation (except for mobile home installations) and only if the unit is installed inside the continental United States, Alaska, Hawaii, and Canada. The warranty applies only if the unit is installed and operated in accordance with the printed instructions and in compliance with applicable installation and building codes and good trade practices.

During the first year after installation, we will provide a replacement for any component part of your unit found to be defective in materials or workmanship. Extended warranties for various components are described on the reverse side of this page. All replacement parts will be warranted for the unused portion of that component's warranty. The part to be replaced must be returned to our distributor or factory branch in exchange for the replacement part.

In lieu of providing a replacement part, we may, at our option, provide the distributor's component purchase price from us or a credit equal to the distributor's component purchase price from us toward the purchase of any new unit which we distribute. If a credit is given in lieu of a replacement part, the rating plate from the unit being replaced must be submitted on a warranty claim, and the unit being replaced must be made available to our distributor or factory branch for disposition.

In establishing the date of installation for any purpose, including determination of the starting date for the term of this limited warranty, reasonable proof of the original installation date must be presented*, otherwise the effective date will be based upon the date of manufacture plus thirty (30) days.

Any labor, material, refrigerant, freight and/or handling charges associated with any repair or replacement pursuant to this limited warranty will be your responsibility. In this warranty the word "installation" means original installation.

We will not be responsible for and you, the user, will pay for: (a) damages caused by accident, abuse, negligence, misuse, riot, fire, flood, or Acts of God (b) damages caused by operating the unit where there is a corrosive atmosphere containing chlorine, fluorine, or any other damaging chemicals (other than in a normal residential environment) (c) damages caused by any unauthorized alteration or repair of the unit affecting its stability or performance (d) damages caused by improper matching or application of the unit or the unit's components (e) damages caused by failing to provide proper maintenance and service to the unit (f) any expenses incurred for erecting, disconnecting, or dismantling the unit (g) parts or supplies used in connection with service or maintenance, such as refrigerant, filters, or belts (h) damage, repairs, inoperation or inefficiency resulting from faulty installation or application (i) electricity or fuel costs or any increase in electricity or fuel cost whatsoever including additional or unusual use of supplemental electric heat.

We shall not be liable for any incidental, consequential, or special damages or expenses in connection with any use or failure of this unit. We have not made and do not make any representation or warranty of fitness for a particular use or purpose, and there is no implied condition of fitness for a particular use or purpose. We make no express warranties except as stated in this limited warranty. No one is authorized to change this limited warranty or to create for us any other obligation or liability in connection with this unit. Any implied warranties shall last for one year after the original installation. Some states and provinces do not allow the exclusion or limitation of incidental or consequential damages or do not allow limitations on how long an implied warranty or condition lasts, so the above limitations or exclusions may not apply to you. The provisions of this limited warranty are in addition to and not a modification of or subtraction from any statutory warranties and other rights and remedies provided by law.

Please refer to reverse side of this page for additional terms.

Model No. _____
Serial No. _____
Date Installed _____ *

EFFECTIVE ON ALL UNITS INSTALLED AFTER 9/1/91.
* To receive advantage of your warranty, you must retain the original records that can establish the installation date of your unit.

FORM: 7680-149
PRINTED: AUGUST, 1991

INTER-CITY PRODUCTS CORPORATION.
(618) 282-6262

FIGURE 19–18 Typical gas furnace warranty. (Courtesy of ARCOAIRE, Inter-City Products Corporation, USA.)

STUDY QUESTIONS

Answers to the study questions may be found in the sections noted in brackets.

19–1. Name 10 items that are included under furnace maintenance. *[Importance of Proper Maintenance]*

19–2. Which parts of the furnace require adjustment? *[Importance of Proper Maintenance]*

19–3. How should the firing rate of the furnace be determined? *[Testing and Adjusting]*

19–4. How is the air quantity determined? *[Servicing Fan-Motor Assembly]*

19–5. What is the relation of the amount of air required for cooling to the amount required for heating? *[Direct-Drive Fans]*

19–6. In balancing the airflow, where are the thermometers located? *[Rebalancing the System]*

19–7. How often should the furnace cycle per hour? *[Adjusting the Thermostat Heat Anticipator and Fan Control]*

19–8. How often should the fan motor be lubricated? *[Servicing Fan-Motor Assembly]*

19–9. What is the proper color for a gas flame? *[Gas Furnace]*

19–10. How frequently should oil burners be serviced? *[Oil Furnace]*

19–11. What is the maximum time that heat exchangers are under warranty? *[Warranty]*

19–12. What are the important areas of concern in customer relations? *[Customer Relations]*

20

Energy

Conservation

OBJECTIVES

After studying this chapter, the student will be able to:

- Recommend construction factors to reduce building exposure losses
- Determine the value of retrofit measures to reduce the use of energy required for heating
- State the types of auxiliary equipment or modifications that are available for energy conservation

ENERGY CONSERVATION MEASURES

Figure 20–1 shows the extent to which space heating contributes to the nation's use of energy. Nearly 18% of the total energy consumed is required for heating. By adding domestic hot water and air conditioning, the proportions of energy used rises to about 25% of the total National consumption. Although heating is an essential element of our existence, only recently has a great deal of attention been directed to conserving the valuable natural resources required for heating.

In other areas of the book a number of ways to conserve energy are shown, including the use of high-efficiency furnaces and heat pumps, the improved use of controls, and so on. This chapter is devoted primarily to describing how the building envelope can be improved to save energy. Included also are other conservation

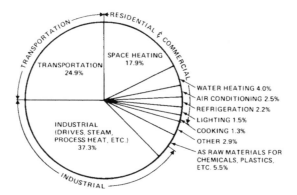

FIGURE 20–1   Heat loss through a typical, conventionally insulated home. (Courtesy of The Dow Company.)

measures for specific applications. This information is divided into the following three areas:

1. Reducing exposure losses
2. Reducing outside air infiltration
3. Using other retrofit measures

Although heating installation and service people are not concerned directly with the construction of the building, they are frequently called upon to offer recommendations for reducing the size of the heating load and for improving comfort levels. An understanding of the construction factors and other modifications to improve performance can be a valuable asset.

Reducing Exposure Losses

Figure 20–2 shows the exposure losses for a typical, well-built house. The construction shown includes fiberboard sheathing, insulated doors, dual-glazed windows, R–19 ceiling insulation, and R–11 wall insulation. Variations in the size and shape of the house and its window area will alter the heat-loss distribution. Typical losses are as follows:

| | *Percent of total* |
Exposure	*heat loss*
Frame walls	17%
Ceiling	5%
Basement walls	20%
Basement floor	1%
Windows	16%
Doors	3%
Air leakage	38%

Some reduction in heat loss can be accomplished by adopting the options shown in Figure 20–3.

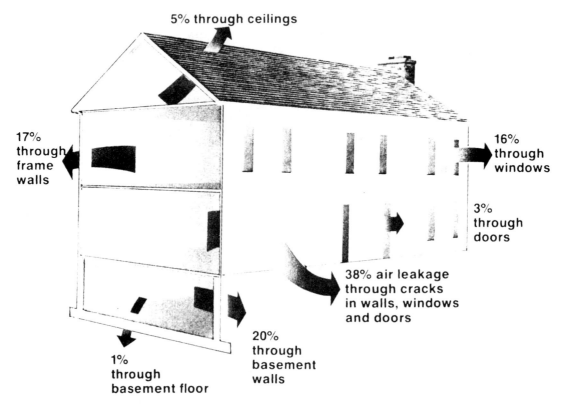

FIGURE 20–2 Heat loss through a typical, conventionally insulated home. (Courtesy of The Dow Company.)

Insulation The insulating values of various types of materials are commonly given in terms of R-factors, where R represents the resistance of the material or materials to thermal loss—that is, the R-value is the ability of the insulation to slow the transfer of heat. Higher R-values represent more insulating ability.

The following table shows the insulating values of certain substances, given in terms of 1 in. of thickness.

Material	Density (lb./ft.^{3})	Thermal resistance, R (in./thickness)
Glass fiber	9.5–11.00	4.00
Vermiculite, expanded	7.0–8.20	2.08
Mineral wool, resin binder	15.00	3.45
Expanded polystyrene, extruded	2.20	5.00

Figure 20–4 shows the amount of either *batts* or *loose fill* material required to achieve various insulating values. For example, 6 in. of glass mineral fiber batts are needed to produce R–19 thermal resistance. Using loose fill, $8^3/4$ in. are required to produce the same R-value. The number of bags of loose fill required per 1000 ft.^{2} to provide the various thicknesses is also shown.

OPTION:	APPROXIMATE SAVINGS ON HOME HEAT LOSS:
CEILING: RAISE INSULATION FROM R-19 TO R-30	2%
WALL (4" STUD): RAISE INSULATION FROM R-11 TO R-13	1%
WALL (6" STUD): RAISE INSULATION FROM R-11 TO R-19	5%
WINDOWS: CHANGE FROM DUAL GLAZING TO TRIPLE GLAZING	5%
SHEATHING: SWITCH FROM CONVENTIONAL FIBERBOARD TO 1 IN. OF R-5.41 SHEATHING AND INSTALL FROM ROOFLINE TO SILL PLATE	14%
SHEATHING: SWITCH FROM CONVENTIONAL FIBERBOARD TO 1 IN. OF R-5.41 SHEATHING AND INSTALL FROM ROOFLINE TO FROSTLINE	24%

FIGURE 20–3   Thermal improvement options. (Courtesy of The Dow Company.)

BATTS OR BLANKETS

INSULATION VALUE	GLASS MINERAL FIBER	ROCK MINERAL FIBER
	INCHES	INCHES
R-11	3½	3
R-13	3⅝	3½
R-19	(6)	5½
R-22	6½	6
R-26	8¼	7
R-30	9½	8½
R-38	12	11

LOOSE FILL (POURED OR BLOWN)

INSULATION VALUE	**GLASS MINERAL FIBER		**ROCK MINERAL FIBER		***CELLULOSIC FIBER
	INCHES	BAGS/1000 SQ. FT.	INCHES	BAGS/1000 SQ. FT.	INCHES
R-11	5	11	3¾	23	3
R-13	6	13½	4¾	28	3½
R-19	(8¾)	20	6½	38	5⅛
R-22	10	22	7½	45	6
R-26	12	27	9½	56	7
R-30	13¾	30	10¼	62	8⅛
R-38	17½	40	12¾	77	10¼

**Blown mineral fiber insulation has both a depth and density relationship. R-values depend upon both number of inches and bags per 1,000 square feet of insulation.

***According to the National Cellulose Insulation Manufacturers Association, blown cellulose insulation shall have an R-value that is greater than or equal to 3.70 per inch of thickness with a density not to exceed 3 pounds per cubic foot.

FIGURE 20–4   R-values related to insulation thickness. (Courtesy of the U. S. Department of Energy.)

Referring to ceiling insulation information shown in Figure 20–5, the optimum thickness of insulation is approximately 4 in. Doubling this thickness to 8 in. increases the insulating value by only 5.5%, and tripling the amount of insulation increases it by only 7.5%. A comparison of the various types of insulation with reference to such qualities as ease of application, fire resistance, and vapor barrier requirements is given in Figure 20–6.

Attic ventilation   Related to the use of attic insulation is the need for adequate attic ventilation. In summer the attic temperature can be excessive unless the attic is well ventilated. Two means are available: (1) natural ventilation and (2) the use of an exhaust fan. The selection depends on the attic construction and the feasibility of providing the necessary openings.

The following two methods of providing *natural ventilation* can be used. In making a selection, the important element to consider is the amount of net vent area each would provide. As noted in Figure 20–7, the recommended net vent area is dependent on the method used.

Natural ventilation method	Recommended net vent area
Continuous ridge vents plus soffit vent	1.5 in.²/ft.² of ceiling area
Gable, roof, or turbine vents plus soffit vent	3.0 in.²/ft.² of ceiling area

Powered ventilation consists of a thermostatically controlled vent placed near the peak of the roof in the center of the attic. If the house is large (over 2000 ft.²) or has a T- or L-shaped configuration, more than one is needed. The fan capacity of the ventilator should provide a minimum of 1.5 cfm per square foot of ceiling area. Soffit vents, which provide intake air, should have a minimum of 80 in. of net free area for each 100 cfm of ventilator capacity. The thermostat should be set to turn on at 100°F and off at 85°F.

Vapor barriers   To protect the insulation against condensation, a vapor barrier is recommended. An excellent example of energy-efficient wall construction is shown in

Inches	Percent Reduction in Ht. Transfer	Percent Gain from Previous Figure	Total Gains Possible Beyond 4 in. of insulation		
0					
1	65.5%	65.5%			
2	79.2%	13.7%			
4	88.3%	9.1%	5.5% from 4 to 8 in.	6.7% from 4 to 10 in.	7.5% from 4 to 12 in.
6	92.0%	3.7%			
8	93.8%	1.8%			
10	95.0%	1.2%			
12	95.8%	0.8%			

Figure 20–5   Energy-loss reduction equated to inches of ceiling insulation.

TYPE	COMMENTS	APPLICATION
BATTS/BLANKETS Performed glass fiber or rock wool with or without vapor barrier backing	Fire resistant, moisture resistant, easy to handle for do-it-yourself installation, least expensive and most commonly available.	Unfinished attic floor, rafters, underside of floors, between studs.
RIGID BOARD 1. Extruded polystyrene bead 2. Extruded polystyrene 3. Urethane 4. Glass fiber	All have high R-values for relatively small thickness. 1, 2, 3: Are not fire resistant, require installation by contractor with $1/2$-in. gypsum board to insure fire safety. 3: Is its own vapor barrier; however, when in contact with liquid water, it should have a skin to prevent degrading. 1, 4: Require addition of vapor barrier. 2: Is its own barrier.	Basement walls, new construction frame walls, commonly used as an outer sheathing between siding and studs.
LOOSE FILL (POURED IN) 1. Glass fiber 2. Rock wool 3. Treated cellulosic fiber	All easy to install, require vapor barrier bought and applied separately. Vapor barrier may be impossible to install in existing walls. 1, 2: Fire resistant, moisture resistant. 3: Check label to make sure material meets federal specifications for fire and moisture resistance and R-value.	Unfinished attic floor, uninsulated existing walls.
LOOSE FILL (BLOWN IN) 1. Glass fiber 2. Rock wool 3. Treated cellulosic fiber	All require vapor barrier bought separately, all require space to be filled completely. Vapor barrier may be impossible to install in existing walls. 1, 2: Fire resistant, moisture resistant. 3: Fills up spaces most consistently. When blown into closed spaces, has slightly higher R-value. Check label for fire and moisture resistance and R-value.	Unfinished attic floor, finished attic floor, finished frame walls, underside of floors.

Figure 20–6   Insulation materials chart. (Courtesy of the U.S. Department of Energy.)

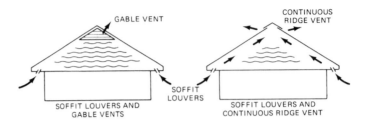

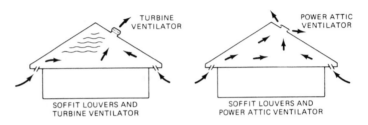

Figure 20–7   Types of attic ventilation. (Courtesy of the U.S. Department of Energy.)

Figure 20–8. Note the position of the polyethylene vapor barrier and the use of sheathing with a high R-factor.

The U-factor   Thus far the discussion of insulation has centered around the R-factor, the resistance of a material to the flow of heat. A more useful factor in determining heat load is the U-factor. The U-factor is the reciprocal of the R-factor; thus,

$$U = \frac{1}{R}$$

The U-factor is an overall heat-transfer coefficient. It represents the amount of heat in Btuh units that will flow through a given material or materials per square foot of surface area per degree of difference in temperature. For example, if the R-value is R 13, the U-factor is

$$U = \frac{1}{R} = \frac{1}{13} = 0.08 \text{ Btuh/ft.}^2/°F$$

Applying this to an exposed wall, the R-factor is the sum total of the R-factors of the individual components in the wall. The following tabulation illustrates the determination of the R-factor for a wall composed of various components. Note that this wall has a total R-factor of 15.18. This amount represents the resistance of the wall to the flow of heat through it.

Material or surface	R-factor
Exterior surface resistance	0.17
Bevel-lapped siding, $1/2 \times 8$ in.	0.81
Fiberboard insulating sheathing, $3/4$ in.	2.10
Insulation, mineral wool batts, $3 1/2$ in.	11.00
$3/8$-in. gypsum lath and $3/8$-in. plaster	0.42
Interior surface resistance	0.68
Total R-factor	15.18

Figure 20–8 Example of energy-efficient wall construction. (Courtesy of Owens/Corning Fiberglas Corporation.)

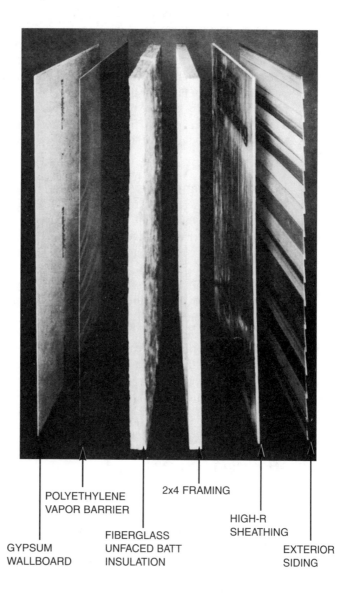

POLYETHYLENE
VAPOR BARRIER

2x4 FRAMING

HIGH-R
SHEATHING

GYPSUM
WALLBOARD

FIBERGLASS
UNFACED BATT
INSULATION

EXTERIOR
SIDING

In most northern climates it is good practice to provide construction of walls with an R-factor of 15.0 or greater and ceilings with a factor of 25.0 or greater. Windows should be constructed with double glass or single glass with a storm window.

To convert to a U-factor in the preceding example, where the R-factor for the exposed wall is 15.18, the heat-transfer coefficient is determined as follows:

$$U = \frac{1}{R} = \frac{1}{15.18} = 0.07 \text{ Btuh/ft.}^2/^\circ\text{F}$$

The U-factor is calculated in Btuh/ft.^{2} of surface per degree of difference in temperature. With this information, the effectiveness of adding insulation can be evaluated in terms of heat savings.

Energy-efficient windows Windows with built-in thermal barriers reduce the heat loss through the glass and the framing, as shown in Figure 20–9. This unique construction system provides the highest level of insulation of any residential glass: R–9. This window blocks more than 99.5% of the damaging ultraviolet radiation that causes fabrics and furnishings to fade. Special attention is paid to the thermal conductivity of the window's edge, since this is normally where condensation will form during the coldest weather.

Energy-efficient doors Energy-efficient doors are available. These are doors that incorporate either polystyrene or polyurethane insulation and a thermal barrier to reduce heat loss through the framing (Figure 20–10). One door manufacturer's rating chart gives the overall R-factor for various types of door construction (Figure 20–11). With the use of a full polyurethane core, the R-factor is 15.15, which is almost equal to the wall factor of 15.18 calculated for the exposed wall in the preceding example. With such a door a storm door is virtually unnecessary. In fact, a storm door might be counterproductive because of the tendency to leave the primary door open at times to avoid the inconvenience of opening and closing two doors.

Weatherstripping Weatherstripping and caulking around doors, windows, and other wall penetrations stop the entry of outside air into a building. Even if no noticeable drafts are present, air movement can be occurring. A typical 3-ft.-wide door with a $^1/_8$-in. separation at the threshold may not produce a noticeable draft, but, nonetheless, $4^1/_2$ in.^{2} of open area exists. This is equivalent to a hole $1^3/_{16}$ in. in diameter (see Figure 20–12).

Reducing Air Leakage

There are many ways to tighten a structure to reduce air infiltration. It is first esssential to find out where the leakage is occurring. A number of contractors are offering a service, which consists of a scientific means of finding the leakage areas and then implementing measures to close the openings.

There are two main sources of leakage: (1) through building materials and (2) at intersections where two building components meet. It is a simple matter to install a

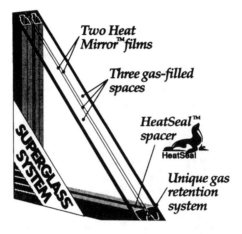

Two Heat
Mirror™ films

Three gas-filled
spaces

HeatSeal™
spacer

Unique gas
retention
system

SUPERGLASS
SYSTEM

FIGURE 20–9   Super-high-efficiency window. (Courtesy of Southwall Technologies.)

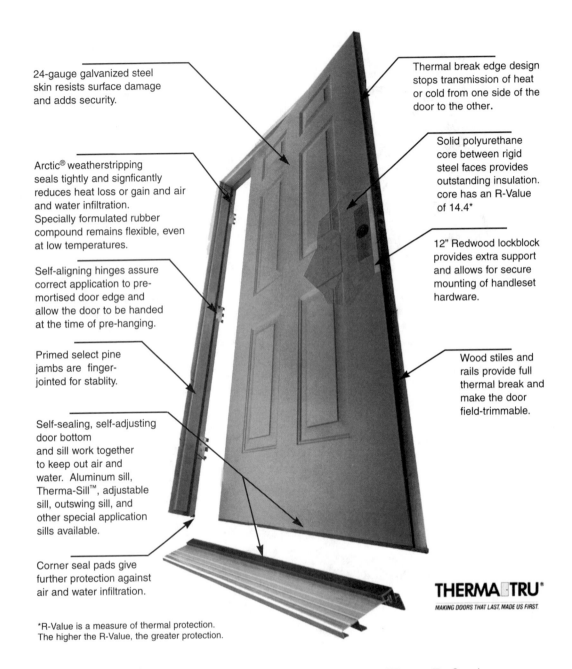

24-gauge galvanized steel skin resists surface damage and adds security.

Thermal break edge design stops transmission of heat or cold from one side of the door to the other.

Solid polyurethane core between rigid steel faces provides outstanding insulation. core has an R-Value of 14.4*

Arctic® weatherstripping seals tightly and signficantly reduces heat loss or gain and air and water infiltration. Specially formulated rubber compound remains flexible, even at low temperatures.

12" Redwood lockblock provides extra support and allows for secure mounting of handleset hardware.

Self-aligning hinges assure correct application to pre-mortised door edge and allow the door to be handed at the time of pre-hanging.

Wood stiles and rails provide full thermal break and make the door field-trimmable.

Primed select pine jambs are finger-jointed for stablity.

Self-sealing, self-adjusting door bottom and sill work together to keep out air and water. Aluminum sill, Therma-Sill™, adjustable sill, outswing sill, and other special application sills available.

Corner seal pads give further protection against air and water infiltration.

THERMA TRU®
MAKING DOORS THAT LAST. MADE US FIRST.

*R-Value is a measure of thermal protection.
The higher the R-Value, the greater protection.

FIGURE 20–10 Example of energy-efficient door construction. (Courtesy of Therma-Tru Corp.)

	R factor
Solid core wood door	2.90*
Stile and rail wood door	2.79*
Hollow core wood door	2.18*
Steel door with polystyrene core	7.14
Steel door with ¾" urethane "honeycomb" core	8.42
Storm door (aluminum)	1.84**
THERMA-TRU door (with a full polyurethane core door)	15.15

*R-factor reference according to ASHRAE (American Society of Heating,
 Refrigeration and Air Conditioning Engineers) figures.
**Based on engineering calculations.

FIGURE 20–11   R-factors for various types of exterior doors. (Courtesy of Pease Company, Ever-Strait Division.)

vapor barrier under plasterboard when a new house is constructed. On existing houses it may be impractical. The use of a vapor barrier greatly reduces the air leakage through building materials.

Some examples of intersections are floors with walls, walls with ceilings, chimneys with floors and walls, and penetrations in the wall, floor, or ceiling to accommodate fixtures for plumbing, electric switches and outlets, or light switches. Air leakage can also occur through bypasses from the basement and the house interior to the attic. These bypasses are most often found in wall cavities and around chimneys, vents, and flue pipes. Wherever the leak is found, it must be eliminated.

Determining the leakage sites. Inspect the house to determine remedial measures to tighten the construction. Some retrofit measures that can be used include the following:

1. Seal holes around pipes and wire.
2. Seal cracks around beams in open beam ceilings.
3. Seal cracks around heating registers and exhaust fan cutouts.
4. Seal cracks around edges of fireplaces and mantelpieces.

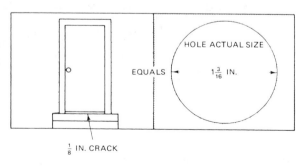

EQUALS

HOLE ACTUAL SIZE

$1\frac{3}{16}$ IN.

$\frac{1}{8}$ IN. CRACK

FIGURE 20–12   Door clearance of $^1/_8$ in. is equivalent to area of $1^3/_{16}$-in. hole.

5. Seal cracks inside and around built-in cabinets and bookshelves.
6. Seal holes in recessed fluorescent light fixtures.
7. Seal gaps beneath baseboards and molding and behind electric baseboard heaters.
8. Install a fireplace seal tight damper in the chimney flue.
9. Weatherstrip and caulk leaky windows and doors and seal cracks around the window and door frames.

Air-to-air heat exchangers   Cutting down infiltration and reducing air leakage can create nearly airtight homes. This can cause problems unless some form of ventilation is provided. Some problems caused by airtight houses are shown in Figure 20–13.

The air-to-air heat exchanger is a device for recovering heat from exhaust air and using it to heat air supplied from the outside for ventilation. Figure 20–14 shows how this heat-recovery unit operates. In winter, fresh, dry cold air is forced through the multipath heat exchanger core and stale, warm indoor air is forced through in the opposite direction. The fresh air temperature rises 80% or more of the indoor-outdoor temperature difference. The rate of airflow can be regulated by the homeowner to meet individual needs. During the colder winter months, some moisture in the exhaust air can freeze when subjected to low outside temperatures. The unit includes automatic defrost to ensure proper operation during severe winter conditions. A humidistat can be provided to switch the fan speed to control indoor humidity levels.

Figure 20–15 illustrates the application of an air-to-air heat-exchanger system in a typical home. The best mounting location is usually the basement adjacent to other mechanical equipment or in the laundry area. Select a location with the best relationship to the ductwork and as close as possible to the outside wall. As provision for a condensate drain will have to be made, a plumbing stack, fixture, or floor drain should be handy. The unit may be mounted between or below the floor joists, on wall brackets, or on the floor.

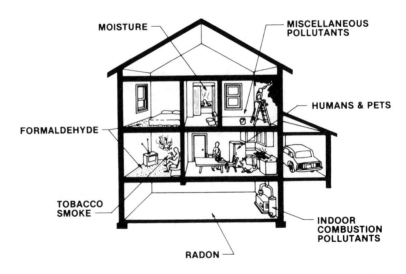

FIGURE 20–13   Sources of indoor pollution. (Courtesy of the U.S. Department of Energy.)

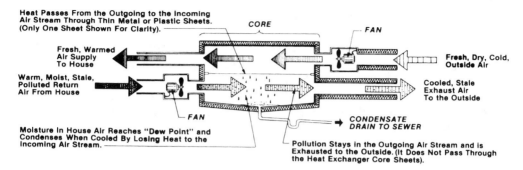

Heat Passes From the Outgoing to the Incoming
Air Stream Through Thin Metal or Plastic Sheets.
(Only One Sheet Shown For Clarity).

CORE

FAN

Fresh, Warmed
Air Supply
To House

Fresh, Dry, Cold,
Outside Air

Warm, Moist, Stale,
Polluted Return
Air From House

Cooled, Stale
Exhaust Air
To the Outside

FAN

*CONDENSATE
DRAIN TO SEWER*

Moisture In House Air Reaches "Dew Point" and
Condenses When Cooled By Losing Heat to the
Incoming Air Stream.

Pollution Stays in the Outgoing Air Stream and is
Exhausted to the Outside.(It Does Not Pass Through
the Heat Exchanger Core Sheets).

FIGURE 20–14   Operation of air-to-air exchanger. (Courtesy of the U.S. Department of Energy.)

Costs can be substantially reduced when installing a central, ducted system in
new construction or retrofitting an existing system if the proper planning takes place
in advance. Exchanger manufacturers should be consulted in the design phase of the
project to facilitate this planning process. Ductwork layout and design must be
planned for, and many problems can be avoided if the system is well integrated into
the house design.

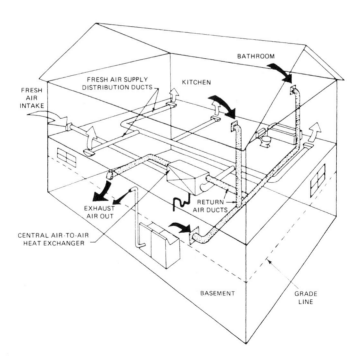

BATHROOM

FRESH AIR SUPPLY
DISTRIBUTION DUCTS

KITCHEN

FRESH
AIR
INTAKE

EXHAUST
AIR OUT

RETURN
AIR DUCTS

CENTRAL AIR-TO-AIR
HEAT EXCHANGER

BASEMENT

GRADE
LINE

FIGURE 20–15   Application of an air-to-air heat exchanger in a typical home. (Courtesy of the
U.S. Department of Energy.)

Using Other Retrofit Measures

There is a continuing effort among manufacturers to offer new products to reduce energy consumption. Some of these products fit specific requirements, while others have more general applications. In the following section various measures that have unique features are described. The list is not complete, due to the dynamic nature of research and development being carried on in this field. The student should be constantly on the alert for new ideas and products that conserve energy. The topics that are discussed in this section include the following:

1. Fireplace treatment
2. Use of heat pump water heaters
3. Use of more efficient lighting
4. Alterations to the heating unit
5. Using programmed thermostats
6. Using solar heating
7. Improved maintenance

Fireplace treatment   The open fireplace can be a source of considerable heat loss. To prevent this, it is recommended that wood-burning fireplaces be installed with separate outside air intake vents for combustion air. This provision replaces the normal drawing of already heated air from within the house. Glass doors on the unit also channel radiant heat into the room while preventing warm air from escaping up the chimney, as shown in Figure 20–16.

Using heat pumps for hot water   Heat-recovery units that use rejected energy for heating water are now available on many residential cooling and heat pump units. These units are valuable for supplementing the conventional water heater. Complete

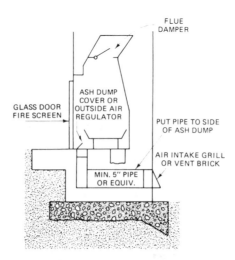

FIGURE 20–16   Example of an energy-efficient fireplace.

package heat pump water heaters are also available. They operate the year around in the heating mode to supplement the standard gas or electric units (see Chapter 24 for information on heat pumps).

Using more efficient lighting   Energy-efficient fluorescent lighting is recommended whenever appropriate. Fluorescent lights produce from 55 to 92 lumens of light per watt, compared to 15 to 25 lumens per watt for incandescent light. A lumen is a measure of the flow of light. Fluorescent lights have a longer life than incandescent bulbs. The average life of a fluorescent bulb is around 20,000 h compared to less than 1000 h for incandescent bulbs.

Alterations to the heating unit   Alterations to the heating unit to improve efficiency have been included in earlier chapters and should be consulted for complete information. Important measures to consider for retrofitting include:

1. Replacing the unit with a high-efficiency furnace (see Chapter 12)
2. Sizing the furnace to fit the load (see Chapter 16)
3. Installing electronic ignition (see Chapter 11)

Using programmable thermostats   The use of an automatic temperature setback thermostat is one example of a system modification that can be made (Figure 20–17). A 5 to 10% savings in fuel can be realized by lowering the temperature in the space 5°F for 8 h each night. A savings of 9 to 16% can be realized by lowering the space temperature 10°F for 8 h at night. Tables showing night setback savings for various parts of the country are shown in Figures 20–18 and 20–19.

Using solar heating   Solar heating is used by a homeowner principally for:

1. Heating space
2. Heating domestic water
3. Heating swimming pool water

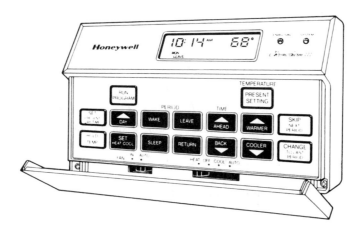

FIGURE 20–17   Seven-day programmable thermostat. (Courtesy of Honeywell Inc.)

Year	Miami Houston	Phoenix Columbus, SC Dallas	St. Louis Atlanta	Philadelphia Chicago Salt Lake City	Buffalo Denver Minneapolis
1	$ 180	$ 278	$ 372	$ 464	$ 556
2	360	556	744	928	1112
3	540	834	1116	1392	1668
4	720	1112	1488	1856	2224
5	900	1390	1860	2320	2780
6	1080	1668	2232	2784	3336
7	1260	1946	2604	3248	3892
8	1440	2224	2976	3712	4448
9	1620	2502	3348	4176	5004
10	1800	2780	3720	4640	5560

YEAR AFTER YEAR, SAVINGS JUST KEEP ADDING UP!

PULSE (95% AFUE) vs. furnace with 60% AFUE
Load @ 70,000 Btuh
Gas Rate = 60¢/therm
Savings figures are cumulative (not allowing for inflation).
Actual figures may vary in your area depending on weather conditions and family lifestyles.

FIGURE 20–18   Annual savings with the use of a programmable thermostat. (Courtesy of Lennox Industries, Inc.)

From an economic standpoint, domestic hot water solar heating has the greatest return for the average homeowner, since hot water is needed year around. This type of heating permits utilization of the summer solar radiation, which is greater than that available in winter for most parts of the country. Figure 20–20 shows a solar closed-system domestic water heating package. This particular package consists of a series of components hooked up and ready to be connected to collectors and a water tank. The collectors and tank are not part of the package, so they must be ordered separately. Any good closed system using collectors of ample capacity can be used. Swimming pool water solar heating also utilizes the summer heat to advantage. A simple hookup is shown in Figure 20–21.

Improved Maintenance

Firing devices should be cleaned and serviced on a regular basis. Throwaway filters should be replaced when dirty. Motors should be oiled. Regular maintenance is important on any heating system. If maintenance is neglected, the efficiency and reliability of the system will decrease. Where efficiency can easily be measured, as on an oil-fired installation, this should be done at least once a year to assure good performance.

Distribution systems should be kept clean. Thermostats should be kept in calibration. Ductwork should be balanced to provide an even distribution of heat. The thermostat location should be changed or the thermostat replaced if it does not provide

City	①	②	③	④	City	①	②	③	④
ALBUQUERQUE, NM	12%	24%	16%	16%	LOS ANGELES, CA	15%	30%	20%	27%
ATLANTA, GA	15%	27%	12%	19%	LOUISVILLE, KY	13%	24%	%	18%
ATLANTIC CITY, NJ	12%	23%	13%	20%	MADISON, WI	10%	19%	%	19%
BILLINGS, MT	10%	20%	9%	16%	MEMPHIS, TN	15%	26%	11%	17%
BIRMINGHAM, AL	15%	28%	12%	17%	MIAMI, FL	18%	30%	11%	17%
BOISE, ID	11%	22%	8%	15%	MILWAUKEE, WI	10%	19%	13%	19%
BOSTON, MA	11%	22%	13%	20%	MINNEAPOLIS, MN	9%	18%	12%	20%
BUFFALO, NY	10%	20%	14%	22%	NEW ORLEANS, LA	16%	30%	11%	17%
BURLINGTON, VT	9%	18%	14%	22%	NEW YORK, NY	12%	23%	13%	20%
CHARLESTON, SC	16%	29%	13%	19%	OKLAHOMA CITY, OK	14%	26%	11%	16%
CHEYENNE, WY	10%	19%	12%	17%	OMAHA, NE	11%	20%	12%	19%
CHICAGO, IL	11%	21%	13%	20%	PHILADELPHIA, PA	11%	24%	13%	20%
CINCINNATI, OH	12%	24%	12%	19%	PHOENIX, AZ	16%	30%	%	11%
CLEVELAND, OH	10%	21%	13%	21%	PITTSBURGH, PA	11%	22%	13%	20%
COLORADO SPRINGS, CO	11%	22%	11%	16%	PORTLAND, ME	10%	19%	15%	21%
COLUMBUS, OH	11%	22%	12%	19%	PORTLAND, OR	13%	24%	11%	20%
CORPUS CHRISTI, TX	17%	30%	10%	15%	PROVIDENCE, RI	11%	21%	16%	24%
DALLAS, TX	15%	28%	9%	14%	ROANOKE, VA	12%	24%	12%	19%
DENVER, CO	11%	22%	10%	17%	SALT LAKE CITY, UT	11%	21%	10%	16%
DES MOINES, IA	11%	20%	12%	19%	SAN DIEGO, CA	16%	30%	25%	33%
DETROIT, MI	11%	21%	13%	22%	SAN FRANCISCO, CA	14%	26%	14%	19%
DODGE CITY, KS	12%	23%	9%	15%	SEATTLE, WA	12%	24%	16%	23%
GREENSBORO, NC	14%	25%	12%	19%	SIOUX FALLS, SD	10%	19%	11%	18%
HOUSTON, TX	16%	30%	9%	14%	SPOKANE, WA	11%	20%	10%	18%
INDIANAPOLIS, IN	11%	22%	12%	19%	SPRINGFIELD, MA	11%	20%	13%	20%
JACKSON, MS	16%	30%	%	17%	ST. LOUIS, MO	12%	23%	11%	18%
JACKSONVILLE, FL	17%	30%	%	17%	SYRACUSE, NY	11%	20%	13%	21%
KANSAS CITY, MO	12%	23%	10%	16%	WASHINGTON, DC	13%	25%	13%	20%
LAS VEGAS, NV	15%	27%	%	11%	WILMINGTON, DE	12%	23%	10%	20%
LITTLE ROCK, AR	15%	27%	10%	16%	©Copyright Honeywell, Inc.				

① 10° * SINGLE HEATING SETBACK 70° TO 60° 8 HOURS/DAY

② 10° * DOUBLE HEATING SETBACK 70° TO 60° 8 HOURS/DAY, TWICE/DAY

③ 5° SINGLE COOLING SETUP 75° TO 80° 11 HOURS/DAY

④ 5° DOUBLE COOLING SETUP 75° TO 80° 9 HOURS/DAY, 7 HOURS/NIGHT

*SAVINGS FOR A 5° HEATING SETBACK ARE AT LEAST $\frac{1}{2}$ OF SAVINGS FOR A 10° SETBACK.

ACTUAL SAVINGS DEPEND ON YOUR HOME, GEOGRAPHIC LOCATION, NUMBER OF SETBACKS AND AMOUNT OF SETBACK DEGREES.

FIGURE 20–19 Percentage of heating-cooling energy savings with thermostat setback in average home. (Courtesy of Honeywell Inc.)

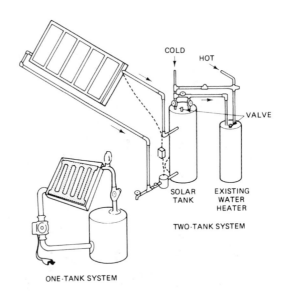

FIGURE 20–20   Solar domestic hot water system. (Courtesy of The Detroit Edison Company.)

adequate temperature control. Proper maintenance is essentially good housekeeping practice, which results in improved performance.

Many new types of energy-saving devices are becoming available on the market because of the urgent need for saving fuel. Anyone involved in the heating business should carefully evaluate these innovations, since fuel should be saved by all practical means.

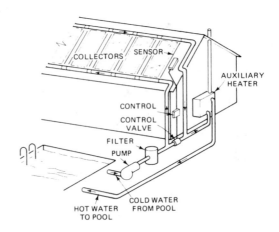

FIGURE 20–21   Solar swimming pool heating system. (Courtesy of The Detroit Edison Company.)

STUDY QUESTIONS

Answers to the study questions may be found in the sections noted in brackets.

20–1. What percentage of the total energy consumed in the United States is used for heating? *[Energy Conservation Measures]*

20–2. What does an R-factor represent in terms of insulating value? *[Insulation]*

20–3. What is the largest factor in the thermal resistance of a properly constructed wall? *[Insulation]*

20–4. What should the R-factor be for a ceiling, in keeping with good practice? *[Insulation]*

20–5. An R-factor of 13 is equivalent to what U-factor? *[Insulation]*

20–6. What percentage of the heat loss of an average house is due to air leakage? *[Reducing Exposure Losses]*

20–7. What is the density of expanded polystyrene in pounds per cubic foot? *[Insulation]*

20–8. What is the increase in insulating value in changing 4 in. of insulation to 12 in.? *[Insulation]*

20–9. What is the recommended net vent area for continuous ridge vents? *[Attic Ventilation]*

20–10. What R-factor is practical for a polystyrene core door? *[Energy-Efficient Doors]*

20–11. How is an air-to-air heat exchanger used? *[Air-to-Air Exchangers]*

20–12. What is the best method of reducing heated-air losses from a fireplace? *[Fireplace Treatment]*

20–13. What types of lighting are most energy-efficient for residences? *[Using More Efficient Lighting]*

21

Indoor Air Quality

OBJECTIVES

After studying this chapter, the student will be able to:

- Define the elements that make up polluted air
- Make a survey of a building to determine the conditions causing air pollution
- Know the procedures required to control pollution
- Make recommendations for improving indoor air quality

INTRODUCTION

Air is a relatively thin layer of mixed gases that surrounds the earth. This atmosphere consists primarily of nitrogen (78%) and oxygen (21%). Air in its pure form is invisible, odorless, tasteless, and required to support life. Oxygen is the active element. Nitrogen is the inactive element and is used to dilute oxygen within limits needed for breathing. By inhaling air, oxygen is supplied to the bloodstream to carry out the metabolic process essential to life. Oxygen is converted to carbon dioxide when it is exhaled. Anyone confined to a closed space must be provided with adequate ventilation. The supply of fresh outside air is as important as exhausting the stale air to maintain normal respiratory functions.

AIR CONTAMINATION

Normal air contains certain foreign material. These *permanent atmosphere impurities* enter the air as a result of natural processes such as wind erosion, sea wave action, and volcanic eruption. Man-made contamination can come from a number of sources, including power plants, industrial factories, transportation, construction, and agriculture.

Since the earth is a closed system, these contaminants stay within the earth's atmosphere and must be accepted and endured, or modified to rid them of undesirable qualities. As these impurities accumulate, the detrimental ones become a problem. To maintain health and safety we must control air quality both inside the buildings we occupy and outside to meet certain standards.

Studies have shown that we spend about 90% of our time indoors. Since the heating and air conditioning industry is highly responsible for indoor climate, we must, therefore, provide equipment and services to maintain a healthy indoor environment.

A distinction needs to be made between the terms *contaminant* and *pollutant*. The word *contaminant* is used to indicate unwanted constituents that may or may not be detrimental to human health. The term *pollutant* is used to indicate contaminants that do present a health risk.

The information that is presented here pertains primarily to pollutants. We define what they are, their source, the health problems they can cause, the limits to which they can be tolerated, and how they can be controlled. We pay particular attention to the services that HVAC service technicians can perform and should perform to provide the healthiest indoor air.

PARTICLE SIZE

Air pollution is not easily detectable. It can escape our normal senses. If we could see the impurities in the air we breathe, it would often be unacceptable. Contaminants can be classified roughly as follows:

1. Dust, fumes, and smokes that are solid particulate matter, although smoke often contains liquid particles.
2. Mists, fogs, and smokes that are suspended liquid particles.
3. Vapor and gases.

These contaminants differ a great deal in size, as shown in Figure 21–1. Only a few are visible to the human eye. Note that the scale at the top of Figure 21–1 is in microns. A micron is one millionth of a meter or one thousandth of a millimeter. For comparison, human hairs have a size range between 25 and 300 microns as shown on the chart.

Particle size is important in determining the type of filter to be used to capture the contamination. Particles 10 microns or larger are visible to the naked eye. Smaller particles are visible only in high concentrations such as smoke or clouds. Hygienists are concerned primarily with particles 2 microns or smaller since this is the range of sizes most likely to be retained in the lungs. Particles larger than 8 to 10 microns are separated and retained by the upper respiratory tract and are rapidly cleared by swallowing or coughing. The size ranges for a few common pollutants are: pollen, 10 to 100 microns; bacteria, 0.4 to 5.0 microns; tobacco smoke, 0.1 to 0.3 microns; and viruses, 0.003 to 0.06 microns. Removal equipment needs to be selected to deal with these contaminants.

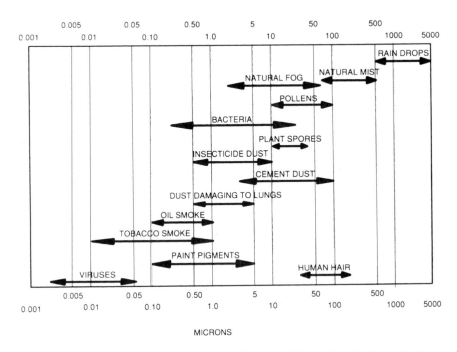

FIGURE 21–1   Sizes and characteristics of airborne solids and liquids. (Compiled from original data in the *ASHRAE Handbook.*)

THE POLLUTANTS

Often it takes a "shocker" or an emergency to focus attention on a prevalent problem. In 1976 several thousand veterans attending an American Legion convention at a large hotel in Philadelphia experienced an outbreak of pneumonia. The bacterium causing the disease was named "Legionella" since it had not previously been recognized. It took two years to determine the cause of the infection. It was found to have spread through the air-conditioning system. The bacteria originated in the cooling towers located on the roof, where the continually wet surface allowed the microorganisms to grow. The cooling towers were located near the fresh air intake of the air-conditioning system, and the infecting bacteria were transferred to the main airstream. This resulted in 182 illnesses and 29 deaths.

One study estimated that about 15% of the admissions to hospital emergency rooms could be attributed to dust mites and other airborne allergens. A few instances such as these help document the importance of indoor air quality.

Pollutants can be separated roughly into three groups: particles, gases or vapors, and combinations. The pollutants of importance falling in each of these groups are as follows:

Particles

1. Bioaerosols
   (a) Allergens: pollen, fungi, mold spores, and insect parts and feces

      (b) Pathogens: bacteria and viruses (almost always contained in or on other particle matter)
2. Respirable particles: 10 microns or less in size
3. Asbestos fibers

Gases and Vapors

1. Formaldehyde (HCHO)
2. Radon: decayed material vapors that become attached to solids
3. Other volatile compounds (VOCs)

Combination (Solid and Liquid Droplets, as well as Gases and Vapors)

1. Environmental tobacco smoke
2. Combustion products

Bioaerosols (Allergens and Pathogens)

Bioaerosols are airborne biological agents, including fungi (yeasts and molds), dander, pollen, insect parts and feces, bacteria, and viruses. Microorganisms common to measles or mumps and "flu" or "colds" fall in this category.

Sources   Biological growth sources include wet insulation or moisture-laden dirty ductwork, ceiling tile, furniture, and stagnant water in air conditioners, humidifiers, cooling towers, or cooling coils. Pets also may bring some of these biological agents into the building. Biological agents may enter the building through the outside air intakes. Due to their small size, they may not be filtered out of the airstream. Frequently, they settle in the ventilation system itself.

Symptoms   Sneezing, watery eyes, coughing, shortness of breath, lethargy, fever, and digestive problems. Prolonged exposure to mold spore allergens may wear down the immune system and increase the individual's susceptibility to infectious disease.

Respirable Particles

Respirable particles are usually considered to be 10 microns or less in size. The smaller particles are breathed deeper into the lungs. They can be either biological or nonbiological. Since particles often are carriers of other contaminants, they can deliver harmful substances to critical areas.

Sources   Common sources are tobacco smoke, kerosene heaters, humidifiers, and wood stoves. Particles are brought indoors on clothing, through the use of household sprays and cleaners, or the deterioration of building materials and furnishings.

Health effects   Particles and substances they carry can cause nose, throat, and lung infections. They can impair breathing. They can increase susceptibility to cancer.

Asbestos

Asbestos is a name used to describe a number of fibers that are used for a common purpose. About 95% of the asbestos used is a mineral called chrysolite. Once in place, the material does not deteriorate easily. The danger occurs to an installer who does not use proper protection or to someone damaging the material and breathing the fibers.

Sources   In building materials it is usually found in boiler insulation, pipe insulation, sprayed-on fireproofing, and floor and ceiling tiles. It is used chiefly for thermal and acoustic insulation and for fireproofing.

Health effects   Three forms of disease have been associated with the inhalation of the fibers: (1) asbestos fibrosis or scarring of the lungs; (2) mesothelioma, a damaging effect to the linings of the lung and abdomen; and (3) lung cancer. There are no immediate symptoms of asbestos exposure. Most of the deaths have occurred as a result of high exposure in industrial locations. Recent studies show that the exposure in schools and homes is below the critical level.

Formaldehyde

Formaldehyde is a colorless gas at room temperatures and has a pungent odor. It is used in a wide variety of building products and becomes effective as a pollutant usually during building construction or remodeling.

Sources   Formaldehyde is used in the manufacture of many building products, including plywood, fiberboard, paneling, particleboard, urea-foam insulation, fiberglass, and wallboard. It is also a product of incomplete combustion.

Health effects   The strength of the concentration as well as the length of exposure can greatly influence the response to formaldehyde. Based on low concentrations, besides a disagreeable odor, it can cause eye and throat irritation and a biting sensation in the nose. A medium dose can cause a strong flow of tears in the eyes. A strong exposure can cause inflammation of the lungs and even danger of death.

Radon

Radon is a colorless, odorless gas that is always present to some degree in ambient air. It is formed by the decay of uranium. It produces radioactive elements which are a major indoor air concern. These elements attach to particles in the air and are inhaled. About 30% of the charged particles are retained in the lungs, providing a source of injury to the tissues.

Source   The principal source of radon is the soil. The gas enters a building through cracks and crevices in the foundation.

Health effects   No immediate symptoms are evident. Radon decay products increase susceptibility to lung cancer.

Volatile Organic Compounds

Some volatile organic compounds (VOCs) are always present in indoor air. They constitute the contaminating vapors that emit from hundreds of household products. Formaldehyde is a VOC, as are products of tobacco smoke, such as benzene and phenols.

Sources   Some of the major sources are building materials, personal hygiene and cosmetic products, gasoline, paints, refrigerants, photocopying materials, disinfectants, and cleaning products.

Health effects   Some of the health effects include sore throat, eye irritation, nausea, drowsiness, fatigue, and headaches. Studies have documented a relationship between certain VOCs and respiratory ailments, heart disease, allergic reactions, and cancer.

Environmental Tobacco Smoke

Environmental tobacco smoke is the sidestream smoke that comes from the burning end of a cigarette, cigar, or pipe, and the secondhand smoke that is exhaled by a smoker. It is sometimes termed *involuntary smoking*. It contains irritating gases and tar particles. Since the tobacco does not burn completely, contaminants are released, such as sulfur dioxide, ammonia, nitrogen oxides, formaldehyde, benzene, and arsenic, to name only a few.

Health effects   Involuntary or passive smoking has been shown to increase the risk of lung cancer in adults. Studies have also indicated that environmental tobacco smoke significantly increases respiratory illness in children. The Environmental Protection Agency conducted tests showing that inhaling tobacco smoke can cause permanent damage to the blood cells.

Combustion Products

Combustion products include respirable particles, carbon monoxide, nitrogen oxides, and VOCs. Some of the particles are exceedingly small and lodge in the lungs. Carbon monoxide is a colorless, odorless, highly poisonous gas. Nitrous oxides are all irritant gases that can have an impact on human health. Other VOCs include hydrocarbons, which act in an addictive fashion with other contaminants.

Sources   Combustion products are released as a result of incomplete combustion that can occur during the burning of wood, gas, and coal stoves, unvented kerosene heaters, fireplaces during downdraft conditions, and environmental tobacco smoking.

Health effects   Carbon monoxide reduces the ability of the blood to carry oxygen to the body tissues. Common symptoms are dizziness, dull headache, nausea, ringing in the ears, and pounding of the heart. An extreme dose can cause death. Nitrogen dioxide can cause irritation to eyes, nose, and throat, respiratory infections, and some lung impairment. Combustion particles can affect lung function.

ENVIRONMENTAL CONDITIONS

Environmental conditions such as temperature and humidity may also have a significant effect on health, particularly when associated with certain pollutants. For example, if the air is too humid, it may facilitate the growth of mold. Also, temperature and humidity can greatly affect the release of formaldehyde from certain building products. More will be presented on this subject later.

ROLE OF HVAC IN CONTROLLING IAQ

A major role in controlling indoor air quality (IAQ) is through the proper design, operation, and maintenance of the heating, venting, air conditioning (HVAC) system. The occupants of the building depend on the HVAC system for comfort, ventilation, temperature, odor, and humidity control. Studies have shown that 50 to 60% of IAQ problems can relate to the HVAC system. About 80% of IAQ problems can be solved through modifications of the HVAC system.

Surveying the HVAC System

If we could see the debris that the air we breathe passes through, we would be alarmed. One investigator examined the inside of ducts in a number of existing buildings. Besides the accumulation of dust and dirt, he found live ticks, dead insects, molds, fungi, and even rodents. Dirt facilitates the breeding of germs, which can cause infection.

About 80% of IAQ problems can be identified by inspection and the use of a few simple instruments. A smoke pencil can be used to determine air currents in a room. Temperature and humidity gauges can be used to determine conditions of comfort. Where more accurate readings of air movement need to be taken, an anemometer or a velometer can be used.

Responsibility of HVAC Technicians in Controlling IAQ

A high percentage of IAQ problems can be determined through inspection by qualified HVAC personnel. One of the first concerns is whether the problem is one of system design, operation and maintenance, or both. A well designed system is essential to a healthy building. If the basic design is inadequate, plans need to be made to improve them. For example, if the original residential installation was a forced warm air heating system and the problem is found to be lack of ventilation air, in most cases the problem can easily be solved. On the other hand, if the original system was gravity warm air, which at some time was modified by installing a forced air furnace, and the problem is poor air distribution, the solution is more difficult and probably more expensive. In the latter case, probably only an improvement can be made at a reasonable expense. A minimum inspection of the system should include:

1. The make and model number of the equipment installed.
2. The type of air distribution system, including the type and location of supply and return grilles.
3. The design of the outside air intake and its location in respect to the system.
4. The cfm delivered by the total system to each room and from the outside air intake.
5. The type of humidifier used, its make and model number, and its condition.
6. The ability of the system to maintain comfort conditions of temperature and humidity.
7. The cleanliness of the system components, particularly the interior of the ductwork, coils, and drain pans.
8. Inspection of the furnace, supply and return ducts, flue pipes, and outside air system for air leakage.
9. Condition of the system in respect to operation and maintenance. Describe any inherent problems.
10. Type of air filters used and the maintenance program in respect to them. Assess their filtering efficiency and determine what would be involved in replacing them with higher-efficiency filters.

Many of IAQ problems are obvious and can readily be improved by such actions as cleaning the ducts or providing better ventilation. A small, significant percentage of the polluting conditions may be difficult to analyze and require extensive testing. Testing equipment can be expensive and its use can require special training. Under these conditions and particularly where serious health problems are involved, outside consultants should be brought in for assistance.

METHODS OF CONTROL

There are two general methods of pollutant control:

1. Elimination at the source
2. Reduction to an acceptable level wherever pollutants may be offensive
   Let's first review the method of controlling each of the pollutants.

Bioaerosols

Bioaerosols form a group of pollutants that contain the bacteria that cause infectious diseases. Potential sources need to be examined, such as potential reservoirs, porous wet surfaces and water-damaged material. Most remedies require good maintenance or preventive maintenance procedures, such as cleaning filters and wet areas located in the airstream, replacing water-damaged carpets and insulation, maintaining relative humidities between 40 and 60%, cleaning and disinfecting drain pans, and so on.

Filtration of bioaerosols is relatively easy, as the size range is in the area that can easily be trapped by good available filters.

Respirable Particles

Respirable particles are generally defined as being 10 microns or less in size. They fall into two categories: biological and nonbiological. Since they are carriers for other pollutants, they represent a strong potential health hazard. Common sources are kerosene heaters, humidifiers, woodstoves, and fireplaces. Control is through the introduction of outside air and the use of quality air filters. High-efficiency particulate arresting (HEPA) filters and electrostatic air cleaners (EACs) can remove particulates effectively. Appropriate filter maintenance, by cleaning or replacing at regular intervals, is essential.

Asbestos

The EPA estimates that about 20% of existing buildings contain some form of asbestos fibers. Tests have shown that the average level in buildings where the fibers are present is well below the accepted level of 0.001 fiber/mL. The primary health risk is to operations and maintenance people, who in the course of their duties disturb the asbestos-containing materials. Therefore, the best method of control may be not to disturb it.

Formaldehyde

Formaldehyde is a colorless gas that has a pungent odor, frequently induced into the building from materials used in construction or renovation. Human reactions vary greatly but it usually produces eye, ear, nose, and throat irritation. The critical level is usually considered 0.1 ppm. Homes older than 5 years without urea-formaldehyde insulation have levels in the range 0.02 to 0.05 ppm. Special equipment is required to monitor the concentration accurately. The odor usually can identify most critical levels.

Control is usually through careful selection of building materials and through an *off-gasing* procedure. This is simply allowing time, after installation, for the undesirable vapors or gases to be emitted from construction materials before the area is occupied. This process can be greatly speeded up by a *bake-out* procedure.

A bake-out is arranged by adjusting three conditions: the indoor temperature is raised, maximum ventilation is provided, and adequate time is allowed for the process to do its work. Materials that emit formaldehyde gas can also be coated to prevent leakage of the gas. A study made by the National Aeronautics and Space Administration found that ordinary house plants can significantly reduce formaldehyde levels.

Radon

Radon, specifically the radioactive elements to which it decays, represents a major concern, particularly in homes. Radon is a colorless, odorless gas that attaches itself to particles that are inhaled. This radiation energy is a major source of injury to the tissues of the lungs. The principal source of radon is the soil. No immediate symptoms are associated with radon exposure. The critical level is very small, about 4 trillionths per liter. Specialized equipment is required for testing.

The most effective way to control radon is to prevent it from entering the building. Cracks in the basement floor and foundation must be sealed. In residences, mechanical ventilation of the crawl space has proved satisfactory. In one location, increased ventilation on the first floor and exhaust out of the basement took care of the problem.

Volatile Organic Compounds (VOCs)

Hundreds of VOCs are found in indoor air. Some common sources include photocopying materials, paints, gasoline, refrigerants, and cleaning products. The critical level seems to be in the area of 3 mg/m^3. Monitoring can be expensive, depending on the material. Many VOCs defy individual treatment. Increased ventilation is frequently used to control concentrations. Where possible these pollutants should be isolated from the building. Selective purchasing of construction materials is always helpful. A bake-out procedure, as described above, can be effective.

Environmental Tobacco Smoke

Environmental tobacco smoke is the smoke that comes directly from burning tobacco or is exhaled by a smoker. It contains numerous pollutants, including sulfur dioxide, ammonia, nitrogen oxides, vinyl chloride, hydrogen cyanide, formaldehyde, radionuclides, benzene, and arsenic. Carbon monoxide, nicotine, and tar particles are known to be the products most injurious to health. Control of environmental tobacco smoke can take many forms: (1) eliminate smoking entirely, (2) confine it to certain areas where separate ventilation is provided, (3) provide adequate ventilation to dilute the smoke to acceptable levels, and (4) filter the contaminants, using high-efficiency particulate air filters (HEPA) and electrostatic precipitators. Since odor and irritation are mainly present where the smoke is produced, ventilation and filtering do not completely solve the problem.

Combustion Products

Combustion products include carbon monoxide, nitrogen oxides, particulate material, and hydrocarbons. Carbon monoxide is very dangerous. The body can only tolerate very small quantities. The OSHA recommended limit is 50 parts per million in an 8-h period or about 40 mg/m^3 in a 1-h period. Acute exposure can be fatal. The effect of nitrous oxides is unclear. Nitrogen oxide can cause irritation to the eyes, ears, and throat.

Control includes maintaining and properly adjusting all fuel-burning equipment. House plants can serve as a living air purifier for volatile organic chemicals. When unusually high levels of combustion products are expected, additional ventilation can be used as a temporary measure. Do not use unvented heaters.

HVAC EQUIPMENT DESIGNED TO IMPROVE IAQ

A number of manufacturers have developed equipment that can be applied to climate control systems that will greatly improve the indoor air quality. Three major pieces of equipment that meet this requirement are as follows:

1. Quality media air filter (Figure 21–2)
2. Advanced electronic air filter (Figure 21–3)
3. Packaged energy recovery ventilator (Figure 21–4)

Media Air Filter

The media air filter removes as much as five times the contaminants as the typical furnace filter. Ordinary filters trap only the largest particles. These filters trap some particles as small as 0.5 microns, removing such contaminants as whole grain pollen and plant spores. Some of the other features include the following:

1. They keep the heating surfaces, fan blades, and air passages clean for more efficient operation.
2. The filters are approximately 6 in. deep and are constructed of pleated media paper. With proper maintenance they can last up to a year.
3. They can be replaced with an electronic air filter to upgrade the system.

Electronic Air Cleaner

There are a number of types of electronic air filters. Even the best ones produce some ozone. The maximum ozone level should be in the range 0.005 to 0.020 ppm. This is well below the limits established by the EPA. Electronic air cleaners have a performance up to 30 times better at cleaning the air than typical furnace filters. They remove irritating allergens such as pollen and dust mites and even microscopic particles such as bacteria, viruses, and tobacco smoke as small as 0.01 μm. Some of the other features include the following:

1. They can save 10 to 15% in operating cost by keeping the parts of the HVAC system clean.
2. There is no cost for filter replacement. Filters are washed and restored to their original efficiency.
3. Home furnishings stay clean longer, effecting additional savings.

FIGURE 21–2 High-efficiency media air filter. (Courtesy of Honeywell Inc.)

FIGURE 21–3 Electronic air cleaner. (Courtesy of Honeywell Inc.)

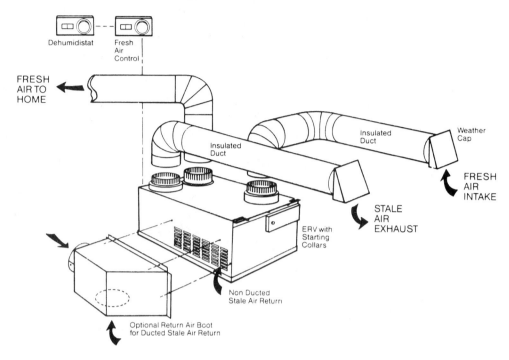

FIGURE 21–4   Energy recovery ventilator (ERV). (Courtesy of Honeywell Inc.)

Energy Recovery Ventilator

This unit is an accessory that can be added to a forced warm air heating system to supply and control the introduction of outside air and to exhaust stale air. It is a type of *air-to-air heat exchanger.* Various sizes are available, to fit individual job requirements. Usually, these units include a desiccant-coated heat transfer disk (Figure 21–5). This disk rotates between two airstreams: incoming fresh air and outgoing stale air. In winter, the rotating disk recovers heat and moisture from stale air. In summer, heat and moisture are removed from incoming air and transferred to stale exhaust air. It provides fresh air the year around at little energy cost.

Some of these units include a heat transfer wheel (Figure 21–6), which recovers enough heat from the exhaust air to warm incoming air to 60°F minimum, when the outside air temperature is as low as 5°F. On subzero days an electric frost control operates an electric preheater to warm incoming air a few more degrees. Heaters of various sizes are available for different design temperature areas. A standard air filter removes most airborne particles down to 5 microns in size before they enter the energy recovery ventilator. These filters are readily replaceable as required.

Figure 21–7 shows a diagrammatic view of the outside air and the exhaust air connections to the heat recovery ventilator. Frequently, dedicated air ducts are run to the bathrooms and laundry rooms to provide exhaust from these areas. Figure 21–8 shows

FIGURE 21–5   Desiccant-coated heat transfer disk rotates between two airstreams and recovers heat and moisture. (Courtesy of Honeywell Inc.)

a schematic of the complete system providing precise indoor temperature, humidity, and air quality control. Also shown in Figure 21–8 is the outside air control and the dehumidistat, which are part of the system. The humidistat is used to control the relative humidity and prevent moisture condensation on the windows in winter. The outside air control permits the building occupants to adjust the speed of the fan to regulate the ventilation rate.

FIGURE 21–6   Heat transfer wheel recovers heat from exhaust air. (Courtesy of Honeywell Inc.)

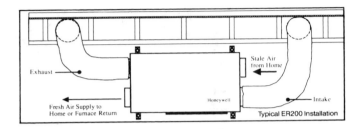

FIGURE 21–7   Diagrammatic view of ERV unit showing outside air and exhaust air connections. (Courtesy of Honeywell Inc.)

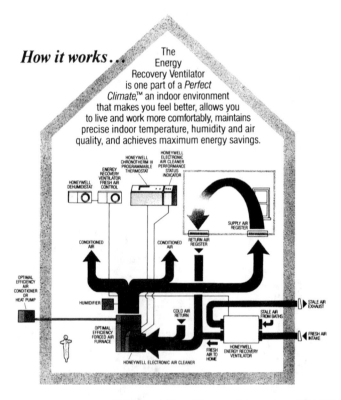

FIGURE 21–8   Diagrammatic view of ERV installed with complete system. (Courtesy of Honeywell Inc.)

STUDY QUESTIONS

Answers to the study questions may be found in the sections noted in brackets.

21–1. What is the difference between contaminated air and polluted air? *[Air Contamination]*

21–2. How small a particle can be seen with the naked eye? *[Particle Size]*

21–3. What caused the disease called "Legionella"? *[The Pollutants]*

21–4. In what category are the microorganisms that cause the common cold? *[Bioaerosols]*

21–5. What pollutant causes scaring of the lungs? *[Asbestos]*

21–6. How is radon formed? *[Radon]*

21–7. What is meant by environmental tobacco smoke? *[Environmental Tobacco Smoke]*

21–8. What percent of IAQ problems can be solved by modifying the HVAC system? *[Surveying the HVAC System]*

21–9. What is meant by respirable particulates? *[Respirable Particles]*

21–10. What pollutants are produced by the combustion of fuels? *[Combustion Products]*

22

Zoning

OBJECTIVES

After studying this chapter, the student will be able to:

- Improve the performance of a heating system using zoning
- Select and install the proper devices to form an operating zone control system
- Program and adjust the system to achieve maximum comfort and efficiency

INTRODUCTION

The availability of high-technology components has made it possible to upgrade residential and small commercial heating and cooling systems. A series of "comfort systems" have evolved all the way from the "potbelly" stove to the "electronic marvels" that can greatly enhance the way we live. To mention a few of these innovations:

1. The high-efficiency furnace, designed to conserve energy, covered in Chapter 12
2. The heat pump, designed to utilize the same apparatus for both heating and cooling, covered in Chapter 24
3. Provision for improved indoor air quality to provide a healthier environment, covered in Chapter 21
4. The application of an integrated comfort system which includes individual zone control, electronic balancing, and computerized monitoring, covered in this chapter

Home owners and small commercial users are demanding more functions from the climate control system. These include heating, cooling, humidity control, improved air cleaning, fresh air regulation, zoned temperature control, and energy conservation. In this chapter we pay particular attention to the use of an integrated system that will supply greater comfort and efficiency through the use of zoned control.

ZONING

Zoning is a type of system design in which the air supply to various areas of the building are separated and controlled individually. The air supply to each zone is fitted with an adjustable zone damper that is controlled by a room thermostat located in the zone. The selection of areas for each zone can be determined by considering the usage or exposure orientation or both. For residential applications the areas for zoning are usually selected based primarily on use, due to 24-h occupancy. For small commercial installations the building orientation is often the controlling factor.

Why is zoning so important? It is because load factors differ in various parts of the building. To maintain comfort conditions in each important area, the system must provide individual zone control. If only one thermostat is used, the service person will balance the system for one set of conditions and find that at another time, rebalancing is required. Controlling each zone according to its needs is essential in maintaining maximum customer satisfaction. For example, in a residence the following zoning may prove favorable:

> *Zone 1:* kitchen, dining room, utility room
>
> *Zone 2:* family room and living room
>
> *Zone 3:* bedrooms

A desirable characteristic of a zoned system is that it often permits the use of a smaller conditioning unit. All zones will not be calling for peak capacity at the same time. It makes possible only conditioning part of the building at one time, the part that needs it. This saves energy.

A recommended procedure for planning a zoned system for a new residence is as follows:

1. Decide on the areas to be included in each zone.
2. Determine the peak heating and cooling demands and peak cfm values for each zone.
3. Determine the heating and cooling equipment size and performance required for the structure, based on the demands for the building and not the sum of the individual zone loads.
4. Lay out and size the supply air ducts and locate the comfort zone dampers. Each zone must be large enough to handle its peak requirements.
5. Decide where to locate the thermostats for each zone in accordance with good practice.
6. Proceed with the installation arrangements.

Figures 22–1 to 22–6 illustrate various applications of zoned systems.

Figure 22–1 shows a three-zone, split-level system. Each zone has a thermostat and zone damper controlling the air flow to that zone.

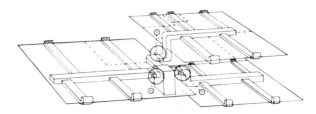

3-ZONE SPLIT LEVEL System in a typical split level house is shown with a damper and thermostat controlling the flow of air through the trunk duct to each zone. Installation requires a 3-Zone Mastertrol, 3 dampers, with thermostats.

FIGURE 22-1 Three-zone, split-level system. (Courtesy of Honeywell Inc.)

Figure 22–2 shows zoned control for a bilevel house: one zone controlling the first-floor living area, another zone controlling the second-floor bedrooms, and a third zone controlling the downstairs recreation room.

Figure 22–3 shows a five-zone radial system with the ductwork located in the slab.

Figure 22–4 shows a two-zone ranch house system with separate zones for the living and sleeping areas.

Figure 22–5 shows a four-zone system for a small office building. Here both building use and orientation were taken into consideration in planning the zoning.

Figure 22–6 shows an individual room control system with a separate thermostat and damper for each room.

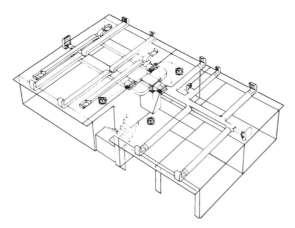

ZONE CONTROL FOR A BI-LEVEL HOUSE is shown with one thermostat and damper controlling the upstairs living area zone, same for the bedroom zone, and same for downstairs recreation area. A three zone Mastertrol Panel, 1 40 VA transformer, plus three dampers and thermostats is the only material required for the installation.

FIGURE 22-2 Zone control for a bilevel house. (Courtesy of Honeywell Inc.)

FIGURE 22–3   Five-zone radial system. (Courtesy of Honeywell Inc.)

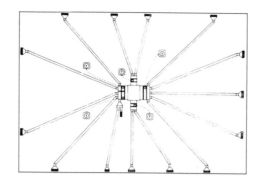

ROOM BY ROOM TEMPERATURE CONTROL is shown in this 5-zone radial system, which may be located either overhead or in slab.

FIGURE 22–4   Two-zone ranch house. (Courtesy of Honeywell Inc.)

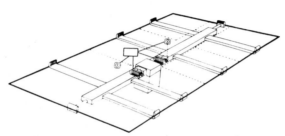

2-ZONE RANCH HOUSE is shown with a thermostat in each zone controlling a corresponding zone damper. For a Mastertrol installation, the following material would be required: One 2-Zone Mastertrol Panel, 2 AOBD Dampers with thermostats, and 1 40 VA Transformer.

FIGURE 22–5   Four-zone system. (Courtesy of Honeywell Inc.)

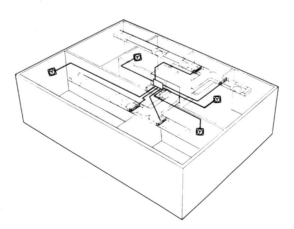

A 4-ZONE SYSTEM for a professional office or home is shown with the air to each room or zone controlled by a damper and thermostat. Installation requires a 4-Zone Mastertrol. 4 dampers and thermostats, and one 40VA transformer.

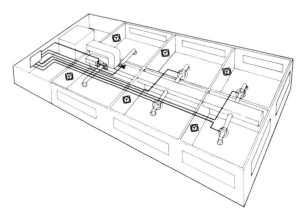

ROOM BY ROOM COMFORT CONTROL may be installed on most any new or existing heating-cooling system by controlling the flow of air at each outlet with automatic square to round transition dampers.

FIGURE 22–6 Individual room zone control system. (Courtesy of Honeywell Inc.)

When considering zoning for an existing system, the supply ductwork must be carefully examined. The ductwork must be readily accessible for the installation of the zone dampers. Ideally, the trunk ducts should be split to supply the required zoning areas. It may be necessary on some jobs to use motorized dampers at the outlets to provide zoning. Often zoning will help a system that is slightly undersized since all zones are seldom calling for peak capacity at the same time. Zoning should not, however, be expected to correct a poorly designed duct system. Important considerations in planning any zoned system are:

1. The airflow over the heating or cooling heat exchangers must not be reduced below limits set by the manufacturer.
2. Air velocities must be held below levels that could produce objectionable noise.
3. Some excess pressure-relieving arrangement needs to be provided to prevent airflow problems when some zones are calling for conditioned air and the rest are shut off.

RELIEVING EXCESS AIR PRESSURE

When a number of zones are satisfied and their dampers shut off, the remaining open zones may be undersized to handle the minimum required airflow from the HVAC unit. To correct this condition, some type of modification needs to be made. One solution is to oversize the ducts for individual zones. By using this arrangement, the duct for the active zone, when others are shut off, may be large enough to handle the required air supply.

Another method of solving the problem, which is usually the preferred solution, is to provide a bypass arrangement. By bypassing some of the air, the total air handled by the conditioner can be held above minimum requirements.

For a retrofit installation, the limitations of an existing system are greater and require more ingenuity on the part of the planner. With proper study, however, zoning can be applied to most systems to improve performance.

It is recommended that the following formula be used in determining bypass airflow:

$$\begin{matrix} \text{air} \\ \textit{handler} \\ \text{(cfm)} \end{matrix} \quad - \quad \begin{matrix} \text{smallest} \\ \textit{zone peak} \\ \text{(cfm)} \end{matrix} \quad - \quad \begin{matrix} \text{leakage of all} \\ \textit{closed dampers} \\ \text{(cfm)} \end{matrix} \quad = \quad \begin{matrix} \text{bypass} \\ \textit{air flow} \\ \text{(cfm)} \end{matrix}$$

There are a number of ways to provide the bypass:

1. Diverting the air to another space inside the building, such as an unoccupied room, utility room, hallway, or basement area. This is usually the preferred arrangement (see Figures 22–7 and 22–8).
2. Returning the bypassed air to the intake side of the HVAC unit (see Figure 22–9). This system works well when the zone or zones calling for conditioned air can be supplied in a reasonable amount of time. With prolonged operation, though, the high-limit temperature may be reached on heating, and the low-limit temperature may be reached on cooling. Either of these conditions can cause the equipment to shut down or short-cycle, which is unsatisfactory.
3. Undersizing the zoned dampers so that there is some leakage past the damper even during normal operation. For example, a 22 ×8 zone damper can be placed in a 24 ×8 zone duct. This arrangement permits a leakage of air past the damper location when the damper is closed. This may be satisfactory on some jobs, but the performance is difficult to predict.
4. Oversize each zone duct to handle 60 to 70% of the air handler cfm and omit any bypass arrangement. This design can only be used on new and relatively small installations.

FIGURE 22–7 Using bypassed air as a supply source. (Courtesy of Carrier Corporation.)

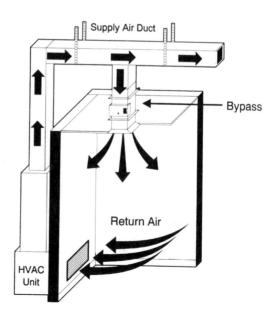

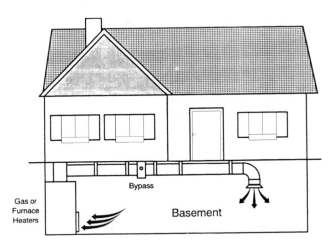

FIGURE 22-8 Bypassed air supplied to the basement area. (Courtesy of Carrier Corporation.)

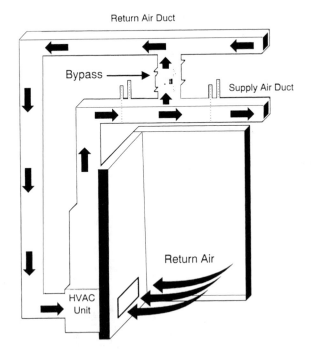

FIGURE 22-9 Returning the bypassed air into the return air plenum or return duct directly. (Courtesy of Carrier Corporation.)

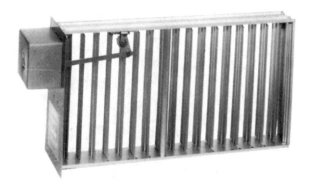

FIGURE 22–10   Zone damper for rectangular duct. (Courtesy of Honeywell Inc.)

TYPES OF ZONE DAMPERS

There are various types of automatic zone dampers available. They are selected to comply with the configuration of the ductwork and the method of control. The types are as follows:

1. Opposed blade damper for rectangular ducts (Figure 22–10)
2. Round duct damper (Figure 22–11)
3. Multivalve supply register damper (Figure 22–12)
4. Square ceiling diffuser damper (Figure 22–13)
5. Round ceiling diffuser damper (Figure 22–14)
6. Floor diffuser damper (Figure 22–15)

FIGURE 22–11   Zone damper for round duct. (Courtesy of Honeywell Inc.)

FIGURE 22–12   Multivalve horizontal register damper. (Courtesy of Honeywell Inc.)

FIGURE 22–13   Square ceiling diffuser damper. (Courtesy of Honeywell Inc.)

Motorized dampers are regulated automatically by the zone thermostats. Some dampers can be fully modulated and others are available only for two-position operation. Either the rectangular or round duct dampers can be used in the fresh air supply duct if regulation is desired.

FIGURE 22–14   Round ceiling diffuser damper. (Courtesy of Honeywell Inc.)

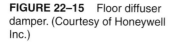

FIGURE 22–15 Floor diffuser damper. (Courtesy of Honeywell Inc.)

FIGURE 22–16   Single blade static pressure-regulating damper. (Courtesy of Honeywell Inc.)

AUTOMATIC BYPASS DAMPERS

There are two types of automatic bypass dampers:

1. *Barometric static pressure relief damper:* requires no electrical connections and operates on low system pressures, usually in a range below 0.5 in. S.P. (static pressure)
2. *Motorized static pressure relief damper:* operates in response to a pressurestat located in the supply duct

A single-blade bypass damper is shown in Figure 22–16.

TYPES OF ZONING SYSTEMS

A number of manufacturers have provided zoning equipment and controls to simplify the installation of a zoned system. These arrangements differ in many respects, such as the number of zones handled, methods of control, and types of adjustments provided. The following information provides a brief review of these systems, so that the HVAC technician can choose the system that best fits the job. The systems presented are as follows:

1. Honeywell Trol-A-Temp zone control system
2. Carrier Comfort Zone system
3. Lennox Zonemaster 11 system
4. Enerstat Zone Control System 2

Honeywell Trol-A-Temp Zone Control System

The Trol-A-Temp zone control system is a series of integrated devices designed to control a multizone HVAC system. The control center is the Mastertrol automatic balancing system (MABS) (Figure 22–17). This device is capable of controlling two or three zones. To control additional zones Mastertrol add-a-zone (MAZ) control panels are used.

Each zone damper is controlled by a room thermostat which is electrically tied to the control center. When any zone calls for heating (or cooling) its zone damper opens and the zones not calling are closed. Automatic changeover from heating to cooling is provided through the zone 1 thermostat. This stat is normally placed in the area that has the greatest use. For example, in a residence, the best location is usually the living room.

In the standard Mastertrol system the zone dampers operate in two positions, fully open when calling for conditioned air and fully closed when satisfied. When all zones are satisfied, all zone dampers go to a fully open position. This permits the fan to dissipate any excess heat left in the furnace after the burner shuts off.

FIGURE 22–17 Mastertrol Mark 11 automatic balancing system, control panel, and related controls. (Courtesy of Honeywell Inc.)

MABS II

TRT and MCRS

(All thermostats and subbases are ordered separately.)

For a single-stage system, a temperature-reversing thermostat (TRT) is used with a Mastertrol changeover subbase (MCRS) in zone 1. The subbase also causes changeover at the other zone thermostats.

For a multistage system a Mastertrol changeover two-stage (NICTS) thermostat is used in zone 1. For a heat pump system a Mastertrol changeover heat pump (MCHP) thermostat is used in zone 1. All other zones use the standard two-stage, heating-cooling thermostat (FICT-2S).

Mode switches   The MABS central control panel has three built-in mode switches:

1. FAN ON IN HEAT
2. TWO COMPRESSOR
3. ONE ZONE COOLING

The FAN ON IN HEAT switch is used primarily for heat pumps. When any zone calls for heat, the switch can be turned on to permit bringing on the fan and the heating at the same time. The TWO COMPRESSOR switch changes the thermostat operation in zones 1 and 2 to operate the first-stage compressor and the zone 3 thermostat to operate the second-stage compressor. The ONE ZONE COOLING switch permits individual zone control for cooling, in the OFF position, or only the zone 1 thermostat to control the cooling, with all the other zones locked open, in the ON position.

Accessory equipment   There are a number of additional controls that can be used, depending on the requirements of the installation.

1. Night setback can be provided in any zone by replacing the standard thermostat with a 7-day time clock and programmable thermostat.
2. Multiposition fresh air dampers (MPFADs) can be provided for placement in both the fresh and return air ducts and be controlled by an automatic multiposition fresh air damper control (AMPFAD-CP), which permits the building occupant to adjust the amount of fresh air entering the building.
3. An economizer control can be provided to regulate the dampers automatically to permit the use of outside air for cooling, when required.
4. An indoor-outdoor reset control can be provided to increase or decrease the supply air temperature based on outside conditions.
5. A Mastertrol minizone (MM-2) two-zone panel can be used in place of the MABS central control panel. This would reduce the cost if only two zones are required.
6. A Mastertrol automatic changeover (MAS) switch can be used. This is a remote system selector switch. The dial has positions HEAT-OFF-COOL-AUTO and the fan switch has positions ON-AUTO. This control is used with a double-pole bulb thermostat (DPBT) located in the return air to sense the changeover temperature. This arrangement is a substitute for the zone 1 changeover function using the MABS panel.
7. A Mastertrol junior (MABS-JR) panel is available for heating only or cooling only systems.

8. A slave damper control relay (SDCR) is available to control two, three, or four dampers simultaneously from a single thermostat.

Wiring for the master control panel A typical wiring diagram for a Mastertrol zone panel with T87F thermostats and single stage heating and cooling is shown in Figure 22–18. Note that the subbase on the zone 1 thermostat has provision for oper-

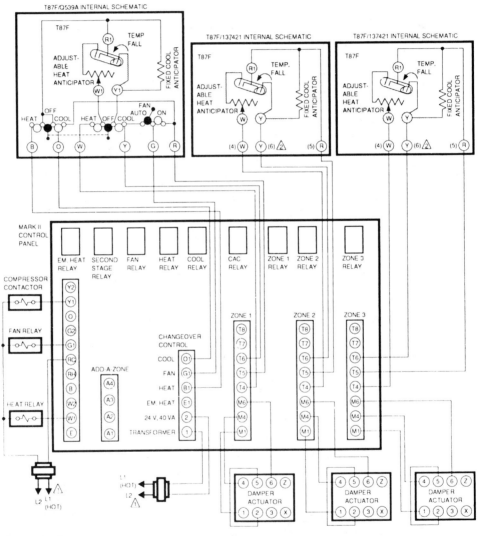

FIGURE 22–18 Typical wiring diagram for the Mastertrol panel with a T87F thermostat and a single-stage, heating-cooling system. (Courtesy of Honeywell Inc.)

ating the changeover control. Note also that two power transformers are required to operate both the panel and the heating, cooling, and fan relays.

Carrier Comfort Zone System

The Carrier Comfort Zone system is designed primarily for residential application. The basic system provides automatic control for four zones with heating only or with heating and cooling. It is recommended for applications requiring 5 tons (2000 cfm) or smaller with a maximum 1 in. W.G. inlet static pressure at the zone dampers. A typical system layout is shown in Figure 22–19.

Each zone is controlled by an individual zone thermostat operating a fully modulating zone damper. All wiring is run to a comfort zone center that is located in any

FIGURE 22–19 Typical four-zone Comfort Zone residential system. (Courtesy of Carrier Corporation.)

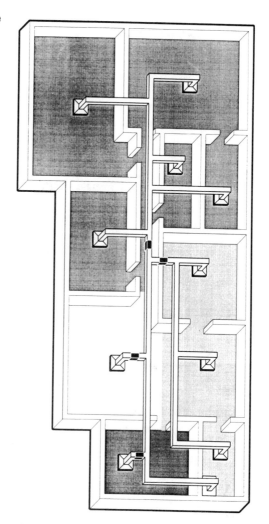

easily accessible location. In the standard system an automatic barometric bypass damper is provided to relieve excess air pressures when a reduced number of zones are calling for conditioned air.

A four-zone controller is placed in zone 1. This zone is considered the most occupied zone of the house, usually the living room or family room. This controller not only controls zone 1 but also provides the programming facility for setting up schedules for all zones. In the standard system remote room sensors are provided for zones 2, 3, and 4. A duct temperature sensor is located between the bypass damper and the heating unit. The standard wiring diagram is shown in Figure 22–20. The wiring for a single-stage heating is shown in Figure 22–21.

Accessories   The accessories available include:

1. Home access module (HAM)
2. Smart sensor
3. Smart sensor power pack
4. Outdoor air temperature sensor
5. Outdoor air damper
6. Motorized bypass damper

The home access module (HAM) is used to detect Comfort Zone system errors. The HAM will report that the system is operating correctly, or if an error does occur it will automatically call an Air Conditioning Service (ACS) dealer or the ACS National Response Center. The HAM must be programmed via report logger or PC command center software prior to installation.

The smart sensor and smart sensor power pack are used together. A smart sensor can be used in place of a remote room sensor. It provides the ability to view and adjust the setpoint in the zone where the sensor is located.

The motorized bypass damper can be used in place of the barometric bypass damper. It senses the position of all zone dampers and opens the bypass, as required, to relieve duct pressure. The outside air damper, activated by the outside air temperature sensor, controls the outside air entering the building. This control operates on an economizer basis, using outside air to cool when temperature conditions permit it. An accessory wiring diagram is shown in Figure 22–22.

Programming and operating the system   The Comfort Zone controller provides the facility for programming the system. From this device the unique demands of each zone can be set for different times of the day and week. The principal parts of this controller are shown in Figure 22–23.

The controller display indicates the zone setpoints zone temperatures and programming information for adjusting the setpoints. The clock display indicates the current time and day. During programming, it shows the start times and weekly periods. The programming adjustment buttons are used for programming weekly periods, start times for each zone and to set the clock. The system switches provide for selection of heat, cool, fan, and emergency heat operation. The zone selector dial provides for the selection of each zone and the vacation mode, for programming. It also has an optional selection area for use in installation and service.

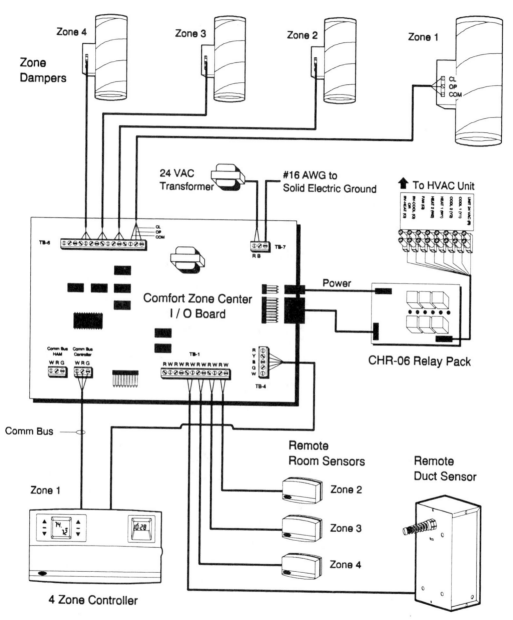

FIGURE 22–20   Standard wiring diagram for a Comfort Zone system. (Courtesy of Carrier Corporation.)

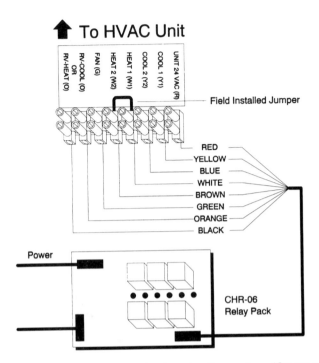

FIGURE 22–21   Wiring diagram for a single-stage heating system. (Courtesy of Carrier Corporation.)

Lennox Zonemaster II Dual-Zone System

The Zonemaster II system is designed for two-zone applications. It provides for separating a residence into two zones. The normal division is a zone for the living quarters and a zone for the sleeping quarters. This is especially useful in cooling since the cooling equipment can be sized to supply only the maximum load in one zone. It saves energy as compared to conditioning an entire building at one time.

The system consists of:

1. A Zonemaster II control panel (Figure 22–24)
2. A HS 14 Power Saver condensing unit with two-speed compressor
3. Two blower coil units (Figure 22–25) or two furnaces with add-on coils
4. Two room thermostats
5. Two expansion valves
6. Two solenoid valves
7. Two refrigerant line kits (optional)
8. Control circuit transformer

Each zone is sized for its heating-cooling load. Each zone is controlled by its room thermostat operating through the control panel. Figure 22–26 shows a schematic view of the control panel connected to the various electrical devices that make up the

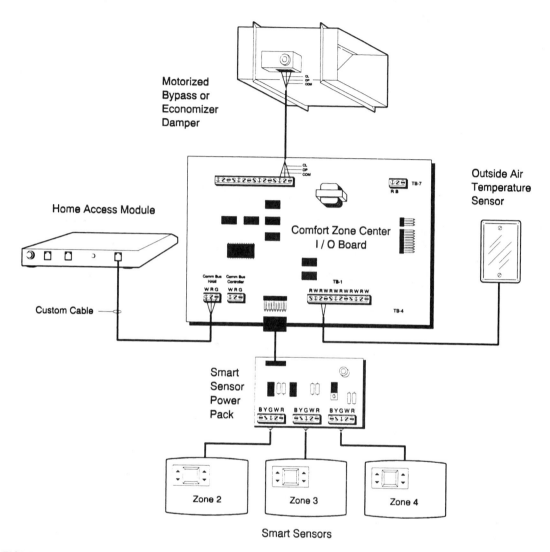

Motorized
Bypass or
Economizer
Damper

Home Access Module

Custom Cable

Comfort Zone Center
I / O Board

Outside Air
Temperature
Sensor

Smart
Sensor
Power
Pack

Zone 2

Zone 3

Zone 4

Smart Sensors

FIGURE 22–22   Accessory wiring diagram. (Courtesy of Carrier Corporation.)

system. Using the two-speed compressor, the control panel provides low-speed operation when one zone is calling for cooling and high-speed operation when both zones are calling for cooling. Each evaporator requires an expansion valve and a solenoid valve. They are picked to match the condensing unit-evaporator selections.

Solid-state control panel   The panel consists of low-voltage terminal blocks and a solid-state printed circuit board. The circuit board includes all the necessary relays and controls to operate the system. The panel has indicator lights (LEDs) which are green when lit. These lights show when the heating or cooling is operating in each

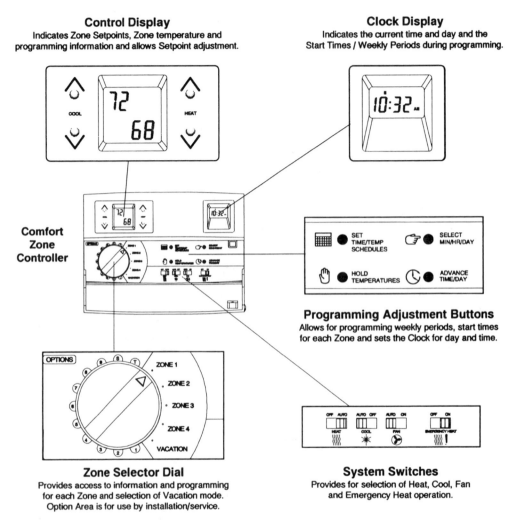

Control Display
Indicates Zone Setpoints, Zone temperature and programming information and allows Setpoint adjustment.

Clock Display
Indicates the current time and day and the Start Times / Weekly Periods during programming.

Comfort Zone Controller

SET TIME/TEMP SCHEDULES
SELECT MIN/HR/DAY
HOLD TEMPERATURES
ADVANCE TIME/DAY

Programming Adjustment Buttons
Allows for programming weekly periods, start times for each Zone and sets the Clock for day and time.

ZONE 1
ZONE 2
ZONE 3
ZONE 4
VACATION
OPTIONS

Zone Selector Dial
Provides access to information and programming for each Zone and selection of Vacation mode. Option Area is for use by installation/service.

System Switches
Provides for selection of Heat, Cool, Fan and Emergency Heat operation.

FIGURE 22–23 Comfort Zone controller. (Courtesy of Carrier Corporation.)

zone and when the compressor is operating on low speed or high speed. A time-delay relay is provided in the control panel to prevent short cycling of the solenoid valves.

Expansion valve kits (optional) The expansion valves are selected to fit the requirements of the condensing unit-evaporator components. The kit includes the expansion valve and the necessary parts for installation. The expansion valve kit can be selected from the information in Figure 22–29.

Refrigerant solenoid valve The solenoid valve is also selected to meet the requirements of the condensing unit-evaporator components. They are ordered separately for field installation. One valve is used for each evaporator.

FIGURE 22–24   Solid-state control panel. (Courtesy of Lennox Industries, Inc.)

Room thermostats   There are a number of choices for room thermostats. The most suitable one is selected for each zone. Any single-stage heating/single-stage cooling or programmable thermostat can be used.

Transformer   A 24-V control circuit transformer is required.

Refrigerant line kits   Refrigerant line kits are available in several sizes and lengths as shown in Figure 22–27. Both the suction and liquid line are supplied refrigerant clean, dried, pressurized, and sealed. The suction line is fully insulated. One end of the lines is furnished with a flare fitting for the evaporator. The other end is stubbed for connection to the condensing unit. Each evaporator requires a separate line kit. The installer must furnish the piping manifold from the condensing unit connection to the beginning of the line sets, as shown in Figure 22–28.

System equipment data   Figure 22–29 shows the typical ARI ratings for various condensing unit evaporator selections. This table also shows the required expansion valve kits. Figure 22–30 shows typical ratings for condensing unit evaporator selections using either low-speed or high-speed compressor operation. An example in the use of Figures 22–29 and 22–30 is as follows:

1. Selecting a HS14-411V condensing unit to be used with one C16-18FF and one C16-21FF evaporator (Figure 22–29).
2. The ARI rating is 31,800 Btuh cooling capacity for the entire system. This is based on an outdoor temperature of 80°F db/67°F wb entering the evaporator and with 25 ft. of connecting refrigerant lines.
3. The required expansion valve kit for each evaporator is part LB-5308 1 CF.

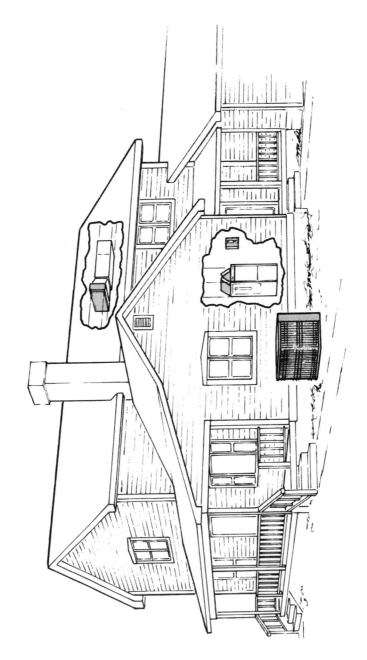

FIGURE 22–25 Two-zone system. (Courtesy of Lennox Industries, Inc.)

FIGURE 22–26 Field wiring. (Courtesy of Lennox Industries, Inc.)

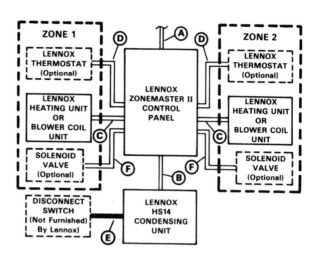

A — Two wire low voltage power (not furnished) 18 ga. minimum
B — Three wire low voltage (not furnished) 18 ga. minimum
C — Four wire low voltage (not furnished) 18 ga. minimum
D — Five wire low voltage (not furnished) 18 ga. minimum
E — Two or three wire power (not furnished)
F — Two wire low voltage (not furnished) 18 ga. minimum
All wiring must conform to NEC and local electric codes.

Evaporator Unit	Line Set Model No.	Length Suction & Liquid Lines (ft.)	Liquid Line (o.d. in.)	Suction Line (o.d. in.)
C16-18FF, C16-21FF, CR16-21FF, CH16-21FF, CB18-21, CBS18-21, CB19-21, CBH19-21	L10-21-20	20	5/16	5/8
	L10-21-25	25		
	L10-21-35	35		
	L10-21-50	50		
C14-26FF, CB18-26, CBS18-26, CB19-26, CBH19-26	L10-26-20	20	3/8	5/8
	L10-26-25	25		
	L10-26-35	35		
	L10-26-50	50		
C16-31FF, C16-31WFF, CR16-31FF, CH16-31FF, CB18-31, CBS18-31, CB19-31, CBH19-31, C14-41FF, C16-41FF, C16-41WFF, CR16-41FF, CH16-41FF, CB18-41, CBS18-41, CB19-41, CBH19-41	L10-41-20	20	3/8	3/4
	L10-41-30	30		
	L10-41-40	40		
	L10-41-50	50		

NOTE — Refrigerant piping from condensing unit to Line Sets must be field furnished.

FIGURE 22–27 Refrigerant line kits. (Courtesy of Lennox Industries, Inc.)

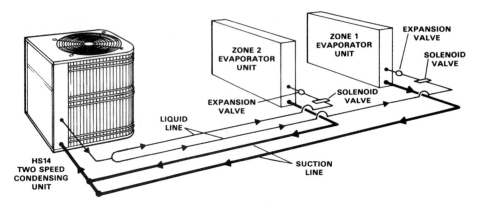

FIGURE 22–28 Typical refrigerant piping. (Courtesy of Lennox Industries, Inc.)

4. Using the same condensing unit with one C16-18FF evaporator, operating the compressor at low speed, 67°F wet bulb air entering the coil, 700 cfm total air volume and with 85°F outdoor air temperature entering the condenser coil, the total cooling capacity is 18,300 Btuh (Figure 22–30).
5. Under similar conditions except by using both the C 16–18FF and C 16–21FF evaporators, and with the compressor operating at high speed and 1200 cfm total air volume, the total cooling capacity is 35,200 Btuh (Figure 22–30).

Enerstat Zone Control System 2

Enerstat offers zone control systems for two-, five-, and 10-zone applications. In view of our limited space, we will describe only the two-zone system. Information on the other system can be obtained from the manufacturer or its sales outlets. System 2 is designed to condition only the occupied half of the residence at one time. It is suggested that the living area be selected for one zone and the bedroom area for the other. Some of the important features included in the system are as follows:

1. Either solid-state programmable or standard thermostats can be used.
2. Solid-state logic panel.
3. Logic panel can be used with heat pumps and gas, oil, or electric furnaces.
4. Will control one- or two-stage heating-cooling system.
5. Auto or manual heating-cooling changeover.
6. Continuous or intermittent fan operation in both zones.
7. Anti-short-cycle protection.
8. Two-position or modulating damper operation.
9. Bypass damper not required for most systems.
10. LED (light) indication on all relays.

Description of the system Two programmable setback/set-up or conventional thermostats are required to control the two-zone damper motors. The thermostats are

ARI RATINGS

Condensing Unit Model No. ★ ARI Standard 270 SRN (bels)	*ARI Standard 210 Ratings				Evaporator Unit			Expansion Valve Kit
	SEER (Btuh/Watt)	EER (Btuh/Watt)	Cooling Capacity (Btuh)	Total Unit Watts	Up-Flo	Down-Flo	Horizontal	
	9.50	8.45	(31,800)	3760	C16-18FF and C16-21FF	....	....	(LB-53081CF) / LB-53081CF
	10.40	8.65	33,200	3840	(2) C16-21FF	(2) CR16-21FF	(2) CH16-21FF	LB-53081CF
	10.50	8.85	34,600	3900	C16-21FF and C14-26FF	....	....	LB-53081CF / LB-53081CD
	11.45	9.25	35,200	3800	**(2) CB18-21	....	**(2) CBS18-21	LB-53081CF
	10.60	9.15	36,400	3970	C16-21FF and C16-28FF or 28WFF or C16-31FF or 31WFF	CR16-21FF and CR16-31FF	CH16-21FF and CH16-31FF	LB-53081CF / LB-53081CA
(HS14-411V) HS14-413V (7.8)	11.55	9.50	37,200	3910	**CB18-21 and **CB18-26	....	**CBS18-21 and **CBS18-26	LB-53081CF / LB-53081CD
	11.55	9.50	37,400	3920	**CB18-21 and **CB18-31	....	**CBS18-21 and **CBS18-31	LB-53081CF / LB-53081CA
	11.60	9.55	37,600	3930	**(2) CB18-26	....	**(2) CBS18-26	LB-53081CD
	12.00	9.55	39,500	4140	(2) C14-26FF	....	....	LB-53081CD
	12.80	11.15	41,500	3725	**(2) CB19-21	**(2) CBH19-21	**(2) CBH19-21	LB-53081CF
	12.85	11.15	41,500	3713	**CB19-21 and **CB19-26	**CB19-21 and **CB19-26	**CBH19-21 and **CBH19-26	LB-53081CF / LB-53081CD
	13.00	11.20	41,500	3701	**(2) CB19-26	**(2) CB19-26	**(2) CBH19-26	LB-53081CD
	12.70	11.10	42,000	3791	**CB19-21 and **CB19-31	**CB19-21 and **CB19-31	**CBH19-21 and **CBH19-31	LB-53081CF / LB-53081CA

★ Sound Rating Number in accordance with ARI Standard 270.
* Rated in accordance with ARI Standard 210 and DOE; 95°F outdoor air temperature, 80°F db/67°F wb entering evaporator air with 25 ft. of connecting refrigerant lines.
** Denotes blower powered evaporator.
  Kit is optional and must be ordered extra for field installation.

FIGURE 22–29   ARI ratings. (Courtesy of Lennox Industries, Inc.)

HS14-411V-413V WITH C16-18FF EVAPORATOR UNIT
(Low Speed Compressor Operation)

Enter. Wet Bulb (°F)	Total Air Vol. (cfm)	Outdoor Air Temperature Entering Condenser Coil (°F)														
		75					95					105				
		Total Cool Cap. (Btuh)	Comp. Motor Watts Input	Sensible To Total Ratio (S/T) Dry Bulb (°F)			Total Cool Cap. (Btuh)	Comp. Motor Watts Input	Sensible To Total Ratio (S/T) Dry Bulb (°F)			Total Cool Cap. (Btuh)	Comp. Motor Watts Input	Sensible To Total Ratio (S/T) Dry Bulb (°F)		
				76	80	84			76	80	84			76	80	84
63	600	17,600	1150	.79	.91	1.00	16,800	1280	.80	.93	1.00	15,200	1540	.82	.95	1.00
	700	18,100	1160	.83	.96	1.00	17,300	1290	.85	.98	1.00	15,600	1550	.87	1.00	1.00
	800	18,400	1160	.87	1.00	1.00	17,700	1290	.89	1.00	1.00	16,200	1560	.91	1.00	1.00
67	600	18,800	1160	.61	.73	.84	18,000	1290	.62	.74	.86	16,100	1560	.63	.76	.88
	700	19,200	1160	.64	.76	.89	18,300	1300	.65	.78	.91	16,400	1570	.66	.80	.94
	800	19,600	1170	.66	.80	.94	18,700	1300	.68	.82	.96	16,700	1570	.69	.85	.99
71	600	20,300	1170	.46	.56	.67	19,300	1310	.46	.57	.69	17,300	1580	.47	.59	.70
	700	20,700	1170	.47	.59	.71	19,700	1310	.47	.60	.72	17,600	1590	.48	.61	.75
	800	21,000	1180	.48	.61	.74	20,000	1320	.49	.62	.76	17,800	1600	.49	.64	.79

NOTE — All values are gross capacities and do not include evaporator coil blower motor heat deduction.

HS14-411V-413V WITH (1) C16-18FF AND (1) C16-21FF EVAPORATOR UNITS
(High Speed Compressor Operation)

Enter. Wet Bulb (°F)	Total Air Vol. (cfm)	Outdoor Air Temperature Entering Condenser Coil (°F)														
		95					105					115				
		Total Cool Cap. (Btuh)	Comp. Motor Watts Input	Sensible To Total Ratio (S/T) Dry Bulb (°F)			Total Cool Cap. (Btuh)	Comp. Motor Watts Input	Sensible To Total Ratio (S/T) Dry Bulb (°F)			Total Cool Cap. (Btuh)	Comp. Motor Watts Input	Sensible To Total Ratio (S/T) Dry Bulb (°F)		
				76	80	84			76	80	84			76	80	84
63	900	31,200	2870	.73	.84	.94	29,700	3020	.75	.86	.96	26,400	3430	.79	.91	1.00
	1200	33,100	2920	.80	.92	1.00	31,400	3090	.82	.95	1.00	27,800	3510	.87	1.00	1.00
	1500	34,300	2950	.86	1.00	1.00	32,700	3140	.89	1.00	1.00	29,300	3600	.95	1.00	1.00
67	900	33,600	2940	.58	.68	.77	31,900	3110	.59	.69	.79	28,200	3540	.61	.73	.84
	1200	35,200	2980	.62	.74	.86	33,400	3160	.63	.76	.88	29,300	3600	.67	.81	.95
	1500	36,300	3010	.66	.80	.94	34,400	3190	.68	.83	.97	30,100	3650	.72	.89	1.00
71	900	36,200	3010	.45	.54	.63	34,300	3190	.45	.54	.64	30,200	3650	.46	.57	.68
	1200	37,800	3050	.46	.57	.69	35,800	3240	.47	.59	.70	31,300	3710	.48	.62	.75
	1500	38,800	3080	.48	.61	.74	36,600	3270	.49	.63	.77	31,900	3750	.51	.67	.83

NOTE — All values are gross capacities and do not include evaporator coil blower motor heat deduction.

FIGURE 22–30 System ratings. (Courtesy of Lennox Industries, Inc.)

programmed or set manually to deliver the required amount of heat or cooling to each area. The system can be set in either manual or automatic heating-cooling changeover. If set in the automatic position, the first thermostat to call for heating or cooling establishes the mode of the system. Short-cycling protection is provided to prevent rapid changeover. A typical system drawing is shown in Figure 22–31.

Sequence of operation   If either the zone 1 or zone 2 thermostat calls for heating or cooling, the fan will start unless delayed by the fan limit control. The heating and cooling equipment will be cycled as needed. The operating sequence for the zone dampers is as follows:

1. If the zone 1 thermostat calls for heating or cooling, the zone 1 damper will remain open and the zone 2 damper will be driven closed.
2. If the zone 2 thermostat calls for heating or cooling, the zone 2 damper will remain open and the zone 1 damper will be driven closed.
3. If both thermostats call for heating or cooling at the same time, both zone dampers will open.
4. If a power failure should occur, the spring return on the damper motors will operate to open both dampers.
5. The system can be programmed to operate in either manual or automatic changeover.
6. If the thermostats are calling for opposite modes (one for heating, one for cooling), the zone calling first is served first. The other zone will be served 5 min. after the first zone stops calling.

Schematic diagram of connections to the logic panel   Figure 22–32 shows the wiring connections from the logic panel to various components, for both the gas/oil and heat pump systems. A key to the terminal designations is shown, as are a series of notes that apply to the operation of these systems.

Design of the Air Distribution System

1. It is recommended that the duct for each zone be sized for approximately 75% of the total air supply cfm. This will increase the outlet velocity for the zone that is

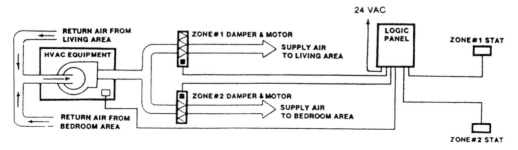

FIGURE 22–31   System drawing. (Courtesy of Enerstat-Valera Corp.)

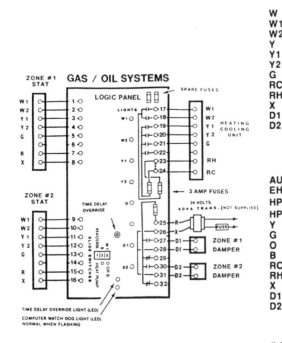

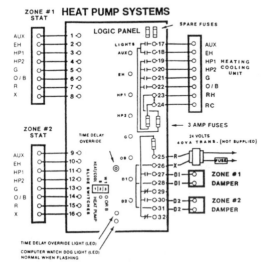

TERMINAL DESIGNATION CHART
(for Heat-Cool systems)

W	- Heating (one stage only)
W1	- First stage Heating
W2	- Second stage Heating
Y	- Cooling (one stage only)
Y1	- First stage Cooling
Y2	- Second stage Cooling
G	- Fan
RC	- 24 Vac Hot (cooling)
RH	- 24 Vac Hot (heating)
X	- 24 Vac common
D1	- Damper zone #1
D2	- Damper zone #2

TERMINAL DESIGNATION CHART
(for Heat Pump systems)

AUX	- Auxiliary Heat
EH	- Emergency Heat
HP1	- Heat Pump 1st stage
HP2	- Heat Pump 2nd stage
Y	- Compressor (heating/cooling)
G	- Fan
O	- Changeover (cooling)
B	- Changeover (heating)
RC	- 24 Vac Hot (cooling)
RH	- 24 Vac Hot (heating)
X	- 24 Vac Common
D1	- Damper zone #1
D2	- Damper zone #2

NOTES

1) Logic panel has built-in minimum on, minimum off time delays and may not appear to respond to a signal from the thermostats for several minutes.

2) All heating and cooling equipment must supply it's own 24 Vac power. If separate transformers for Heating and Cooling are used, remove jumper between 23 and 24 (RH-RC).

3) If only two zone dampers are required, contractor should furnish and install a 40VA control transformer and a Buss SSU box with a 0.5 Amp fuse.

4) If system 2 is installed in a residence, one stat should be located in the living area (not in a hall). The other stat should be located in the master bedroom (not in the hall).

5) It is normal for D2 light (LED) to come on when power is connected to panel even if there are no calls from the thermostat.

6) Damper motors are powered closed and spring return open. Lights D1 or D2 will be lit if damper is open.

Up to 3 motors may be connected in parallel on each zone (must use 75VA transformer).

Damper motor power requirements: 24Vac at 0.5 Amp, 12VA.

Logic Panel power requirements: ~~24Vac at~~ 0.6 Amp, 15VA. (add 12VA for each damper)

FIGURE 22–32 Logic panel connections. (Courtesy of Enerstat-Valera Corp.)

calling only a small amount. The important result is that the cfm of air across the cooling coil is kept above minimum requirements.

2. Often, all that is necessary is to increase the branch size from 6 in. round to 7 in. round and to increase the supply grilles from 8 in. × 4 in. to 12 in. × 4 in.
3. If the condition exists where one zone is considerably larger than the other, it is recommended that some leakage be provided past the larger zone damper when it is in closed position (about 20%) to release excess air pressure.
4. Balance dampers are recommended on all branch runs to facilitate balancing.

Preparing the logic panel for operation   Refer to the manufacturer's instructions for:

1. Setting up the logic panel.
2. Overriding the compressor time delay during testing.
3. Use with special heat pump equipment.

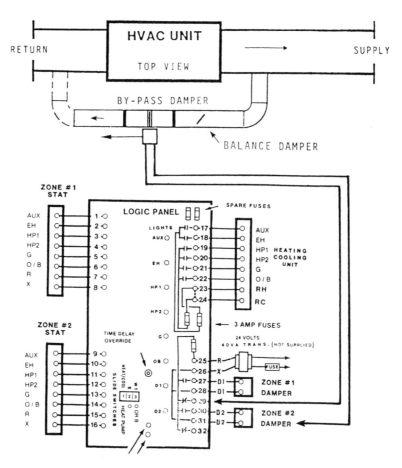

FIGURE 22–33   Bypass damper connections to logic panel. (Courtesy of Enerstat-Valera Corp.)

Special Zone Damper Applications

1. In a few applications, individual dampers must be installed in some or all branch runs. The logic panel is set up to handle up to three damper motors per zone. Additional dampers may be added by installing an auxiliary relay and transformer.
2. If needed, an additional zone can be added by installing an extra thermostat, damper, transformer, and relay.

Bypass dampers If one zone is substantially larger than another, it may be advisable to install a bypass damper to relieve the air pressure. Provision is made in the logic panel for this addition. High- and low-limit discharge bulb stats should also be installed. It is recommended that the low limit be set at 50°F and the high limit at 150°F. The wiring connections to the logic panel are shown in Figure 22–33.

Two-speed fan operation Two DPST 24-V a.c. relays are required to control a two-speed fan. If one zone damper is open, the fan will run at low speed. If both zone dampers are open, the fan will run at high speed. If the unit is equipped with two-stage cooling, only one stage will come on when a single zone is calling. See Figure 22–34 for wiring connections of a two-speed fan to the logic panel.

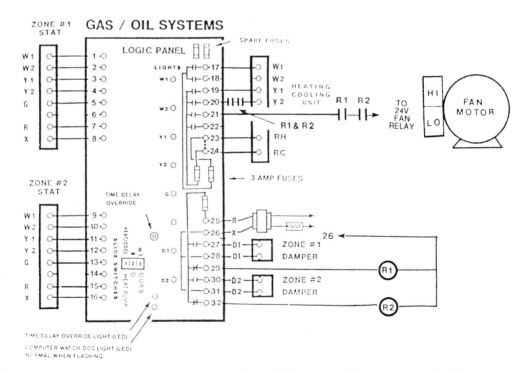

FIGURE 22–34 Two-speed fan connections to logic panel. (Courtesy of Enerstat-Valera Corp.)

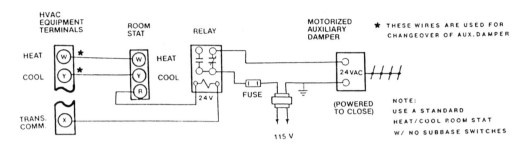

FOR USE WITH HEAT PUMP SYSTEMS

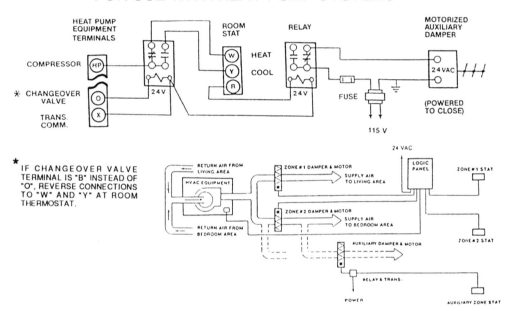

FIGURE 22–35   Auxiliary damper control wiring. (Courtesy of Enerstat-Valera Corp.)

Auxiliary zones   An auxiliary zone is used to serve a light-load area, such as a basement or single room. It has no direct control of the heating or cooling equipment. The branch duct to the auxiliary zone can be taken off ahead of or after the existing zone damper. Wiring diagrams for the auxiliary zone controls are shown in Figure 22–35.

STUDY QUESTIONS

Answers to the study questions may be found in the sections noted in brackets.

22–1. What is meant by *zoning? [Zoning]*

22–2. What is the procedure for planning a zoned system? *[Zoning]*

22–3. For a two-zone system, how is the residence usually divided? *[Zoning]*

22–4. How is excess air pressure controlled? *[Relieving Excess Air Pressure]*

22–5. Describe the types of zone dampers available. *[Types of Zone Dampers]*

22–6. Describe the types of automatic bypass dampers. *[Automatic Bypass Dampers]*

22–7. Describe a mode switch. *[(Honeywell) Mode Switches]*

22–8. What accessories are available for the Trol-A-Temp system? *[(Honeywell) Accessory Equipment]*

22–9. What accessories are available for the Comfort Zone system? *[(Carrier) Accessories]*

22–10. Describe the essential parts of the Comfort Zone system controller. *[(Carrier) Programming and Operating the System]*

23

Hydronic Heating

OBJECTIVES

After studying this chapter, the student will be able to:

- Determine the proper design for a residential hot water heating system
- Select the system components required for an installation
- Troubleshoot a system and solve problems

INTRODUCTION

There are certain areas of the country where there is a preference for the use of hot water for residential heating. Modern hot water heating systems require an understanding of hydronic technology, such as the physics of heat transfer, piping circuitry, control operation, and combustion characteristics. The hydronic heating system uses boiler heated water as a heat transfer medium. The hot water is pumped through the radiation located in the spaces to be heated. The comfort received from this type of system is highly desirable.

The following is a brief review of some of the features:

1. Heat is supplied along the outside wall where the heat loss occurs. The outside walls and window areas are heated, reducing the radiation loss from the body to these cold surfaces.
2. Convection air movement from the baseboard heat source rises toward the ceiling. Then it circulates through the room, returning along the floor to the bottom of the

baseboard (Figure 23–1). This produces a gentle movement of warm air, without drafts, that adds to the comfort of the system.

3. The mass of hot water being heated creates a "flywheel" effect. The room temperature heats up and cools down slowly. This prevents sudden changes in room temperature that can be uncomfortable. It prevents the "cold 70" condition that is common to many forced air heating systems where the thermostat is satisfied and the occupants are uncomfortable.

In spite of these advantages, there are a few disadvantages:

1. It is not usually feasible to provide humidification with a hot water heating system.
2. If summer cooling is desired, a separate air system needs to be provided. Cold water cannot be circulated satisfactorily through the baseboard.
3. The installed cost of a hot water heating system is usually higher than an equivalent forced warm air system.

TYPES OF SYSTEMS

There are five common piping configurations employed in a residential hot water heating system: the series loop, one pipe or single main, two-pipe reverse return, two-pipe direct return, and panel. These piping layouts are described as follows.

A series-loop baseboard system is shown in Figure 23–2. A single pipe or main enters directly into a section of baseboard, then continues to the opposite end of the section, then to the next section. In this manner all of the water flowing through the circuit flows through all series-connected baseboard sections.

The one-pipe or single-main system, using diverter fittings to control the water flow through the individual sections of radiation, is shown in Figure 23–3. A simple one-pipe system utilizes a single pipe or main from the boiler outlet to the boiler return connection.

When connecting the radiation branches to the main, one standard tee is used on one radiation branch and a special diverter tee is used to connect the other. This will create a pressure drop, thus a flow, through the connected section of radiation.

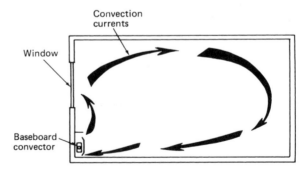

FIGURE 23–1   Convection current.

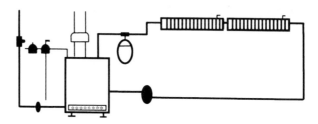

FIGURE 23–2   Series-loop baseboard system, single-circuit layout.

The two-pipe reverse-return system uses one pipe or main from the boiler to supply hot water to the radiation and a second pipe or main to return the water to the boiler. The piping configuration is in reverse order. The hot water to the first radiation off the main is the last one to return to the boiler. This piping design is said to be self-balancing, as shown in Figure 23–4.

The two-pipe direct-return layout is shown in Figure 23–5. The direct return is rarely used in residential heating because of the balancing problems that could arise. The piping follows the principle of "first in" and "first out," as shown in the figure, and is run as short as possible. To prevent short-circuiting of the water, balance valves are used on each section of radiation.

Panel hot water systems are installed in floors or ceilings, utilizing a supply and return main to which all the coils can be connected. Balancing valves and vents on each of the coils can then be made accessible in a floor pit or in the ceiling of a closet. The panel system is shown in Figure 23–6. This type of design uses panels or serpentine coils. A system can be designed for snow removal. Freeze protection can be provided by using a glycol solution as the transfer medium in place of pure water.

In the series-loop system, all the water from the boiler flows through every baseboard or convector. The same-sized piping is used throughout to keep the pressure drop as low as possible. The water temperature is reduced somewhat as it enters successive convectors. This may require adding additional lineal feet to convectors located farthest from the boiler. This is the simplest and least expensive type of system. It has the disadvantage of not providing individual convector control.

In the zoned system, an individual supply main is run from each zone valve to the zone convector. Each zone valve is controlled by an individual thermostat located in

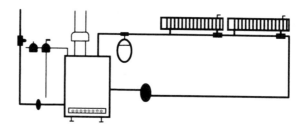

FIGURE 23–3   One-pipe or single-main system with diverter fittings.

FIGURE 23–4 Two-pipe reverse-return system, showing equalized circuits.

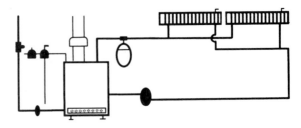

FIGURE 23–5 Two-pipe, direct-return system. Note that each radiator circuit is a different length.

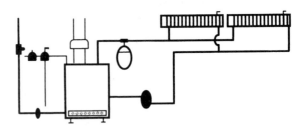

FIGURE 23–6 Panel hot water system with balancing valves.

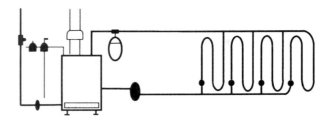

that zone. The control system is arranged so that the circulator operates when any zone calls for heating. The boiler burner is cycled "on" when any of the zones call for heat. Boiler water temperature is maintained by an immersion aquastat which operates the gas valve or oil burner. The high-limit aquastat is set to override the burner operation should the water temperature exceed the limit setting. The supply water main is pitched upward from the boiler. The return main is pitched downward to the boiler. Air vents are provided for each convector and at the end of the supply main.

BOILER RATINGS

Residential boilers are rated in accordance with procedures set up by the U.S. Department of Energy (DOE). Manufacturers follow these guidelines and publish the heating capacity for a boiler. This heating capacity rating is the useful heat output available for space heating. It is given in Btuh or in MBh (thousands of Btu per hour).

Some manufacturers also give a net $I = B = R*$ rating, which is the DOE heating capacity minus an allowance for piping and pickup losses. This reduction in capacity for forced hot water heating systems is 13%.

---

*Institute of Boiler and Radiator Manufacturers.

For cast-iron boilers with a slow thermal recovery rate it is usually advisable to select the boiler using the net rating. For high-efficiency steel boilers, which have a relatively small water content in most cases, the DOE heating capacity rating can be used. In both selections the piping losses are a minimum since all piping is within the building.

SELECTING THE EQUIPMENT FOR A TYPICAL SYSTEM

We will now consider some of the design aspects of hot water heating systems, lay out a typical residential system, and select suitable equipment. The following is an outline of topics to be covered:

1. Determine the heating load.
2. Sketch the piping layout.
3. Select the circulator pump.
4. Select the boiler.
5. Select the radiation.
6. Select the accessories.
7. Select the control system.

Determining the Heating Load

Refer to Chapter 16 for calculating the heating load for the building. This information provides not only the total load in Btuh under design conditions, but also the loads for individual rooms.

For our typical house we will use the first-floor layout shown in Figure 16–1. We will assume a full or partial basement with space for the boiler and the piping. A breakdown of the individual loads for the rooms is as follows:

Room	Btuh heat loss
Family room	13,934
Bedroom	5342
Kitchen-dining room	7932
Bathroom	2560
Entire house	29,768

Sketching the Piping Layout

For our example we will select a series-loop system using baseboard fin-tube radiation (Figure 23–7). The heating element will be installed along the outside wall, covering as much exposure as possible. In this type of layout the main trunk is run within the baseboard enclosure, using sufficient fin-tube material necessary to meet the load requirements. The total length of pipe and fin-tube measures 170 ft.

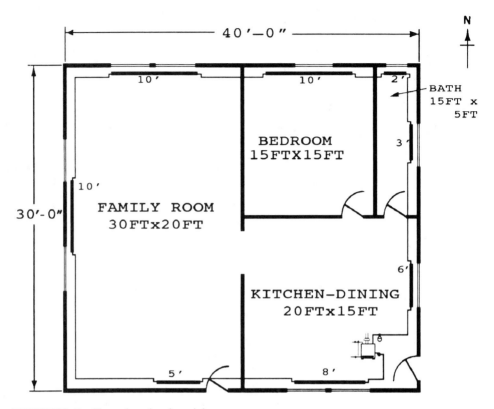

FIGURE 23–7 Floor plan showing piping.

Selecting the Circulator and Trunk Lines

The Btu capacity of a hot water heating (HWH) system is equal to the gallons of water circulated per minute (gpm) times the temperature drop (TD) of water times a factor of 500. The 500 is a conversion factor, being the product of the pounds of water per gallon (8.33) times the number of minutes in an hour (60). In formula form,

$$Btu = gpm \times TD \times 500$$

or

$$gpm = Btu / (TD \times 500)$$

For the typical system example,

$$circulator\ gpm = 29,768\ Btu / (20 \times 500) = 3.0\ gpm$$

Note: A TD of 20°F is considered good practice.
We then need to determine the pressure head in feet required for the pump.

$$1\ ft.\ of\ head = 0.433\ psi\ (pounds\ per\ square\ inch)$$

or

$$1\ psi = 2.31\ ft.\ of\ head$$

Circuit or Trunk Pipe Size	GALLON PER MINUTE CAPACITY OF CIRCUIT														
½"	2.3	2.0	1.9	1.8	1.7	1.7	1.6	1.5	1.5	1.4	1.3	1.2	1.2	1.1	0.9
¾"	5.0	4.3	4.1	3.8	3.7	3.6	3.4	3.2	(3.1)	2.9	2.8	2.6	2.4	2.2	2.0
1"	9.6	8.3	7.7	7.3	7.0	6.8	6.5	6.3	5.9	5.7	5.5	5.0	4.6	4.3	3.8
1¼"	..	18	17	16	15	15	14	14	13	12	11	11	9.7	9.0	8.3
Available Head in Ft. of Water	TOTAL LENGTH OF CIRCUIT (AS MEASURED ON PIPING LAYOUT)														
4	35	45	50	60	65	70	75	80	90	100	110	130	150	180	220
5	45	60	65	70	80	90	95	100	120	130	140	160	190	230	290
6	55	70	80	90	100	110	120	130	140	160	180	200	240	290	350
(7)	65	90	100	110	120	130	140	150	(170)	190	210	240	290	340	420
8	75	100	110	130	140	150	160	180	200	220	250	290	330	400	490

FIGURE 23–8   Table for sizing the circulator. (Courtesy of the Hydronics Institute, Inc.)

First we determine the available head of the system by referring to Figure 23–8. The ³/4-in. size is most commonly used for a series-loop system. Locate the ³/4-in. trunk size, and then move to the right to a number equal to or larger than 3.0 gpm, which is 3.1. Follow that column down to a number equal to or larger than the 170-ft. measured length of piping. Follow that row to the left to obtain the available head of 7 ft. of water. Referring to the pump curves, shown in Figure 23–9, an LR-20BF circulator exceeds our requirements and can be used.

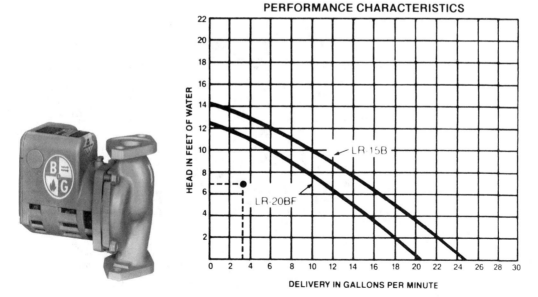

FIGURE 23–9   Typical circulator pump and pump curves. (Courtesy of ITT Fluid Handling Sales.)

Selecting the Boiler

Several types of boilers are available. Boilers can be either gas or oil-fired. They can be cast iron or steel in construction. Figure 23–10 shows a conventional gas-fired cast-iron boiler with an output efficiency of 80%. This boiler has an internal draft diverter and a removable burner tray. The sections can be inspected through a top access panel. It comes completely assembled with a circulator and controls. The capacity of the circulator can be verified using the above information.

Figure 23–11 illustrates a standard oil-fired, cast-iron boiler. It is supplied as a package, with circulator pump, oil burner, and completely wired controls. It has an output efficiency of 80%. This boiler features horizontal sections and a specially designed air separator. It is very compact, with a height of only $48^{1}/_{2}$ in. with heating capacities ranging from 84 to 303 MBh.

Figure 23–12 shows a high-efficiency steel gas boiler available in three sizes for output capacities of 47, 88, and 134 MBh. The annual fuel utilization efficiency (AFUE) is above 90%. This unit uses pulse combustion. The fuel-gas mixture is initially ignited by a spark plug. Thereafter, it is ignited by the previous cycle's heat.

FIGURE 23–10   Typical cast-iron gas boiler. (Courtesy of H.B. Smith.)

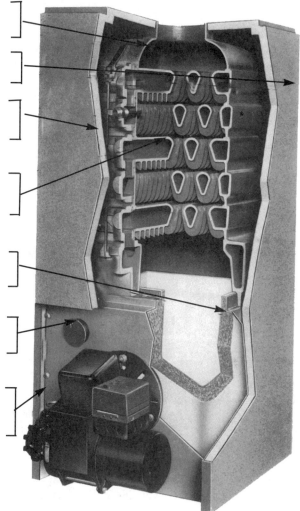

Dome is of the same quality cast iron as the absorption unit.

Gray hammertone steel jacket.

Throughly insulated with 1" thick fiberglass insulation.

Absorption unit provides maximum heat transfer in minimum space. It is constructed of gray cast iron, factory-tested at 150 psi and is fully assembled.

One-piece soft cushion combustion chamber.

Front plate equipped with observation port.

UL Listed flame retention burner. Equipped with factory-installed and wired cadium sulfide flame detector and primary flame safety control. Equipped with swing-away transformer.

FIGURE 23–11   Typical cast-iron oil boiler. (Courtesy of HydroTherm Corporation.)

Exhaust gases are vented through a $1^{1}/_{2}$ to 2-in. chlorinated polyvinyl chloride (CPVC) pipe. Condensed water vapor from the flue gases is removed through a $^{1}/_{4}$-in. ID pipe. In selecting a boiler, the net IBR output capacity must be equal to or slightly greater than the heating load for the structure.

Selecting the Room Radiation

There are three different types of room radiation that can be applied: baseboard fin tube, convectors, and radiators. For most residences, fin-tube radiation is most popular. It spreads out the supply of heat over a large area and is usually more attractive.

How the Hydro-Pulse® Works

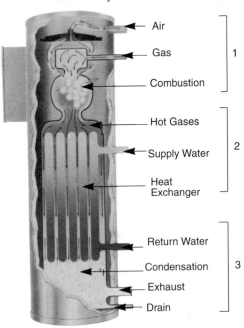

Air

Gas

Combustion

1 The boiler draws air from outside the structure through a small diameter poly-vinyl-chloride (PVC) pipe into its combustion chamber, where it's mixed with gas and ignited by a spark plug on the initial cycle only. Each mixture/burn cycle, thereafter, is ignited by the previous cycle's heat.

Hot Gases

Supply Water

Heat Exchanger

2 The pressure resulting from the combustion process forces the hot gases down through heat exchanger tubes inside the boiler. Here, the heat is transferred to the boiler water, which is circulated throughout the structure's heating system (or hot water heat exchanger coil) much in the same manner as with a conventional boiler.

Return Water

Condensation

Exhaust

Drain

3 As the hot gases are cooled below the dew point, condensation of the water vapor in the flue gases takes place, releasing the latent heat of vaporization, amounting to an increase in efficiency equalling about 9½% of the fuel input. The condensate is removed by a drain at the boiler's base. And the low temperature exhaust is safely vented outside through a small diameter chlorinated-poly-vinyl-chloride (CPVC) pipe.

FIGURE 23–12   Typical high-efficiency boiler. (Courtesy of HydroTherm Corporation.)

In rooms where baseboard space is at a premium, however, such as a bath or kitchen, it may be advisable to use convectors (radiators).

The amount of radiation required depends on the flow rate of the hot water, the average water temperature, and the type of radiation being used. For an example of the rating supplied by the manufacturer, please refer to Figure 23–13. This chart shows the ratings for typical baseboard radiation in Btu/linear foot with the damper wide open. Flow rates of 1 and 4 gpm are given, also average water temperatures ranging from 100° to 220°F.

For our example, where we use one continuous loop, you will recall that the flow rate was 3.0 gpm. Since the 3.0 gpm is less than the listed 4.0 gpm flow rate shown on the chart, the smaller 1-gpm flow rate must be used. If we assume a water temperature leaving the boiler of 190°F and a boiler return temperature of 170°F, the average water temperature would be 180°F. Reading from this table, the Btu/linear foot is 580. The total amount of radiation required for our example is the heating load divided by this figure:

$$total\ radiation = 29{,}768/580 = 51.32\ linear\ feet$$

This radiation is distributed in each room according to room load as follows:

Room	Btuh	Sections of fin tube
Family room	13,934	Two 10 ft. and one 5 ft.
Kitchen and dining room	7932	One 8 ft. and one 6 ft.
Bedroom	5342	10 ft.
Bath	2560	3 ft. and one 2 ft.

Model	Flow Rate		Pressure Drop (Mil. Ins.)	BTU/Hr/Linear Foot with Damper Fully Open												
				Average Water Temperature F												
	GPM	Lbs/Hr		100°	110°	120°	130°	140°	150°	160°	170°	180°	190°	200°	210°	220°
740	1	500	47	107	157	207	265	323	381	450	510	580	640	700	760	830
	4	2000	525	114	167	220	281	343	404	480	540	610	680	740	800	880
750	1	500	47	105	154	203	259	316	373	430	490	560	620	680	740	810
	4	2000	525	112	163	215	275	335	396	450	520	590	660	720	780	860

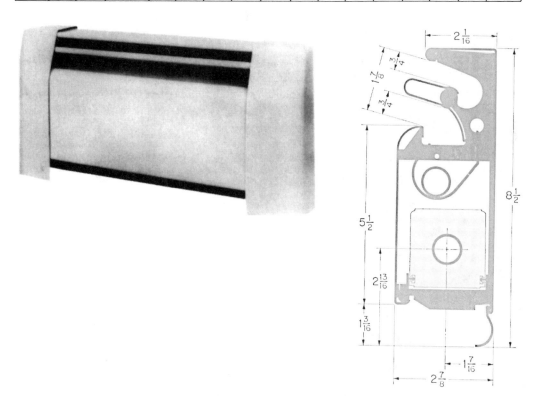

FIGURE 23–13   Baseboard radiation rating chart, dimensional data and enclosure. (Courtesy of HydroTherm Corporation.)

Figure 23–7 shows the location of these various sections of radiation on the floor plan. The maximum gallons per minute for $^3/4$-in. copper tubing is 3.5 gpm. Should the system require a greater total flow than this, it would be necessary to split the supply circuit, as shown in Figure 23–14, to stay within this requirement. See recommended flow rates for copper tubing, p. 519.

Selecting the Accessories

Although most boiler packages are supplied completely assembled, some system components are selected and installed on the job. The design of the piping and the placement of accessories is critical to the operation of the system.

FIGURE 23–14 Double-circuit series-loop system.

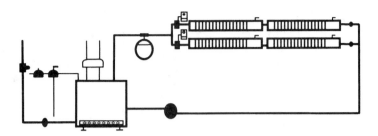

Location of the circulator pump The circulating pump can be located on either the return side (Figure 23–16) or discharge side of the boiler. Figure 23–15 shows the boiler room piping with the discharge side configurations. The placement of the feed-water line and expansion tank connections to the system are critical and the arrangements shown in Figure 23–15 should be followed.

Location of valves In Figure 23–15, note that shutoff valves are used in the system to isolate accessories or the boiler in case service is required, without draining

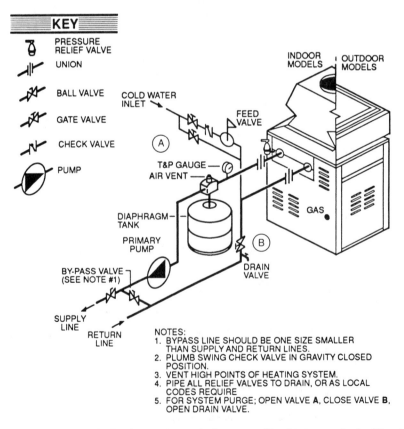

FIGURE 23–15 Piping hydronics system; single-zone with diaphragm tank. (Courtesy of Raypak, Inc.)

the system. Valves are also used to provide a proper path for filling the system. The supply line furnishing city water has three valves: a shutoff valve, a check valve and a pressure-regulating valve. The pressure-regulating valve is adjustable to maintain a system pressure of 12 psig. The check valve is required by code to prevent contaminating the water supply in case the system pressure should exceed the city water pressure. Use of the bypass valve shown is included where straight-through zone valves are used. The bypass could be eliminated using three-way zone valves.

Filling the system   One good way to fill the system and at the same time purge out the air is to open valve A, shown in Figure 23–15, close valve B, and open the drain valve. This arrangement uses city water pressure to fill the system. Care must be taken to return the system from city water pressure to 12 psig when the automatic feed is placed in control.

Air purging arrangement   The piping must be filled with a continuous supply of water. Air pockets must be eliminated. The high points of the system must have vents for removing any air that may be collected. Depending on the selection of accessories, entrained air can be vented at the expansion tank. Even if the air is completely exhausted when the system is filled, air will continue to be generated when the water is heated. Some air must remain in the expansion tank to act as an air cushion to allow for the change in volume of water (Figure 23–16).

Water volume control   The expansion tank allows for the change in volume of the water as the temperature changes. The tank holds water and air. The space occupied by the air will vary as the water volume changes. There are two types of tanks, the air cushion (Figure 23–17) and the pressurized diaphragm types. The arrangement for connecting a diaphragm-type tank is shown in Figure 23–16.

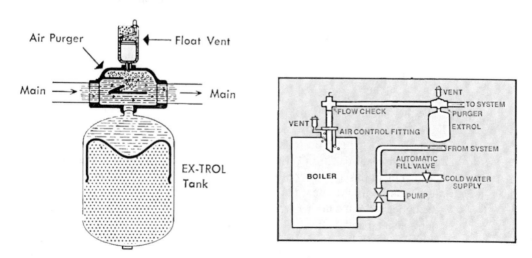

FIGURE 23–16   Diaphragm-type tank and installation system. (Courtesy of ANITROL Inc.)

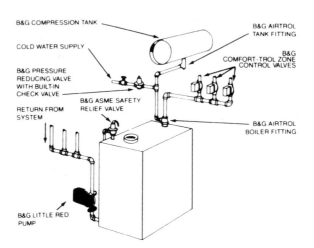

B&G COMPRESSION TANK

COLD WATER SUPPLY

B&G PRESSURE
REDUCING VALVE
WITH BUILT-IN
CHECK VALVE

RETURN FROM
SYSTEM

B&G ASME SAFETY
RELIEF VALVE

B&G LITTLE RED
PUMP

B&G AIRTROL
TANK FITTING

B&G
COMFORT-TROL ZONE
CONTROL VALVES

B&G AIRTROL
BOILER FITTING

FIGURE 23–17   Boiler room piping with zone valves. (Courtesy of ITT Fluid Handling Sales.)

Safety controls and gauges   Figure 23–15 shows a good location for the safety pressure/temperature relief valve and T&P gauge. The gauge measures water pressure, equivalent altitude in feet, and boiler water temperature. The safety pressure relief valve is usually set to discharge at 30 psig or 210°F into an approved drain.

Special provisions for zoning   Zone valves are placed in the supply line to one or more sections of radiation as shown in Figure 23–17. A separate thermostat controls each zone valve. Zone valves can either be the straight-through type or a three-way design. Usually, zone valves are supplied with a manual lever that is useful for fully opening the system for balancing or in the event of zone valve failure.

Selecting the Control System

Some of the common arrangements in selecting control sequence for a hot water heating system are:

1. The thermostat can control operation of the circulator. The boiler water temperature can be maintained by an operating aquastat. This is particularly suitable in an installation where domestic hot water is furnished using boiler heat.
2. The thermostat can turn on the boiler and the circulator at the same time. This arrangement has a distinct advantage in mild weather since lower water temperatures can be used to heat the building. Also, energy is saved by not fully heating the boiler when the higher-temperature water is not required. New energy code requirements mandate this as the preferred method.
3. Where zone valves are used, opening any zone valve should start the circulator. Boiler temperature is controlled as described in arrangement 1 or 2 above.

Aquastats   Aquastats can be either the immersion type or the surface type. The immersion type is preferred where it can be used. A safety temperature-limiting aquastat is always required. An operating aquastat can be used to maintain boiler water temperature.

Relays   Since the circulator operates on line voltage (120 V) and the thermostat is usually low voltage (24 V), a relay is required. Relays are often combined with an aquastat and transformer to form an aquastat relay.

Wiring Diagrams

The following figures show a number of typical wiring diagrams for hot water heating systems. The controls included in these diagrams depend on the components of the system used. Figure 23–18 illustrates a gas-fired boiler with 24-V controls using an aquastat relay and standing pilot. A gas-operated boiler with 24-V controls using an aquastat relay and electronic pilot is shown in Figure 23–19. The wiring diagram shown in Figure 23–20 is for zoning with zone valves using an aquastat relay.

FIGURE 23–18   Wiring diagram with standing pilot and aquastat relay. (Courtesy of HydroTherm Corporation.)

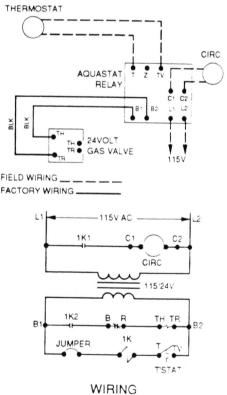

WIRING
BOILERS w/ L8148E AQUASTAT RELAY

Selection of control sequence for a hot water heating
ments are:

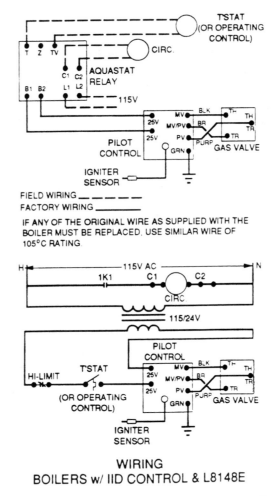

FIELD WIRING _ _ _ _ _

FACTORY WIRING _____

IF ANY OF THE ORIGINAL WIRE AS SUPPLIED WITH THE
BOILER MUST BE REPLACED, USE SIMILAR WIRE OF
105°C RATING.

WIRING
BOILERS w/ IID CONTROL & L8148E

FIGURE 23–19 Wiring diagram with electronic pilot and aquastat relay. (Courtesy of Hydro-
Therm Corporation.)

BOILER INSTALLATION, OPERATION, AND MAINTENANCE

A boiler must be installed in accordance with national and local codes. These codes
apply to the fuel supply, the venting requirements, and the safety provisions. The manufacturer's instructions shipped with the equipment should be followed carefully regarding the location and setting of the boiler, installion of water piping, and hydronic
components, wiring the boiler, providing combustion air requirements, startup procedure, and maintenance.

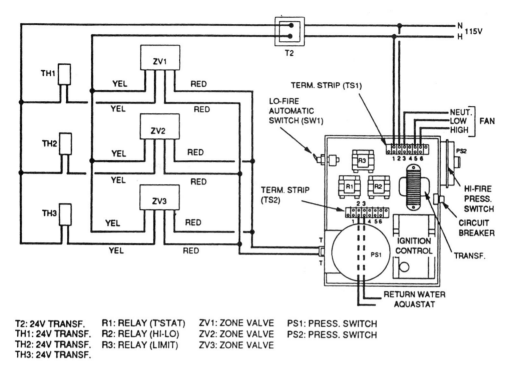

FIGURE 23-20 Wiring diagram showing zone valves with aquastat relay. (Courtesy of HydroTherm Corporation.)

T2: 24V TRANSF.	R1: RELAY (T'STAT)	ZV1: ZONE VALVE	PS1: PRESS. SWITCH
TH1: 24V TRANSF.	R2: RELAY (HI-LO)	ZV2: ZONE VALVE	PS2: PRESS. SWITCH
TH2: 24V TRANSF.	R3: RELAY (LIMIT)	ZV3: ZONE VALVE	
TH3: 24V TRANSF.			

INTEGRATED HOT WATER SYSTEM

The integrated hot water system utilizes a water heater to supply hot water to the air handler or heat exchanger. Hot water is tapped off near the top of the water heater and is circulated through a fin-tube heat exchanger in an air handler or duct coil that will force circulation of warm air to the conditioned space. Figure 23–21 shows two airflow systems. One is a horizontal air handler which includes a fan, heat exchanger coil, and a circulating pump, and the other is a vertical air handler with similar equipment.

The basic operation is as follows: On a call for heat, the hot water circulator is energized through a relay, as is the blower motor. Hot water at 140°F begins to circulate through the heat exchanger, returning to the hot water tank at about 120°F. This would result in a 20°F temperature drop (TD) in the hot water circulated. The typical air temperature leaving the air handler would be between 100° and 105°F. Special fittings, including check valves, are used at the hot and cold water connections.

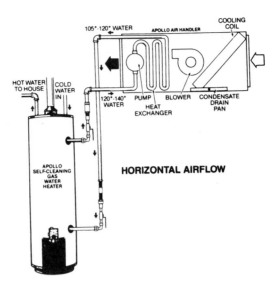

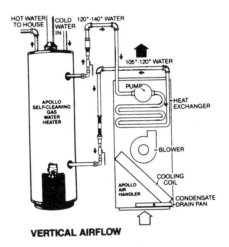

FIGURE 23–21   Integrated hot water system and air handlers. (Courtesy of Apollo Hydro Heat, Division of State Industries.)

STUDY QUESTIONS

Answers to the study questions may be found in the sections noted in brackets.

23–1. Describe the series-loop piping system. *[Types of Systems]*

23–2. Describe the piping method used in a two-pipe reverse-return system. *[Types of Systems]*

23–3. Are the piping and pickup losses considered in selecting a boiler? *[Boiler Ratings]*

23–4. Where should the circulatory pump be located? *[Location of the Circulator Pump]*

23–5. What factors are considered in selecting fin-tube radiation? *[Selecting the Room Radiation]*

23–6. What formula is used for determining the gpm circulated? *[Selecting the Circulator]*

23–7. What valves are used in the automatic water feed system? *[Water Volume Control]*

23–8. What safety controls are required in a typical hydronic system? *[Safety Controls and Gauges]*

23–9. What allowance is made for the change in system water volume? *[Water Volume Control]*

23–10. Explain briefly the operation of the integrated hot water system. *[Integrated Hot Water Systems]*

24

Heat Pumps and Integrated Systems

OBJECTIVES

After studying this chapter, the student will be able to:

- Describe the various types of heat pumps
- Explain the operation of a heat pump
- Read a wiring diagram of a heat pump control system
- Troubleshoot a defective heat pump system

CHARACTERISTICS

The heat pump system is a modification of a cooling system using the refrigeration cycle not only to cool the building but also to heat it. Electrical heating using resistance-type elements is usually prohibitive from an operating cost standpoint. The heat pump, however, uses a heat-transfer principal to greatly improve electrical heating efficiency. Using strictly resistance heat, a watt of electricity is converted into 3.4 Btu of heat. Using the heat pump under most favorable conditions, 1 W of power can produce 12 or 13 Btu.

TYPES OF HEAT PUMPS

The heat pump is a mechanical device used to transfer heat from a *heat source* and discharge it to a *heat sink*. Heat is absorbed from one medium, added to the heat of compression (produced by the refrigeration Compressor), and rejected to a second medium (usually air). There are two types of heat pumps in common use: air-to-air and the water-to-air designs. The air-to-air type uses air both as a heat source and as a heat sink. The water-to-air type uses water for the heat source and air for the heat sink. The air-to-air design is more frequently used due to easier accessibility of air than of water.

The two types of heat pumps are similar in that they both utilize the refrigeration cycle to transfer or move heat from one area to another. There are, however, some important differences. For one thing, the air-to-air heat pump uses an outdoor heat exchanger (a finned tube coil) to pick up heat for the heating cycle. Under certain conditions this coil requires defrosting. On the water-to-air heat pump the heat source is a constant or near constant temperature water supply, always above freezing temperatures, which does not require a defrost cycle.

A second important difference is the use of supplementary heat. With the air-to-air design, as the outdoor temperature drops and the need for heat is increased, supplementary heat must be added. With the water-to-air system a constant temperature supply of water is available, and the heating capacity is not affected by the outside temperature. Supplementary heat is added only when the normal heating capacity of the unit is insufficient to handle the load. Since the unit is usually selected based on its cooling capacity, it is not considered good practice to oversize the unit more than approximately 20% to handle the heating. Therefore under extreme weather conditions supplementary heat is required.

Refrigeration Cycle

The refrigeration cycle is shown in Figure 24–1. Starting with the compressor, high-temperature/high-pressure refrigerant vapor is delivered to the condenser. The vapor is cooled by air (for an all-air system), changing the vapor into liquid refrigerant. The liquid is then passed through an orifice (metering device) attached to the inlet side of the evaporator, reducing its temperature and pressure and permitting it to boil and absorb heat. The low-temperature/low-pressure refrigerant vapor then flows back to the compressor and the cycle is repeated.

Heat is exchanged in three places: in the condenser, where the heat is dissipated; in the evaporator, where heat is absorbed; and in the compressor, where electrical energy from the motor and compression cycle are converted into heat and added to the refrigerant. The heat produced by the compressor is added to the heat absorbed by the evaporator and is exhausted to the outside air. The heat absorbed by the evaporator causes the indoor air to be cooled.

Using the refrigeration cycle as a heat pump, the position of the two coils is reversed. The condenser is placed inside the building to heat the air, and the evaporator is placed in the outdoor air to absorb heat. Needless to say, it is not practical physically to alter the position of these coils in changing from cooling to heating. To accomplish the same thing, a reversing (switchover) valve is used in the heat pump, as shown in Figure 24–2.

With a reversing valve in the position shown in Figure 24–2a, the cycle cools the indoor air. Note the arrangement at the bottom of the drawing for reversing the direction

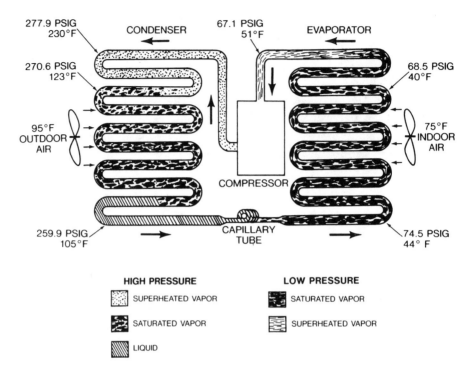

FIGURE 24–1 Typical refrigeration cycle used for cooling. (Courtesy of the Trane Company Unitary Products Group.)

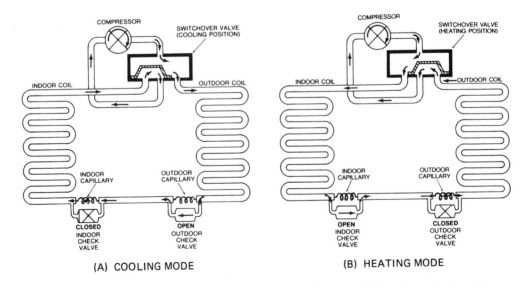

FIGURE 24–2 Basic heat pump circuits. (Courtesy of the Trane Company Unitary Products Group.)

of refrigerant flow through the metering device when changing from cooling to heating. A check valve in parallel with each metering device functions to direct the flow through the metering device being used, bypassing the unused one.

Defrost Cycle

Another necessary element in the air-to-air heat pump design is the defrost arrangement for the outside coil. There are times during heating when the refrigerant temperature in the outdoor coil is below freezing temperatures and ice forms on the coil, restricting the airflow. To prevent inefficient heating as a result of this condition, the outdoor coil is automatically defrosted when necessary.

One way to control the defrost cycle is to use a Dwyer defrost arrangement as shown in Figure 24–3. The control system must accomplish two functions to initiate the defrost cycle:

1. The temperature of the refrigerant must be below 32°F.
2. The coil must be sufficiently frosted to restrict the airflow 70 to 90%.

Position B in Figure 24–3 shows the defrost termination switch open, indicating that the refrigerant temperature is above 32°F. Position A shows the vacuum-operated switch contacts open, indicating that the coil is not iced up sufficiently to require defrost. Position C shows the defrost termination switch closed, indicating that the refrigerant temperature is below 32°F. Position D shows

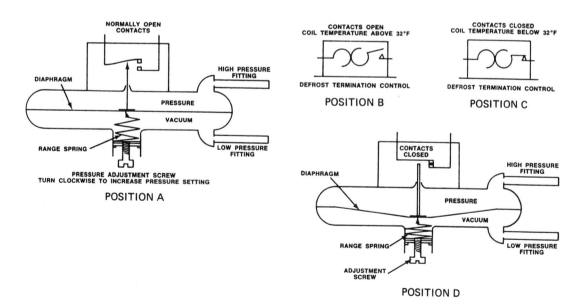

FIGURE 24–3 Dwyer defrost system's mechanical operation. (Courtesy of the Trane Company Unitary Products Group.)

the vacuum-operated switch contacts closed, indicating the need for defrosting the coil.

Based on the two switches (positions C and D) in defrost, the reversing valve automatically places the cycle in the cooling mode (Figure 24–2a), supplying hot gas from the compressor to the outside coil and defrosting it. The defrost cycle continues until the refrigerant temperature reaches 55°F, opening the defrost termination switch (position B) and automatically placing the system back in the heating mode (Figure 24–2b).

Supplementary Heat

The air-to-air heat pump is the most effective in absorbing heat from the outdoor air when it is relatively warm outside. For example, on a typical 5-horsepower (hp) unit, the relationship of watts input, total Btu output, and outside air temperature, based on an outdoor condition of 70% relative humidity and indoor temperature of 70°F, are as follows:

Outdoor Temperature (°F)	Compressor Motor (watts input)	Total Output (Btuh)
60	4520	57,100
50	4060	50,100
47*	3920	48,000
40	3570	40,800
30	3200	32,900
20	2960	27,500
17*	2890	25,900
10	2670	22,500
0	2360	17,600
−10	2045	12,700
−20	1735	7800

*Department of Energy (DOE) standard test points

The heat pump produces more heat even at -20°F (7800 Btuh) than resistance heating (1735 W × 3.4 = 5899 Btuh). Thus the control system continues to operate the heat pump even at low outside temperature.

Since the amount of heat required by a building increases as the outside temperature becomes lower, supplementary heat must be added. This additional heat could come from a gas furnace or an electric strip heater.

The electric source is more common. Figure 24–4 shows an electric strip heater package being inserted into a packaged heat pump. The heating element is compact and can be installed without a chimney, thus simplifying installation. Heat pumps are more popular in the warmer climates, since less supplementary heat needs to be added. When the supplementary heat is from a gas furnace, the system is normally referred to as an "add-on" heat pump.

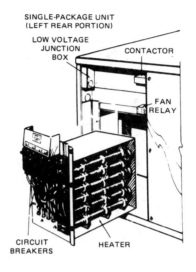

FIGURE 24–4   Electric strip heater package used for supplementary heat. (Courtesy of Heil-Quaker Corporation.)

AIR-TO-AIR SYSTEM

Many of the items included in this section, such as certain rating definitions, the calculations for supply air temperature rise, the type of thermostat used, the refrigeration piping, and details of condensate drains, also apply to the water-to-air heat pump. For the sake of completeness these sections can be referred to in studying the water-to-air systems.

There are two principal arrangements of equipment available:

1. Split system
2. Single package

The *split system* normally has two components, as shown in Figure 24–5. The compressor section, sometimes called the condensing unit, is located outside the building. The furnace and coil section or air handler is located inside the building. Together they provide systems capable of delivering a maximum HSPF of 8.70 in the heating mode or a maximum standard SEER of 12.20 in the cooling mode.

A typical *single-package system* is shown in Figure 24–6. All components are housed in a single enclosure, which is installed outside the building. Where this arrangement can be applied, field labor is reduced.

FIGURE 24–5   Components of a heat pump.

Ratings

Figure 24–7 shows typical heat pump performance data. Ratings are based on Air Conditioning and Refrigeration Institute (ARI) standards. Standards and terms for rating heat pumps are as follows:

1. *Cooling standard:* 80°F db, 67°F wb temperature of the air entering indoors and 95°F db air entering the outdoor unit.
2. *High-temperature heating standard:* 70°F db temperature of air entering indoors and 47°F db, 43°F wb air entering the outdoor unit.
3. *Low-temperature heating standard:* 70°F db temperature of air entering indoors and 17°F db, 15°F wb air entering the outdoor unit.
4. *Coefficient of performance (C.O.P.):* rating given to heat pumps that is equivalent to the ratio of output over input. Output is in Btuh and input is converted to Btuh

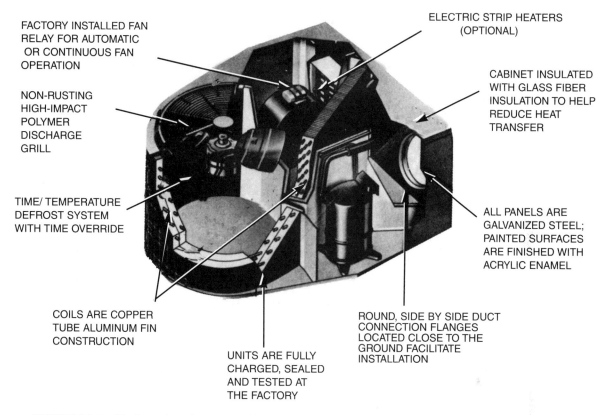

FACTORY INSTALLED FAN
RELAY FOR AUTOMATIC
OR CONTINUOUS FAN
OPERATION

NON-RUSTING
HIGH-IMPACT
POLYMER
DISCHARGE
GRILL

TIME/ TEMPERATURE
DEFROST SYSTEM
WITH TIME OVERRIDE

COILS ARE COPPER
TUBE ALUMINUM FIN
CONSTRUCTION

UNITS ARE FULLY
CHARGED, SEALED
AND TESTED AT
THE FACTORY

ELECTRIC STRIP HEATERS
(OPTIONAL)

CABINET INSULATED
WITH GLASS FIBER
INSULATION TO HELP
REDUCE HEAT
TRANSFER

ALL PANELS ARE
GALVANIZED STEEL;
PAINTED SURFACES
ARE FINISHED WITH
ACRYLIC ENAMEL

ROUND, SIDE BY SIDE DUCT
CONNECTION FLANGES
LOCATED CLOSE TO THE
GROUND FACILITATE
INSTALLATION

FIGURE 24–6   Single-package heat pump. (Courtesy of Heil-Quaker Corporation.)

by multiplying watts input by 3.413 Btu per watt. For example, the C.O.P. for a nominal 2-hp unit, operating with 47°F air entering the outdoor coil, is as follows:

$$C.O.P. = \frac{25,200 \text{ Btuh}}{24,500 \text{ W} \times 3.4 \text{ Btu/W}} = 3.02$$

Nominal Tons	Indoor Compressor Section	Outdoor Section	Indoor Fan Section	ARI Standing Ratings (1–Ph)							
					Cooling		Hi-Temp Heat		Lo-Temp Heat		
				CFM	TC	SEER w/lls	TC	C.O.P.	TC	C.O.P.	HSPF
2.0	IC-024	OS-940	IF-024	850	23.8	9.80	(25.2)	2.90	15.3	2.05	7.65
2.5	IC-030	OS-940	IF-030	1025	27.6	9.55	29.6	2.90	18.0	2.05	7.55
3.0	IC-036	OS-940	IF-036	1175	32.4	9.85	(34.0)	2.95	20.0	2.00	7.65

FIGURE 24–7   Typical heat pump performance data.

5. *Heating season performance factor (HSPF):* ratio of heat output in Btu to watts input.
6. *Seasonal energy efficient ratio (SEER):* applied to the cooling performance and is also a ratio of Btu output to watts input.
7. *Sound rating number (SRN):* noise-level rating (decibels).
8. *Total capacity (T.C.):* thousands of Btuh.
9. *Units rated with accessory liquid line solenoid.*
10. *Cubic feet per minute:* air volume rating of the indoor fan.

All ratings are based on ARI Standard 240 and U.S. Department of Energy (DOE) test procedures at 450 cfm indoor air volume per ton (12,000 Btuh) cooling capacity with 25 ft. of connecting refrigerant lines.

Indoor-Air-Temperature Rise

Referring to Figure 24–7, note that at top performance the largest unit shown, with 47°F outside air, delivers 34,000 Btu using 1175 cfm. To determine the temperature rise (TR) on heating, the following formula is applied:

$$Btu = cfm \times 1.08 \times TR$$

$$TR = \frac{34,000}{1175 \times 1.08} = 27°F$$

Based on a return air temperature of 70°F, the delivered air is 97°F (70°F + 27°F). Thus, a heat pump delivers relatively low-temperature air compared to a conventional furnace. This fact is important to keep in mind when designing the distribution system. Otherwise, discomfort can be the result.

Locating the Outdoor Coil Sections

The outdoor coil section must be installed free of obstructions to permit full airflow to and from the heat exchange surface, illustrated in Figure 24–8. It should be not closer than 30 in. from a wall or 48 in. from a roof overhang. It should be mounted on a base separate from the structure of the building to isolate any vibration.

Heat Pump Thermostat

The heat pump thermostat differs from the normal furnace thermostat in that it has an emergency position. This is used to operate the supplementary heat manually when the heat pump requires service.

Outdoor Thermostat

An outdoor thermostat is provided to restrict the use of supplementary heat. This is usually set at 26°F to prevent the supplementary heat from being used until the outside temperature drops below this point.

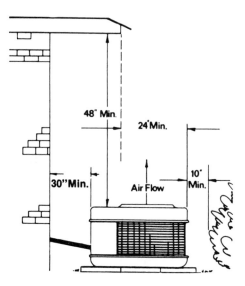

FIGURE 24–8 Typical outdoor coil section location. (Courtesy of Addison Products Company and Knight Energy Institute.)

Condensate Drain

The inside coil section must be provided with a condensate drain. The drain pan must be level or sloping slightly toward the drain connection. The flow is actuated by gravity and must be trapped, as shown in Figure 24–9.

Refrigerant Piping Connections

It is good practice to use preinsulated tubing for the refrigerant lines with brazed connections at each end. If the condensing unit is below the inside coil, the line should slope toward the outside unit, as shown in Figure 24–10. If the condensing unit is above the inside coil, the suction line should be trapped, as shown in Figure 24–11.

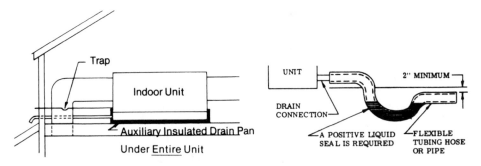

FIGURE 24–9 Typical condensate drain trap installation. (Courtesy of Addison Products Company and Knight Energy Institute.)

FIGURE 24–10 Refrigerant lines connected to outdoor unit located below indoor unit. (Courtesy of Addison Products Company and Knight Energy Institute.)

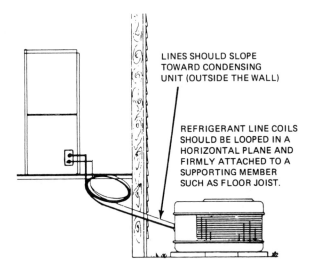

LINES SHOULD SLOPE TOWARD CONDENSING UNIT (OUTSIDE THE WALL)

REFRIGERANT LINE COILS SHOULD BE LOOPED IN A HORIZONTAL PLANE AND FIRMLY ATTACHED TO A SUPPORTING MEMBER SUCH AS FLOOR JOIST.

FIGURE 24–11 Vertical discharge piping. Note trap in suction line below indoor unit and pipe sloping at outdoor unit. (Courtesy of Addison Products Company and Knight Energy Institute.)

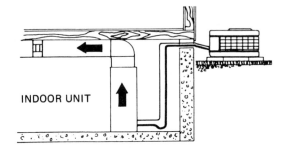

INDOOR UNIT

Suction accumulator A suction accumulator (Figure 24–12) is often placed in the suction line between the evaporator and the compressor. This device traps liquid refrigerant that may damage the compressor. The liquid gradually evaporates in the accumulator and enters the compressor as a vapor. Any trapped oil is allowed to enter the suction line slowly through a metering orifice located in the lower portion of the U-tube in the accumulator.

Refrigerant metering devices As shown in Figure 24–2, the heat pump uses two metering devices, one for the cooling cycle and one for the heating cycle. There are two types of metering devices used by the various manufacturers: the capillary tube (see Figure 24–2) and the thermostatic expansion valve (TEV) (see Figure 24–13). The TEV has a sensing bulb on the suction line that controls the flow of refrigerant. Under ideal conditions it provides complete evaporation of the liquid before the refrigerant enters the compressor.

FIGURE 24–12 Suction line accumulator. (Courtesy of the Trane Company Unitary Products Group.)

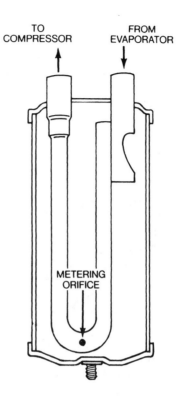

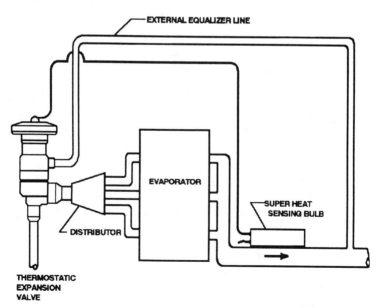

FIGURE 24–13 Thermostatic expansion valve.

In the *emergency heating mode,* when the outdoor temperature falls below 26°F, supplementary heat is supplied in stages to meet the requirements of the thermostat. The heat pump portion of the unit, consisting of the compressor, outdoor fan, and reversing valve, is inoperative. The heat is supplied by electric strip heaters.

In the *defrost mode,* the compressor, the outdoor fan, and the indoor fan are in operation in the same manner as in the cooling mode. This is done to supply heat to the outdoor coil to defrost it. The air pressure drop, the refrigerant temperature, and time are all factors in controlling the defrost cycle on a demand basis.

Wiring Diagrams and Sequence of Operation

The wiring diagrams shown in this section are strictly electrical (not solid-state). Some manufacturers have effectively used solid-state controls. These will be described later. Since the majority of heat pump service problems are electrical, a thorough understanding of the electrical system is essential.

Cooling mode   The wiring diagram for a typical heat pump, operated in the cooling mode, is shown in Figure 24–14. The thermostat is shown in the lower left, the indoor unit is on the right (top and bottom), and the outdoor unit is at the upper left. The energized circuits for cooling are highlighted. The key to the symbols for the wiring diagram is shown in Figure 24–15.

When the system switch on the thermostat is set to cooling, the fan switch is set on auto, and the room temperature is above the thermostat setting, three low-voltage circuits are made:

1. Circuit to the cooling relay (CR)
2. Circuit to the fan motor relay (FMR)
3. Circuit to the compressor contactor (CC)

The CR relay energizes the reversing valve in the outdoor unit. The FMR relay starts the indoor fan at high speed.

The CC contactor starts the compressor and outdoor fan. The cooling cycle is in operation.

Heating mode   When the system switch on the thermostat is set to heating, the fan switch is set on the auto position, and the room temperature is below the thermostat setting, two low-voltage circuits are made (see Figure 24–16):

1. Circuit to the fan motor relay (FMR)
2. Circuit to the compressor contactor (CC)

The system operates just as it did on cooling, *except that the reversing valve is de-energized.*

With the heat pump operating and if the room temperature continues to drop 1° or 2° below the thermostat setting, the second-stage heating (the supplementary heat) is

FIGURE 24–14 Wiring diagram for a typical heat pump, cooling mode. (Courtesy of Addison Products Company and Knight Energy Institute.)

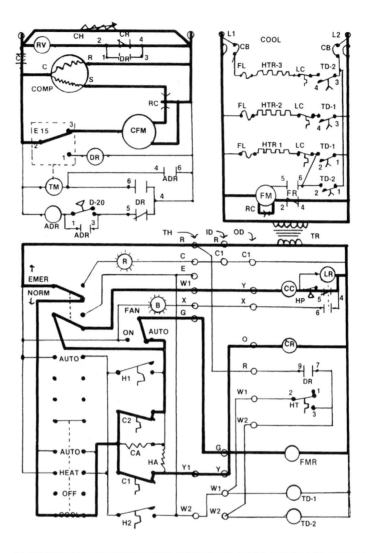

FIGURE 24–15 Key to symbols used in wiring diagrams. (Courtesy of Addison Products Company and Knight Energy Institute.)

KEY TO SYMBOLS			
ADR	Auxiliary Defrost Relay	E15	Defrost Control
FM	Fan Motor	FL	Fuse Link
FMR	Fan Motor Relay	HA	Heating Anticipator
FR	Fan Relay (Contacts)	HP	High Pressure Control
B	Blue "Check" Light	HTR	Heater, Auxiliary Electric
CA	Cooling Anticipator	HT	Holdback Thermostat
CB	Circuit Breaker	H1	1st Stage Heating
CC	Compressor Contactor	H2	2nd Stage Heating
CFM	Condenser Fan Motor	LC	Limit Control
CH	Crankcase Heat	LR	Lockout Relay
CR	Cooling Relay	R	Red "Emerg" Heat Light
C1	1st Stage Cooling	RC	Run Capacitor
C2	2nd Stage Cooling	RV	Reversing Valve
DR	Defrost Relay	TD	Time Delay Relay
D-20	Pressure Switch—Defrost	TM	Time Motor (Part of E15)
		TR	Control Transformer

FIGURE 24–16 Wiring diagram for a typical heat pump, first-stage heating (heat pump only). (Courtesy of Addison Products Company and Knight Energy Institute.)

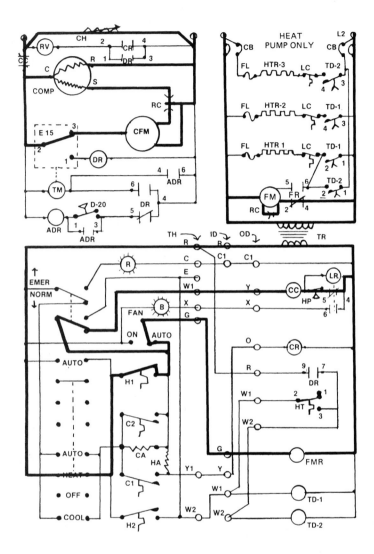

activated. When the secondary heat contacts (H2) are made in the room thermostat, the following sequence takes place (see Figure 24–17):

1. The first time-delay relay (TD-1) is energized, closing the circuit in the indoor unit to two or more electric strip heaters.
2. If the outdoor temperature measured on the hold-back thermostat (HT) is below 26°F, a circuit is made to the second time-delay relay (TD-2). This closes the circuit to the remaining electric strip heaters. The unit is now in maximum heat position.

In the emergency heating mode, the heat pump is inoperative and the system is manually switched to emergency heat, as shown in Figure 24–18. Three low-voltage circuits are energized:

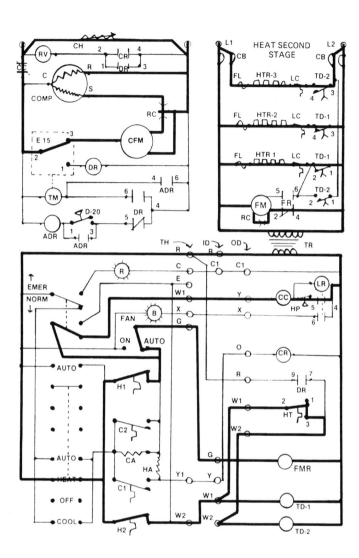

FIGURE 24–17 Wiring diagram for a typical heat pump, second-stage heating. (Courtesy of Addison Products Company and Knight Energy Institute.)

1. Fan motor relay (FMR)
2. First time-delay relay (TD-1)
3. *Red* light, indicating that emergency heat is on

The inside fan is operated by the FMR relay. The heater elements are energized through the TD-1 relay and the TD-2 relay if the outside temperature is below 26°F.

Defrost mode   In the defrost mode the system is primarily in the cooling cycle (see Figure 24–19). The only difference is that the indoor fan is operating and part of the resistance heat is turned on to offset the cooling effect. The *demand defrost control*

FIGURE 24–18 Wiring diagram for a typical heat pump, emergency heat. (Courtesy of Addison Products Company and Knight Energy Institute.)

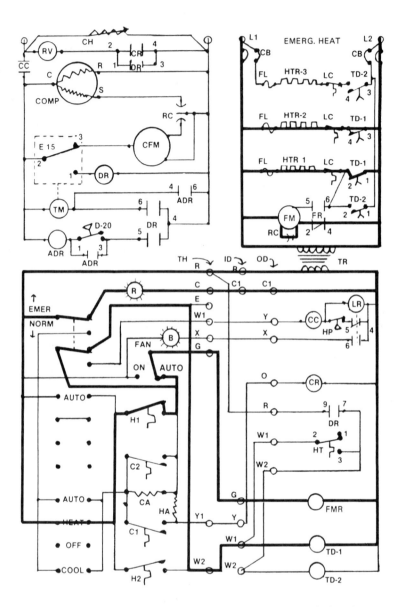

system is used to assure defrosting only when necessary. The defrost initiation is a function of:

1. Air pressure drop across the outdoor coil
2. Refrigerant coil temperature (26°F)
3. Defrost time (not to exceed 10 min.)

There are four controls used to initiate and terminate the defrost cycle:

1. Pressure switch (D-20)
2. Auxiliary defrost relay (ADR)

FIGURE 24–19 Wiring diagram for a typical heat pump, defrost mode. (Courtesy of Addison Products Company and Knight Energy Institute.)

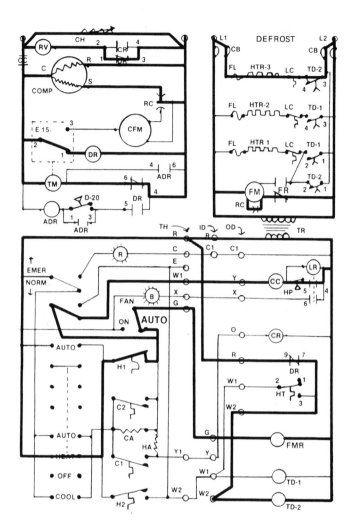

3. Defrost relay (DR)

4. Defrost control (E-15), as shown in wiring diagram (Figure 24–19)

The D-20 *demand-defrost pressure switch,* shown in Figure 24–20, senses the air pressure difference across the indoor coil. If the pressure difference is between 0.4 and 0.7 in. (W.C.), the switch is closed.

The *ADR,* shown in Figure 24–21, is a magnet relay with a 208/240-V holding coil and two normally open (NO) switches. When the coil is energized, a circuit is completed between terminals 1 and 3 and another circuit between 4 and 6.

The *defrost relay,* shown in Figure 24–22, has three normally closed (NC) switches and three (NO) switches.

The E-15 *defrost control,* shown in Figure 24–23, is a single-pole, double-throw switch (SPDT). The switch is activated by two forces, one from the movement of pressure cam A and the other by the pressure arm C created by the temperature

FIGURE 24–20 Demand-defrost pressure switch for heat pump defrost system. (Courtesy of Addison Products Company and Knight Energy Institute.)

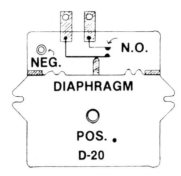

FIGURE 24–21 Auxiliary defrost relay for heat pump defrost system. (Courtesy of Addison Products Company and Knight Energy Institute.)

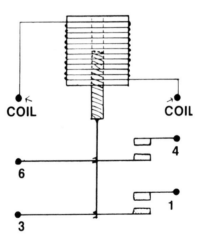

FIGURE 24–22 Defrost relay for heat pump defrost system. (Courtesy of Addison Products Company and Knight Energy Institute.)

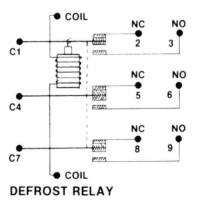

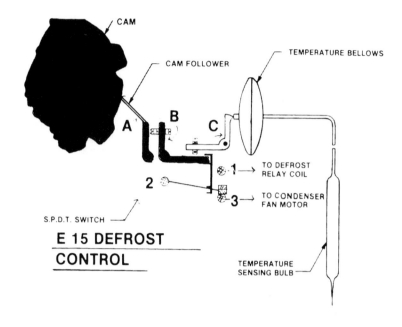

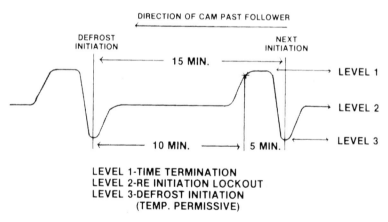

FIGURE 24–23 Operating cam configuration and sequence for the E-15 defrost control. (Courtesy of Addison Products Company and Knight Energy Institute.)

sensor. During the normal cycle, the switch is held closed by these two forces. For the switch to open, both of these forces must be removed from pressure arm B. The cam is moved by a timing motor and reaches a low point every 15 min. The force exerted by pressure arm C is removed when the coil temperature reaches 26°F as sensed by the temperature-sensing bulb.

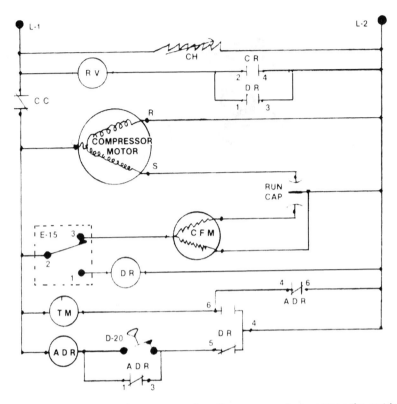

FIGURE 24–24 Defrost control sequence when the pressure drops across the outdoor coil. (Courtesy of Addison Products Company and Knight Energy Institute.)

The first indication of the need for defrost is by the D-20 pressure switch closing, caused by a buildup of frost on the outdoor coil. This energizes the ADR, closing two switches (see Figure 24–24):

1. Energizing the timer motor (TM)
2. Forming a holding circuit to keep the ADR energized in case the D-20 opens prematurely

Assuming that the pressure drop is caused by frost, the timer cam advances to the low point, the coil temperature reaches 26°F, and the defrost timer (E-15) switch opens, turning off the outdoor condenser fan motor (CFM) and energizing the defrost relay (DR). This causes the following action, as shown in Figure 24–25.

1. The reversing valve (RV) is energized.
2. The ADR is de-energized.
3. A circuit is formed to continue energizing the TM.
4. The second-stage heater (HTR-3) is turned on through the time-delay relay (TD-2), as shown in Figure 24–19.

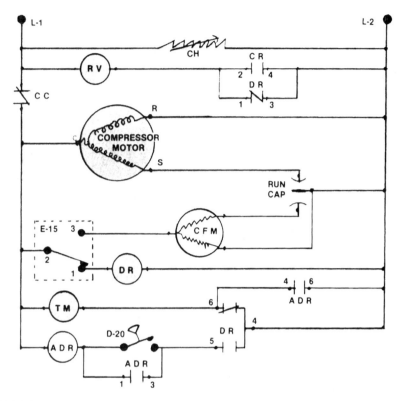

FIGURE 24–25 Defrost control sequence when the coil temperature drops to 26°F or lower. (Courtesy of Addison Products Company and Knight Energy Institute.)

When the outdoor coil temperature reaches 55°F or the timer cam advances to the high point (a maximum of 10 min. defrost), the defrost cycle is terminated and the E-15 switch returns the system to normal operation.

REFRIGERATION SYSTEM SERVICING

A useful method of diagnosing refrigeration service problems is to refer to Figure 24–26. This chart lists the more frequent problems and suggested solutions. The same methods used for evacuating, leak testing, and refrigerant charging air-conditioning systems are also used to service heat pumps. Remember that a heat pump must have proper air flow and proper refrigerant charge.

Solid-state control A solid-state control module is used by certain manufacturers to replace some of the standard electrical or mechanical controls. A typical control system of this type is shown in Figure 24–27. This logic module responds to the demand signal of the thermostat, examines the input from four sensors ("outdoor,"

Problem		Suction Pressure	Head Pressure	Superheat	Compressor Amperage	Temp. Diff. Over Indoor Coil	Possible Solutions
Low Refrigerant Charge		LOW	LOW	HIGH	LOW	LOW	Possible icing of evaporator. Repair leak, evacuate and Charge by Weight.
RESTRICTION		LOW	LOW	HIGH	LOW	LOW	Most Restrictions occur in strainer. Possible icing of evaporator.
Low Air Flow Over Indoor Coil	Heating	HIGH	HIGH	LOW	HIGH	HIGH	Cause: Dirty Filter; Dirty Blower Wheel; Duct too small. Supply outlets closed.
	Cooling	LOW	LOW	LOW	LOW	HIGH	
Low Air Flow Over Outdoor Coil	Heating	LOW	LOW	LOW	LOW	LOW	Cause: Dirty Coil; Bad Fan Motor; Fan Blade; Ice on coil; air blocked by building, etc.
	Cooling	HIGH	HIGH	LOW	HIGH	LOW	
Leaking Check Valve Heating or Cooling Mode		HIGH	HIGH	LOW	HIGH	LOW	Switch System to opposite Mode. If conditions correct themselves this proves check valve was leaking.
Compressor running but not pumping		HIGH	LOW	HIGH OR NONE	LOW	LOW	If not pumping at all, suction and head pressure will be equal and no refrigeration.
Reversing Valve Leaking or Stuck Mid Position		HIGH	LOW	HIGH OR NONE	LOW	LOW	All four lines of reversing valve will be hot.
Unit Not Defrosting		LOW	LOW	LOW	LOW	LOW	Outdoor Coil will be iced over. Check Refrigerant Charge, defrost controls.

FIGURE 24–26 Heat pump service problems and possible solutions. (Courtesy of Addison Products Company and Knight Energy Institute.)

"discharge," "defrost," and "liquid"), and determines when the heat pump or the supplementary heaters will operate.

Balance-point adjustment The location of the balance-point adjustment is shown in Figure 24–27. The balance point is the lowest ambient temperature at which the heat pump can operate without the use of supplementary heat. The balance point is set by the local contractor based on:

1. Outdoor design temperature
2. Building heat loss
3. Unit capacity

Low ambient cutoff adjustment Figure 24–27 shows the location of the low ambient cutoff adjustment. This is the minimum outside temperature at which it is no longer economical to operate the heat pump. Below this temperature all heating is performed by the secondary heat source. This setting is supplied by the manufacturer at −10°F, but it can be adjusted upward by the contractor.

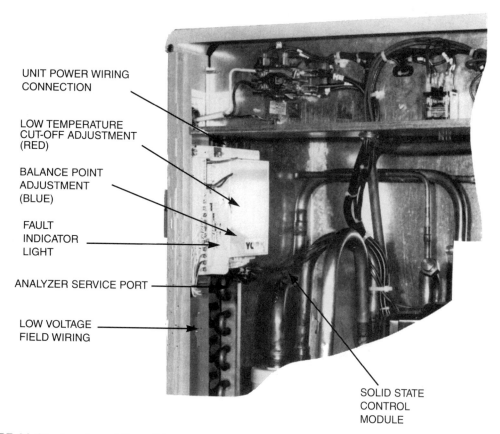

UNIT POWER WIRING
CONNECTION

LOW TEMPERATURE
CUT-OFF ADJUSTMENT
(RED)

BALANCE POINT
ADJUSTMENT
(BLUE)

FAULT
INDICATOR
LIGHT

ANALYZER SERVICE PORT

LOW VOLTAGE
FIELD WIRING

SOLID STATE
CONTROL
MODULE

FIGURE 24–27   Location of the solid-state control module in the outdoor compressor unit of a heat pump system. (Courtesy of York Corporation.)

Wiring diagram   A typical wiring diagram is shown in Figure 24–28. The defrost timer (DB) is factory set for 90-min. cycles. The timer can be field-set for 30- and 50-min. cycles, depending on defrost conditions in your geographical location. On startup be sure to energize the crankcase heater (CH) a minimum of 24 h before starting the unit. To energize the heater only, set the thermostat at the "off" position and close the electrical disconnect to the outdoor unit. The field wiring must comply with local and national fire, safety, and electrical codes.

Fault Code	Failure Mode
2	Discharge pressure reaches approximately 400 psig
3	Discharge temperature reaches approximately 275 °F
4	Discharge temperature did not reach approximately 90 °F within 1 h of compressor operation
5	Defrost failure
7	Outdoor temperature sensor failure
8	Liquid line temperature sensor failure
9	Bonnet sensor shorted

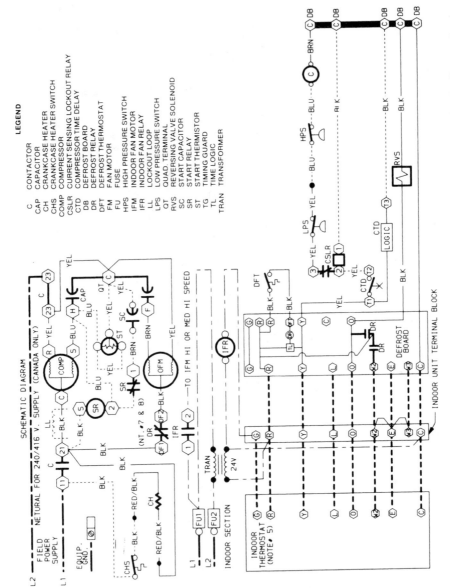

FIGURE 24–28 Typical wiring diagram with legend for an air-to-air heat pump. (Courtesy of Carrier Corporation.)

FIGURE 24–29   Service analyzer attached to solid-state control module in outdoor compressor unit. (Courtesy of York Corporation.)

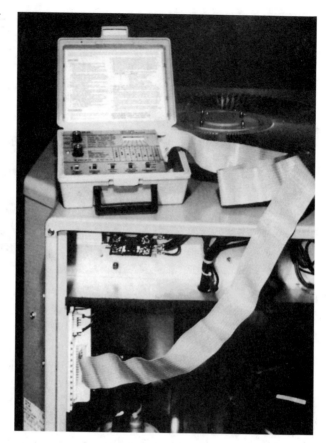

Service analyzer   The service analyzer, shown in Figure 24–29, is used by the service person to determine any malfunction in the operation of the heat pump. The analyzer indicates the service problem by a fault code:

ADD-ON HEAT PUMP SYSTEM

The major advantages of having a high-efficiency heat pump and a gas furnace combined in one system are:

1. Heating costs are reduced.
2. A comfort level is maintained.
3. The source of heat can be either gas or electricity.

The add-on heat pump system is shown in Figure 24–30. High-efficiency heat pumps produce a more "even" heat at milder outdoor temperatures, above 30°F.

With the lower discharge air temperature of approximately 100°F, the heat pump allows the indoor room temperature to remain more constant. Even though the heat

FIGURE 24–30 Cutaway view of a typical add-on heat pump system. (Courtesy of the Trane Company Unitary Products Group.)

pump may run for extended periods, its efficiency remains high. The efficiency begins to decrease at outdoor temperatures lower than 30°F.

The advantage of a gas furnace lies in the fact that its efficiency does not change. As the outdoor temperature drops, the furnace will run longer to maintain the desired indoor temperature but the operating efficiency (Btu of heat produced per cubic feet of gas consumed) does not change.

Figure 24–31 illustrates the comparison of heat pump and gas furnace heating. These curves depict operating costs compared with outdoor temperature. Actual operating costs depend on the efficiency of the heat pump and the gas furnace, the hours of operation, and the cost of gas and electricity. In general, the heat pump operates most efficiently in the temperature range from 65°F down to approximately 30°F. Below

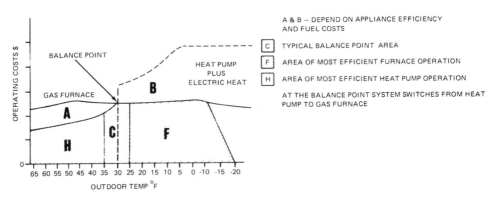

FIGURE 24–31 Performance curve for an add-on heat pump system.

this temperature, the gas furnace takes over, operating more efficiently at the lower temperatures when compared to a heat pump plus electric heat.

WATER-TO-AIR SYSTEM

Water-to-air heat pump systems use a water-to-refrigerant heat exchanger on the water side and an air-to-refrigerant heat exchanger on the air side. The water-to-refrigerant coil is usually of the coaxial type (tube-in-tube), located inside the building. There are two types of piping arrangements: the open-loop system and the closed-loop system.

On the open-loop system, water is continuously supplied at the rate of 1 to 5 gpm per ton from a deep well, lake, or river. A common source consists of drawing well water through the heat pump and then discharging into a lake, river, or disposal well. This is an excellent system for areas where plentiful, high-quality ground water can be obtained inexpensively. The coefficient of performance is usually 3.00 or better and is not affected by outdoor air temperature.

On the closed-loop system, water is circulated through a coil buried in the earth. Coils are placed in trenches 4 to 6 ft. deep. Since the earth's temperature will decrease as heat is removed, the coefficient of performance is reduced during operations. Thus, the closed-loop system is not as efficient as the open-loop system and requires longer piping. If temperatures below freezing may be encountered, an antifreeze solution must be used.

A flow diagram for the cooling cycle is shown in Figure 24–32; for the heating cycle, in Figure 24–33. Water valves are used to furnish more precise water flow for

FIGURE 24–32 Flow diagram for well water system: cooling cycle. (Courtesy of WeatherKing, Inc.)

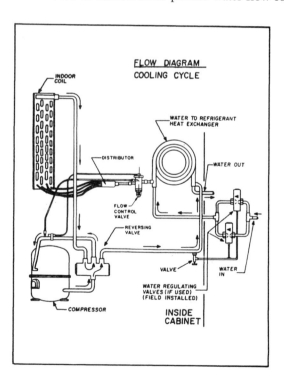

FIGURE 24–33 Flow diagram for well water system: heating cycle. (Courtesy of WeatherKing, Inc.)

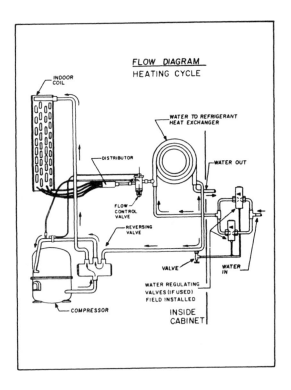

both heating and cooling. On cooling, the valve controls compressor discharge pressure. On heating, the valve controls compressor suction pressure. Note that the thermal expansion valve used is capable of controlling refrigerant flow in both directions.

Performance Data

Figure 24–34 shows typical performance data for both heating and cooling on the closed-loop system. The capacity of the unit is dependent both on the entering water temperature (EWT) and the water flow in gallons per minute. Ratings for heat absorbed by the condenser (QA) and heat rejected by the condenser (QR) are given in thousands of Btu per hour (MBh). Note the standard conditions on which these ratings are based. Figure 24–35 shows typical performance data on both heating and cooling for the open-loop system.

Water Piping

Figure 24–36 shows a typical ground-loop piping system. Gate valves and unions should be used on each side of components requiring removal for service. The expansion tank must be large enough to handle the change in volume of the liquid due to temperature variations. A relief valve is required by local codes. A purge valve located

COOL

EWT	GPM	LWT	QR	PS	PD
45	2	75	29.8	69-75	151-166
	3	65	30.5	67-73	137-151
	4	60	30.8	67-73	130-144
55	2	84	29.0	70-76	168-185
	3	75	29.6	70-76	156-171
	4	70	29.9	69-75	148-163
65	3	84	28.7	71-77	176-193
	4	79	29.0	70-76	168-185
	5	77	29.1	70-76	166-182
75	3	94	27.9	73-79	199-217
	5	86	28.3	71-77	187-205
	7	83	28.4	71-77	184-202
85	4	99	27.2	74-81	217-236
	6	94	27.5	74-81	211-229
	8	92	27.5	73-79	208-226

At standard rated air flow and 80 / 67 air entering cooling coil.

Depending upon return air conditions air flow temperature drops should be from 14° to 20°.

HEAT

EWT	GPM	LWT	QA	PS	PD
45	6	40	14.5	52-57	208-226
	8	41	15.0	53-59	211-229
	10	42	15.1	55-60	214-233
55	4	47	16.5	60-65	220-239
	6	49	17.3	64-70	226-245
	8	51	17.7	65-72	230-250
65	4	56	18.8	71-77	236-256
	6	58	19.9	74-81	243-263
	8	60	20.3	78-84	246-267
75	3	61	20.5	81-87	250-272
	4	64	21.6	84-91	256-278
	5	66	22.2	87-93	260-282

NOTE 1 - At standard rated air flow and 70°F return air
NOTE 2 - Indoor air temperature difference in heating °F = 25 to 40°F depending on water temperature, GPM and air flow.

FIGURE 24–34 Performance data, water-source heat pump, closed loop. (Courtesy of WeatherKing, Inc.)

at the highest point of the system is convenient for removing air during charging. The circulating pump must be adequate to supply the required gallons per minute against the total pressure drop of the system.

Knowing the water quality is important in determining the treatment required. Corrosion, scale formations, biological growths, and suspended solids can present real problems. For single-water-source units, manufacturers usually supply a cupronickel condenser, since some types of corrosion attack all copper tubes.

E.W.T.	GPM	BTUH TOTAL	BTUH SENS.	WATTS	EER W/OUT PUMP	EER WITH PUMP	HEAT REJ.
45	2.0	24800	16700	1730	14.3	13.4	29800
	3.0	25700	17100	1660	15.5	14.0	30500
	4.0	26100	17300	1630	16.0	14.0	30800
50	2.0	24200	16500	1770	13.7	12.8	29300
	3.0	25100	16900	1710	14.7	13.3	30000
	4.0	25500	17000	1670	15.3	13.4	30300
55	2.0	23700	16300	1820	13.0	12.2	29000
	3.0	24500	16600	1750	14.0	12.7	29600
	4.0	24900	16800	1720	14.5	12.7	29900
60	3.0	23900	16400	1800	13.3	12.1	29100
	4.0	24300	16500	1770	13.7	12.1	29400
	5.0	24500	16600	1750	14.0	12.0	29600
65	3.0	23300	16100	1850	12.6	11.5	28700
	4.0	23700	16300	1820	13.0	11.5	29000
	5.0	23900	16400	1790	13.4	11.4	29100
70	•3.0	22700	15900	1900	11.9	10.9	28300
	5.0	23300	16100	1840	12.7	10.9	28700
	7.0	23600	16300	1820	13.0	10.5	28900
75	3.0	22100	15600	1950	11.3	10.4	27900
	5.0	22700	15900	1900	11.9	10.3	28300
	7.0	22900	16000	1880	12.2	10.0	28400

EWT	GPM	BTUH TOTAL	WATTS	COP W/OUT PUMP	HEAT OF ABSORP.
25	6	13500	1480	2.7	9300
	8	13800	1490	2.7	9600
	10	14000	1500	2.7	9800
30	• 6	15000	1550	2.8	10500
	8	15300	1570	2.9	10800
	10	15500	1580	2.9	11000
35	6	16400	1620	3.0	11800
	8	16800	1640	3.0	12100
	10	17100	1660	3.0	12300
40	6	18000	1700	3.1	13100
	8	18400	1720	3.1	13500
	10	18700	1740	3.2	13700

FIGURE 24–35 Performance data, water-source heat pump, open loop. (Courtesy of WeatherKing, Inc.)

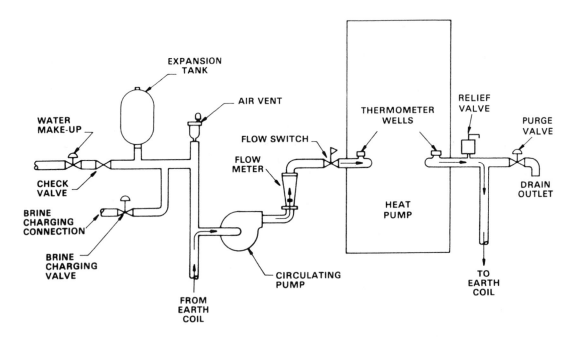

FIGURE 24–36   Typical ground-loop heat pump piping system.

For a single-source system on small installations, it is advisable to use an inexpensive filter that can be cleaned periodically. For a multiple-unit system on a larger building with a closed-loop recirculating water system, an automatic chemical treatment arrangement should be considered. Each system must be considered individually on its own merits.

STUDY QUESTIONS

Answers to the study questions may be found in the section noted in brackets.

24–1. How many Btus are converted into heat per watt of input by a heat pump? *[Characteristics]*

24–2. Describe the two types of heat pumps used for residential applications. *[Types of Heat Pumps]*

24–3. Describe how the refrigeration cycle operates during the heat pump mode. *[Refrigeration Cycle]*

24–4. Why is the defrost cycle necessary? *[Defrost Cycle]*

24–5. When is supplementary heat used? *[Supplementary Heat]*

24–6. For the air-to-air system, what is the difference between a single package and a split system? *[Air-to-Air System]*

24–7. What are the conditions for a high-temperature and low-temperature rating? *[Ratings]*

24–8. How is the air temperature rise determined for a heat pump? *[Indoor-Air-Temperature Rise]*

24–9. For a typical 5-hp air-to-air heat pump with outside temperature of 47°F, what would be the output? *[Supplementary Heat]*

24–10. At what refrigerant temperature is the defrost cycle usually terminated? *[Defrost Cycle]*

24–11. What does C.O.P. mean? *[Ratings]*

24–12. Describe the control sequence for the heating mode. *[Heating Mode]*

24–13. Describe the control sequence for the defrost mode. *[Defrost Mode]*

24–14. How is the service analyzer used? *(Service Analyzer]*

24–15. Name the three major advantages of an add-on heat pump system. *[Add-on Heat Pump System]*

24–16. Above what temperature does the heat pump operate most efficiently? *[Add-on Heat Pump System]*

Appendices

INDEX FOR APPENDICES SERVICE INFORMATION

SERVICE GUIDE FOR GAS-FIRED FURNACES

CONDITIONS	POSSIBLE CAUSES	POSSIBLE CURES
FLAME TOO LARGE	1. PRESSURE REG. SET TOO HIGH. 2. DEFECTIVE REGULATOR 3. BURNER ORIFICE TOO LARGE.	1. RESET, USING MANOMETER 2. REPLACE 3. REPLACE WITH CORRECT SIZE.
NOISY FLAME	1. TOO MUCH PRIMARY AIR. 2. NOISY PILOT 3. BURR IN ORIFICE	1. ADJUST AIR SHUTTERS 2. REDUCE PILOT GAS· 3. REMOVE BURR OR REPLACE ORIFICE
YELLOW TIP FLAME	1. TOO LITTLE PRIMARY AIR. 2. CLOGGED BURNER PORTS 3. MISALIGNED ORIFICES 4. CLOGGED DRAFT HOOD	1. ADJUST AIR SHUTTERS 2. CLEAN PORTS 3. REALIGN 4. CLEAN
FLOATING FLAME	1. BLOCKED VENTING 2. INSUFFICIENT PRIMARY AIR	1. CLEAN 2. INCREASE PRIMARY AIR SUPPLY

DELAYED IGNITION	1. IMPROPER PILOT LOCATION.
	2. PILOT FLAME TOO SMALL.
	
	3. BURNER PORTS CLOGGED
	   NEAR PILOT
	4. LOW PRESSURE
		1. REPOSITION PILOT.
		2. CHECK ORIFICE, CLEAN,
		   INCREASE PILOT GAS.
		3. CLEAN PORTS
		
		4. ADJUST PRESSURE REGULATOR.

FAILURE TO IGNITE	1. MAIN GAS OFF 2. BURNED OUT FUSE 3. LIMIT SWITCH DEFECTIVE 4. POOR ELECTRICAL CONNECTIONS. 5. DEFECT GAS VALVE. 6. DEFECTIVE THERMOSTAT.	1. OPEN MANUAL VALVE. 2. REPLACE 3. REPLACE 4. CHECK, CLEAN AND TIGHTEN. 5. REPLACE 6. REPLACE

BURNER WON'T TURNOFF	1. POOR THERMOSTAT LOCATION.
	2. DEFECTIVE THERMOSTAT.
	
	3. LIMIT SWITCH MALADJUSTED.
	4. SHORT CIRCUIT
	
	5. DEFECTIVE OR STICKING AUTOMATIC
	   VALVE
		1. RELOCATE
		2. CHECK CALIBRATION. CHECK
		   SWITCH AND CONTACTS.
		   REPLACE.
		3. REPLACE
		4. CHECK OPERATION AT
		   VALVE. LOOK FOR
		   SHORT AND CORRECT.
		5. CLEAN OR REPLACE.

RAPID BURNER CYCLING	1. CLOGGED FILTERS. 2. EXCESSIVE ANTICIPATION. 3. LIMIT SETTING TOO LOW. 4. POOR THERMOSTAT LOCATION.	1. CLEAN OR REPLACE. 2. ADJUST THERMOSTAT ANTICIPATOR FOR LONGER CYCLES. 3. READJUST OR REPLACE LIMIT. 4. RELOCATE.
RAPID FAN CYCLING	1. FAN SWITCH DIFF. TOO LOW. 2. BLOWER SPEED TOO HIGH.	1. READJUST OR REPLACE. 2. READJUST TO LOWER SPEED.
BLOWER WON'T STOP	1. MANUAL FAN "ON". 2. FAN SWITCH DEFECTIVE. 3. SHORTS	1. SWITCH TO AUTOMATIC. 2. REPLACE 3. CHECK WIRING AND CORRECT.

II   MOTOR AND BLOWER

CONDITION·	POSSIBLE CAUSES	POSSIBLE CURES
NOISY	1. FAN BLADES LOOSE. 2. BELT TENSION IMPROPER. 3. PULLEYS OUT OF ALIGNMENT. 4. BEARINGS DRY. 5. DEFECTIVE BELT. 6. BELT RUBBING.	1. REPLACE OR TIGHTEN. 2. READJUST (USUALLY 1 INCH SLACK) 3. REALIGN 4. LUBRICATE 5. REPLACE 6. REPOSITION

Source: Courtesy of Robertshaw Controls Company.

S87 DIRECT-SPARK IGNITION SYSTEM TROUBLESHOOTING

Start the system by setting the temperature controller to call for heat. Observe the system response and establish the type of malfunction or deviation from normal operation using the appropriate table.

Use the table by following the instructions in the boxes. If the condition is true or okay (answer: yes), go down to the next box. If the condition is not true or not okay (answer: no), go to the box to the right. Continue checking and answering conditions in each box until a problem and/or repair is explained. After any maintenance or repair, the troubleshooting sequence should be repeated until normal system operation is obtained.

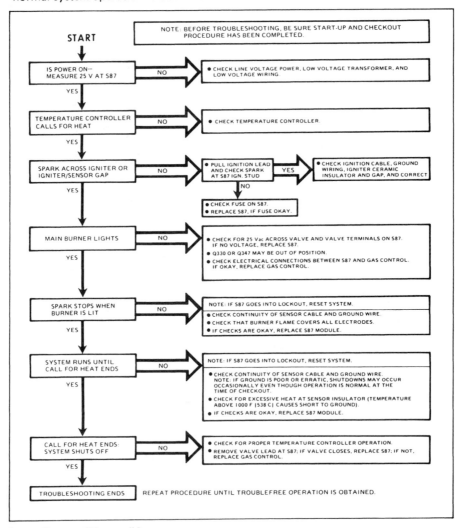

Source: Courtesy of Honeywell Inc.

S89A DIRECT-SPARK IGNITION GAS PRIMARY TROUBLESHOOTING

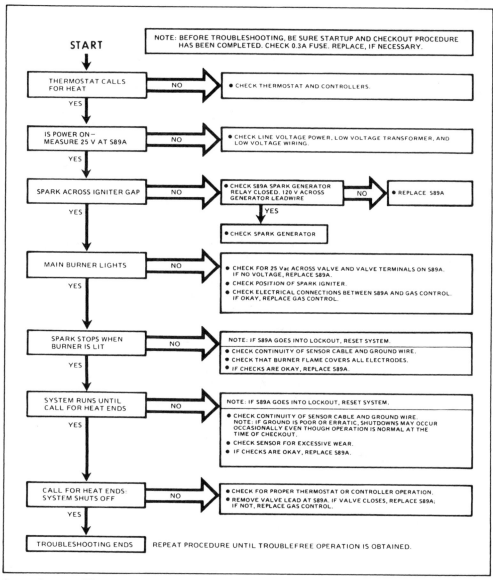

Source: Courtesy of Honeywell Inc.

S86 INTERMITTENT PILOT SYSTEM TROUBLESHOOTING

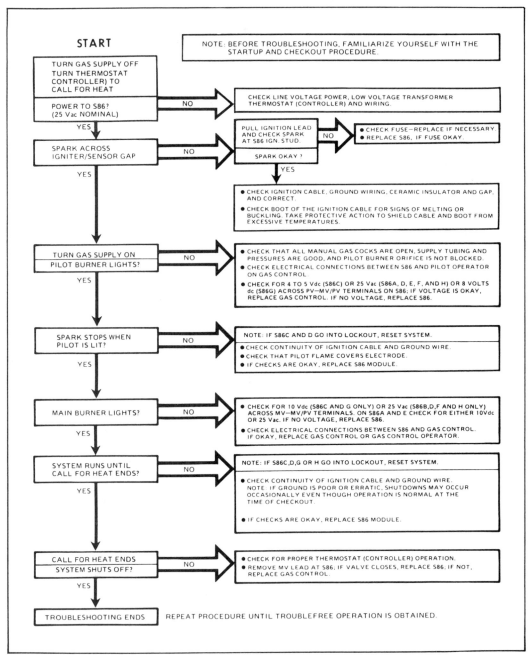

Source: Courtesy of Honeywell Inc.

S89C HOT-SURFACE IGNITION-CONTROL TROUBLESHOOTING

Start the system by setting the thermostat (temperature controller) to call for heat. Observe the system response and establish the type of malfunction or deviation from normal operation by using the flow chart below.

Follow the instructions in the boxes. If the condition is true or okay (answer is yes), go down to the next box.

If the condition is not true or not okay (answer is no), go to the box at right. Continue checking and answering conditions in each box until a problem and/or repair is explained. After any maintenance or repair, the troubleshooting sequence should be repeated until normal system operation is obtained.

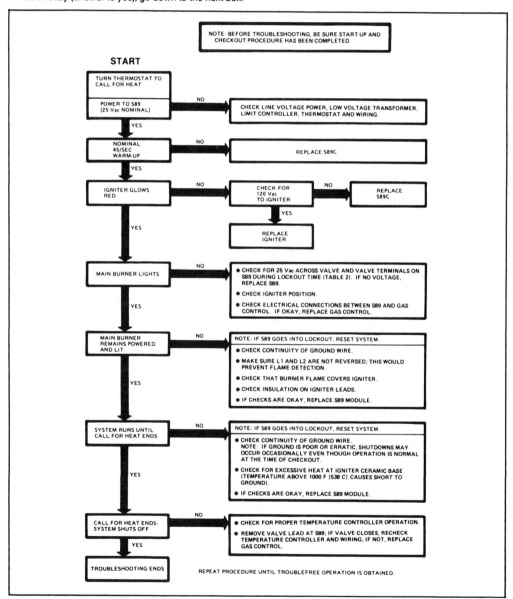

Source: Courtesy of Honeywell Inc.

MAIN BURNER AND PILOT BURNER, ORIFICE SIZE CHART

Input (Btu/h) per spud	Natural gas: 1020 Btu – 0.65 SG 3¹/₂ in. WC manifold		Propane: 2500 Btu – 1.5 SG 11 in. WC manifold	
	Drill size	Decimal tolerance	Drill size	Decimal tolerance
12,000	51	0.064–0.067	60	0.038–0.040
15,000	48	0.073–0.076	58	0.040–0.042
20,000	43	0.086–0.089	55	0.050–0.052
25,000	41	0.093–0.096	53	0.056–0.059
27,500	39	0.097–0.100	53	0.060–0.063
40,000	32	0.113–0.116	49	0.070–0.073
50,000	30	0.124–0.128	46	0.078–0.081
60,000	27	0.140–0.144	43	0.086–0.089
70,000	22	0.153–0.157	42	0.090–0.093
80,000	20	0.156–0.161	40	0.095–0.098
90,000	17	0.168–0.173	38	0.098–0.101
100,000	13	0.180–0.185	35	0.107–0.110
105,000	11	0.186–0.191	34	0.108–0.111
110,000	10	0.188–0.193	33	0.109–0.113
125,000	5	0.200–0.205	1/8	0.121–0.125
135,000	3	0.208–0.213	30	0.124–0.128
140,000	7/32	0.214–0.219	30	0.124–0.128
150,000	1	0.223–0.228	29	0.132–0.136
160,000	A	0.229–0.234	28	0.136–0.140
175,000	C	0.237–0.242	27	0.140–0.144
190,000	E	0.245–0.250	25	0.145–0.149
200,000	F	0.252–0.257	23	0.150–0.154
210,000	H	0.261–0.266	21	0.154–0.159
220,000	I	0.267–0.272	20	0.156–0.161
240,000	K	0.276–0.281	18	0.164–0.169
260,000	M	0.290–0.295	16	0.172–0.177
280,000	5/16	0.307–0.312	13	0.180–0.185
300,000	O	0.311–0.316	11	0.186–0.191
310,000	P	0.318–0.323	9	0.191–0.196
320,000	21/64	0.323–0.328	7	0.196–0.201

Source: Courtesy of Luxaire, Inc.

OIL FURNACE ROUTINE PERFORMANCE CHECKS AND TROUBLESHOOTING

1. Check Shut-Off Valve and Line Filter. Replace or clean cartridge in line filter if dirty. Be sure to open shut-off valve.

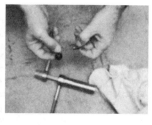

2. Check Nozzle Assembly. Replace the nozzle according to manufacturer's recommendations when needed.

Important: Use proper designed tools for removal of nozzle from firing head.

3. Check Strainer. Clean strainer using clean fuel oil or kerosene. Install new cover gasket. Replace strainer if necessary.

4. Check Connections. Tighten all connections and fittings in the intake line and unused intake port plugs.

5. Pressure Setting. Insert pressure gage in gage port. Normal pressure setting should be at 100 PSI. Check manufacturer's pressure setting recommendation on each installation being serviced.

6. Insert Vacuum gage in unused intake port. Check for abnormally high intake vacuum.

TROUBLESHOOTING

	cause	remedy
NO OIL FLOW AT NOZZLE	Oil level below intake line in supply tank	*Fill tank with oil.*
	Clogged strainer or filter	*Remove and clean strainer. Repack filter element.*
	Clogged nozzle	*Replace nozzle.*
	Air leak in intake line	*Tighten all fittings in intake line. Tighten unused intake port plug. Tighten in-line valve stem packing gland. Check filter cover and gasket.*
	Restricted intake line (High vacuum reading)	*Replace any kinked tubing and check any valves in intake line.*
	A two pipe system that becomes airbound	*Check and insert by-pass plug.*
	A single-pipe system that becomes airbound (Model J unit only)	*Loosen gage port plug or easy flow valve and drain oil until foam is gone in bleed hose.*
	Slipping or broken coupling	*Tighten or replace coupling.*
	Rotation of motor and fuel unit is not the same as indicated by arrow on pad at top of unit	*Install fuel unit with correct rotation.*
	Frozen pump shaft	*Return unit to approved service station or Sundstrand factory for repair. Check for water and dirt in tank.*

Source: Courtesy of Sunstrand Hydraulics, Inc.

OIL FURNACE ROUTINE PERFORMANCE CHECKS
AND TROUBLESHOOTING continued

	cause	remedy
OIL LEAK	Loose plugs or fittings	*Dope with good quality thread sealer.*
	Leak at pressure adjusting end cap nut	*Fibre washer may have been left out after adjustment of valve spring. Replace the washer.*
	Blown seal (single pipe system)	*Check to see if by-pass plug has been left in unit. Replace fuel unit.*
	Blown seal (two pipe system)	*Check for kinked tubing or other obstructions in return line. Replace fuel unit.*
	Seal leaking	*Replace fuel unit.*
NOISY OPERATION	Bad coupling alignment	*Loosen fuel unit mounting screws slightly and shift fuel unit in different positions until noise is eliminated. Retighten mounting screws.*
	Air in inlet line	*Check all connections.*
	Tank hum on two-pipe system and inside tank	*Install return line hum eliminator.*
PULSATING PRESSURE	Partially clogged strainer or filter	*Remove and clean strainer. Replace filter element.*
	Air leak in intake line	*Tighten all fittings and valve packing in intake line.*
	Air leaking around cover	*Be sure strainer cover screws are tightened securely.*
LOW OIL PRESSURE	Defective gage	*Check gage against master gage, or other gage.*
	Nozzle capacity is greater than fuel unit capacity	*Replace fuel unit with unit of correct capacity.*

IMPROPER NOZZLE CUT-OFF

To determine the cause of improper cut-off, insert a pressure gage in the nozzle port of the fuel unit. After a minute of operation shut burner down. If the pressure drops and stabilizes above 0 P.S.I, the fuel unit is operating properly and air is the cause of improper cut-off. If, however, the pressure drops to 0 P.S.I, fuel unit should be replaced.

Filter leaks	*Check face of cover and gasket for damage.*
Strainer cover loose	*Tighten 8 screws on cover.*
Air pocket between cut-off valve and nozzle	*Run burner, stopping and starting unit, until smoke and after-fire disappears.*
Air leak in intake line	*Tighten intake fittings and packing nut on shut-off valve. Tighten unused intake port plug.*
Partially clogged nozzle strainer	*Clean strainer or change nozzle.*

Source: Courtesy of Sundstrand Hydraulics, Inc.

OIL NOZZLE SELECTION

OIL BURNER NOZZLE INTERCHANGE CHART

STEINER 30°-90°	DELAVAN 30° — 90°
H/PH	A
S (.5 — 2.0) or Q	A or W
S/SS (2.25 +)	B
HAGO 30°-90°	DELAVAN 30° — 90°
SS	A
H	A or W
ES/P	B
MONARCH 30°-90°	DELAVAN 30° — 90°
R/NS/PL	A
AR	A or W
PLP	B

EFFECTS OF PRESSURE ON NOZZLE FLOW RATE

NOZZLE RATING AT 100 PSI	NOZZLE FLOW RATES IN GALLONS PER HOUR (Approx.)					
	80 PSI	120 PSI	140 PSI	160 PSI	200 PSI	300 PSI
.50	0.45	0.55	0.59	0.63	0.70	0.86
.65	0.58	0.71	0.77	0.82	0.92	1.12
.75	0.67	0.82	0.89	0.95	1.05	1.30
.85	0.76	0.93	1.00	1.08	1.20	1.47
.90	0.81	0.99	1.07	1.14	1.27	1.56
1.00	0.89	1.10	1.18	1.27	1.41	1.73
1.10	0.99	1.21	1.30	1.39	1.55	1.90
1.20	1.07	1.31	1.41	1.51	1.70	2.08
1.25	1.12	1.37	1.48	1.58	1.76	2.16
1.35	1.21	1.48	1.60	1.71	1.91	2.34
1.50	1.34	1.64	1.78	1.90	2.12	2.60
1.65	1.48	1.81	1.95	2.09	2.33	2.86
1.75	1.57	1.92	2.07	2.22	2.48	3.03
2.00	1.79	2.19	2.37	2.53	2.82	3.48
2.25	2.01	2.47	2.66	2.85	3.18	3.90
2.50	2.24	2.74	2.96	3.16	3.54	4.33
2.75	2.44	3.00	3.24	3.48	3.90	4.75
3.00	2.69	3.29	3.55	3.80	4.25	5.20
3.25	2.90	3.56	3.83	4.10	4.60	5.63
3.50	3.10	3.82	4.13	4.42	4.95	6.06
4.00	3.55	4.37	4.70	5.05	5.65	6.92
4.50	4.00	4.92	5.30	5.70	6.35	7.80
5.00	4.45	5.46	5.90	6.30	7.05	8.65
5.50	4.90	6.00	6.50	6.95	7.75	9.52
6.00	5.35	6.56	7.10	7.60	8.50	10.4
6.50	5.80	7.10	7.65	8.20	9.20	11.2
7.00	6.22	7.65	8.25	8.85	9.90	12.1
7.50	6.65	8.20	8.85	9.50	10.6	13.0
8.00	7.10	8.75	9.43	10.1	11.3	13.8
8.50	7.55	9.30	10.0	10.7	12.0	14.7
9.00	8.00	9.85	10.6	11.4	12.7	15.6
9.50	8.45	10.4	11.2	12.0	13.4	16.4
10.00	8.90	10.9	11.8	12.6	14.1	17.3
11.00	9.80	12.0	13.0	13.9	15.5	19.0
12.00	10.7	13.1	14.1	15.1	17.0	20.8
13.00	11.6	14.2	15.3	16.4	18.4	22.5
14.00	12.4	15.3	16.5	17.7	19.8	24.2
15.00	13.3	16.4	17.7	19.0	21.2	26.0
16.00	14.2	17.5	18.9	20.2	22.6	27.7
17.00	15.1	18.6	20.0	21.5	24.0	29.4
18.00	16.0	19.7	21.2	22.8	25.4	31.2
19.00	16.9	20.8	22.4	24.0	26.8	33.0
20.00	17.8	21.9	23.6	25.3	28.3	34.6
22.00	19.6	24.0	26.0	27.8	31.0	38.0
24.00	21.4	26.2	28.3	30.3	34.0	41.5
26.00	23.2	28.4	30.6	32.8	36.8	45.0
28.00	25.0	30.6	33.0	35.4	39.6	48.5
30.00	26.7	32.8	35.4	38.0	42.4	52.0
32.00	28.4	35.0	37.8	40.5	45.2	55.5
35.00	31.2	38.2	41.3	44.0	49.5	60.5
40.00	35.6	43.8	47.0	50.5	56.5	69.0
45.00	40.0	49.0	53.0	57.0	63.5	78.0
50.00	44.5	54.5	59.0	63.0	70.5	86.5

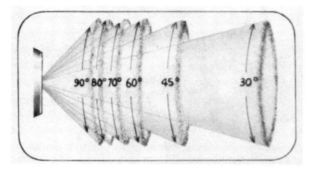

90° 80° 70° 60°   45°   30°

Source: Courtesy of Delavan Corporation.

DETERMINING OIL-FLOW RATES AND COMBUSTION CHAMBER SIZE

PROPER FLOW RATES

Oil burner nozzles are available in a wide selection of flow rates, all but eliminating the need for specially calibrated nozzles. For example, between 1.00 GPH and 2.00 GPH inclusive, seven different flow rates are available. The following guidelines may be used for determining the proper flow rates:

The proper size nozzle for a given burner unit is sometimes stamped on the name plate of the unit.

If the unit rating is given in BTU per hour input, the nozzle size may be determined by . . .

$$GPH = \frac{BTU\ Input}{140,000}$$

If the unit rating is given in BTU output . .

$$GPH = \frac{BTU\ Output}{(Efficiency\ \%) \times 140,000}$$

On a steam job, if the total square feet of steam radiation, including piping, is known.

$$GPH = \frac{Total\ Ft^2\ of\ Steam \times 240}{(Efficiency\ \%) \times 140,000}$$

If the system is hot water operating at 180° and the total square feet of radiation, including piping, is known . . .

$$GPH = \frac{Total\ Ft^2\ of\ Hot\ Water \times 165}{(Efficiency\ \%) \times 140,000}$$

Generally, with hot water and warm air heat, the smallest flow rate that will adequately heat the house on the coldest day is the most economical in operation.

Source: Courtesy of Delavan Corporation.

RECOMMENDED COMBUSTION CHAMBER DIMENSIONS

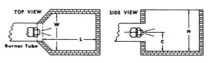

Nozzle Size or Rating (GPH)	Spray Angle	Square or Rectangular Combustion Chamber				Round Chamber (Diameter in inches)
		L Length (in.)	W Width (in.)	H Height (in.)	C Nozzle Height (in.)	
0.50 – 0.65	80°	8	8	11	4	9
0.75 – 0.85	60°	10	8	12	4	*
	80°	9	9	13	5	10
1.00 – 1.10	45°	14	7	12	4	*
	60°	11	9	13	5	*
	80°	10	10	14	6	11
1.25 – 1.35	45°	15	8	11	5	*
	60°	12	10	14	6	*
	80°	11	11	15	7	12
1.50 – 1.65	45°	16	10	12	6	*
	60°	13	11	14	7	*
	80°	12	12	15	7	13
1.75 – 2.00	45°	18	11	14	6	*
	60°	15	12	15	7	*
	80°	14	13	16	8	15
2.25 – 2.50	45°	18	12	14	7	*
	60°	17	13	15	8	*
	80°	15	14	16	8	16
3.00	45°	20	13	15	7	*
	60°	19	14	17	8	*
	80°	18	16	18	9	17

* Recommend oblong chamber for narrow sprays.

NOTES: These dimensions are for average conversion burners. Burners with special firing heads may require special chambers.

Higher backwall, flame baffle or corbelled backwall increase efficiency on many jobs.

Combustion chamber floor should be insulated on conversion jobs.

For larger nozzle sizes, use the same approximate proportions and 90 sq. in. of floor area per 1 gph.

For FlameCone installations, use approximately 65 sq. in. of floor area per 1 gph.

OIL BURNER SETUP AND TROUBLESHOOTING GUIDE

1. Check the pump oil pressure with a ¼" NPT pressure gauge. Pressure should be a steady 100 PSI. Adjust, if necessary.
2. An oil filter must be installed on all furnace installations to insure reliable service and a clean oil supply. It should be located as close to the furnace as possible and have the following minimum capacities.
   A. One Pipe System—5 gal/hr
   B. Two Pipe System—20 gal/hr
3. Proper instrumentation must be used to set the correct smoke and draft readings.
   A. Allow the furnace to fire for at least five minutes.
   B. Use a smoke tester to adjust the air band setting to achieve a 0+ smoke.
   C. Use a draft gauge to adjust the barometric draft regulator to achieve a stack draft between −.025" w.c. and −.035" w.c. The pressure differential for the over the fire draft should be +.005" w.c. to +.015" w.c. (For firing rates from 1.5 GPH to 3.0 GPH, a pressure differential of up to +.02" w.c. is acceptable.)
   D. If these readings and differential cannot be attained, a problem exists which must be solved before proceeding further.
4. Make sure that the furnace is level (or tilted up to 3° backwards) and is flat on the floor. If the furnace must be mounted on blocks then it must be supported along its entire length with a frame and additional blocking.
5. A one pipe system is recommended for gravity feed only. Up to an eight foot lift is allowable if the system is absolutely airtight.
   Rule of Thumb: Allow 1" HG (mercury) of vacuum for each foot of vertical lift and 1" HG (mercury) of vacuum for each 10' of horizontal run.

For a two pipe system, follow the chart below.

Figures in body of table are total allowable feet of line length (Vertical + Horizontal) given feet of lift in column at left for pumps set 2 pipe.

FEET VERTICAL LIFT	1 Stage		2 Stage		WEBSTER 1 Stage "J" ONLY	
	⅜" OD TUBING	½" OD TUBING	⅜" OD TUBING	½" OD TUBING	⅜" OD TUBING	½" OD TUBING
0	50	100	75	100	100	100
1	46	100	71	100	93	100
2	42	100	68	100	85	100
3	39	100	64	100	78	100
4	35	100	60	100	70	100
5	31	95	56	100	63	100
6	27	83	53	100	55	100
7	24	72	49	100	48	100
8	20	60	45	100	40	100
9	16	49	41	100	33	99
10	12	38	38	100	25	76
11		27	34	100	18	53
12		15	30	91		31
13			26	80		
14			23	68		
15			19	57		
16				46		
17				34		
18				23		

This chart does not allow for any added restrictions such as line filter, elbows, sharp bends, check valves, etc.

Problem	Solution
Excessive oil dripping from nozzle after shutdown	Slight amount of oil normal. All air must be purged from oil line. —turn burner on, then open purge valve on pump. —close purge valve on pump before burner is shut down. Check all fittings (especially on suction side of pump) for tightness. —all connections should be flare type rather than compression type.
Oil running back down blast tube	Check above solutions for excessive oil dripping. Check tightness of nozzle. Check if nozzle is cross threaded. Check if furnace is level or up to a 3° tilt backwards.
Oil dripping into burner housing or between blast tube and burner housing	Check above solutions. Check if gasket is between mounting plate and housing. Check if screws holding mounting plate to housing are tight.
Misalignment of nozzle	Check locking nut on electrode assembly. Should be only hand tight plus 1/4 turn.
End cone distortion	Check alignment of electrode/oil pipe assembly. Check nozzle to face of end cone dimension. Should be 1". If distortion is severe, check above and replace end cone. Check oil spray pattern—replace nozzle if necessary.
Delayed ignition	Check electrode to nozzle dimension. —0 to 1/16" in front of nozzle. —1/2" above nozzle ₵. —1/8" between electrodes. Check oil spray pattern replace nozzle if necessary.

OIL BURNER TROUBLESHOOTING GUIDE

Most oil burner service calls fall into one of 4 basic categories:
1. No heat.
2. System overheats house.
3. System underheats house.
4. Miscellaneous complaints.

The following troubleshooting summary provides a guide to common possible causes of each of these complaints.

NO-HEAT COMPLAINTS

When troubleshooting a "no-heat" complaint, always check the following basic points first.

1. Make sure power is on at the main switch.
2. Make sure burner motor fuse isn't blown.
3. Check burner on-off switch. If switch is off, make sure combustion chamber is free of oil or oil vapor, then turn switch to ON position.
4. Check oil supply.
5. Make sure manual oil valves are open.
6. Make sure limit switches are closed.
7. Reset safety switch and set thermostat to call for heat.

After completing these checks, run through starting procedure. If system still does not operate properly, note point at which sequence fails.

Check the appropriate table to determine which parts of the system are most likely to be the cause of the trouble.

BURNER MOTOR DOESN'T START

CAN INDICATE	POSSIBLE CAUSE	CORRECTIVE ACTION
Trouble in primary	See cad-cell troubleshooting, or stack relay troubleshooting, as applicable.	
Trouble in thermostat	1. Broken wires, loose connections. 2. Dirty contacts. 3. Defective thermostat.	1. Replace broken wires, tighten connections. 2. Clean contacts. 3. Replace thermostat.
Faulty burner components	1. Broken wires, loose connections. 2. Motor start switch or thermal overload switch open. 3. Defective motor. 4. Defective pump.	See instructions supplied with heating equipment.

Source: Courtesy of Honeywell Inc.

OIL BURNER TROUBLESHOOTING GUIDE continued

BURNER MOTOR STARTS—NO FLAME IS ESTABLISHED

CAN INDICATE	POSSIBLE CAUSE	CORRECTIVE ACTION
Trouble in primary	See cad-cell troubleshooting, or stack relay troubleshooting, as applicable.	

Trouble in ignition system	1. Loose connection, broken wires between ignition transformer and primary.
	2. Defective transformer.
	3. Ignition electrodes
	  a. improperly positioned.
	  b. spaced too far apart.
	  c. loose.
	  d. dirty.
	4. Ceramic insulators dirty, shorted, damaged.
		1. Replace broken wires, tighten connections.
		2. Replace transformer.
		3. Check manufacturer's instructions.
		
		4. Replace electrode asssembly.

Faulty burner components	1. Dirty nozzle. 2. Nozzle loose, misaligned, worn. 3. Clogged oil pump strainer. 4. Clogged oil line. 5. Air leak in suction line. 6. Defective pressure regulator valve. 7. Defective pump. 8. Improper draft. 9. Water in oil. 10. Oil too heavy.	See instructions supplied with heating equipment.

BURNER MOTOR STARTS, FLAME GOES ON AND OFF AFTER STARTUP

CAN INDICATE	POSSIBLE CAUSE	CORRECTIVE ACTION
Trouble in primary	1. Dirty ignition or motor relay contacts. 2. Burned out contacts.	1. Clean appropriate contacts. 2. Replace primary.
Trouble in limit control(s)	1. Dirty contacts. 2. High and low limit settings too close or differential set too wide.	1. Clean contacts. 2. Readjust setting(s) and/or differential.
Trouble in thermostat	1. Broken wires, loose connections. 2. Differential set too close. 3. Anticipator defective. 4. Thermostat defective.	1. Replace broken wires, tighten connections. 2. Reset differential. 3. Replace thermostat. 4. Replace thermostat.
Faulty burner components	1. Clogged or dirty oil lines. 2. Fluctuating water level (hydronic systems).	See instructions supplied with heating equipment.

Source: Courtesy of Honeywell Inc.

HYDRONIC TROUBLE ANALYSIS

Troubleshooting

Preliminary Checks

Supply Voltage

To check the voltage being supplied to the motor, use a voltmeter. **Be careful, since power is still being supplied to the pump.** Do not touch the voltmeter leads together while they are in contact with the power lines.

Three Phase Motors
Touch a voltmeter lead to:
- Power leads L1 and L2
- Power leads L2 and L3
- Power leads L3 and L1

These tests should give a reading of full line voltage.

Single Phase Motors
Touch one voltmeter lead to each of the lines supplying power to the pump L1 and L2. (or L1 and N for 115V circuits).

Checking Single Phase Power

L1 L2

Evaluation

When the motor is under load, the voltage should be within 5% (+ or -) of the nameplate voltage. Any variation larger than this may indicate a poor electrical supply and can cause damage to the motor windings. The motor should not be operated under these conditions. Contact your power supplier to correct the problem or change the motor to one requiring the voltage you are receiving.

Current Measurement

To check the current, use an ammeter. To do so, follow these steps:
1. Make sure the pump is operating.
2. Set the ammeter to the proper scale.
3. Place the tongs of the ammeter around the leg to be measured.
4. Compare the results with the amp draw information on the motor nameplate.
5. Repeat for the other legs.

Evaluation

If the current draw exceeds the listed nameplate amps, or if the current imbalance is greater than 5% between each leg on three-phase units, then check the following:
- The voltage supplied to the pump maybe too high or too low.
- The contacts on the motor starter may be burned.
- The terminals in the starter or terminal box may be loose.
- There may be a winding defect. Check the winding and insulation resistance.
- The motor windings may be shorted or grounded.
- The pump may be damaged in some way and may be causing a motor overload.
- A voltage supply or balance problem may exist.

Troubleshooting

Insulation Resistance (lead-to-ground)

APPLIES TO THREEPHASE 460 V MODELS ONLY

To check the insulation resistance of the motor and leads, a megohmmeter is required.

1. Turn the **POWER OFF**.
2. Disconnect all electrical leads to the motor.
3. Set the scale selector on the megohmmeter to R x 100K, touch its leads together, and adjust the indicator to zero.
4. Touch the leads of the megohmmeter individually to each of the motor leads and to ground (i.e. L1 to ground; L2 to ground, etc.):

Evaluation: The resistance values for new motors must exceed 1,000,000 ohms. If they do not, replace the motor.

Note: Insulation resistance tests cannot be performed on multi-speed models, since the overload relay opens when power is disconnected.

Source: Grundfos Pumps Corporation

HYDRONIC TROUBLE ANALYSIS continued

Troubleshooting

Troubleshooting

Diagnosing Specific Problems

If The Pump...	It May Be Caused By...	Check This By...	Correct It By...
Does Not Run	1. No power at motor	Check for voltage at terminal box	If no voltage at motor, check feeder panel for tripped circuits
	2. Fuses are blown or circuit breakers are tripped.	Remove fuses and check for continuity with an ohmmeter.	Replace blown fuses or reset circuit breaker. If new fuses blow or circuit breaker trips, the terminal box wiring must be checked.
	3. Defective controls	Check all safety and pressure switches for operation. Inspect contact in control devices.	Replace worn or defective parts.
	4. Motor is defective (3 x 460V only)	Turn off power. Disconnect the wiring. Measure the lead-to-lead resistance with an ohmmeter (set at R1). Measure lead-to-ground values with a megohmmeter (R100K). Record the measured values.	If the motor windings are open or grounded, replace the motor.
	5. (On 1-phase pumps) Defective capacitor	Turn off the power, then discharge the capacitor. Disconnect the leads and check them with an ohmmeter (R100K).	When the meter is connected, the needle should jump toward "0" ohms and slowly drift back to infinity. Replace capacitor if defective.
Pump Runs, But At A Reduced Capacity	1. Wrong rotation (3 phase only)	Check for proper electrical connections in terminal box.	Correct wiring and change leads as required.
	2. Leak in discharge piping or valve.	Examine system for leaks.	Repair leaks.
	3. Clogged strainer	Remove screen and inspect.	Clean, repair, rinse out screen and re-install.
	4. Worn pump	Install pressure gauge, start the pump, gradually close the discharge valve and read pressure at shut-off.	Refer to the specific pump curve for shut-off head for that pump model. If head is close to curve, pump is probably OK. If not, remove pump and inspect.
	5. Foreign material lodged in impeller.	Shut isolation valves. Drain the pump. Remove the powerhead housing allen screws and remove the impeller/rotor assembly.	Inspect impeller for foreign material. Remove and reassemble pump. Check to insure the O-ring between the powerhead housing and pump housing is not damaged during reassembly.
Fuses Blow or Circuit Breakers Trip	1. High or low voltage	Check voltage at the starter panel or terminal box.	If not within + or - 5%, check wire size and length of run to pump panel.
	2. 3-phase current imbalance.	Check the current draw on each lead.	Must be within + or - 5%. If not, contact the power company.
	3. Terminal box wiring	Check that actual wiring matches wiring diagram. Check for loose or broken wires or terminals.	Correct as required.
	4. (On 1-phase pumps) Defective capacitor	Turn off power, then discharge the capacitor. Disconnect leads and check with an ohmmeter (R100K)	When the meter is connected, the needle should jump towards "0" ohms and slowly drift back to infinity. Replace capacitor, if defective.

Source: Grundfos Pumps Corporation

AIR ELIMINATION IN HYDRONIC SYSTEMS
B&G Airtrol
Tank Fittings

For proper operation, the air cushion Compression Tank(s) should be the only air space within a closed hydronic system. This air cushion can then provide adequate pressurization for all fluctuations of water volume.

However, because air can be absorbed in water, some means of restricting the flow of cooler water (gravity circulation) from the tank into the system is needed without restricting passage of free air into the tank. Compression tank size can be reduced considerably by reducing vapor pressure if this can be achieved.

B&G Airtrol Tank Fittings fill this need. The cross section of the ATF fitting illustrates how air bubbles can rise directly into the tank, but water flow is restricted by a baffle or trap. ATF fittings are available for tanks up to and including 24" diameter.

For tanks of 100 gallons and larger, the 1" ATFL fitting is recommended. As illustrated, air bubbles form an air trap at the bridge and rise unobstructed into the tank. Water will not circulate across this air trap so must return to the system via the "U" tube. A small differential in pressure between the system and the tank will move the non-ferrous ball past the small port, permitting tank water to return to the system. A large difference in pressure will force the ball to either end of the tube, thus permitting full flow through the tube to or from the system.

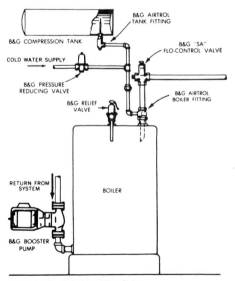

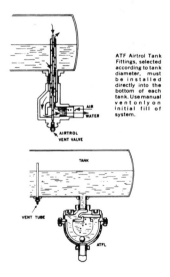

ATF Airtrol Tank Fittings, selected according to tank diameter, must be installed directly into the bottom of each tank. Use manual vent only on initial fill of system.

Source: ITT Fluid Handling Sales.

AIR ELIMINATION IN HYDRONIC SYSTEMS continued

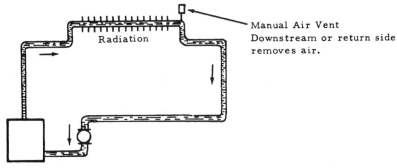

Manual Air Vent
Downstream or return side
removes air.

Radiation

System Vented at High Point

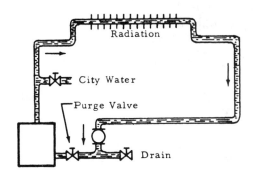

Radiation

City Water

Purge Valve

Drain

1. Close Purge Valve
2. Open City Water Valve
3. Open Drain Valve Until Water
   Runs Free of Air
4. Close Drain and City Water
5. Adjust System Pressure

Source: ITT Fluid Handling Sales.

RECOMMENDED FLOW RATES (GAL/MIN) FOR COPPER TUBING

Nominal tubing size (in.)	Minimum (gal/min)	Velocity (ft/sec)	Maximum (gal/min)	Velocity (ft/sec)
1/2	–	–	1.5	2.1
3/4	1.5	1.0	3.5	2.3
1	3.5	1.4	7.5	3.0
1 1/4	7	1.9	13	3.5
1 1/2	12	2.1	20	3.6

Series 100 Circulator Pump

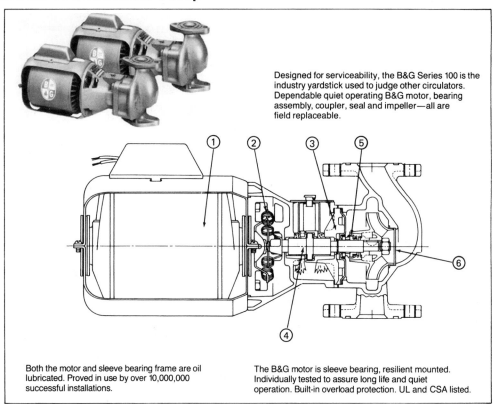

Designed for serviceability, the B&G Series 100 is the industry yardstick used to judge other circulators. Dependable quiet operating B&G motor, bearing assembly, coupler, seal and impeller—all are field replaceable.

Both the motor and sleeve bearing frame are oil lubricated. Proved in use by over 10,000,000 successful installations.

The B&G motor is sleeve bearing, resilient mounted. Individually tested to assure long life and quiet operation. Built-in overload protection. UL and CSA listed.

 ① B&G Motor - The heart of the Booster. The finest circulator motor available. Sleeve bearing, oil lubricated with replaceable resilient motor mount. Two-piece bracket makes service a snap.

 ② Noise dampening coupler. B&G's own flexible spring design adds to quiet operation. Do not accept a substitute.

 ③ Long bronze sleeve bearings maintain exact shaft alignment. Provides for constant circulation of oil over bearing surfaces.

 ④ Precision ground pump shaft is over-sized to provide large bearing surfaces. Hardened integral thrust collar prevents end-thrust to ensure long seal and bearing life.

 ⑤ The B&G mechanical seal is designed to withstand the wide range of water temperatures, pressures, additives and dissolved solids common in hydronic systems.

 ⑥ Patented centrifugal impeller prevents accumulation of air at seal faces to assure long life. Close impeller/body tolerances minimize water slippage and maximizes efficiency.

Source: ITT Fluid Handling Sales.

SUPPLY AND RETURN PIPING FOR HOT WATER HEATING SYSTEM

Source: Hydro Therm Corporation.

521

MEASUREMENT OF PRESSURE WITH A MANOMETER

Pressure is defined as a force per unit area — and the most accurate way to measure low air pressure is to balance a column of liquid of known weight against it and measure the height of the liquid column so balanced. The units of measure commonly used are inches of mercury (in. Hg.), using mercury as the fluid and inches of water (in. W.C.), using water or oil as the fluid.

Instruments employing this principle are called manometers. The simplest form is the basic and well-known U-tube manometer (Fig. 1). This device indicates the difference between two pressures (differential pressure), or between a single pressure and atmosphere (gage pressure), when one side is open to atmosphere.

If a U-tube is filled to the half way point with water and air pressure is exerted on one of the columns, the fluid will be displaced. Thus one leg of water column will rise and the other falls. The difference in height "h" which is the *sum* of the readings above and below the half way point, indicates the pressure in inches of water column.

The U-tube manometer is a primary standard because the difference in height between the two columns is always a true indication of the pressure regardless of variations in the internal diameter of the tubing.

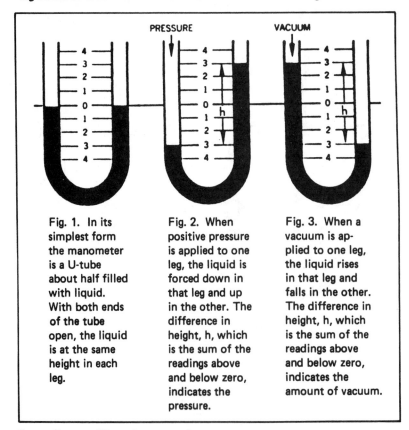

Fig. 1. In its simplest form the manometer is a U-tube about half filled with liquid. With both ends of the tube open, the liquid is at the same height in each leg.

Fig. 2. When positive pressure is applied to one leg, the liquid is forced down in that leg and up in the other. The difference in height, h, which is the sum of the readings above and below zero, indicates the pressure.

Fig. 3. When a vacuum is applied to one leg, the liquid rises in that leg and falls in the other. The difference in height, h, which is the sum of the readings above and below zero, indicates the amount of vacuum.

Source: Courtesy of Dwyer Instruments, Inc.

MEASUREMENT OF AIR VELOCITY
WITH A MANOMETER

To measure air velocity, connect a Dwyer Durablock inclined manometer to a Pitot tube in the air stream as shown. This method requires only a static tap plus a simple tube in center of duct to pick up total pressure. The differential pressure reading on the manometer is velocity pressure, which may be converted to air velocity by calculation or reference to conversion charts.

Dwyer stainless steel Pitot tubes are made in numerous lengths and configurations to serve in the smallest to the largest duct sizes.

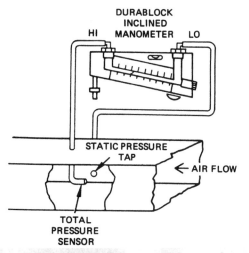

Source: Courtesy of Dwyer Instruments, Inc.

CONVERSION FACTORS

MULTIPLY	BY	TO OBTAIN	MULTIPLY	BY	TO OBTAIN	MULTIPLY	BY	TO OBTAIN
Atmospheres (Std.) 760 MM of Mercury at 32°F.	14.696	Lbs./sq. inch	**Feet of water**	0.02950	Atmospheres	**Liters**	0.2642	Gallons
Atmospheres	76.0	Cms. of mercury	Feet of water	0.8826	Inches of mercury	Liters	2.113	Pints (liq.)
Atmospheres	29.92	In. of mercury	Feet of water	0.03048	Kgs./sq. cm.	Liters	1.057	Quarts (liq.)
Atmospheres	33.90	Feet of water	Feet of water	62.43	Lbs./sq. ft.	**Meters**	100	Centimeters
Atmospheres	1.0333	Kgs./sq.cm.	Feet of water	0.4335	Lbs./sq. inch	Meters	3.281.	Feet
Atmospheres	14.70	Lbs./sq. inch	**Feet/min.**	0.5080	Centimeters/sec.	Meters	39.37	Inches
Atmospheres	1.058	Tons/sq. ft.	Feet/min.	0.01667	Feet/sec.	Meters	1000	Millimeters
Brit. Therm. Units	0.2520	Kilogram-calories	Feet/min.	0.01829	Kilometers/hr.	Meters	1.094	Yards
Brit. Therm. Units	777.5	Foot-lbs.	Feet/min.	0.3048	Meters/min.	**Ounces (fluid)**	1.805	Cubic inches
Brit. Therm. Units	0.000393	Horse-power-hrs.	Feet/min.	0.01136	Miles/hr.	Ounces (fluid)	0.02957	Liters
Brit. Therm. Units	0.293	Watt-hrs.	**Foot-pounds**	0.001286	BTU	**Ounces/sq. inch**	0.0625	Lbs./sq. inch
BTU/min.	12.96	Foot-lbs./sec.	**Gallons**	3785	Cu. centimeters	Ounces/sq. inch	1.73.	Inches of water
BTU/min.	0.02356	Horse-power	Gallons	0.1337	Cubic feet	**Pints**	0.4732	Liter
BTU/min.	0.01757	Kilowatts	Gallons	231	Cubic inches	**Pounds (avoir.)**	16	Ounces
BTU/min.	17.57	Watts	Gallons	128	Fluid ounces	**Pounds of water**	0.01602	Cubic feet
Calorie	0.003968	BTU	Gallons	3.785	Liters	Pounds of water	27.68	Cubic inches
Centimeters	0.3937	Inches	**Gallons water**	8.35	Lbs.water@60°F.	Pounds of water	0.1198	Gallons
Centimeters	0.03280	Feet	**Horse-power**	42.44	BTU/min.	**Pounds/sq. foot**	0.01602	Feet of water
Centimeters	0.01	Meters	Horse-power	33,000	Foot-lbs./min.	Pounds/sq. foot	0.006945	Pounds/sq. inch
Centimeters	10	Millimeters	Horse-power	550	Foot-lbs./sec.	**Pounds/sq. inch**	0.06804	Atmospheres
Centmtrs. of Merc.	0.01316	Atmospheres	Horse-power	0.7457	Kilowatts	Pounds/sq. inch	2.307	Feet of water
Centimtrs. of merc.	0.4461	Feet of water	Horse-power	745.7	Watts	Pounds/sq. inch	2.036	In. of mercury
Centimtrs. of merc.	136.0	Kgs./sq. meter	**Horse-power (boiler)**	33,479	BTU/hr.	Pounds/sq. inch	27.68	Inches of water
Centimtrs. of merc.	27.85	Lbs./sq. ft.	Horse-power (boiler)	9.803	Kilowatts	**Temp.(°C.) + 273**	1	Abs. temp. (°C.)
Centimtrs. of merc.	0.1934	Lbs./sq. inch	**Horse-power-hours**	2547	BTU	Temp.(°C.) + 17.78	1.8	Temp.(°F.)
Cubic feet	2.832x10⁴	Cubic cms.	Horse-power-hours	0.7457	Kilowatt-hours	Temp.(°F.) + 460	1	Abs. temp. (°F.)
Cubic feet	1728	Cubic inches	**Inches**	2,540	Centimeters	Temp.(°F.) −32	5/9	Temp.(°C.)
Cubic feet	0.02832	Cubic meters	Inches	25.4	Millimeters	**Therm**	100,000.	BTU
Cubic feet	0.03704	Cubic yards	Inches	0.0254	Meters	**Tons(long)**	2240	Pounds
Cubic feet	7.48052	Gallons U.S.	Inches	0.0833	Foot	**Ton, Refrigeration**	12,000.	BTU/hr.
Cubic feet/ minute	472.0	Cubic cms./ sec.	**Inches of mercury**	0.03342	Atmospheres	**Tons (short)**	2000	Pounds
Cubic feet/minute	0.1247	Gallons/sec.	Inches of mercury	1.133	Feet of water	**Watts**	3.415	BTU
Cubic foot water	62.4	Pounds @ 60°F.	Inches of mercury	13.57	Inches of water	Watts	0.05692	BTU/min.
Feet	30.48	Centimeters	Inches of mercury	70.73	Lbs./sq. ft.	Watts	44.26	Foot-pounds/min.
Feet	12	Inches	Inches of mercury	0.4912	Lbs./sq. inch	Watts	0.7376	Foot-pounds/sec.
Feet	0.3048	Meters	**Inches of water**	0.002458	Atmospheres	Watts	0.001341	Horse-power
Feet	1:3	Yards	Inches of water	0.07355	In. of mercury	Watts	0.001	Kilowatts
			Inches of water	0.5781	Ounces/sq. inch	**Watt-hours**	3.415	BTU/hr.
			Inches of water	5.202	Lbs./sq. foot	Watt-hours	2655	Foot-pounds
			Inches of water	0.03613	Lbs./sq. inch	Watt-hours	0.001341	Horse-power hrs.
			Kilowatts	56.92	BTU/min.	Watt-hours	0.001	Kilowatt-hours
			Kilowatts	1.341	Horse-power			
			Kilowatts	1000	Watts			
			Kilowatt-hours	3415	BTU			

PRESSURE CONVERSION TABLES

Equivalent Inches		Pressure Per Square Inch		Equivalent Inches		Pressure Per Square Inch	
Water	Mercury	Pounds	Ounces	Water	Mercury	Pounds	Ounces
0.10	0.007	0.0036	0.0577	8.0	0.588	0.289	4.62
0.20	0.015	0.0072	0.115	9.0	0.662	0.325	5.20
0.30	0.022	0.0108	4.173	10.0	0.74	0.361	5.77
0.40	0.029	0.0145	0.231	11.0	0.81	0.397	6.34
0.50	0.037	0.0181	0.289	12.0	0.88	0.433	6.92
0.60	0.044	0.0217	0.346	13.0	0.96	0.469	7.50
0.70	0.051	0.0253	0.404	13.6	1.00	0.491	7.86
0.80	0.059	0.0289	0.462	13.9	1.02	0.500	8.00
0.90	0.066	0.325	0.520	14.0	1.06	0.505	8.08
1.00	0.074	0.036	0.577	15.0	1.10	0.542	8.7
1.36	0.100	0.049	0.785	16.0	1.18	0.578	9.2
1.74	0.128	0.067	1.00	17.0	1.25	0.614	9.8
2.00	0.147	0.072	1.15	18.0	1.33	0.650	10.4
2.77	0.203	0.100	1.60	19.0	1.40	0.686	10.9
3.00	0.221	0.109	1.73	20.0	1.47	0.722	11.5
4.00	0.294	0.144	2.31				
5.0	0.368	0.181	2.89	25.0	1.84	0.903	14.4
6.0	0.442	0.217	3.46	27.2	2.00	0.975	15.7
7.0	0.515	0.253	4.04	27.7	2.03	1.00	16.0

Source: Courtesy of Robertshaw Controls Company.

Abbreviations for Text and Drawings

A	Amperes
AC	Auxiliary contacts
ACCA	Air Conditioning Contractors of America
ACS	Air Conditioning Service, National Response Center
AFUE	Annual fuel utilization efficiency
AGA	American Gas Association
ALS	Auxiliary limit switch
AMP	Amperes
API	American Petroleum Institute
ARI	Air Conditioning and Refrigeration Institute
ASHRAE	American Society of Heating, Refrigerating, and Air Conditioning Engineers, Inc.
AWG	American wire gauge
BK	Black-wire color
BL	Blue-wire color
BLWM	Blower motor
BOCA	Building Officials & Code Administrators International, Inc.
Btu	British thermal unit
Btuh	British thermal units per hour
C	Degrees Celsius
C	24V Common connection
C.A.	California seasonal efficiency percent

CAD	Cad cell
CAP	Capacitor
CB	Circuit breaker
CBR	Cooling blower relay
CC	Compressor contactor
CCH	Compressor crankcase heater
CFC	Chlorofluorocarbon
cfh	Cubic feet per hour
cfm	Cubic feet per minute
CGV	Combination gas valve
CH	Crankcase heater
CO	Carbon monoxide
CO_2	Carbon dioxide
COMP	Compressor
COP	Coefficient of Performance
CPVC	Chlorinated polyvinyl chloride
CR	Control relay
cu	Cubic
dB	Decibel
db	Dry bulb
DEG	Degree
DOE	Department of Energy
DOT	Department of Transportation
DPDT	Double-pole double-throw switch
DPST	Double-pole single-throw switch
DSI	Direct spark ignition
DSS	Draft safeguard switch
E	Electromotive force (volts)
EAC	Electrostatic air cleaner
EMF	Electromotive force
EP	Electric pilot
EPA	Environmental Protection Agency
ESP	External static pressure
ERV	Energy recovery ventilator
EWT	Entering water temperature
F	Degrees Fahrenheit
F	Farad
F	Fuse
FC	Fan control

FD	Fused disconnect
FL	Fuse link
FLA	Full load amperes
FM	Fan motor
FR	Fan relay
ft.	Feet
ft.^{3}	Cubic feet
ft.^{3}/h	Cubic feet per hour
ft.^{3}/min.	Cubic feet per min.
FU	Fuse
g	Grams
G	Green-wire color
G	Neutral-ground
GFCI	Ground fault circuit interrupter
gph	Gallons per hour
gpm	Gallons per minute
GV	Gas valve
H	Humidistat
H_2O	Water
HAM	Home access module
HCFC	Hydrochlorofluorocarbon
HCHO	Formaldehyde
HCT-2S	Two-stage heating-cooling thermostat
HE	High efficiency
HEF	High efficiency furnace
HEPA	High efficiency particulate arresting (filter)
HFR	Heating blower relay
HI	High speed
HP	High pressure (control)
HP	Horsepower
HR	Heat relay
HS	Humidification system
HSPF	Heating season performance factor
HTM	Heat transfer multiplier
HTM™	Heat Transfer Module™
HU	Humidifier
HVAC	Heating, ventilating, and air-conditioning
Hz	Cycles/second
I	Amperes

IAQ	Indoor air quality
I=B=R	Institute of Boiler and Radiator Manufacturers
ID	Inside diameter
IDM	Induced draft motor
IDR	Induced draft relay
IFR	Inside fan relay
in.Hg	Inches of mercury
IPS	Iron pipe size
J	Joule
kcal	Kilocalorie
kg	Kilogram
kW	Kilowatt
kWh	Kilowatt-hours
L	Change in latent heat per pound, Btu
L	Limit
L1 L2	Power supply
LA	Limit auxiliary
lb.	Pound
LED	Indicator lights
LO	Low speed
LP	Liquid petroleum
LR	Lockout relay
LRA	Locked rotor amperes
LS	Limit switch
m	Meter
M	One thousand
m/s	Meters per second
mA	Milliampere
MABS	Mastertrol automatic balancing system
MAZ	Mastertrol add-a-zone control panels
MBh	Thousand of BTU/hour
MCHP	Mastertrol changeover heat pump thermostat
MCTS	Mastertrol changeover two-stage thermostat
MFD	Microfarads
mm	Millimeter
mu m	Micrometer or micron
MuF	Microfarads
mV	Millivolt
N	Neutral

N	Nitrogen
NC	Normally closed
NFPA	National Fire Protection Association
NO	Normally open
O	Oxygen
OBM	Oil burner motor
OD	Outside diameter
OL	Overload
OSHA	Occupational Safety and Health Administration
OT	Outdoor thermostat
PC	Printed circuit
PCB1	Inducer motor controller
PCB2	Blower motor controller
PCB3	Microprocessor board
PF	Power factor
Ph	Phase
PPC	Pilot power control
ppm	Parts per million
PRS	Pressure switch
PSC	Permanent split phase capacitor
psi	Pressure per square inch
psia	Pressure per square inch, absolute
psig	Pounds per square inch gauge
PVC	Polyvinyl chloride
Q	Quantity of heat, Btu
R	Red-wire color (24-V power terminal)
R	Refrigerant
R	Resistance, Ohms
rev/min	Revolutions per minute
rh	Relative humidity
RH	Resistance heater
RV	Reversing valve
S	Cad cell relay terminal
s	Seconds
SAE	Society of Automotive Engineers
SEER	Seasonal energy efficient ratio
SH	Specific heat
SI	International System Units
Sol	Solenoid valve

SP	Static pressure
SPDT	Single-pole double-throw switch
SPST	Single-pole single-throw switch
SQ	Sequencer
SRN	Sound rating number
T	Thermostat terminal
T.C.	Total capacity
TD	Temperature difference, degrees F
TEL	Total equivalent length
TEV	Thermal expansion valve
TFS	Time fan start
THR	Thermocouple
TR	Temperature rise
TR	Transformer
TRAN	24-volt transformer
TRT	Temperature-reversing thermostat
U	Overall heat transfer coefficient
UBC	Uniform Building Code
UL	Underwriters' Laboratories
V	Volt (electromotive force)
VA	Volt-amp
VAC	Volts alternating current
VOCs	Volatile compounds
W	Watt
w	Weight, lb
W	White-wire color
W.C.	Water column
W/lls	(Units rated) with (accessory) liquid line solenoid
W1	First stage heat-thermostat
W2	Second state heat-thermostat
wb	Wet bulb
wc	Water column in inches
Y	Yellow-wire color
Y, R, G, W	Thermostat terminals

INDEX